The Columbia Guide to South African Literature in English Since 1945

COLUMBIA GUIDES TO LITERATURE SINCE 1945

The Columbia Guides to Literature Since 1945

The Columbia Guide to the Literatures of Eastern Europe Since 1945, ed. Harold B. Segel
The Columbia Guide to American Indian Literatures of the United States Since 1945, ed. Eric Cheyfitz
The Columbia Guide to Contemporary African American Fiction, Darryl Dickson-Carr
The Columbia Guide to Asian American Literature Since 1945, Guiyou Huang
The Columbia Guide to East African Literature in English Since 1945, Simon Gikandi and Evan Mwangi
The Columbia Guide to Central African Literature in English Since 1945, Adrian Roscoe
The Columbia Guide to West African Literature in English Since 1945, Oyekan Owomoyela

The Columbia Guide to South African Literature in English Since 1945

Gareth Cornwell, Dirk Klopper,
and Craig MacKenzie

Columbia University Press
New York

Columbia University Press
Publishers Since 1893
New York Chichester, West Sussex

Library of Congress Cataloging-in-Publication Data
Cornwell, Gareth.
The Columbia guide to South African literature in English since 1945 / Gareth Cornwell, Dirk Klopper and Craig MacKenzie.
p. cm. — (The Columbia guides to literature since 1945)
Includes bibliographical references and index.
ISBN 978-0-231-13046-2 (cloth : alk. paper)
1. South African literature (English)—Dictionaries. 2. Authors, South African—20th century—Biography—Dictionaries. I. Klopper, Dirk. II. MacKenzie, Craig, 1960– III. Title. IV. Series.
PR9350.2.C67 2009
820.9'9680904503—dc22
[B]

2009018408

Columbia University Press books are printed on permanent and durable acid-free paper.
This book was printed on paper with recycled content.
Printed in the United States of America
c 10 9 8 7 6 5 4 3 2 1

Contents

Preface

This book is a product of the collaboration of three university professors, but it is not intended solely or even primarily for an academic readership. It is a general reference work whose natural home is the library—the public library and the school library no less than the college library.

There is need for an up-to-date reference work in the field of South African literature in English. The 1986 *Companion to South African English Literature* was the first work of this nature, and it marked the coming of age of South African English literature after the intellectual and political ferment of the 1970s and early 1980s. But the *Companion* has never been updated, and many of the writers featured in this *Guide* have made their names during the more than twenty years that have elapsed since its publication.

The authors on whom the *Guide* contains entries are South African either by birth or by domicile, or they have written works relating to South Africa. They have all published at least one work, and this has been in English or has been translated into English from another South African language. There have inevitably been cases to test these criteria, but we have nonetheless attempted to apply them as consistently as possible.

The entries themselves range from under one hundred words to three thousand words. The subject entries—novel, short story, drama, and so on—have generally been accorded more space, and the major writers—Coetzee, Gordimer, Fugard, and Bosman, for instance—have all been given entries of between one thousand and two thousand words. In making such discriminations, we have been guided largely, but not solely, by our sense of whose work has attracted the most attention and debate. In other words, we have seen our role as one of recording rather than creating a context or history of reception.

It is impossible to be comprehensive in an undertaking of this nature, and the present volume has no such ambition. In a review of a comparable project, Randall Stevenson's *Oxford English Literary History, Vol. XII: 1960–2000*, the critic James Wood complained in the *London Review of Books* about the way that the author "drags a very large net through contemporary waters, apparently fearful of missing the slightest sardine." His discussion is therefore "sabotaged by the complete lack of selectivity." We have tried to avoid this by including only those writers whose work, in our opinion, has helped shape (or is helping to shape) the corpus of South African literature in English and has continuing relevance to South African life and culture. More selective still is the ground covered in the introduction, a personal account of over sixty years of literary production that unashamedly reflects my own interests, assumptions, likes, and dislikes. (My coauthors therefore bear no responsibility for its shortcomings.)

Our principal source of information has been the NISC CD-ROM *SA Studies* (now incorporated into the Africa-Wide NiPAD database aggregation), the main contributor to which—as far as South African English literature is concerned—is the National English Literary Museum in Grahamstown. We are indebted to NELM for the invaluable service it provides. Members of its staff, most especially Thomas Jeffery, Crystal Warren, and Lynne Grant, have also been helpful in answering more specific queries relating to elusive details like birth and death dates. Other key sources are the *Companion to South African English Literature* (1986), the *Encyclopedia of Post-Colonial Literatures in English* (1994), the *Companion to African Literature* (2000), and the *Dictionary of Literary Biography: South African Writers*, vol. 225 (2000). We are grateful also to the following South African publishers for information relating to recent publications: Umuzi, Human & Rousseau, Kwela, Jacana, Penguin, Picador, Zebra, Random, Jonathan Ball, Snailpress, and Oxford University Press.

The authors wish to thank those writers who responded to requests for biographical details. We also owe a debt of gratitude to several editors at Columbia University Press, who have been unfailingly patient and gracious in the face of the interruptions and delays impeding our progress over the past several years: Plaegian Alexander, Jamie Warren, Juree Sondker, and Afua Adusei. I should like to record my personal thanks to my coauthors, Craig MacKenzie and Dirk Klopper, who came to my rescue when it dawned on me that I was congenitally incapable of tackling the A–Z entries on my own. Craig and Dirk resurrected a project on which they had previously collaborated, comprehensively amending, augmenting, and updating their work to meet the needs of the present volume.

Warmest thanks of all must go to my wife, Judy, who makes everything worthwhile.

Gareth Cornwell

Chronology

25,000 BCE	Earliest dated rock art.
15,000 BCE	San hunter-gatherers distributed widely across southern Africa.
1300–1500 CE	Khoisan are the dominant society in the southern and southwestern Cape; Nguni speakers occupy areas along Drakensberg and the south-eastern coast; Tswana and Sotho speakers settle on the highveld.
1488	Portuguese navigator Bartolomeu Dias rounds the Cape of Good Hope.
1497	Vasco da Gama sails along the South African coast.
1572	Luis de Camoëns publishes the epic poem *The Lusiads*, which describes Vasco da Gama's journey around the Cape and will later inspire many South African literary and literary-critical responses.
1652	Dutch East India Company founds a refreshment station at the Cape.
1658	First slaves arrive at the Cape.
1690s	Dutch settlers (*trekboers*) begin moving into the Cape hinterland.
1790	François le Vaillant's *Travels Into the Interior Parts of Africa* is published.
1779	First Frontier War.
1795	First British occupation of the Cape.
1801	John Barrow's *An Account of Travels into the Interior of Southern Africa in the Years 1797 and 1798* is published.
1803	Dutch reassume control of the Cape.
1806	Second British occupation begins.
1820	5,000 British settlers arrive in the Eastern Cape, among them Thomas Pringle.
1822 and 1824	William Burchell's *Travels in the Interior of Southern Africa* is published in two volumes.
1824	Thomas Pringle and John Fairbairn's *South African Journal* appears.
1834	Slavery abolished at the Cape.

1834	Thomas Pringle's *African Sketches* (incorporating *Narrative of a Residence in South Africa* and *Poems Illustrative of South Africa*) is published.
1835–37	The Great Trek: Cape Boers cross the Orange River in large numbers.
1836	Nathaniel Isaacs's *Travels and Adventures in East Africa* is published.
1843	British annex Natal as a colony.
1848	Harriet Ward's two-volume *Five Years in Kaffirland* is published.
1856–57	Xhosa cattle killing and crop burning; famine ensues, causing mass starvation.
1857	David Livingstone's *Missionary Travels and Researches in Southern Africa* published.
1860	First indentured Indian laborers arrive in Natal.
1864	W. H. I. Bleek's *Hottentot Fables and Tales* is published.
1866	British Kaffraria is annexed to the Cape Colony.
1867	Discovery of diamonds in Griqualand West.
1868	Henry Callaway's *Nursery Tales, Traditions and Histories of the Zulus* is published.
1870–71	Diamond rush to Kimberley.
1877	Proclamation of Transvaal as British Crown Colony.
1879	Anglo-Zulu War.
1880–81	First Anglo-Boer War.
1880	Frances Colenso's *My Chief and I* is published.
1883	Olive Schreiner's *The Story of an African Farm* is published.
1885	Henry Rider Haggard's *King Solomon's Mines* is published.
1886	Discovery of main gold reef on the Witwatersrand.
1890	Cecil Rhodes becomes prime minister of the Cape.
1895	Dr. Jameson launches a raid into Transvaal.
1897	Annexation of Zululand to Natal.
1899–1902	Second Anglo-Boer War.
1899–1900	Sol Plaatje writes his diary recording events during the siege of Mafeking (eventually published as *The Boer War Diary of Sol T. Plaatje* in 1973).
1907	J. Percy FitzPatrick's *Jock of the Bushveld* is published.
1910	Union of South Africa proclaimed.
1912	South African Native National Congress (SANNC) formed; later changes its name to the African National Congress (ANC); Sol Plaatje is one of the founding members.
1913	Natives' Land Act promulgated, in terms of which Africans are prohibited from owning land outside of designated reserves and allocated 7 percent of the total land area of South Africa (subsequently increased to about 13 percent).
1914–18	First World War.
1916	Sol Plaatje's *Native Life in South Africa* is published.
1922	White miners strike; Rand Revolt.
1924	Sarah Gertrude Millin's *God's Step-Children* is published.
1925	Thomas Mofolo's *Chaka* is published in Sesotho (published in English translation in 1931); Pauline Smith's *The Little Karoo* is published.

1926 The first issue of the literary review *Voorslag* appears under the editorship of Roy Campbell, William Plomer, and Laurens van der Post; Plomer's *Turbott Wolfe* and Pauline Smith's *The Beadle* are published.

1928 R. R. R. Dhlomo's *An African Tragedy*, the first novella by a black South African writer in English, is published.

1929 The satirical journal *The Sjambok* appears under Stephen Black's editorship; Deneys Reitz's *Commando: A Boer Journal of the Boer War* is published.

1930 Sol Plaatje's *Mhudi: An Epic of South African Native Life a Hundred Years Ago*, the first full-length novel by a black South African writer in English, and Roy Campbell's *Adamastor* are published; the literary magazine *The Touleier* appears under the editorship of Herman Charles Bosman and Aegidius Jean Blignaut.

1939–45 Second World War.

1946 Peter Abrahams's *Mine Boy* and Es'kia Mphahlele's first collection, *Man Must Live and Other Stories*, are published.

1947 Herman Charles Bosman's *Mafeking Road* is published.

1948 Herenigde Nasionale Party (later Nasionale Party) wins the general election with its policy of apartheid; Alan Paton's *Cry, the Beloved Country* is published.

1949 Prohibition of Mixed Marriages Act; Nadine Gordimer's *Face to Face*, her first collection of short stories, is published.

1950 The Population Registration Act, in terms of which South Africans are classified White, Black, Coloured,[1] or Indian (though petty apartheid will mostly distinguish only between "whites" (Afrikaans, *blankes*) and "non-whites" (*nie-blankes*); the Immorality Act Amendment, banning all sexual relations between whites and other groups; the Suppression of Communism Act; and the Group Areas Act, enforcing residential apartheid, are passed into law; Doris Lessing's *The Grass Is Singing* is published; the stage show *King Kong*, with music by Todd Matshikiza, is first performed.

1951 The first issue of *Drum* magazine is published (in Cape Town) as *African Drum*.

1952 Guy Butler's first poetry collection, *Stranger to Europe: Poems 1939–1949*, is published.

1953 Bantu Education Act, aimed at preparing blacks to be unskilled laborers, segregates education at all levels; the South African Communist Party (SACP) is formed underground.

1955 The removal of people from Sophiatown, a black "location" northwest of Johannesburg, begins. By the end of 1963, the ghetto would be completely razed and work on a new white working-class suburb, Triomf, begun. This was part of the government's resettlement program, which continued through the 1960s and 1970s and involved the forced removal to designated "group areas" of up to three million people. Those moved were inhabitants of inner-city slums, labor tenants on white-owned farms, the inhabitants of so-called black spots (areas of black-owned land surrounded by white farms), the families of workers living in townships close to the homelands, and "surplus people" from urban areas, including thousands of people from the Western Cape (declared a "Coloured Labor Preference Area"), who were dumped in the Transkei and Ciskei homelands. Sophiatown was the home or temporary abode of many artists and musicians, and featured in the work of numerous prominent writers, including Can Themba, Casey Motsisi, Alan Paton, Nadine Gordimer, and Don Mattera. Anglican priest Trevor Huddleston was also resident there, and his *Naught for Your Comfort* (1956) portrays the township as he knew it. Famous as a meeting place for the different races, until its brutal eradication it represented a vibrant microcosm of a multiracial and multiclass South African society.

1956 ANC approves the Freedom Charter (later to form the basis of the new South African Constitution); 20,000 women march to the Union Buildings in Pretoria to protest against the extension of the pass laws to women; Nadine Gordimer's *Six Feet of the Country* is published.

1959 The Pan Africanist Congress (PAC) is formed; Es'kia Mphahlele's *Down Second Avenue* is published.

1960 Peaceful PAC-led campaign to protest the pass laws provokes the infamous Sharpeville massacre; State of Emergency declared; ANC and PAC banned; Douglas Livingstone's first poetry collection, *The Skull in the Mud*, is published.

1961 South Africa withdraws from the Commonwealth and becomes a republic; ANC adopts armed struggle.

1963 Bloke Modisane's autobiography *Blame Me on History* and Dennis Brutus's poetry collection *Sirens, Knuckles, Boots* are published.

1966 Verwoerd assassinated; Vorster becomes prime minister; District Six cleared and declared a white area. Like Sophiatown, District Six was the home or meeting place of numerous writers and musicians, including Dollar Brand (Abdullah Ibrahim), Richard Rive, Bessie Head, James Matthews, Alex La Guma, Adam Small, and Jack Cope. It, too, was a powerful symbol of a multiracial South Africa and has featured prominently in numerous literary and artistic renderings. Sydney Clouts's *One Life*, the only collection of poems to appear in his lifetime, is published.

1969 Athol Fugard's *Boesman and Lena* is published.

1971 Mbuyiseni Oswald Mtshali's *Sounds of a Cowhide Drum* is published.

1972 Mongane Serote's *Yakhal'inkomo* is published.

1973 Athol Fugard's *Sizwe Bansi Is Dead* and Bessie Head's *A Question of Power* are published.

1974 J. M. Coetzee's *Dusklands* and Nadine Gordimer's *The Conservationist* are published.

1976 Police fire on Soweto schoolchildren protesting against being forced to learn some subjects in Afrikaans; the unrest spreads to other cities and broadens into a political uprising against oppression; hundreds are killed, thousands more go into exile. The events of 1976 give rise to a new Black Consciousness–rooted aesthetic, which involves a rejection of Western cultural models in favor of African ones. Poetry collections in the 1970s and 1980s by Mafika Gwala, Oswald Mtshali, Mongane Serote, Sipho Sepamla, Ingoapele Madingoane, and others reflect a new urgency of tone and a more militant artistic agenda.

1976 Sipho Sepamla's *The Blues Is You in Me* is published.

1977 Steve Biko is murdered in detention, sparking an international outcry.

1978 Ahmed Essop's *The Hajji and Other Stories* is published; the first issue of *Staffrider*, founded and edited by Mike Kirkwood and espousing a workerist, egalitarian aesthetic, appears: it will go on to publish the work of Njabulo Ndebele, Mtutuzeli Matshoba, Miriam Tlali, Ahmed Essop and Mothobi Mutloatse, among many others.

1979 Mtutuzeli Matshoba's *Call Me Not a Man* is published.

1981 Mongane Serote's *To Every Birth Its Blood* and Achmat Dangor's *Waiting for Leila* are published.

1982 Ruth First is assassinated by parcel bomb in Maputo.

1983 Jeremy Cronin's *Inside* and Njabulo Ndebele's *Fools and Other Stories* are published.

1985 Ellen Kuzwayo's autobiography, *Call Me Woman*, is published.

1986 The government responds to rising levels of political violence in the urban townships by declaring a National State of Emergency, giving the police sweeping powers and clamping down on the media.

1989 P. W. Botha suffers a stroke; F. W. de Klerk becomes state president; De Klerk meets Nelson Mandela for the first time.

1990 De Klerk unbans ANC, SACP, and other opposition parties; Mandela's unconditional release announced; political censorship of literature in terms of the Publications Act and the Internal Security Act effectively ceases; Ivan Vladislavić's *Missing Persons* is published.

1991 De Klerk announces that all apartheid laws will be repealed; Mandela elected president of the ANC; Nadine Gordimer wins the Nobel Prize in literature.

1993 Mandela and De Klerk are announced joint winners of the Nobel Peace Prize.

1994 First democratic elections held; Mandela becomes president; his autobiography *Long Walk to Freedom* is published.

1996 Truth and Reconciliation Commission (TRC) begins hearings. The TRC was set up in terms of the Promotion of National Unity and Reconciliation Act of 1995, and comprised three committees charged with investigating human rights abuses that occurred between 1960 and 1994, restoring victims' dignity and formulating proposals to assist with rehabilitation, and considering applications from individuals for amnesty in accordance with the provisions of the Act. Hundreds of victims and violators testified before Archbishop Desmond Tutu and his commissioners in an emotional process generally believed to have brought healing and reconciliation to the nation.

1998 TRC report is published; Antjie Krog's *Country of My Skull* is published.

1999	Thabo Mbeki succeeds Mandela as president; J. M. Coetzee's Booker Prize–winning *Disgrace* is published.
2003	J. M. Coetzee awarded the Nobel Prize in literature.
2005	Jacob Zuma dismissed as deputy president because of allegations of corruption relating to the arms deal of the late 1990s; later in the year he is charged with rape.
2006	Ivan Vladislavić's *Portrait with Keys: Joburg and What-What* is published.
2007	Doris Lessing awarded the Nobel Prize in literature.
2009	Jacob Zuma becomes president of South Africa.

NOTE

1. The term *Coloured* (not always capitalized) has a particular meaning in the South African context and is therefore orthographically differentiated from the American "Colored." According to the *Dictionary of South African English on Historical Principles* (Cape Town: Oxford University Press, 1996), the word as adjective means: "Of mixed ethnic origin, including Khoisan, African, slave, Malay, Chinese, white, and other descent"; as noun: "A person of mixed black (or brown) and white descent who speaks either English or Afrikaans as home language." Some of those classified as Coloured in terms of apartheid legislation rejected the nomenclature, calling themselves "black" (a gesture of political alignment) or insisting on the distancing qualifier "so-called," as in "so-called coloured." Others "self-identified" as Coloured, especially those belonging to long-settled communities in the Western Cape (Cape Coloureds). Today the term has less of a stigma attached to it, though the use of racial terminology is generally frowned upon in polite or public discourse and is almost never used in the print and broadcast media.

The Columbia Guide to South African Literature in English Since 1945

South African Literature in English Since 1945

Long Walk to Ordinariness

THIS INTRODUCTORY ESSAY IS a modest exercise in literary history, and since literary history continues to be a controversial domain of academic enquiry, some initial statement of intent seems appropriate. Literary history—the life story, encoded in books, of a suprapersonal entity (the national culture, "the spirit of an age," "the mind of a people," and so on)—has been treated with extreme skepticism by almost every literary-critical movement since the early twentieth century. From Russian Formalists to New Critics to poststructuralists, the complaint has been that literary history is (necessarily?) about virtually anything and everything *except literature*:

> It presents names, titles, groups, movements, influences, and external information of all kinds—biographical, political, social, *geistesgeschichtlich*—but, as Roland Barthes says in attacking Gustave Lanson, "the work *escapes*," for the work is "*something else* than its history, the sum of its sources, influences, or models."[1]

To this objection, postmodernism has added its strong suspicion of the normative and exclusionary effects of narrative itself, so that in recent years the would-be literary historian has tended deliberately to eschew consecutiveness and coherence. The typical result is the multiauthored collection of essays or "microhistories" of a focused or thematized kind, purposively and self-consciously restricted in range and perspective.[2] But as fertile as this form of enquiry may be, like travelers abroad in need of a basic map, we may find ourselves missing a sense of the general picture. In other words, there remains a place for the selective ordering and clarifying narrative of literary emergence. In such a narrative, a body of writing sharing a place of origin, a time, and a language is treated as an evolving entity—as what Dilthey, referring to historiography more generally, called an "ideal unity" or "logical subject." This is the kind of literary history that this introduction attempts, in full awareness that its project is logically and cognitively compromised.[3]

To this conceptual incoherence may be added the practical impossibility presented by the sheer complexity of the field known as South African literature. As Leon de Kock, in his reader's report on this manuscript, commented, "its origins have, over the years, proved too diverse, its languages too many, its intersections too speculative, and its trajectories too multifarious for any attempt at comprehensive—or even adequate—historical capture to succeed."

Necessarily negotiating the shadow of its own impossibility, then, this essay had better get under way.

Setting the Scene

Like many states that came into being as a consequence of European expansionism and imperialism, South Africa is the product of a history of physical and epistemic violence in which, from the mid-seventeenth century until toward the end of the twentieth, different peoples coexisted in the same geographical space—sometimes peacefully, sometimes not—without fusing into a single social or cultural formation. A conspicuous sign of this rooted and persistent difference is the country's multilingualism. South Africa's postapartheid constitution of 1996 recognizes no fewer than eleven "official" languages (and mentions the need to "promote and ensure respect" for some fourteen others). Each official language (together with residual indigenous tongues, such as those spoken by the Khoi, Nama, and San peoples) subtends a distinct culture, and each culture has a literary tradition, whether oral or written, or both. An obvious consequence of this linguistic and cultural diversity is that South Africa does not have—has never had, may well never have—a single national literature, in the sense of a coherent body of writings to which all its citizens have access and with whose representations they can all identify.

In recent decades, beginning with the revisionist wave of scholarship in South African historiography and literary studies in the 1970s, it has been customary to deplore this fact and treat it as a consequence of the apartheid government's race policies. Thus, in his pioneering study *Southern African Literatures: An Introduction*, Stephen Gray compares "Southern African literature" (in this context, not even national territorial borders signify real division) to an "archipelago," suggesting that "the islands with their peaks protrude in set positions, even if one does not readily see the connections between them beneath the surface." It is the task of literary scholarship, says Gray, to uncover these "internal interconnections" and so restore integrity to what has been fragmented by the vagaries of politics.[4] Although Gray continued to pursue this project in his subsequent anthologies *The Penguin Book of Southern African Stories* (1985) and *The Penguin Book of Southern African Verse* (1989), all he succeeded in demonstrating was the existence of broad thematic similarities among texts written in different languages or by authors of different races. Nevertheless, as the 1980s gave way to the decade that saw Mandela's release and a negotiated political settlement in South Africa, the concept of a single national literature—like that of a shared national culture—beckoned ever more invitingly. In 1994, the newly founded Centre for the Study of South African Literature and Languages (CSSALLS) committed itself to the compilation of a vast, multilingual, interdisciplinary database from which a single, encyclopedic narrative of South African literary history might emerge.[5] Then, in 1996, Michael Chapman published his sweeping historical survey *Southern African Literatures*, an avowedly "integrative" history committed to redressing the consequences of the fact that "in the countries of southern Africa the texts of politics have wanted to overwhelm the texts of art."[6]

This desire to move away from cultural apartheid, from racial and linguistic separatism, is of course admirable. But the efforts of scholars such as Gray, Chapman, and, most recently, Christopher Heywood,[7] in fact demonstrate that it remains little more than that, a desire, an optimistic gesture in the optative mood—the expression of a political ideology rather than an objectively existent state of affairs. It is an ideology forged in principled opposition to the policies of racial separatism implemented by the National Party government over a period of forty years. It is therefore understandably suspicious of difference and differentiation, especially when these coincide with racial, cultural, or linguistic demarcations; in this sense it remains an essentially reactive mode of thinking, inescapably implicated in the binarism to which it responds. It is thus salutary to remind ourselves not to conflate or confuse the categories *postapartheid* and *antiapartheid*, but rather to open ourselves to the full potentiality of the present moment by recognizing it as postapartheid, certainly; but as also and equally *postantiapartheid*.[8]

The first decisive step in this direction was taken by Malvern van Wyk Smith, who pointed out that the putative "underlying unity of South African literature" was merely a function of the texts' "exploring the same subject matter because they happen to have been written in the same part of the world."[9] He noted that the various literary traditions had evolved independently within boundaries both linguistic and (in the case of English writing) racial: until recently, there has been little evidence of intertextuality, cross-fertilization or influence between, for instance, Afrikaans and English writing, or between any of the African language literatures and either Afrikaans or English, or even between "White Writing" and "Writing Black" in English.[10] Although the subtitle of his essay—"The Anxiety of Non-Influence"—made reference to Harold Bloom's influential theorizing of literary succession, van Wyk Smith was implicitly appealing to an essentially formalist conception of what Jurij Tynjanov called "literary evolution"—the notion that the history of literature unfolds according to an immanent logic of formal properties and possibilities.[11] In other words, whatever "history" South African literature shares, this is not the "idiogenetic" system of formal exhaustion and renewal known as literary history, but the "allogenetic" history of social and political events and conditions.[12]

Leon de Kock has quite usefully described these "events and conditions" as constitutive of "a crisis of writing in and about one of the great seams of the modern world."[13] In terms of his metaphor, the South African author takes the reality of rags and tatters and seeks to write the fabric of the nation into existence: "the sharp point of the nib [is] a stitching instrument that seeks to suture the incommensurate," rendering the seam "the place where difference and sameness are hitched together—where they are brought to self-awareness, denied or displaced."[14] But more recently, de Kock has suggested that the metaphor no longer applies: the seam—"South African literature," an essentially political construct—has effectively been abrogated by historical developments and ought to yield to the recognition of what he calls "literature *in* South Africa."[15]

The phrase "literature in South Africa" serves also to remind us that the literary education of South African writers has by no means been confined to South African writing. The colonial cultural matrix—as embodied, for instance in school English syllabuses—has meant that generations of South Africans of every color have been exposed to the same formative literary influences: Shakespeare's plays, Romantic poetry, Victorian fiction. In this perspective, South African literature is merely a local manifestation of a much vaster cultural and historical phenomenon, and the distinctions that we are making between idiogenetic and allogenetic influence might seem precious, even otiose. But the difference remains, and the difference is crucial. To give but one example: Guy Butler and Can Themba were contemporaries, and both writers were steeped in Shakespeare. But Butler was a white university professor, Themba a black Sophiatown journalist, and while aspects of Shakespearean influence might be identified in the writings of both, those aspects are different from each other, and the writings themselves appear to have nothing in common.

To bring an expectation of heterogeneity rather than homogeneity to the "fantastically diverse body of writing"[16] that has emanated from South Africa is not to ignore or repudiate the possibilities for affinity and pattern, but rather to place oneself in a better position to recognize and respect the singularity of individual works and authors; works and authors, it must be said, which and whom it has been customary to read back into the general discourse of history, to subsume under broad generalizations of a sociological and political kind.[17]

I have offered this brief account of recent thinking about South African literature for three related reasons. First, it provides a rationale for what might otherwise seem the arbitrary restriction of this *Guide* to writing published in English (including, of course, translations from other languages). To attempt to extend coverage to literature in the other South African languages is to court incoherence, perhaps even necessarily to falsify the object of enquiry.[18] As the linguistic medium for the most prolific literary tradition in South Africa, English is the only world language spoken extensively in South Africa—and also the only South African language spoken extensively outside of the country. And—however regrettable the situation may be—it is only through translation into English that works in languages such as isiXhosa, isiZulu, Sesotho, Setswana, and even Afrikaans become accessible to a general readership, both within the country and abroad. It is worth adding that, mainly for reasons of access to the wider world, the vast majority of black South African writers have from the earliest times chosen English as their literary lingua franca.

Second, the emphasis on the realities of cultural difference in the South African context gives notice that it will be appropriate in this introduction—however much it may be regretted—to treat the writings of black and white South Africans up to the year 1990 as comprising two largely distinct systems (or corpora, or traditions).

Third, the reference to formalist notions of literariness indicates the basic set of assumptions upon which the various kinds of selection and discrimination informing this introduction depend. These assumptions are as follows: that there exists in literature (or in some literature, at any rate), a species of artistic value that we shall call *literary merit*; that there is sufficient consensus in the English-speaking world concerning the criteria for recognizing literary merit that it makes sense to regard it as effectively inhering objectively in literary texts;[19] that literary merit is essentially aesthetic in nature and the most significant factor in the assessment of the overall worth of literary texts; and finally, that it is the responsibility of literary critics—including those who, in the role of literary historian, offer cursory overviews like the present one—to make discriminations of value and significance based on perceptions of literary merit. The purpose of this introduction, then, and indeed of the volume as a whole, is, as its title suggests, to *guide* the reader to what is in the opinion of the authors most important—best, most worth bothering with, remembering or going back to—in South African writing since 1945.

Those unfamiliar with this literature and its context might find it odd that such a series of commonplaces should have been presented with all the flourish of a new and subversive polemic. But the fact of the matter is that—not only in South Africa but, to an extent, in the Western academy at large—in recent decades a generalized suspicion of "literature" (perceived as a privileged and therefore potentially discriminatory category in a nexus of social power relations), together with the rise of multiculturalism, have injected sufficient political capital into the business of making attributions of literary value as to scare away most critics (and certainly academic critics) from doing it in public. In the overheated arena of cultural politics in South Africa in the 1980s, compelling arguments for the redundancy of the aesthetic, or at least its strict subordination to the political, were routinely made, and more than a trace of this puritanical attitude continues to inform the public discourse on the arts in South Africa today.[20]

Such, indeed, has been the towering role of politics in South African writing that it has become customary to periodize it according to political events. Thus, the latter half of the twentieth century is divided up as follows: 1948 (the first National Party election victory) to 1960 (the Sharpeville killings); 1960 to 1976 (the Soweto uprising); 1976 to 1994 (the first democratic election); and 1994 to date (the postapartheid era). Although I have chosen rather to use literary events to organize the commentary that follows, there is in fact nothing inappropriate about the standard periodization, because there has been so little in the way of idiogenetic development in South African writing: the texts quite patently respond more directly to historical events and conditions than they do to other texts.

If, however, one attempts to make sense of this bare chronology by having recourse to descriptive or definitional terms drawn from current critical discourse, the picture is rather less straightforward. To define South African writing in the period before 1994 as "colonial" and writing thereafter as "postcolonial" is an easy but unsatisfactory option. Although it used to be fashionable to describe the South African system under National Party rule as "internal colonialism," the fact is that South Africa achieved independence from Britain with the Act of Union in 1910. From the perspective of Afrikaner nationalism, the National Party electoral victory in 1948 marked the liberation of a hitherto colonized people, their "independence" sealed by a symbolically important act of severance: South Africa's departure from the Commonwealth in 1961. Introducing the entry for the "Novel (South Africa)" in the Routledge *Encyclopedia of Post-Colonial Literatures in English*, Stephen Clingman acknowledges the cultural anomaly generated by this history: "As South Africa is a society that is, properly speaking, neither colonial nor post-colonial, yet participates in features of both, so too its literature has been caught up in an extended historical interregnum involving repeated explorations of a delayed transition between these two conditions."[21]

It makes sense to introduce at this point a second pair of terms: the modern and the postmodern. Here I am persuaded by Robert Thornton's argument that South Africa today is neither a colonial nor a postcolonial polity but a postmodern one. In this perspective, apartheid was a postcolonial system that, with its ambitious policies of social engineering and its aggressive *administrative* drive was "a form of rampant modernism," and "post-Apartheid is therefore postmodern."[22] Although Thornton is speaking in the first instance about political "settlements" of social difference, anyone familiar with the kaleidoscopic and often bizarre collage of styles, identifications, traditions, and practices that constitute contemporary South African culture will recognize the unmistakable stamp of the postmodern. Traditional folkways of course remain, but media saturation—popular music, radio, television, advertising—together with the myriad zones of contact encountered in everyday life increasingly ensure that the cultural identity of South Africans is defined by what Sarah Nuttall has recently characterized as varying degrees of mutual "entanglement."[23] But I wish to make a point about South African literature in particular that will involve the introduction of yet another contested term—that of nationalism.

Looking back at the latter half of the twentieth century from the present point of vantage, one is inclined to see in South Africa (and no doubt elsewhere as well) the flowering and subsequent rapid demise of the idea of a national literature, meaning a cultural reservoir containing a reasonably coherent reflection and embodiment of the history, character, and aspirations of a unitary nation state. The globalization of economics and politics, the contempt for borders implicit in mass media and cyberspace communications, the trend toward an internationally homogenized consumer culture—all these things have conspired to make literature an increasingly cosmopolitan commodity produced by authors for a virtual or world readership rather than a specific local one. Nationalism was in some senses *the* project of modernism, and the waning of national literatures is undoubtedly evidence of Lyotard's "incredulity" toward the kind of master narrative on which both modernism and nationalism depend.

This perspective lends a certain valedictory flavor to this book, as though its purpose were to record the rise and fall of an era in which South Africans (or some of them, at least) believed that their literature revealed to them, or would one day reveal to them, certain truths about themselves as a national community with a common history, culture, and destiny. Although this hope has not of course disappeared entirely, it would certainly seem that the era of postapartheid, nonracial South African nationalism—seen as a positive phenomenon, a popular spirit of unity, rather than a legal default position underwritten by the Constitution—has been brief indeed. (There is, of course, a huge and hitherto officially for the most part unrepresented, or underrepresented, *African* nationalism, but this pertains to ethnic identity and a historical sweep that far exceeds the geography and chronology proper to the nation-state.) The yielding of the national to the global is in this context somehow emblematized by the decision by J. M. Coetzee, South Africa's illustrious Nobel laureate, to emigrate to Australia in 2002, news to which most South Africans reacted with a shrug of the shoulders.

But if one were to attempt to date with any precision the transition in South Africa to the postnational sort of postmodernism I am seeking to adumbrate, one would have to point to the year in which Nelson Mandela retired to make way for Thabo Mbeki, 1999. With the departure of Mandela—a living symbol as much as a man of great gifts—a certain kind of hope and idealism died: his disappearance from politics seems to have spelled the end (or at least the muting) of the new national narrative of harmony and upliftment whose promise found perfect expression in the uncertain optimism of the phrase "the *new* South Africa." Because of Mbeki's initial rhetoric of "African Renaissance," it was not at first clear that a different sort of "new" era had dawned. But by now, despite the many radical and real manifestations of social transformation, it would seem that South Africans have lost that sense of exceptionalism that the more or less peaceful transition of power in the early 1990s seemed to have conferred upon them, in the eyes of the world as well as their own. They are getting used to the inflated promises of politicians and the disappointment of non-delivery; they are getting used to the idea that their well-being ultimately depends upon the vagaries of international economic trends; they are getting used to the fact that they will be governed, like everyone else in the world, by unimaginative self-serving bureaucrats, and that what "freedom" means to the poor is little more than the freedom to assume personal responsibility for their poverty. Nevertheless, as Thornton suggests, "South Africa seems likely to remain in permanent transition, just as it once seemed to exist perpetually just ahead of apocalypse,"[24] and the postmodern open-endedness of this orientation to the future endows South African culture with a keen consciousness of possibility that must bode well for the arts, including literature.[25]

Reflection of this sort leads us to consideration of the force of the term "South African" in this context. It raises a question not so much of who qualifies as South African, although the considerable exodus of writers from this country from the 1960s on does pose certain problems of classification. For instance, if a South African writer ceases to write about South Africa—ceases to set his or her novels in South Africa, for instance—does he or she still qualify? It is impossible to make fixed rules in such matters, and I intend to use, here and elsewhere, an entirely situational and pragmatic approach to the question: any work that is generally regarded as falling into the category "South African" will be treated as such.

More interesting in this context is the question of the way in which the label "South African" has for so long not only designated a national identity but also implicitly privileged writing which is in some important sense *about* South Africa, about "the South African experience" or some variety thereof. Fredric Jameson's well-known postulate that "third-world" novels are in some historically necessary sense "national allegories" may or may not be valid, but it is certainly an expectation that the international reading public brings to bear on nonmetropolitan literatures. It is, moreover, an expectation long shared by South African readers, eagerly waiting for the Great South African Novel finally to *represent* them, to represent the truth about their identity in all its myriad and fractured inflections. Certainly, such expectations cannot but influence the sort of choices and prioritizing that a project of this nature inevitably involves. However, in light of the argument in the previous paragraph, it would seem that the era in which the Great South African Novel beckoned to writers and readers alike, akin to a holy grail, as desirable as it seemed unattainable, seems now to have passed; as far back as 1983, Coetzee was cautioning that the very idea of a Great South African Novel was a pipe dream because of the limitations imposed on the writer's experience and vision by the terminally fragmented nature of South African society.[26]

One final point: in the commentary that follows, the emphasis falls largely on the narrative prose genres of the novel, short story, and autobiography. This is not because I wish to devalue or further marginalize poetry and drama, but simply in recognition that the latter are minority pursuits, both in South Africa and in the world at large, and likely to become increasingly so as the visual media continue their triumphant conquest of popular culture.

White Writing, 1948–1973

One of the most memorable characterizations of South African literature is to be found in J. M. Coetzee's Jerusalem Prize acceptance speech:

> The deformed and stunted relations between human beings that were created under colonialism and exacerbated under what is loosely called apartheid have their psychic rep-

> resentation in a deformed and stunted inner life. All expressions of that inner life, no matter how intense, no matter how pierced with exultation or despair, suffer from the same stuntedness and deformity. I make this observation with due deliberation, and in the fullest awareness that it applies to myself and my own writing as much as to anyone else. South African literature is a literature in bondage, as it reveals in even its highest moments, shot through as they are with feelings of homelessness and yearnings for a nameless liberation. It is a less than fully human literature, unnaturally preoccupied with power and the torsions of power, unable to move from elementary relations of contestation, domination, and subjugation to the vast and complex human world that lies beyond them. It is exactly the kind of literature that you would expect people to write from a prison. And I am talking here not only about the South African *gulag.* As you would expect in so physically vast a country, there is a South African literature of vastness. Yet even that literature of vastness, examined closely, reflects feelings of entrapment, entrapment in infinitudes. [27]

This harsh assessment was made in 1987, midway through the State of Emergency declared by the Botha regime, and it clearly bears the imprint of that dark and desperate time. Coetzee nevertheless articulates several unarguable truths about South African writing, most notably the "deformity" of its preoccupation with the politics of race, or with the consequences of this politics. Coetzee intends "deformed" to mean "less than fully human," but it makes sense to interpret the verb also in the formalist sense. According to Tynjanov, a work "enters into literature and takes on its own literary function through [its] dominant," and this "dominant" element or function "involves the deformation of the remaining elements."[28] Much of the writing emanating from South Africa in the period under review sought primarily to document political oppression and stir the reader into doing something about it. To use the terms popularized by Roman Jakobson, the "referential" and "conative" functions of this literature threaten to usurp the dominance of its "poetic" or aesthetic function (especially in so-called protest writing):[29] the result is a *less than fully literary* literature, a literature deformed by its slavish deference to the discourse of history and to the representational mode privileged by history, social realism.

No doubt this was to some extent inevitable: Coetzee concluded the Jerusalem Prize speech by conceding that "in South Africa there is now too much truth for art to hold, truth by the bucketful, truth that overwhelms and swamps every act of the imagination."[30] But he saw no reason to make of inevitability a virtue: a year later, in an address to a *Weekly Mail* Book Week audience, he deplored what he saw as the prevailing tendency in South Africa "to subsume the novel under history, to read novels as . . . imaginative investigations of real historical forces and real historical circumstances," and consequently to privilege texts that "*supplement* the history text."[31] The problem with texts that perform the politically useful function of supplementing history ("committed" literature, *littérature engagé*) is that they are in a sense incomplete without the history that they are supplementing: they require a real-world context coeval with and identical to their representations in order to perform their referential-cum-ethical function of bearing witness. Once that context is removed (by political change, by the simple efflux of time), it is as if the text is deprived of a crucial and even life-sustaining support. This seems the most obvious explanation for why so much South African writing dating from the decades of oppression and resistance now seems irredeemably dull, stale, flat, clichéd, melodramatic, or sensational—dead, or just plain bad; of continuing value, like a corpse in a mortuary, only as a source of forensic evidence for the crime of which it is the product. I will return to the subject of writing and political responsibility in due course, but it seems appropriate to turn now to the first real exception, from the years immediately following World War II, to the generalizations made earlier: Alan Paton's novel *Cry, the Beloved Country*.

Paton trained as a schoolteacher and was appointed principal of Diepkloof Reformatory for African boys, near Johannesburg, in 1935. He became well known for his successful liberalization of that institution, implementing a series of reforms based on respect for the individual and reward for responsibility taken—key values for the Liberal Party of which he was years later to become the leader. *Cry, the Beloved Country* was published in 1948, the very year in which the National Party won the general election and set South Africa on the path toward the (in retrospect, increasingly insane-seeming) dispensation of apartheid.

Although its local "white" reception was initially somewhat cautious (readers apparently found it "too political"), the novel was an instant success abroad, especially in the United States, where it was received as "an urgent, poetic and profound spiritual drama, universal in its implications" (*New York Times Book Review*).[32] Within a few years it was deemed sufficiently canonical to be prescribed for study in schools. The novel's reputation in South Africa has been less secure, and its changing fortunes offer an exemplary illustration of the extent to which judgments of literary value have in South Africa over the past half-century and more been formed—or deformed—by considerations of a political kind.

Cry, the Beloved Country tells the story of one black family's suffering in the context of institutionalized racial discrimination and the migrant labor system. It is a powerful and affecting story, memorably told in an elevated and lyrical style. When it was serialized in the new magazine *The African Drum* (later just *Drum*) in 1951, it was warmly welcomed and praised by the magazine's black readers for its realism and moral courage. These readers were clearly recognizing themselves and the conditions of their lives in Paton's representations, and they felt empowered by the experience.

But by the late 1950s, after a decade of increasingly forthright mass resistance to government laws and policy, reaction had set in. Although Paton's novel recognizes the irreversibility of urbanization and the necessity for blacks to assume responsibility for their political future, black readers now reacted angrily to the pastoral nostalgia of its evocations of rural Natal. Seeking more assertive and militant role models, they excoriated the passive subservience of the black characters, especially Reverend Kumalo, and scoffed at the novel's "liberal" political agenda.[33] By the late 1980s, the novel's reputation in South African had sunk yet lower. According to one critic, *Cry, the Beloved Country* had "become the perfect example of all that Black Consciousness was not,"[34] while the critique of the novel's perceived political quietism had become more trenchant under the influence of Marxist ideology. As Stephen Watson argued, "through the mouthpieces of Stephen Kumalo and Msimangu, Paton attempts to solve what is clearly and statedly a material, sociological problem by means of metaphysics; against the multiple problems caused by detribalization and urbanization he advances the solution of love."[35]

Indeed it must have seemed, at the time that Watson was writing, that the Reverend Msimangu's famous misgiving had been realized: "I have one great fear in my heart, that one day when they are turned to loving, they will find we are turned to hating."[36] But just prior to saying this, Msimangu has paid memorable tribute to the power of love, concluding: "I see only one hope for our country, and that is when white men and black men, desiring neither power nor money, but desiring only the good of their country, come together to work for it."[37] Later on, Kumalo remarks that experience has taught him that "kindness and love can pay for pain and suffering," and in this way redeem people from "the fear of bondage and the bondage of fear."[38]

It is possible to argue that history has subsequently vindicated Msimangu's and Kumalo's (and Paton's) Christian faith in the power of love. Although many factors led to the event, the hope that whites might have a change of heart and abandon the ideology of white supremacy, for no better reason—in the final analysis—than because it was the right thing to do, became reality in 1990 when President F. W. de Klerk announced the unbanning of the ANC and the unconditional release of Nelson Mandela. Then the belief that love can conquer fear became reality when Mandela emerged from twenty-seven years of incarceration, astonishingly unembittered, advocating not vengeance but reconciliation and brotherhood. De Klerk, Mandela, and their respective parties then proceeded to "come together" for "the good of their country" in the Codesa negotiations that resulted in political settlement. The rehabilitation of the novel was completed by the posthumous award to Paton by President Mbeki of South Africa's highest decoration for civic achievement, the Order of Ikhamanga (Gold), in 2006. (Cynics might prefer to say that this rehabilitation had already been achieved by the novel's selection by Oprah Winfrey as her Book Club Classics choice in October 2003; for the next two months, fifty-five years after it first appeared, Paton's novel was once again the best-selling book in the United States.)

Cry, the Beloved Country inaugurated a period lasting well into the 1960s when South African prose fiction was dominated by a mode of writing that has come to be known as "liberal realism."[39] In liberal realist novels, characters might be divided or defeated by social and political circumstances, but the values they (or their creators) both assume and advocate—individual freedom and autonomy, justice and fair play, the rule of law, the nonviolent resolution of conflict, and so on—tend nevertheless to achieve symbolic vindication. In this way, the white authors of these novels expressed their outrage at and opposition to the indignity, disadvantage, and persecution suffered by their black countrymen, and they did so in the name of humanist values shared by enlightened liberals the world over. At the same time, born as whites into a caste from which it was impossible for them to resign, they were attempting to write into existence a viable identity and role for themselves in the apartheid state. Among the more important voices in this context were those of Nadine Gordimer and Dan Jacobson.

For most of her writing career, Gordimer has been a reluctant liberal. Evincing awareness from her earliest writings of the structurally compromised position of the white liberal in South Africa, she later repudiated "liberalism" as it was, or could be, practiced in the apartheid state. Gordimer's first novel, *The Lying Days* (1953), uncompromisingly exposes the kinds of complicity and self-deception to which white South Africans of conscience must resort simply in order to continue to function in an oppressive social and political environment. The voice of the novel's first-person narrator, Helen Shaw, anticipates the dominant characteristics of Gordimer's writing over the next three decades: dry, brittle irony; the searching scrutiny and clinical dissection of motives and feelings; an unrelenting insistence on the extent to which private lives and relationships are in South Africa inevitably infiltrated, defined and warped by politics; and, increasingly, a determination to demonstrate the futility of liberal sentiments and gestures in the face of state-sponsored violence and cruelty.

In her second novel, *A World of Strangers* (1958), Gordimer consolidated her trademark narrative stance by presenting the world from an outsider's point of view—in this case, that of the expatriate Englishman Toby Hood. Toby's detached perspective, in terms of which all things South African are implicitly measured and found wanting in contrast with an enlightened Western "normality," essentially became Gordimer's own: a "Martian" viewpoint, as it were, adopted as a defense against corruption or corrosion by the habitual and the familiar.

The problem with such a point of view is that it seems necessarily to result in bleak and unforgiving narratives. Gordimer is in effect repeatedly posing the question of what a white South African is supposed to do, only repeatedly to demonstrate that all the available options are wrong. Kathrin Wagner has pointed out that there are three distinct groups of liberals under attack in Gordimer's fiction: "Firstly, there is a large group made up of those who do little more than embrace alternative attitudes and lifestyles which incorporate a disapproval of apartheid and an awareness of and respect for the idea of fundamental human rights for all." These characters are presented as frauds and cowards. Then there is a second group "made up of those who attempt to involve themselves directly in some sort of anti-apartheid activism"; but these individuals are, however well-meaning, invariably exposed as ineffectual and in search of a private absolution that benefits no one but themselves. Meanwhile, the third group, comprising those who "clumsily risk life itself for their beliefs," is seemingly "rejected for its very willingness to further change through violent action."[40]

Gordimer's 1966 novel *The Late Bourgeois World* is probably typical in its embodiment of this set of attitudes, and—unusually short and tautly constructed—is perhaps the best book for a beginning reader of Gordimer to tackle. It is also a pivotal text in the evolution of Gordimer's politics: the title announces the Marxist perspective that was, particularly after the emergence of the Black Consciousness movement, to become dominant among leftist whites in South Africa, while the novel's epigraphs point toward both the present and the future. The first, from Kafka, evokes the existential impasse of the man or woman whom Albert Memmi famously dubbed "the colonizer-who-refuses":[41] "There are possibilities for me, certainly; but under what stone do they lie?" The second is from Gorky, an expression of revolutionary romanticism that anticipates the freedom struggle proper: "The madness of the brave is the wisdom of life."

The Late Bourgeois World is narrated by a white woman in her thirties, Elizabeth Van Den Sandt, who shares with the reader a single day in her life: the day she receives word that her ex-husband and revolutionary-turned-state-witness, Max, has committed suicide. The time is the early 1960s: in the wake of the Sharpeville killings and the ensuing brutal state clampdown, hope for political change in South Africa has for the moment been shut down. Society as depicted in the novel seems only half-alive, shocked by repression into a condition of impotent stasis.

Elizabeth is a typical Gordimer narrator: cold, knowing, even smug, but frustrated, desperate, full of self-loathing. She sardonically caricatures the hypocrisy and materialism of the white petit bourgeoisie, reserving her most bilious observations for her own grandmother; she ruthlessly dissects her sterile relationship with Graham, her liberal lawyer boyfriend;

and she scornfully dismisses as embarrassingly "priggish" Max's speech at his sister's wedding, when he diagnoses a condition of "moral sclerosis. Hardening of the heart, narrowing of the mind"[42] among the well-heeled guests. Elizabeth's disaffection is repellent because it is futile: it changes nothing and helps no-one in the world around her, failing even to assuage her own feelings of complicity: "Oh we bathed and perfumed and depilated white ladies, in whose wombs the sanctity of the white race is entombed. What concoction of musk and boiled petals can disguise the dirt done in the name of that sanctity?"[43] Elizabeth may have no illusions, but her life has no meaning.

There is, however, a glimpsed possibility of the recovery of agency and purpose at the novel's end: Elizabeth is asked by a black activist to use her grandmother's bank account as a conduit for funds for the liberation movement, and the novel ends with her lying awake in the dark, as "the slow, even beats of my heart repeat to me, like a clock; afraid, alive, afraid, alive, afraid, alive."[44]

The alienation and frustration that define Elizabeth Van Den Sandt are qualities that recur in Gordimer's fiction—though tempered in *Burger's Daughter* (1979), arguably her finest novel, by the dramatization of political commitment as an ethical imperative—until a certain antirealist, whimsical, or "apocalyptic" trend manifests itself in *July's People* (1981), *Something Out There* (1984), and *A Sport of Nature* (1987). Subsequent novels, from *My Son's Story* (1990) to *The House Gun* (1998), return to a dour and politicized realism; however, there are signs in *The Pickup* (2001) of another new phase in Gordimer's career, one marked by a greater creative freedom on the part of an author less in thrall to the political history of her country.

Nadine Gordimer was awarded the Nobel Prize in literature in 1991 in recognition of her long career as a literary artist and voice of conscience in South Africa. Stephen Clingman's influential study of Gordimer's fiction was subtitled *History from the Inside*, and indeed it is hard not to construe her work as paradigmatic of those narratives that, according to Coetzee, are content to "supplement" history rather than seek to "rival" it.[45] As time passes, her novels will continue to be useful sources of historical data—South African society chronologically cross-sectioned, as it were—but are unlikely ever again to be as compelling to read as they were during the dark years of apartheid. One would like to be able to say that the "insider's" perspective that they afford is an intimate one charged with the textures of real life; or that the characters and situations represented are so fresh and free from cliché that they acquire an (as it were) independent life in the reader's imagination. But unfortunately, as the vast majority of her South African readers have attested, neither postulate is true, and Gordimer's reputation within the country, both critical and popular, appears to be in decline.[46] If it is to be revived, it may well be by way of her substantial and unjustly neglected oeuvre of short stories, a genre to which her voice and gifts as a writer seem better suited.

Dan Jacobson's status as a South African writer rests upon a handful of realist novels, mostly set in South Africa, that he published in the 1950s and 1960s (having emigrated to England in 1954, he later turned his hand to a more experimental kind of fiction, fabulous and recondite, beginning with *The Rape of Tamar*, published in 1970).

Jacobson's best-known South African novel is *A Dance in the Sun*. His characteristic estimation of white English-speaking South Africans as "mean-spirited, self-serving or cowardly"[47] is here concentrated in the character of Fletcher, a bigoted Karoo farmer who offers the student narrator and his friend, Frank, stranded hitchhikers, a bed for the night.

They are approached by a humble but dignified black man, Joseph, who asks them to help him find out what has become of his sister, banished from the farm—it later emerges—after giving birth to a child fathered by Mrs. Fletcher's brother Nasie. The awkwardness of the young men in this unusual situation is well portrayed: turning with relief from the vile Fletchers to Joseph, they are dismayed to find that their interaction with him soon reverts to the familiar pattern of the master-servant relationship. The narrator has earlier given memorable expression to the perceived absence of shared cultural fabric, of *relationship*, in all the human encounters depicted:

> By that time I felt not only that I had lost my curiosity about what was happening in the house—I felt something else too—I wouldn't call it fear—it was nothing as grand as that. Deserted would be a better word. Or lonely. Miles from any place I knew, and with my companion asleep. It was a kind of homesickness, I felt then, but it was a sickness for a home I had never had, for a single cultivated scene, for people whose manners and skins and languages were fitted peaceably together. The lorry on which we had hitched a lift from that young couple, whose little history I had just heard, had hurled us towards the man next to whom I stood, and whom I had never seen before, across endless countrysides of heat-seized, silent veld; now we stood together for a moment before the next day would hurl us apart again. And so Louw himself had come, and Frank who was sleeping, and the African outside who had been to Johannesburg—a multi-tongued nation of nomads we seemed to be, across a country too big and silent for us, too dry for cultivation, about which we went on roads like chains. We were caught within it, within this wide, sad land we mined but did not cultivate.[48]

I doubt that there are many white English-speaking South Africans whose hearts will not be touched by this haunting evocation of the "colonial melancholy" of virtual exile so intrinsic to their experience. A later and even more plangent expression of it is to be found in Stephen Watson's essay "A Version of Melancholy,"[49] where visceral recoil from "thinness"—the aesthetic and cultural starvation of all things South African, the abjection of the stunted, pinched, ersatz, arbitrary, futile—is implicitly predicated upon a nameless longing for the plenitude and security that Yeats invoked in his poem "A Prayer for My Daughter" as "custom and . . . ceremony."[50]

In the period under review, the only sustained intellectual and artistic attempt to reimagine the identity of the white English-speaking caste in South Africa in terms more positive than these was made by the poet, dramatist and academic Guy Butler, from the late 1950s to the early 1970s. His early poetry, powerfully affected by his experience with the British Army in Italy in 1944–45, includes such lyrical gems as "Stranger to Europe."[51] His finest achievement, however, is arguably the long poem "Ode: On First Seeing Florence," inspired by his first glimpse of the city as a soldier in August 1944. In later work Butler sought a voice to realize the African elements of his experience in the English poetic idiom: in "Home Thoughts" he figures this as a rapprochement between the rational European Apollo and the passionate African Dionysus:

> . . . Apollo, come!
> O cross the tangled scrub, the uncouth ways,
> Visit our vital if untamed abysm

Where your old rival in the lustrous gloom
Fumbles his drums, feels for a thread of rhythm
To dance us from our megalithic maze.

— so that "From his brimming drum / [there might] spill waves of words, articulate!"

This mythmaking in fact furnishes the coordinates of the story that Butler would go on to tell about the history and role of English-speaking whites in South Africa. In essays and addresses such as "The Republic and the Arts" (1964), Butler saw the historical destiny of white English-speaking South Africans as that of rational mediators, bringing enlightened Western values to bear in the violent clash between the (equally irrational) nationalisms of Afrikaners and Africans. In the Eastern Cape where he lived and taught at Rhodes University, Butler tirelessly popularized the history and legacy of the 1820 British settlers, presenting them as a naturalized or indigenized South African tribe, rooted in the barren soil that they had attempted to cultivate with so little success, and possessed of a proud heritage.

If all this sounds more than a little colonial in its assumptions and terms of reference, it is because—from the position of vantage afforded by postcolonialism as it has subsequently developed—it must be seen as such. In 1974, a vigorous attack by Ravan Press Director Mike Kirkwood on what he hypostasized as "Butlerism" removed English-speaking whites from the neutral ground where Butler had placed them and returned them to their rightful discursive and political home—behind the frontier stockade with the rest of the colonizers. But if this account was more truthful than settler myths of entitlement, it was also not the whole truth: English speakers had more often than not in the long sorry history of the conquest and dispossession of native Africans had a liberalizing affect on legal and political—if not always social—structures and practices. But by the 1970s, the liberation struggle was under way and the values of liberalism were in total eclipse.

Three other writers deserve mention here, one world-renowned, the other two virtually unknown outside South Africa. Athol Fugard has for decades been one of the most respected among contemporary dramatists, perhaps especially in the United States, where his *'Master Harold' . . . and the Boys* (1982) has been a huge success. But among Fugard's best work are early plays such as *Boesman and Lena* and *Hello and Goodbye*, which poignantly evoke the resilience of those cast out from life's feast. Especially fine are plays workshopped with the actors John Kani and Winston Ntshona, *Sizwe Bansi Is Dead* and *The Island*, which depict both the dehumanizing effect of apartheid on black South Africans and their courageous resistance in the face of it. Fugard has the gift of endowing his thoroughly "authentic" South African characters with universal appeal, and the broad humanism of his approach has not wavered in a career now over four decades long.

Herman Charles Bosman is sui generis: a man of mixed Afrikaner and English heritage who wrote mainly in English about "Bushveld" Afrikaner farmers. Although he published two novels, some distinguished verse, a volume of autobiography and quantities of literary journalism, it is for his Oom Schalk Lourens series of short stories that he is chiefly known. These are variously witty, humorous, satirical and lyrical, "oral-style"[52] tales about rural Afrikaner life narrated by the wily Oom ("Uncle," a general term of respect) Schalk. Immensely popular in South Africa—Bosman's oeuvre has remained in print since the 1960s, and in the past few years a multivolume "Centenary Edition" has added previously unpublished and uncollected work—the stories apparently depend too much for their characteristic effects on "insider" understanding to travel successfully. This is partly because Oom Schalk's (and Bosman's) tone is difficult for a non–South African to recognize and respond to, for instance in the opening sentences of the story "Makapan's Caves:"

> Kaffirs? (said Oom Schalk Lourens). Yes, I know them. And they're all the same. I fear the Almighty, and I respect His works, but I could never understand why He made the kaffir and the rinderpest. The Hottentot is a little better. The Hottentot will only steal the biltong hanging out on the line to dry. He won't steal the line as well. That is where the kaffir is different.[53]

Even today, a white South African will probably find this funny, while a non–South African will almost certainly not. Even after it has been explained that the joke is on the bigoted speaker rather than the objects of his racist stereotyping, it is unlikely that the outsider will be amused. Moreover, this "explanation" would not cover the full resonance of the South African reader's response to Oom Schalk's words: part of the joke *is* the racist stereotyping, which means that at least part of the joke is at the expense of the "kaffirs" and the "Hottentots." Bosman is a gifted writer, but the problem with the Oom Schalk stories is that they are shot through with an ambiguity that has usefully been characterized as "unstable irony,"[54] meaning that the relationship between the author and his narrator is inconsistent, shifting and ambivalent.

Although many of his stories were published only after World War II, Bosman began writing a decade before the war. Roy Campbell was still publishing poetry in the 1950s, but his career, like the South African career of William Plomer, essentially belongs to the 1920s and 1930s. In addition to Guy Butler, several accomplished poets emerged in the postwar years—F. T. Prince, Charles Eglington, Ruth Miller—but the most original and distinctive voice after Campbell in South African poetry is that of Sydney Clouts. Clouts's poems are situated at the interface between the individual consciousness and what he called the "thingbedded" reality that surrounds it; as critics have noted, the poems embody a strong sense of Heidegger's *Dasein* or "Being-in-the-world."[55] Formally experimental and thoroughly modernist in its oblique communicative strategies, Clouts's verse evinces also a thoroughly Romantic yearning for transcendence: there is no room in the poems for the news of the day, the contingencies of politics or ideology. The opening poem in his *Collected Poems* might serve as example:

> A pool for the image,
> A cool image of sun.
> Desiring more than reflection,
> What shall I take?
> Flowerstem, clod, or a bouncing stone?
> A plain round pebble is best.
> The rings glance backward to their rest.
> Round, round, round.
> Bright heaven, lap the ground.[56]

Writing Black, 1946–1972

The narrative in this section begins in 1946 because that is the year in which appeared both Es'kia Mphahlele's first slender collection of short stories, *Man Must Live and Other Stories*, and Peter Abrahams's third novel, *Mine Boy*.[57]

Within the South African system of racial classification, Abrahams was Coloured: a person of mixed race or—in the sinisterly pedantic words of the Population Registration Act—a person "not obviously white" nor "obviously black." Partly as a result of his father's Ethiopian heritage, and partly as a consequence of his early acquaintance with writers of the Harlem Renaissance, Abrahams seems—for a time at least—to have solved the vexed question of identity by proudly self-identifying as a black writer.[58] At the same time, his work evinces throughout an impatience with racial categories and a keen awareness of the suffocating effect of generic identifications on the individual's sense of self.

Mine Boy, which was later to reach a wide readership through its reprinting in Heinemann's African Writers Series, is—like *Cry, the Beloved Country*—a classic example of the South African narrative genre that has come to be known (after a film of that name released in 1949) as the "Jim comes to Jo'burg" story. It was an especially topical genre in the years immediately following World War II, when the government was obliged to grapple with problems posed by the massive influx of black work-seekers to the urban areas. Conservative whites saw blacks as unwelcome "visitors" in the city, needing strict control and tolerable only because of the needs of the labor market. Liberals were ambivalent. On one hand, like Paton in *Cry, the Beloved Country*, they acknowledged that "the tribe was broken" and that black people were fast becoming a permanent demographic feature of city life.[59] On the other hand (and again like Paton), they deplored what they saw as the corruption of the pastoral innocence of blacks, through their exposure both to the seamy side of city life and to an increasingly naked and brutal white racism; they felt that Africans were better off returning to the countryside to resume their "traditional" lives. Arguably, both perspectives conduced to the political vision of apartheid, as manifest in measures ranging from the notorious Pass Laws ("influx control,") to the Bantustan system of ethnic "homelands." Urbanized black people, on the other hand, soon saw themselves as irreversibly (if not unproblematically) city folk. As Es'kia Mphahlele puts it in his autobiography, *Down Second Avenue*:

> [In the 1930s] the Black people conditioned themselves by the day, so as to survive. And the more the white man needed them for his work, the more he hated them. More people poured into Pretoria from the north and the east. The more insecure people felt, the more permanent they looked, as they burrowed into location life, putting up tin shacks on the small plots allowed to the residents. Perpetual refugees seeking life and safety in Jim Crow town.[60]

In *Mine Boy*, Johannesburg is represented as a school of hard knocks, characterized by both squalor and opportunity. The novel envisages a class alliance among workers of different races as offering resistance to the depredations of the exploitative mining houses and their racist white champions. But Abrahams's Marxist ideas are subsumed under an overarching liberal humanist perspective that, as in Paton's novel, imagines individuals finding mutual understanding through sympathetic acts of imaginative identification.[61]

Michael Chapman has aptly written of Abrahams that he was "one of the earliest black writers in English to have been given the license to be any kind of radical rather than the one thing he wanted to be: a writer without color."[62] The extent to which only exile (in Jamaica) could resolve the ambiguity and assuage the pain of being a Coloured South African is made clear in Abrahams's autobiography, *Tell Freedom* (1954), the first of several notable achievements in that genre to emanate from South Africa in the 1950s and 1960s:

"Perhaps life had a meaning that transcended race and colour. If it had, I could not find it in South Africa. Also, there was the need to write, to tell freedom, and for this I needed to be personally free."[63]

Although he was later to write two novels, the fact that the first publication by Es'kia Mphahlele was a collection of short stories is significant. Mphahlele would himself argue that the preeminence of the short fictional form in black South African writing in the 1950s was a direct consequence of the dislocated lives led by the writers: "the stringent socio-political conditions to which the African is subjected in South Africa make very difficult the sustained organization of the total personality and effort on the writer's part required for the novel." The short story, on the other hand, was a medium particularly suited to and expressive of a "fugitive urban culture."[64] To an oppression that bore down with unrelenting intensity and afforded only a fragmentary sense of selfhood, black writers reacted with brief, often angry and overblown, cameos of experience.

Publication outlets that became available in the 1950s also conduced to the flourishing of the short story. Magazines such as *Drum* actively solicited short fictional contributions by running regular competitions, and several writers who later achieved prominence were first published in the pages of *Drum* in Johannesburg and other, more overtly political journals and newspapers like *New Age* and *Fighting Talk* in Cape Town: Can Themba, Casey Motsisi, Arthur Maimane, Alex La Guma, Richard Rive, James Matthews.[65] It is no accident that these writers were mostly journalists and based either in Sophiatown (Johannesburg) or District Six (Cape Town), multiracial ghettoes destroyed by forced removals—"slum clearance"—in the late 1950s and early 1960s.[66]

These writers also—usually, from the subsequent perspective of exile—told their own life stories. In addition to Peter Abrahams, in the 1950s and 1960s Es'kia Mphahlele, Bloke Modisane, Todd Matshikiza, and Alfred Hutchinson wrote full-length autobiographies, while Nat Nakasa, Casey Motsisi, and Can Themba, among others, penned autobiographical sketches and vignettes.[67]

Autobiographical writing was for these men in an unusually literal sense an act of self-invention. As a generation, their lives were effectively defined by change, fracture and frustration: to the dislocation of rapid urbanization and cultural change (most were only first- or second-generation city dwellers) was superadded the burden of ever-increasing state regulation and oppression. The autobiographies reveal that their authors experienced selfhood as something not fully owned, as incoherent and problematic because ostensibly "authored" by the apartheid state (cf. the title of Modisane's *Blame Me on History*). In the absence of any preexisting discourse capable of providing adequate self-representation, each individual effectively uses the medium of autobiography to write himself (and the community to which he belongs) into existence. Mphahlele's *Down Second Avenue* is paradigmatic in this regard.

Between the ages of five and thirteen, Mphahlele lived with his paternal grandmother in the rural village of Maupaneng, near present-day Polokwane in the Northern Province. He devotes a scant ten pages to these years, concluding:

> Looking back to those first thirteen years of my life—as much of it as I can remember—I cannot help thinking that it was time wasted. I had nobody to shape them into a definite pattern. Searching through the confused threads of that pattern a few things

> keep imposing themselves on my whole judgment. My grandmother; the mountain; the tropical darkness which glow-worms seemed to try in vain to scatter; long black tropical snakes; the brutal Leshoana river carrying on its broad back trees, cattle, boulders; world of torrential rains; the solid shimmering heat beating down on yearning earth; the romantic picture of a woman with a child on her back and an earthen pot on her head, silhouetted against the mirage.
>
> But all in all perhaps I led a life shared by all other country boys. Boys who are aware of only one purpose of living; to be.[68]

What is of particular interest is the essentially static nature of this time as Mphahlele remembers it, a time when he was possessed of an identity that he can only in retrospect characterize as generic. His move to the house in Second Avenue, Marabastad (in Pretoria), at the age of thirteen was nothing less than a standing jump into the modern, into time experienced as becoming rather than being, into the whole process of individuation. Another way of putting this is to say that it required physical relocation into the space of urban modernity for Mphahlele to acquire a sense of self commensurate with the raw material of autobiography.

The remainder of *Down Second Avenue* records Mphahlele's growing understanding of and bitterness toward the political barriers in the way of his personal freedom and achievement: to be stuck "down Second Avenue" becomes a metaphor for the lot of the black man trapped in the township ghettoes of apartheid South Africa.[69] Particularly memorable are the chapters scattered through the text that Mphahlele entitles "Interlude," and in which he uses various modes of interior monologue to attempt to recapture the immediacy of remembered feelings.[70] A climax in the narrative is reached with Mphahlele's decision to emigrate, and the last part of the book, written in Nigeria in late 1957, celebrates his first taste of "downright individualism."[71]

Mphahlele's experience of race or ethnicity as an artificially imposed and arbitrarily limiting identity helps to explain his and other black South Africans' fierce opposition to essentialist African ideologies such as négritude (and indeed, beyond that, the general resistance of South Africa to description according to the "postcolonial" template).[72] In *Down Second Avenue*, Mphahlele uses an idiom with sharp contemporary resonance to evoke the rapid acculturation of his generation: referring to segregationist insistence that blacks be encouraged to "develop along their own lines," he writes: "We retreated to our townships 'to develop along our own lines.' We couldn't see the lines and the footprints. They had got so mixed up with other footprints in the course of time, and the winds had been blowing away some, too."[73]

Alex La Guma, perhaps the most prominent black South African writer of the 1960s,[74] was also a staunch nonracialist, but the source of his conviction was his lifelong commitment to the ideology of Marxism-Leninism. Having joined the Communist Party of South Africa at an early age, he became, as a so-called listed Communist, a de facto enemy of the South African state when the party was banned under the Suppression of Communism Act in 1950. After several spells in detention and under house arrest, he left South Africa on an exit permit in 1966 and remained abroad until his death in Cuba in 1985. Many other writers fled the country in the state clampdown that followed the Sharpeville shootings, and in subsequent decades two distinct South African literary traditions or systems existed, one inside the country and the other outside. In addition to La Guma, Abrahams and Mphahlele, the exiles included (to name just a few) Dennis Brutus, Keorapetse Kgositsile, Bessie Head, Mazisi Kunene, Daniel P. Kunene, and Lewis Nkosi. While their names became well known abroad, because of the provisions of both the Suppression of Communism Act (later the Internal Security Act) and the Publications Act, the work of these writers was prohibited from being distributed or even read within the borders of the country.

In the five novels he published between 1962 and 1979, La Guma consistently emphasizes the category of class rather than race and thus gives fictional form to a rigorous Marxist analysis of the South African social formation.[75] His enduring theme is the suffering under oppression and revolutionary awakening of black South Africans. In the early novels—*A Walk in the Night* and *And a Threefold Cord*—the characters, lacking rudimentary political awareness, are doomed by the identity imposed on them by the social order to be little more than links in a chain of cause and effect, their consciousness radically determined by the material forces of a coercive political system. In later works such as *In the Fog of the Seasons' End* and *Time of the Butcherbird*, La Guma dramatizes the consolidation of political understanding among the victims of apartheid capitalism and the growth of their commitment to armed struggle.

La Guma's highly detailed descriptive style has been labeled "journalistic," but is more properly seen as a latter-day avatar of literary naturalism, perhaps even of the "socialist realism" promoted in the Soviet Union in the 1930s. His best work is probably *A Walk in the Night*, a tale of moral inversion set in the ghetto of District Six, which portrays the inhabitants as little more than a feature of their dilapidated environment:

> He turned down another street, away from the artificial glare of Hanover, between stretches of damp, battered houses with their broken-ribs of front-railings; cracked walls and high tenements that rose like the left-overs of a bombed area in the twilight; vacant lots and weed-grown patches where houses had once stood; and deep doorways resembling the entrances to deserted castles. There were children playing in the street, darting among the overflowing dustbins and shooting at each other with wooden guns. In some of the doorways people sat or stood, murmuring idly in the fast-fading light like wasted ghosts in a plague-ridden city.[76]

The action of the novel spans a few fateful hours in the life of Michael Adonis, who, having been fired from his job for insubordination to a white foreman, vents his frustration on a harmless old white man, bludgeoning him to death with a wine bottle. An innocent bystander is suspected of the murder and shot dead by racist, trigger-happy police. By the story's end, Adonis has agreed to join a gang of toughs and appears to be drifting into a life of crime.

There are several indications in the course of the narrative as to how these "tragic" events are to be interpreted by the reader (the finger quite clearly points to the structural violence of economic exploitation, reinforced by political oppression). But because the characters, lacking even the most rudimentary political insight, are oblivious to these indications, they are portrayed as little more than ghosts (like that of Hamlet's father), "doom'd for a certain term to walk the night."

The novel is bleakly affecting, and La Guma is perhaps the most accomplished of a group of writers whose work has become known as "protest writing." Although Njabulo Ndebele has rejected the label on the grounds of its being misleading and reductive, as we will see, "protest" nevertheless remains a useful generic descriptor for most of the writing by black South Africans that appeared in the 1960s and early 1970s.

The first stirrings of black literary activity after the bannings and general exodus of intellectuals in the early-to-mid 1960s were notable for the prominence of lyric poetry, a genre almost wholly neglected in the 1950s. The reemergence in print of verse by black South Africans is clearly traceable in contributions to the literary magazine *The Classic*, beginning with four poems in 1968 by Oswald Joseph Mtshali. In a watershed special poetry issue the following year, Mtshali was joined by Njabulo S. Ndebele, Wally Mongane Serote, and M. Pascal Gwala. Mtshali, Serote, Gwala, and a fourth writer, Sydney Sipho Sepamla, were the major authors of what became known as "Soweto poetry," a catchall phrase for a variety of township-based, politically incisive, often blues- or jazz-influenced, sometimes declamatory verse.[77] The impulse animating Soweto Poetry appears to have been the same deep need—in the face of the unrelenting negation of state oppression—for the recovery or invention of human agency (individual self-expression, self-definition, self-creation) that, as we have already noted, characterizes the autobiographies from Abrahams's *Tell Freedom* onwards. A major difference is that historical developments in the 1960s, including widespread decolonization in Africa, the rise of the civil rights movement in the United States, and—most especially—the emergence and gathering momentum of Black Consciousness in South Africa, serve to endow the writing with a new tonal range, considerably more culturally confident and politically assertive. All this history, together with an anticipation of much that was yet to come, is implicit in the opening poem of Serote's first and most memorable collection, *Yakhal'inkomo*:

Do not fear Baas.
It's just that I appeared
And our faces met
In this black night that's like me.
Do not fear—
We will always meet
When you do not expect me.
I will appear
In the night that's black like me.
Do not fear—
Blame your heart
When you fear me—
I will blame my mind
When I fear you
In the night that's black like me.
Do not fear Baas,
My heart is vast as the sea
And your mind as the earth.
It's awright Baas,
Do not fear.[78]

In a poetic reflection on the conditions of poetic production in South Africa, Jeremy Cronin has observed: "Between, let's say, May 1984 and May 1986 / . . . There was a shift out there/ From lyric to epic."[79] David Attwell has more recently approved and elaborated on this diagnosis of generic drift, but shifted its moment back a decade, to 1974, the year of the watershed "Poetry '74" conference.[80] If by the move to "epic" is meant, at the very least, the change from an individual perspective and voice to a communal, national, even world-historical one, then I would suggest that there are distinct traces of the epic to be found in *Yakhal'inkomo*—most especially in angry affirmations of shared black experience in the sequence that closes the volume.[81] It would not be long before Serote was producing epic-length poems dedicated to the heroic struggle for freedom into which his countrymen and women were effectively plunged after June 1976.

White Writing, 1974–1990

In the same year that Serote's *Yakhal'inkomo* was published, John Maxwell Coetzee took up a post as lecturer in English at the University of Cape Town, where he was to remain until his retirement in 2000. Coetzee was born in Cape Town in 1940 and grew up there and in the nearby town of Worcester; some idea of his younger years may be gained from his "autobiographical novel" *Boyhood*.[82] He then studied and worked in England and the United States for some years, obtaining a PhD degree from the University of Texas at Austin.

Coetzee published his first novel, *Dusklands*, in 1974. Juxtaposing two narratives, one with a contemporary Vietnam War setting and the other an eighteenth-century frontier tale, the text exposes and condemns colonial violence as the product of an underlying psychopathology of Western life, seemingly a product of the Cartesian dualism engrained in characteristic modes of perception and relationship. In his novel *In the Heart of the Country* (1977), a lonely spinster searches unavailingly for a language of mutuality to end her isolation on a deserted Karoo farm; while in *Waiting for the Barbarians* (1980), a liberal magistrate in the service of an unnamed empire experiences a crisis of conscience when he is made to choose between loyalty to his masters and protection of their alleged "barbarian" enemies.

In these and subsequent novels, Coetzee makes clear reference to the situation in South Africa without restricting his fiction to the "realist" terms dictated by the discourse of history which, he has suggested, serves only to reinforce the authority of the status quo. Yet the clarity of this reference—the formal manner of the fiction's (non)representation of social and political realities—was insufficient for the taste of South African readers who, increasingly in the aftermath of June 1976, demanded of their writers a more literal demonstration of commitment to the liberation struggle. In 1988, the academic critic Michael Chapman lambasted Coetzee's novel *Foe* for not "speaking to Africa" and serving to provide little more than "a kind of masturbatory release for the Europeanising dreams of an intellectual coterie."[83] The atmosphere of crisis was such that the following year Chapman could effectively dismiss literature's right to be taken seriously by claiming that: "In a State of Emergency [declared by President P. W. Botha in 1986 in response to rising civil unrest], the authority of experience, rather than its transformation into the art object, has become the real locus of power."[84]

In fact, Coetzee had already answered his critics in two articles, "Into the Dark Chamber" and "The Novel Today."[85] Both are partly indebted to T. W. Adorno's 1962 essay "Commitment," which champions what Adorno called the "autonomous" literary work over against the manifestly "committed" one.[86] In "The Novel Today," this distinction is rendered as the difference between the novel that "supplements" history and the novel that "rivals" history, the latter being "a novel that operates in terms of its own procedures and issues in its own conclusions, not one that operates in terms of the procedures of history and eventuates in conclusions that are checkable by history (as a child's schoolwork is checked by a schoolmistress)."[87] This asseveration of the value of the aesthetic in the face of what Coetzee called "the appropriating appetite of the discourse of history"[88] is a quintessentially modernist gesture in which his writing is implicitly identified with the "avant-garde" work of Kafka and Beckett that was applauded by Adorno.[89]

Meanwhile, in the world outside, Coetzee's standing as an author rose ever higher, his books garnering one international literary award after another. Perhaps his most memorable creation from this era is *Life & Times of Michael K* (1983), a novel set in a futuristic South Africa embroiled in civil war. The beleaguered state has taken to herding the poor and unemployed into fenced "camps" so as to control the movement of people about the country. Michael K, the novel's protagonist, is incarcerated in a camp but finds that he cannot bear the loss of freedom. He escapes and for a time leads a solitary existence, first on an abandoned farm and then in the mountains, effectively removed from the linear time of history:

> But most of all, as summer slanted to an end, he was learning to love idleness, idleness no longer as stretches of freedom reclaimed by stealth here and there from involuntary labor, surreptitious thefts to be enjoyed sitting on his heels before a flowerbed with a fork dangling from his fingers, but as a yielding up of himself to time, to a time flowing slowly like oil from horizon to horizon over the face of the world, washing over his body, circulating in his armpits and his groin, stirring his eyelids.[90]

He realizes during this sojourn in nature that he is not a freedom fighter but a "gardener," one whose role it is "to stay behind" while others go to war and "keep gardening alive, or at least the idea of gardening; because once that cord was broken, the earth would grow hard and forget her children."[91] Eventually he is recaptured and sent to a rehabilitation camp in Cape Town, where a military doctor takes a special interest in his case. To the doctor, the taciturn Michael K seems in his utter self-sufficiency to hold the key to genuine freedom, perhaps the secret of life itself.

The opacity of the character is mirrored in the novel's resistance to interpretation. Readers have attempted to allegorize K in a number of ways—as a figure for the author or artist in a time of war; as a figure for the otherness of the text in which he appears, and of literature more generally; as embodying the possibility of dwelling in holistic and respectful harmony with other living things. But K somehow contrives to evade all these "camps," an enigmatic yet poignant presence in a hauntingly beautiful narrative.

Coetzee's next book, *Foe* (1986), rewrites Daniel Defoe's *Robinson Crusoe* by imagining it as the corruption of a story told to Defoe by a woman, Susan Barton, a story focusing in part on the tongueless servant Friday. *The Master of Petersburg* (1994) is similarly "literary" in that it portrays a fictional incident from the life of the Russian novelist Fyodor Dostoyevsky. But Age *of Iron* (1990) is clearly set in Cape Town during the State of Emergency in the late 1980s, and—like the award-winning *Disgrace* (1999)—employs an essentially realist narrative mode to stage ethical dilemmas of universal application.

A recurrent theme in Coetzee's writing is the failure of mutuality, of love, in relations corrupted by the abuse of power: between the white (colonizing) subject and his or her (colonized) Other, between men and women, between humans and other animals. Coetzee's core ideal is justice, and the essential value in terms of which its absence is registered is the suffering human body.[92] Increasingly, however, *metafiction* has become the overarching rubric for Coetzee's work, for a kind of fiction that—mesmerized by its own self-reflexivity—presents itself as a series of meditations on the enigmatic relations among writing, representation and the self.

The work of other white writers from this period tended to respond to the impact of apartheid in a more direct way. During these years, Nadine Gordimer published her politically most incisive novels, *The Conservationist* (1974), *July's People* (1981), and her masterpiece, *Burger's Daughter* (1979), a novel that memorably captures, in the choices made by the protagonist Rosa Burger, the irruption of politics into every aspect of private life in South Africa. The epigraph to *July's People* is a passage from the *Prison Notebooks* of Antonio Gramsci: "The old is dying and the new cannot be born; in this interregnum there arises a great variety of morbid symptoms." The following year, Gordimer gave a public lecture in New York entitled "Living in the Interregnum." This bold acknowledgment that South Africa was already engaged in an irreversible process of revolutionary change captured the imagination of intellectuals and commentators and was frequently cited in the years leading up to February 1990.

Much of the writing by white South Africans from this period registers "morbid symptoms" of one sort or another: mordant guilt, frustration, alienation, apprehension, thralldom to a crippling irony. The overall mood of the white South African populace was memorably captured by the American anthropologist Vincent Crapanzano, who wrote, "Wittingly or unwittingly, the whites wait for something, anything to happen. They are caught in the peculiar, the paralytic time of waiting. . . . Waiting—the South African experience—must be appreciated in all its banality. Therein lies its pity—and its humanity."[93]

A memorable exception to these generalizations is David Muller's novel *Whitey*, which depicts a drunken weekend in the life of a white sailor who fetches up in a Coloured *smokkelhuis* or shebeen in Cape Town. In its haunting evocations of a partly demolished District Six, the novel is an obvious companion piece to La Guma's *A Walk in the Night* and Achmat Dangor's *Waiting for Leila*. But its chief strength is its gut-wrenching and wholly convincing dramatization of the physical and psychological degeneration of an alcoholic *in extremis*.[94]

Meanwhile—as the contents of little magazines such as *New Coin Poetry* attest—white South African poets continued their love affair with the country's rugged landscape and the flora and fauna (especially chameleons) of their suburban gardens.[95] To be sure, as the years pass, their sense of relationship to the land becomes increasingly uneasy and self-doubting, and several interesting poets from this era respond in complex ways to the social crises attendant on the rise of black nationalism and the imminent demise of the Nationalist government.[96] Nevertheless, two of the most memorable voices from these years focus rather on the typical terrain of the modern lyric: personal experience and the place of the individual in an uncertain and seemingly indifferent cosmos.

Don Maclennan came to poetry relatively late—his first collection, *Life Songs*, appearing in 1977, when he was forty-eight—and arguably his best work postdates the period under review, issuing from a prodigiously productive phase lasting from the 1990s to the present. However, it was in the pared-to-the-bone minimalism of *Collecting Darkness* (1988) that Maclennan found his characteristic voice: a voice in love with language but eschewing verbal frippery, confessional, self-deprecating but also forgiving; endlessly questioning, skeptical, or rueful even in celebration; spare, gnomic, sometimes amused and amusing. The poem "Letter in a Bottle" features a typically terse and modest credo that effectively labels an entire oeuvre:

> All I've ever wanted to make—
> a few clean statements
> on love and death,
> things you cannot fake.[97]

Of all South Africa's cities, Cape Town is undoubtedly most deserving of its own poet laureate. In 1986, with the publication of his collection *In This City*, Stephen Watson emerged to fulfill the role. In this and subsequent volumes, Watson sought to capture both the visual beauty and what he calls the spiritual "melancholy" or "thinness" of the city and its inhabitants, "torn between its cloud-light, pine-light, the serene nihilism of its skies, / and its unending, all-negating, word-exhausting human cries."[98] Watson's lyrical gifts, his romantic, elegiac cadences and rhetorically spacious narrative lines, create an unforgettable portrait of a city that somehow accommodates the pain of its troubled history and its immense material inequalities in the poignant evocation of one individual's overwhelming sense of belonging.

Writing Black, 1972–1990

The appearance in 1972 of James Matthews's poetry collection *Cry Rage!* announced a tightening of the nexus between politics and writing by black South Africans.[99] Matthews has commented:

> 1972 became too much for me. The Dimbazas, Ilinges, Sadas and Limehills [resettlement areas]. Dying children—starvation, their sickness. The uprooting of people; the harvesting of crops of crosses, the only fruit the land would bear. Detention and the deaths in detention. It became too much for me. . . . I wrote. It was not prose. Critics hyena-howled. It was not poetry, they exclaimed. I never said it was. I was writing expressions of feelings.[100]

In this way Matthews self-consciously rejected both the forms and the function of the literary tradition in which his use of the English language had placed him. The final piece in the collection is paradigmatic:

> To label my utterings poetry
> And myself a poet
> Would be as self-deluding
> As the planners of parallel development
> I record the anguish of the persecuted
> Whose words are whispers of woe
> Wrung from them by bestial laws
> They stand one chained band
> Silently asking one of the other
> Will it never be the fire next time?

While there is more than a modicum of traditional poetic technique in Matthews's "expressions of feelings," there is no denying that in this and subsequent volumes his writing is deliberately deformed to allow its "emotive" and "conative" functions to usurp the dominance of its "poetic" or aesthetic function (to revert to the structuralist terminology of Roman Jakobson).[101]

While the "feelings" to which Matthews gives vent in *Cry Rage!* are clearly informed by a knowledge of African American writing and the successes of the civil rights movement in the United States, they invoke the authority of a "universal" human-rights discourse. But within two years, Matthews's work in both poetry and prose was to evince a new and fierce commitment to the ideology of Black Consciousness and its program for the psychological rehabilitation and liberation of the oppressed.[102] The elaboration and dissemination of Black Consciousness ideology, with its catchphrase, "You're on your own, Blackman," was mostly the work of the Black Peoples' Convention and the South African Students' Organization, whose charismatic president Steve Biko was the movement's intellectual leader. Biko was tortured to death by the security police in September 1977, an event that outraged the world and led to an intensification of the international campaign against the apartheid government. Biko's speeches and occasional writings were collected as *I Write What I Like* and published in the year after his death.[103] (The book, recently reissued, is still widely read in South Africa today, and is probably the most important publication by a black South African to have appeared in the period under review.)

There is therefore a direct line from Matthews's poetic diatribe against "white syphilization" (1974),[104] via events following the Soweto uprising of 1976 and the death of Biko the following year, to the much-quoted repudiation of Western literary convention in Mothobi Mutloatse's introduction to the 1980 anthology of new writing, *Forced Landing*:

> We will have to *donder* conventional literature: old-fashioned critic and reader alike. We are going to pee, spit and shit on literary convention before we are through; we are going to kick and pull and push and drag literature into the form we prefer. We are going to experiment and probe and not give a damn what the critics have to say. Because we are in search of our true selves—undergoing self-discovery as a people.[105]

But by that time, the Black Consciousness rhetoric of Mutloatse's last sentence had been partly co-opted into an uneasy alliance with the idiom of a revolutionary Marxism, in terms of which black South Africans were rendered as "the masses" engaged in a "liberation struggle" (and using literature as a means of prosecuting that struggle). This process of radical politicization (of which more, below) famously imprinted itself in the form of Mongane Serote's novel, *To Every Birth Its Blood*.[106] The alienated artist-figure Tsi has his world turned upside down by the events of Soweto 1976, and discovers a new and more authentic identity in commitment to his "comrades" in "the struggle;" the ironic lyricism of the first part of the novel gives way to epic celebration in the second.

In 1978, Ravan Press launched *Staffrider*, a literary magazine with a radically democratic editorial policy: writing groups or areas organized by the Association of African Writers submitted batches of material that were published as is, ostensibly without further (white) editorial intervention or mediation.[107] This policy of "grassroots" editorial democracy ensured that new (if unpolished) work by young writers achieved wide and immediate circulation; it also played an important role in popularizing writing in English and demonstrating its increasingly public role as both witness to and actor in the unfolding drama of communal solidarity and historical agency. In his introduction to *Forced Landing*, Mutloatse thus pays tribute to "an age of experimental literature vibrantly expressing communal experience," and even announces the birth of a new literary genre to match the heroic temper of the times, the "proemdra: Prose, Poem and Drama in one!"[108]

A few examples of this "committed" hybrid form appeared in *Staffrider* and culminated in the book-length *Seeds of War* by Mtutuzeli Matshoba.[109] But what had emerged more conspicuously in the late 1970s and early 1980s were a number of volumes of well-crafted stories of township experience, including *Mzala* (later reissued as *My Cousin Comes to Joburg and Other Stories*) by Mbulelo Mzamane (1980) and *Call Me Not a Man* by Mtutuzeli Matshoba (1979).[110] While *Call Me Not a Man* is more earnestly didactic than the often-jokey *Mzala*, both collections offer oral-style narration and irony-laced snapshots of township life that ridicule the pretensions and contradictions of a vicious but tottering apartheid system.[111] Both anthologies also include rewritings of the "Jim comes to Jo'burg" theme for a new generation of black readers. In the story sequence that comprises the first half of *Mzala*, the narrator's cousin Mzal' uJola from the Transkei is a stereotypical naïf when he arrives in eGoli, but (unlike, for example, Absalom in *Cry, the Beloved Country*) he soon adapts to city ways and carves out for himself a robustly vital existence in defiance of the demeaning panoply of rules and restrictions to which black people are subjected. On the other hand, in the final story in *Call Me Not a Man*, "Three Days in the Land of a Dying Illusion," Matshoba inverts the migrant's journey by having his urbane, Johannesburg-bred narrator travel to the "independent" Transkei and register his disgust at the poverty and backwardness of the "homeland"—of which, being Xhosa, he is expected to claim citizenship.[112] The story develops into a sustained exposé of the bankruptcy of grand apartheid's geopolitical ambitions.

Also published in the *Staffrider* series was Achmat Dangor's brilliant debut collection, *Waiting for Leila*.[113] The title novella is set in the crumbling wasteland of an all-but-demolished District Six (the Cape Town ghetto forcibly cleared of its Coloured residents from the late 1960s). In the drink-and drug-battered mind of the protagonist, Samad, feelings evoked by a lost love and the destruction of the Malay community gain weight and resonance from the parallel story of a rebellious slave forebear. The increasingly disjunctive narrative memorably enacts the historical fracture that it represents.

Dangor's and Matshoba's and Mzamane's stories were first published in *Staffrider*, so it was appropriate that some the earliest and most influential critical responses appeared there too. The predominant critical stance at the time, and the one that continued to gain authority and consolidate its orthodoxy until the sea change of 1990, has been usefully characterized as "solidarity criticism."[114] Solidarity criticism is not a literary category at all but a political one, an epiphenomenon of the intensification of "the struggle" against the South African government. It finds its purest expression in the slogan, "Culture is a weapon of the struggle," which meant that writers and artists and other "cultural workers" were required to devote their energies and expertise to furthering political ends. In this perspective, the more blatant and trenchant (and hence more "effective") its propaganda effect, the better the writing.[115]

The Marxist rhetoric adopted by what became the Mass Democratic Movement (MDM) in the 1980s was less a demonstration of commitment to dialectical materialism (as events subsequent to 1994 have shown only too clearly) than it was part of a revolutionary toolkit whose effectiveness had already been extensively demonstrated elsewhere in Africa and Latin America. Meanwhile, academic Marxists worried about the ("petit-bourgeois") class position of writers like Matshoba—and hence the legitimacy of their representations of black working-class experience—and deplored their "humanist" privileging of color rather than class as the primary category of social analysis.[116]

In the context of this politically charged but intellectually dreary climate of reception, the interventions of Njabulo S. Ndebele were, and remain, absolutely seminal. Ndebele's essay "Turkish Tales and Some Thoughts on South African Fiction" appeared in *Staffrider* in 1984.[117] In this piece, Ndebele extols the example of the Turkish short-story writer Yashar Kemal as one who is "rooted firmly in the timeless tradition of storytelling." His tales do not offer social commentary on or political analysis of the situations they depict because Kemal does not presume to "reduce [the] humanity" of his characters by "[turning] them into mere items in a moral or political debate."[118] Ndebele contrasts this with the generality of black South African fiction, which, "built around the interaction of surface symbols of the South African reality," has resulted in "a tradition of almost mechanistic surface representation."[119]

This is the core observation that Ndebele develops in an essay subsequently canonized in the South African critical tradition, "The Rediscovery of the Ordinary: Some New Writings in South Africa."[120] The first part of this essay identifies the "spectacular" as the characteristic mode of black South African "protest" fiction:

> The spectacular, documents; it indicts implicitly; it is demonstrative, preferring exteriority to interiority; it keeps the larger issues of society in our minds, obliterating the details; it provokes identification through recognition and feeling rather than through observation and analytical thought; it calls for emotion rather than conviction; it establishes a vast sense of presence without offering intimate knowledge; it confirms without necessarily offering a challenge. It is the literature of the powerless identifying the key factor responsible for their powerlessness.[121]

Ndebele suggests that "the convention of the spectacle has run its course" and proposes that writers rather seek their material in the "ordinary" aspects of black South African life. Widely misunderstood at the time as a call for the abolition of the liberation aesthetic, Ndebele's arguments are in fact entirely consonant with the Black Consciousness roots of his intellectual project. What he is advocating is a literature sufficiently insightful and attuned to quotidian reality as to be able effectively to assist its readers toward the maturity of consciousness necessary for psychological and political liberation. What is absolutely vital is that black characters be portrayed as free agents, rather than as contingent subjects reacting to a situation not of their own making, or enmeshed in a relationship of submission or antagonism with their white Others. Another way of putting this is to say that, for Ndebele, it is the task of writers to demonstrate that black life is sufficiently dense and complex and suffused with value as to be treatable as *ordinary*, in the way that modern Western fiction had made of ordinary life a seemingly inexhaustible source of subject matter. Yet another (skeptical, yet no less apposite) way of construing Ndebele's critical project is to see it as an attempt to create a suitably sympathetic climate of reception for his own collection of short stories published in late 1983, *Fools and Other Stories*.[122]

Fools is a polished collection of five stories. The first four follow a fairly standard Bildungsroman pattern in tracing the growth of a boy's consciousness as he acquires what David Attwell has aptly described as "the kind of social imagination out of which an appropriately subject-centered activism is possible."[123] In keeping with this focus, there is an emphasis on interiority in the characterization and an insistence that what is unique about the experience of the individual *matters*—but matters, importantly, only in relation to the community to which the individual belongs and from whose historical situation his destiny cannot (and must not) be separated. As Attwell puts it, by adapting to his requirements the forms and concerns of Western literary modernism, Ndebele "is laying claim to . . . the symbolic goods of modern selfhood, on behalf of black South Africans."[124]

The sheer drama of *identity*, of the winning of what Ndebele has elsewhere called "the ultimate right: the right to determine the future with our minds and our hands,"[125] is memorably captured, through a rewriting of the Hegelian trope of master/slave dependency, in the climactic scene in the title story, "Fools." The hitherto cynical and less than entirely admirable narrator, Zamani, has accidentally hit a white man's car with a stone. The "Boer" gets out of his car, brandishing a whip. Zamani's companions flee, but he stands his ground as the whipping begins, thinking to himself that "[he] would not give [the Boer] the kind of victory he wanted."[126] Zamani unflinchingly absorbs the blows until the Boer starts to weep:

> And he seemed to weep louder, the fainter the power of his lashing became.
>
> The blows stopped; and I knew I had crushed him. I had crushed him with the sheer force of my presence. I was there, and would be there to the end of time: a perpetual symbol of his failure to have a world without me. And he walked away to his car, a man without a shadow.[127]

Of the three stories that Ndebele himself identifies in the "Rediscovery" essay as evidencing a new concern for the "ordinary," by far the most interesting is "Man Against Himself" by Joël Matlou. In this and the other sketches collected in *Life at Home and Other Stories*, Matlou evinces a baffling blend of naivety and sophisticated reflexivity that in fact reaches way beyond the "ordinary."[128]Like segments of an hallucinatory autobiography, these intermittently surreal narratives lay bare the originary displacement of black South Africans, staging the disjunction and disorder that characterize their attempts at identity construction. The most memorable story is undoubtedly "My Ugly Face," a disturbing parable of alienation and atonement in which the narrator appears finally to be reconciled with his racial identity, his "ugly face" forgotten in the joy of reunion with his long-lost mother.

The contribution of black women to South African literature was spearheaded from the late 1960s by Bessie Head, writing from her situation of exile in Serowe, Botswana.[129] Although she soon acquired an international reputation, Head's uneven output may not in the end be as interesting as her idiosyncratic life history and the issues of identity politics that it raises. In 1975, Miriam Tlali's account of a young woman's experiences as a clerk for a furniture company, *Muriel at Metropolitan*, became the first novel to be published in English by a black African South African woman.[130] Tlali and others not only brought a gendered perspective to bear on the by now familiar themes of oppression and struggle, but also began to reclaim domestic space and the domain of the family as legitimate material for fictional treatment. In *You Can't Get Lost in Cape Town* (1988), Zoë Wicomb adds to a sensitive exploration of her female protagonist's consciousness a sophisticated fictional self-consciousness. Although she never pauses to explain her allusions and assumptions for the benefit of a non–South African reader, Wicomb's short-story cycle offers accessible and incisive insights into the complicated predicament of the Cape Coloured community in the 1970s. Mention must also be made of Ellen Kuzwayo's autobiography, *Call Me Woman* (1985). Although only a minor figure in political terms, Kuzwayo made an exemplary contribution to her people's long struggle for a better life: as Nadine Gordimer says in her preface, "Ellen Kuzwayo is history in the person of one woman."[131]

As the 1980s ground on, black creative expression became increasingly visible in the public sphere of intensifying physical resistance, with its characteristic *toyi-toyi* dancing, black power salutes, and triumphalist rhetoric. Public or performance poetry, of which Ingoapele Madingoane and, later, Mzwakhe Mbuli, are just two of the better-known practitioners, became a standard feature at political meetings, trade union rallies, and the funerals of those killed in political violence. Many have attested to the electric effect of Madingoane's recital of "Black Trial," an epic evocation of the black man's travails and triumph.[132]

The strategic conjoining of Black Consciousness and the "workerist" activism of the MDM is evident in a collection of performance poetry by three Zulu "worker poets" from the COSATU Durban Workers Cultural Local, *Black Mamba Rising: South African Worker Poets in Struggle.*[133] The verse, especially that of Alfred Temba Qabula, is notable for its recourse to the heroic idiom and the forms of the traditional Zulu *izibongo* or praise poem.

By the end of the 1980s, with the State of Emergency renewed for a fifth consecutive year, South Africa was embroiled in a low-grade but escalating civil war. The African National Congress (ANC)—like any political organization sponsoring an army—had developed a strong command structure and strict policy protocols, which included an orthodoxy of radical militancy for its "cultural workers." Perhaps it was not to be wondered at, then, that veteran ANC activist Albie Sachs set the cat among the pigeons with a position paper prepared for an ANC in-house seminar on culture held in Lusaka in late 1989. In "Preparing Ourselves for Freedom," Sachs deplored the impoverishing effects of political orthodoxy on art and suggested that it was time to abandon the slogan "culture is a weapon of struggle." Although couched in the idiom of liberation politics, his argument was essentially a plea for artistic freedom, for writers and other artists to be allowed to prioritize their craft rather than its political message.[134]

While there was nothing particularly original in Sachs's argument, the fact that it came from an influential member of the ANC stirred wide controversy and resulted in the publication of two book-length collections of response and debate.[135] While the majority of "cultural workers" (academics, critics, writers, and artists) welcomed Sachs's intervention as consonant with the spirit of emancipation abroad in the nation as a whole, it was viewed with suspicion by structures within the ANC and other left-wing political groupings, which—well into the 1990s—continued to regard art as a means to liberation rather than a form of liberation in itself. Nevertheless, the signs were out that a new day in the history of the country and of its literature was about to dawn.

Postapartheid Writing, 1990–2008

Although the era commonly referred to as "postapartheid" technically dates from after the first democratic general election on April 27, 1994, it was in February 1990 that a process of far-reaching and irrevocable change was set in motion. In a parliamentary address on February 2, President de Klerk announced the unbanning of the ANC and other organizations, and the release, without precondition, of the world's most famous political prisoner, Nelson Mandela. It seemed that events would finally complete the figure in terms of which the South African polity had long naturalized its relation to history: waiting, apocalypse and liberation. But what was truly "revolutionary" about the denouement that was about to unfold—or had unfolded, or was in the process of unfolding—was that it was more or less peaceful, and the result of negotiation rather than violent revolution.[136]

February 1990 was also the month in which Albie Sachs's so-called position paper appeared in the Johannesburg *Weekly Mail*. That it can today be dismissed as "largely irrelevant"[137] is because the desiderata that it sets out for a culturally liberated South Africa have effectively been realized in the intervening years. Nevertheless, the paper is worth returning to in order to glean some understanding of the cultural implications of this moment in South African history. To the extent that Sachs was making a case for the depoliticization of the arts in South Africa (or for the ANC to embrace a much broader concept of the political), he also seemed to be arguing for the dismantling of the binary oppositions on which the discourse of the antiapartheid movement had been based. In their stead, anticipating Archbishop Tutu's "rainbow nation," he advocates or recognizes the necessity of a new cultural tolerance and pluralism: "Black is beautiful, Brown is beautiful, White is beautiful."[138] But to the extent that the discourse of opposition to apartheid was also the discourse in terms of which post-1948 South African literature in English had for decades understood itself, implicit in Sachs's plea is the recognition that the "freedom" for which South Africans were to prepare themselves would effectively mean the end of "South African literature" as it had come to be known. To the extent that "apartheid" inescapably remains the primary term in the phrase "antiapartheid," it is even possible to argue that "South African literature in the old sense was a function of our subject-positioning as fellow-travelers with apartheid and its schisms."[139] This "subject-positioning" was further undone by the fact that the demise of apartheid coincided with the collapse of the Soviet Union and the onset of a new phase of globalization that seemed to create an unprecedented fluidity for human subjectivity throughout the world.

But what, indeed, would this mean—does this mean, has this meant—for the culture of letters in the new South Africa? This is a question that has exercised the minds of readers and writers both within the country and without since 1991, and it is a question to which there is still no clear answer (nor, perhaps, should one want there to be, "clear answers" having been the stock in trade of the discursive regime of apartheid South Africa and its opponents). Nevertheless, a few general observations are in order.

Initially, there was a sense of an empty stage, of a space recently vacated, as it were, by the dramatis personae of a previous production. Early attempts to fill this space had recourse to rapidly obsolescent terms of contestation: for instance, in a finger-wagging public address given in July 1990, ANC Culture Desk Chair Barbara Masekela warned,

> The Freedom Charter and the Constitutional Guidelines make it clear that any artist who wishes to sing his or her own song must in the future be free to do so—so long as that song does not pretend to a representativeness it does not have. Those who wish to speak on behalf of the South African people must be part of structures which can join with them

in shaping and giving mandate to their message, so that when it reaches the world, it truly represents us as a nation.[140]

And both politicians and academics continued for some time to make futile attempts to derive a cultural "model" for the new South Africa from political principles.[141]

However, in the years since 1994 there has been a general move away from doctrinaire or authoritarian approaches to "cultural production" in the country, to the extent that the notion of a "party line" in literature or any other art would today seem—no less than it would elsewhere in West—a flagrant encroachment on the civil liberties of the individual. In retrospect, one cannot help but be struck by the extent to which political structures and influences continued to dominate developments in literature and literary criticism in the early 1990s; an obvious comparison can be made with the slow process of military demobilization after an armed conflict.

Two other broadly political developments affecting literature at this time deserve mention here. The first was the return of exiled writers and academics, the second the rapid erosion of repressive state censorship. By the mid-1990s, censorship—which had for thirty years maimed the production and circulation of writing in South Africa—was so liberalized as effectively to be over, and scores of writers and texts became once more, or for the first time, available to the South African reading public. (An important collection of reflective essays on the subject of censorship by the novelist J. M. Coetzee, *Giving Offense*, appeared in 1996.) One of the signal effects of these developments was to bring to an end the division entrenched during the apartheid years between an "internal" South African literature and an "external" one (the latter produced and promoted by exiled writers, critics and academics)—too late, regrettably, for authors such as Dennis Brutus and the late Alex La Guma, who had built up substantial reputations abroad. Their work—like so much other "protest" and "resistance" writing of the 1960s and 1970s—has dated rapidly and seems unlikely ever to enjoy a wide popular readership in South Africa.

Throughout the 1990s, there were calls for new directions and initiatives in South African literature commensurate with the changes in society at large. It was widely argued that, now that South African fiction had at last been released from its oppositional obligation to document, to bear witness, it should also shrug off its long allegiance to the conventions of realism—as André Brink put it, the challenge was to "[re]imagine the real" itself.[142] And indeed, a number of South African writers have obliged, taking their cue either from the metafictional self-consciousness of postmodernism or the "magic realist" precedent of Europe and South America.[143] Probably the most impressive experimental work has come from the pen of Ivan Vladislavić, whose writing acknowledges a debt to Kafka and Borges but revels in an absurdist idiom that is quintessentially South African. The early collections of short fiction *Missing Persons* and *Propaganda by Monuments and Other Stories* are particularly recommended; the novels *The Folly* and *The Restless Supermarket* have interesting premises but simply go on for too long, like good jokes pedantically told. However, the hybrid form and surrealist menace of *The Exploded View* (2004) suggest that this intriguing writer has recently found a way of matching his highly original voice to the demands of extended narrative.

Black South African writers have not found it quite so easy to dismiss the claims of realism, facing as they do the challenges of both attesting to the social legacy of inequality and deprivation, and making a "usable past" out of the years of political struggle. Established novelists Mandla Langa, Mongane Serote, and Lewis Nkosi all weighed in with solid "documentary" performances;[144] more formally innovative were first novels by Phaswane Mpe (*Welcome to Our Hillbrow*) and K. Sello Duiker, whose *Thirteen Cents* offers a haunting account of a street child's experience in the gangland of the Cape Flats that builds to a magnificent apocalyptic climax.[145]

But arguably the most interesting postapartheid development in black South African fiction can be dated to 1995, when the established playwright Zakes Mda published two hugely entertaining novels: *Ways of Dying* and *She Plays with the Darkness*. Both are distinguished by a mixture of social realism and a variety of folkloric magic realism in terms of which traditional African myths blend with everyday life on the same plane of experience. Mda's texts effectively enact the vitality (rather than confusion or fragmentation) of the culturally hybridized identity of contemporary Africa, and decisively signpost a new bearing in a literary tradition long inhibited by a narrowly political conception of human destiny. Mda continued to subject South African experience to carnivalesque review in *The Madonna of Excelsior* (an update on the infamous 1971 Immorality Act prosecutions) and *The Heart of Redness*, an encyclopedic novel that juxtaposes a revisioning of the nineteenth-century Great Cattle Killing with a contemporary ecological perspective on the perennial conflict between tradition and modernity/modernization. Unfortunately, Mda has recently had to face serious accusations of plagiarism (namely, that he makes extensive verbatim borrowing from Jeff Peires's historical account *The Dead Will Arise*), and *The Heart of Redness*—hailed by many as *the* postapartheid historical novel—must now unfortunately be regarded as a compromised text.[146]

The restoration of hope and promise to South Africans' sense of the future has, perhaps not surprisingly, prompted many writers to turn to the past—to retrieve memories buried, feelings suppressed, voices silenced, by the hitherto authorized or dominant discourses of history. A notable subgenre to have emerged is the white "confessional" novel that probes the roots of individual white complicity in the evils of the apartheid years through depictions of coming-of-age experiences: among the more readable are Mark Behr's *The Smell of Apples*, Troy Blacklaws's *Karoo Boy*, and Rachel Zadok's *Gem Squash Tokoloshe*.[147]

The essentially postcolonial gesture made by such books, that of revisiting the past in order to rehabilitate the present and thus make the future imaginable, was memorably enacted from 1996 to 1998 by the Truth and Reconciliation Commission. Although both violators and victims testified under the rubric of reconciliation, it was the narrativization of the past from the perspective of the victims, and the relatives of victims, that assumed a truly performative weight and dignity and seemed to effect at least a measure of catharsis and healing. One of the most celebrated books of the decade was Antjie Krog's *Country of My Skull* (1998), a journalist's notebook that movingly combines documentary coverage of the workings of the TRC with exploration of the author's complex personal responses to it. In the opening pages, the author's friend Professor Kondlo tries to explain the significance of the wordless cry of Fort Calata's widow Nomonde at an early session of the TRC:

> The academics say pain destroys language and this brings about an immediate reversion to a pre-linguistic state—and to witness that cry was to witness the destruction of

> language . . . was to realize that to remember the past of this country is to be thrown back into a time before language. And to get that memory, to fix it in words, to capture it with the precise image, is to be present at the birth of language itself. But more practically, this particular memory at last captured in words can no longer haunt you, push you around, bewilder you, because you have taken control of it—you can move it wherever you want to. So maybe this is what the Commission is all about—finding words for that cry of Nomonde Calata.[148]

The revelation that "Professor Kondlo" is a fictional character and that some of his pronouncements were lifted by Krog, almost verbatim and unacknowledged, from other sources, further complicates (some have said, compromises) *Country of My Skull*'s self-conscious grappling with notions of truth, authority and responsibility.[149] And while Krog has undoubtedly performed a valuable service in making some of the TRC testimony accessible to a wide audience, some readers may find the juxtaposition of her gonzo journalism and the harrowing accounts of cruelty and carnage in questionable taste.

Country of My Skull can in some ways be regarded as a riposte to an earlier, equally celebrated, autobiographical plumbing of the soul of South Africa by a writer of Afrikaner stock, *My Traitor's Heart* by Rian Malan. Set during the troubled 1980s, *My Traitor's Heart* is a sustained meditation on the ethical scandal of human behavior in South Africa, in particular the acts of savage, excessive violence that people, white and black, routinely inflict upon one another. Malan's attempt to understand this behavior produces an enormously complex portrait of its historical roots that in the end serves only to emphasize the limits of Western rationality and psychology in the face of the irreducibly "anthropological."[150] *Country of My Skull*, on the other hand, seeks to demythologize racial otherness and play down political difference by maintaining an unwavering focus on the suffering human body, at once the common denominator that transcends all discriminations of human difference and the ultimate authority for ethical judgment.[151]

Even more different from each other are the two best-known postapartheid narratives, Nelson Mandela's autobiography *Long Walk to Freedom* and J. M. Coetzee's novel *Disgrace*. Although Mandela acknowledges the assistance of a number of cowriters and editors, a vivid sense of his voice animates the narrative. He tells his heroic story—which is also the story of the ANC and the struggle—in a modest, restrained, and dignified way that invests every sentence with an unassailable moral authority. And although *Long Walk* is in every sense a political biography, it is remarkably free of the jargon and euphemistic abstractions about which George Orwell so memorably cautioned his readers in "Politics and the English Language."

Despite his occasional doubts and misgivings (most of which concern his private role as a husband, father, and friend), there is simply no room for ambiguity in Mandela's world: things, as the phrase has it, are either black or white. In the world of Coetzee's fiction, on the other hand, all is doubt, indeterminacy, ambiguity. *Age of Iron* (1990) is set in Cape Town during the late 1980s, juxtaposing life in the white suburbs with the civil war raging in the townships. It is not clear whether the protagonist, Mrs. Curren, dying of cancer, has been fatally stricken also by the moral disease peculiar to her time and place and race; or whether her various acts of charity have been sufficient to redeem her—or indeed, whether redemption of any kind is possible. Similar issues are raised in the dark but magnificently imagined *The Master of Petersburg* (1994), a fictional account of an episode in the life of the nineteenth-century Russian novelist Fyodor Dostoevsky. But the most controversial and talked-about South African novel of recent times is undoubtedly *Disgrace* (1999), which won Coetzee his second Booker Prize. The novel poses uncomfortable questions about just what kind of adjustments whites will be required to make in order to earn admission to the postapartheid national community—and whether these adjustments are feasible or desirable. How the reader responds to the novel as a whole depends to a large extent on how sympathetic he or she finds the protagonist, David Lurie. Fired from his job as lecturer at the Cape Technical University for seducing a Coloured student (and also raping her, depending on how one of their sexual encounters is construed), an unrepentant Lurie goes to visit his daughter Lucy, who lives on a smallholding near Grahamstown in the Eastern Cape. Shortly afterward, he is assaulted and his daughter raped by three black men, who seem to be motivated by racial hatred. Lucy reports the attack as a robbery, refusing to make public the rape on the grounds that it is "a purely private matter," explaining to her skeptical father:

> But isn't there another way of looking at it, David? What if . . . what if *that* is the price one has to pay for staying on? Perhaps that is how they look at it; perhaps that is how I should look at it too. They see me as owing something. They see themselves as debt collectors. Tax collectors. Why should I be allowed to live here without paying?[152]

In order to secure the patronage and protection of her black neighbor, Petrus (who seems to have had a hand in planning the attack), Lucy cedes her patch of land to him and even agrees to be his nominal third wife. Her hitherto self-centered father, meanwhile, appears to be finding redemption of sorts in voluntary service at an animal shelter, assisting in the euthanasia of unwanted dogs and disposing of the corpses. But even this activity is shadowed by the "disgrace" of the novel's title, the universal spiritual condition of humanity in the fallen world that the novel evokes.

Good art seldom brings glad tidings, and the bleakness of *Disgrace* is shared by two other postapartheid novels of quality, Damon Galgut's *The Good Doctor* and Justin Cartwright's *White Lightning*. In their different ways, these texts revisit the colonial trope of Europe's bruising encounter with the "Dark Continent," portraying characters "broken or beaten or besotted with the almighty violence of Africa."[153]

Looking ahead, it is only to be expected that South African writers—black and white, male and female—will continue to be preoccupied with the question of identity, perhaps best seen as an ongoing process of negotiation between residual ethnic cultural patterns and allegiance to the principles and values of citizenry within a modernizing, multiethnic nation-state. For the foreseeable future, the fault line in the social imaginary will be the tension between a permanently resurgent African nationalism and the nonracialism embedded in the national Constitution. The inglorious past will continue to cling and demand reimagining, and the task of wresting the continent of Africa from the discursive grasp of the West must remain a work in progress.

Thus the challenges and opportunities for South African writers have never been greater. The compiler of what is at the time of writing the most recent comprehensive annual bibliography of South African writing in English, looking back on the year 2005, had this to say:

> The literature has continued to move away from a literature of apartheid, and South African authors are increasingly exploring different themes and times. Identity, for individuals and society, preoccupies many writers, with the problems of AIDS, crime, violence, poverty and women's rights being the common themes. Yet, there are still many authors who are looking into the past, or exploring notions of memory and loss, while others are recording aspects of daily life in contemporary South Africa.[154]

These bromides will seem disappointing or bathetic only to those who belong to societies long habituated to freedom of expression. To South Africans, they are real news, announcing as they do that their literature has at last shrugged off the obligation constantly to rehearse what Fredric Jameson famously called the "national allegory."[155] Or, to put it another way, the signs are out that South African literature is at last enjoying the luxury of being "ordinary."

NOTES

1. David Perkins, *Is Literary History Possible*? (Baltimore: Johns Hopkins University Press, 1992), 7–8.
2. The *Cambridge History of South African Literature*, edited by David Attwell and Derek Attridge and currently in preparation, is just such a project.
3. According to Ackbar Abbas, Paul de Man accorded literary history "the paradoxical status of being an ever-present impossibility." Abbas, "Metaphor and History," in *Rewriting Literary History*, ed. Tak-Wai Wong and M. A. Abbas (Hong Kong: Hong Kong University Press, 1984), 177.
4. Stephen Gray, *Southern African Literatures: An Introduction* (Cape Town: David Philip, 1979), 14.
5. A conference was held and some draft documents were prepared, but at the time of writing the project appears to have been abandoned. See Jean-Philippe Wade, "Introduction," *AlterNation* 1, no. 1 (1994): 1–7. The Centre for South African Literature Research (CENSAL), a division of the HSRC in Pretoria, announced a similar project in the mid-1990s. Restructuring within the HSRC saw the demise of CENSAL shortly afterward. Perhaps the Centre's most useful initiative was the *SA Literature/Literatuur* annual survey series (1980–87).
6. Michael Chapman, *Southern African Literatures: An Introduction* (London: Longman, 1996), xv, 1.
7. Christopher Heywood, *A History of South African Literature* (Cambridge: Cambridge University Press, 2004).
8. See Loren Kruger, "'Black Atlantics,' 'White Indians,' and 'Jews': Locations, Locutions, and Syncretic Identities in the Fiction of Achmat Dangor and Others," *Scrutiny2* 7, no. 2 (2002): 39.
9. Malvern van Wyk Smith, "White Writing/Writing Black: The Anxiety of Non-Influence," in *Rethinking South African Literary History*, ed. Johannes A. Smit, Johan van Wyk, and Jean-Philippe Wade (Durban: Y Press, 1996), 75.
10. The phrases derive from the titles of collections of essays by J. M. Coetzee, *White Writing: On the Culture of Letters in South Africa* (New Haven: Yale University Press, 1988), and Richard Rive, *Writing Black* (Cape Town: David Philip, 1981).
11. See Jurij Tynjanov, "On Literary Evolution," in *Readings in Russian Poetics: Formalist and Structuralist Views*, ed. Ladislav Matejka and Krystyna Pomorska (Cambridge, Mass.: MIT Press, 1971), 66–78; see also Boris Ejxenbaum, "Literary Environment," ibid., 56–65.
12. This useful distinction is made by Stefan Morawski, "The Aesthetic Views of Marx and Engels," *Journal of Aesthetics and Art Criticism* 28, no. 3 (1970): 301–314. The terms denote, respectively, "the stimulus of past aesthetic achievement upon the present aesthetic project," and "the stimulus given the aesthetic field by that which is in other respects external to it" (303).

13. Leon de Kock, "South Africa in the Global Imaginary: An Introduction," in *South Africa in the Global Imaginary*, ed. Leon de Kock, Louise Bethlehem, and Sonja Laden (Pretoria: UNISA Press, 2004), 11.
14. Ibid., 11, 12.
15. Leon de Kock, "Does South African Literature Still Exist? Or: South African Literature Is Dead, Long Live Literature in South Africa," *English in Africa* 32, no. 2 (2005): 69–83. See also Leon de Kock, "'Naming of Parts,' or, How Things Shape Up in Transcultural Literary History," *Literator* 26, no. 2 (2005): 1–15.
16. De Kock, "Does South African Literature Still Exist?" 71.
17. Although his conclusions are not the same as ours, David Attwell gives extended and sophisticated coverage to this basic literary-historiographical question in "South African Literature in English," *The Cambridge History of African and Caribbean Literature*, ed. F. Abiola Irele and Siman Gikandi (Cambridge: Cambridge University Press, 2004), 2:504–510.
18. A good example of this is that the reader of Christopher Heywood's *History* is seldom informed as to the original language of composition of a text: all quotations appear in English, unflagged and thus redolent of a perfect seamlessness in the literary corpus. Contextual misunderstanding and historical distortion are bound to result.
19. Terry Eagleton is probably the scholar to have argued most cogently that value is not inherent in texts, but something that communities of readers "read into" them: "It is quite possible," he maintains, that "we may in future produce a society which is unable to get anything at all out of Shakespeare . . . [where] Shakespeare would be no more valuable than present-day graffiti" (*Literary Theory: An Introduction* [Oxford: Basil Blackwell, 1983], 11). But a failure to recognize value is not identical with the absence of value. I would share the intuitive and tentative perspective of Frank Kermode, who, giving qualified endorsement to Stanley Fish's notion of the power of interpretive communities, insists that "some element of literary value is at least as-if immanent"; Kermode, *History and Value* (Oxford: Clarendon Press, 1988), 104. A useful distinction suggested recently by Peter D. McDonald would characterize my position as that of "enchanted antiessentialist": "Unlike the skeptical antiessentialists, who tended to locate all the performative authority on the side of the interpretive community, class ideology, or the literary field, they figured X in the formulation 'X said, "This is literature"' as writing itself"; McDonald, "Ideas of the Book and Histories of Literature: After Theory?" *PMLA* 121, no. 1 (2006): 219.
20. For example, Michael Chapman, "The Liberated Zone: The Possibilities of Imaginative Expression in a State of Emergency," *English Academy Review* 5 (1988): 23–53.
21. Stephen Clingman, "Novel (South Africa)," *Encyclopedia of Post-Colonial Literatures in English*, ed. Eugene Benson and L. W. Connolly (London: Routledge, 1994), 1148.
22. Robert Thornton, "The Potentials of Boundaries in South Africa: Steps Towards a Theory of the Social Edge," in *Postcolonial Identities in Africa*, ed. Richard Werbner and Terence Ranger (London: Zed, 1996), 136.
23. Sarah Nuttall, *Entanglement: Literary and Cultural Reflections on Post-Apartheid* (Johannesburg: University of Witwatersrand Press, 2008). A useful concept in this context is that of "transculturality." The cultural identity of all South Africans is characterized by a complexity and hybridization so thorough that "authenticity has become folklore, it is ownness simulated for others—to whom the indigene himself belongs"; Wolfgang Welsch, "Transculturality: The Puzzling Form of Cultures Today," *Spaces of Culture: City, Nation, World*, ed. Mike Featherstone and Scott Lash (London: Sage, 1999), 200.
24. Thornton, "Potentials of Boundaries," 158.
25. It must at once be conceded that the preceding argument is overstated for polemical purposes: there are indeed writers in South Africa still working to a forward-looking, nationalistic agenda, and with a collective sense of history, and it goes without saying that in a number of important senses South Africa is—and will continue for some time to be—a polity at once modern, postmodern, and postcolonial.

26. J. M. Coetzee, "The Great South African Novel," *Leadership SA* 2, no. 4 (1983): 74, 77, 79.
27. J. M. Coetzee, *Doubling the Point: Essays and Interviews*, ed. David Attwell (Cambridge, Mass.: Harvard University Press, 1992), 98.
28. Tynjanov, "On Literary Evolution," 72.
29. See Roman Jakobson, "Closing Statement: Linguistics and Poetics," in *Style in Language*, ed. Thomas A. Sebeok (Cambridge, Mass.: MIT Press, 1960), 350–377. For an application of Jakobson's theorizing to South African writing, see Gareth Cornwell, "Evaluating Protest Fiction," *English in Africa* 7, no. 1 (1980): 51–70.
30. Coetzee, "Jerusalem Prize," 99.
31. J. M. Coetzee, "The Novel Today," *Upstream* 6, no. 1 (1988): 2.
32. Susan VanZanten Gallagher, "Historical Location and the Shifting Fortunes of *Cry, the Beloved Country*," in *African Writers and Their Readers: Essays in Honor of Bernth Lindfors* (Trenton, N.J.: Africa World Press, 2002), 2: 378, 375.
33. One of the more memorable expressions of such attitudes toward the novel and liberalism more generally is that of Lewis Nkosi in the ad-libbed shebeen scene in Lionel Rogasin's 1960 movie *Come Back, Africa*.
34. Quoted in Gallagher, "Historical Location," 382.
35. Stephen Watson, "Cry, the Beloved Country and the Failure of Liberal Vision," *English in Africa* 9, no. 1 (1982): 35.
36. Alan Paton, *Cry, the Beloved Country: A Story of Comfort in Desolation* (Harmondsworth: Penguin, 1958), 38.
37. Ibid., 37.
38. Ibid., 193, 236.
39. See, among others, Paul Rich, "Liberal Realism in South African Fiction, 1948–1966," *English in Africa* 12, no. 1 (1985): 47–81.
40. Kathrin Wagner, *Rereading Nadine Gordimer: Text and Subtext in the Novels* (Bloomington: Indiana University Press, 1994), 16–18.
41. Albert Memmi, *The Colonizer and the Colonized* (London: Earthscan, 2003). Of the position of the "left-wing colonizer," Memmi writes: "There are, I believe, impossible historical situations and this is one of them" (83).
42. Nadine Gordimer, *The Late Bourgeois World* (Harmondsworth: Penguin, 1982), 31.
43. Ibid., 25.
44. Ibid., 95.
45. Stephen R. Clingman, *The Novels of Nadine Gordimer: History from the Inside* (Johannesburg: Ravan, 1986); Coetzee, "The Novel Today," 2.
46. For a typically negative critical view, see Don Maclennan, "The Vacuum Pump: The Fiction of Nadine Gordimer," *Upstream* 7, no. 1 (1989): 30–33.
47. Sheila Roberts, "Dan Jacobson 7 March 1929–," *Dictionary of Literary Biography*, vol. 225, *South African Writers*, ed. Paul A. Scanlon (Farmington Hills, Mich.: Gale, 2000), 226.
48. Dan Jacobson, *The Trap and A Dance in the Sun* (Harmondsworth: Penguin, 1968), 140–141.
49. Stephen Watson, "A Version of Melancholy," *Selected Essays 1980–1990* (Cape Town: Carrefour, 1990), 173–188.
50. W. B. Yeats, *The Collected Poems of W. B. Yeats* (London: Macmillan, 1950), 214.
51. The title is instructive but a trifle misleading: what the speaker in fact records is the enfolding in his experiential memory of European things hitherto encountered only in books: "brown hawthorn berry, red dog-rose"; Guy Butler, *Collected Poems*, ed. Laurence Wright (Cape Town: David Philip, 1999).
52. See Craig MacKenzie, *The Oral-Style South African Short Story in English: A. W. Drayson to H. C. Bosman* (Atlanta: Rodopi, 1999).
53. Herman Charles Bosman, *Mafeking Road and Other Stories* (Cape Town: Human & Rousseau, 1998), 64.

54. Rebecca Davis, "Unstable Ironies: Narrative Instability in Herman Charles Bosman's 'Oom Schalk Lourens' Series," M.A. thesis (Grahamstown, South Africa: Rhodes University, 2006). The term "unstable irony" is Wayne C. Booth's.
55. See Stephen Watson, "Sydney Clouts and the Limits of Romanticism," *Selected Essays*, 57–81.
56. Sydney Clouts, *Collected Poems*, ed. M. Clouts and C. Clouts (Cape Town: David Philip, 1984), 1.
57. Ezekiel Mphahlele, *Man Must Live and Other Stories* (Cape Town: The African Bookman, 1946); Peter Abrahams, *Mine Boy* (London: Dorothy Crisp, 1946).
58. See Peter Abrahams, *Tell Freedom* (London: Faber, 1954), 61, 193, 197.
59. Paton, *Cry the Beloved Country*, 79.
60. Es'kia Mphahlele, *Down Second Avenue* (London: Faber, 1959), 105–106.
61. See Abrahams, *Tell Freedom*, 250–251, for an account of Abrahams's ambivalence toward Marxism.
62. Chapman, *Southern African Literatures*, 229.
63. Abrahams, *Tell Freedom*, 311.
64. Ezekiel Mphahlele, "South Africa," *Kenyon Review* 31 (1969): 476, 474. The argument first appears in *The African Image* (London: Faber, 1962), 37–38.
65. See Michael Chapman, ed., *The Drum Decade: Stories from the 1950s*, 2nd ed. (Pietermaritzburg: University of Natal Press, 2001). Es'kia Mphahlele was for a time fiction editor at *Drum* magazine, where he sought to encourage a less sensational, more "realist" mode of writing (see Mphahlele, *Down Second Avenue*, 188).
66. A whole mythology—some might say, nostalgia industry—has grown up surrounding these vanished places: see, among others, Adam Small and Jansje Wissema, *District Six* (Johannesburg: Forntein, 1986); Jan Greshoff, *The Last Days of District Six* (Cape Town: District Six Museum, 1996); Norman G. Kester, *From Here to District Six: A South African Memoir with New Poetry, Prose and Other Writings* (Toronto: District Six Press, 2000); Junction Avenue Theatre Company, *Sophiatown: A Play* (Cape Town: David Philip, 1988); Don Mattera, *Memory Is the Weapon* (Johannesburg: Ravan, 1987); and Jurgen Schadeberg, ed., *Sof'town Blues: Images from the Black '50s* (Johannesburg: Jurgen Schadeberg, 1994).
67. Es'kia Mphahlele, *Down Second Avenue*; Bloke Modisane, *Blame Me on History* (New York: Dutton, 1963); Todd Matshikiza, *Chocolates for My Wife* (London: Hodder & Stoughton, 1961); Alfred Hutchinson, *Road to Ghana* (London: Gollancz, 1960); Nat Nakasa, *The World of Nat Nakasa* (Johannesburg: Ravan, 1985); Casey Motsisi, *Casey & Co.: Selected Writings* (Johannesburg: Ravan, 1978); Can Themba, *The Will to Die* (London: Heinemann, 1972).
68. Mphahlele, *Down Second Avenue*, 18.
69. As James Olney observes in *Tell Me Africa: An Approach to African Literature* (Princeton: Princeton University Press, 1973), what is most distinctive about African autobiography is its concern to present not a unique existence but a representative life that helps to explain the historical circumstances that engendered it (see especially chapter 6, "Politics, Creativity and Exile").
70. David Attwell cites these passages as evidence of the existence of a neglected "experimental line" in black South African writing, in *Rewriting Modernity: Studies in Black South African Literary History* (Scottsville: University of KwaZulu-Natal Press, 2005), 174.
71. Mphahlele, *Down Second Avenue*, 220.
72. For a penetrating discussion of this and Mphahlele's subsequent career, see Attwell, "Fugitive Pieces: Es'kia Mphahlele in the Diaspora," *Rewriting Modernity*, 111–136.
73. Mphahlele, *Down Second Avenue*, 166.
74. La Guma was, in terms of the South African nomenclature, a Coloured man. To the extent that he was "non-white," he was black, although he was always adamant that his writing was first and foremost concerned with his own Cape Coloured community. From the late 1970s onward, the majority of (politicized) Coloureds self-identified as black.
75. *A Walk in the Night* (Ibadan: Mbari, 1962); *And a Threefold Cord* (Berlin: Seven Seas, 1964); *The*

Stone Country (Berlin: Seven Seas, 1967); *In the Fog of the Seasons' End* (London: Heinemann, 1972); *Time of the Butcherbird* (London: Heinemann, 1979).

76. La Guma, *A Walk in the Night* (London: Heinemann, 1967), 21. The deterministic connection between material environment and character is thus made clear.
77. The poets all "Africanized" their names over the next decade: thus Mbuyiseni Mtshali, Mongane Serote, Mafika Gwala, and Sipho Sepamla. Each writer published at least two volumes of lyric poetry in the 1970s.
78. Wally Mongane Serote, *Yakhal'inkomo* (Johannesburg: Renoster & Bateleur Press, 1972), 9. For an astonishingly perceptive analysis of this poem, see Derek Attridge, *The Singularity of Literature* (Oxford: Routledge, 2004), 111–118.
79. Jeremy Cronin, "Three Reasons for a Mixed, Umrabulo, Round-the-Corner Poetry," *Even the Dead: Poems, Parables and a Jeremiad* (Cape Town: Mayibuye Books and David Philip, 1997), 1.
80. Attwell, *Rewriting Modernity*, 137ff.
81. Serote, *Yakhal'inkomo*, 51–62.
82. J. M. Coetzee, *Boyhood: Scenes from Provincial Life* (London: Secker & Warburg, 1997). His experience as a young man working in London is described in *Youth* (London: Secker & Warburg, 2002).
83. Michael Chapman, "The Writing of Politics and the Politics of Writing: On Reading Dovey on Reading Lacan on Reading Coetzee on Reading . . . (?)" Review of Teresa Dovey, *The Novels of J. M. Coetzee: Lacanian Allegories*, *Journal of Literary Studies* 4, no. 3 (1988): 335.
84. Michael Chapman, "Writing in a State of Emergency," *Southern African Review of Books* (December 1988–January 1989): 14. See also Chapman, "The Liberated Zone: The Possibilities of Imaginative Expression in a State of Emergency," *English Academy Review* 5 (1988): 23–55.
85. "Into the Dark Chamber: The Writer and the South African State" first appeared in the *New York Times Book Review*, January 12, 1986, and was later reprinted in expanded form in *Doubling the Point*, 361–368. "The Novel Today" was the text of an address given at the 1987 *Weekly Mail* Book Week and appeared in *Upstream* 6, no. 1 (1988): 2–5.
86. Reprinted in *The Essential Frankfurt School Reader*, ed. Andrew Arato and Eike Gebhardt (Oxford: Blackwell, 1978), 300–318.
87. Coetzee, "The Novel Today," 3. Perhaps the best example of South African fiction that (quite deliberately) "supplements" history is the work of Nadine Gordimer.
88. Ibid.
89. Kafka and Beckett are unarguably the most obvious influences on Coetzee's fiction.
90. J. M. Coetzee, *Life & Times of Michael K* (London: Penguin, 1985), 115.
91. Ibid., 109.
92. See Coetzee, *Doubling the Point*, 248.
93. Victor Crapanzano, *Waiting: The Whites of South Africa* (New York: Vintage, 1986), 43. Other writers of fiction from this period whose work invites rereading include Christopher Hope, *A Separate Development* (Johannesburg: Ravan, 1980) and *Private Parts and Other Stories* (London: Routledge & Kegan Paul, 1982); Peter Wilhelm, *At the End of a War* (Johannesburg: Ravan, 1981), *Some Place in Africa* (Johannesburg: Ad Donker, 1987), and *The Healing Process* (Johannesburg: Ad Donker, 1988); Sheila Roberts, *Outside Life's Feast* (Johannesburg: Ad Donker, 1975) and *This Time of Year and Other Stories* (Johannesburg: Ad Donker, 1983); and Damon Galgut, *Small Circle of Beings* (Johannesburg: Lowry, 1988) and *The Beautiful Screaming of Pigs* (London: Scribners, 1991).
94. David Muller, *Whitey* (Johannesburg: Ravan, 1977). Its wider 1969 setting is perfectly referenced in the characterization of a teenage hippie or "flower child" encountered by the protagonist.
95. In his "Jerusalem Prize Acceptance Speech" (1987), Coetzee observed acerbically that "at the heart of the unfreedom of the hereditary masters of South Africa is a failure of love. . . . Their talk, their excessive talk, has consistently been directed towards the land, that is, towards what is

least likely to respond to love: mountains and deserts, birds and animals and flowers" (*Doubling the Point*, 97).

96. See, for example, Kelwyn Sole, *The Blood of Our Silence* (Johannesburg: Ravan, 1988) and *Love That Is Night* (Durban: Gecko Poetry, 1998); Ingrid de Kok, *Familiar Ground* (Johannesburg: Ravan, 1988) and *Transfer* (Cape Town: Snail Press, 1997).
97. Maclennan, *Letters* (Cape Town: Carrefour Press, 1992), 50.
98. Watson, "Coda," *In This City* (Cape Town: David Philip, 1985), 34.
99. James Matthews, *Cry Rage!* (Johannesburg: Spro-Cas, 1972). The original edition credits Gladys Thomas as coauthor; the reprint in *Cry Rage: Odyssey of a Dissident Poet* (Athlone: Realities, n.d.) makes no mention of her.
100. James Matthews, "James Matthews," in *Momentum: On Recent South African Writing*, ed. M. J. Daymond, J. U. Jacobs, and Margaret Lenta (Pietermaritzburg: University of Natal Press, 1984), 73.
101. Jakobson, "Closing Statement: Linguistics and Poetics."
102. James Matthews, *Black Voices Shout!* (Athlone: BLAC, 1974) and *The Park and Other Stories* (Athlone: BLAC, 1974).
103. Steve Biko, *I Write What I Like* (London: Heinemann, 1978).
104. Matthews, *Black Voices Shout!* 29.
105. Mothobi Mutloatse, ed., *Forced Landing—Africa South: Contemporary Writings* (Johannesburg: Ravan, 1980), 5.
106. Mongane Serote, *To Every Birth Its Blood* (Johannesburg: Ravan, 1981).
107. There is unfortunately no space to document fully the heroic role played by independent South African publishers—in Johannesburg, Ravan, Ad Donker, and Skotaville; in Cape Town, David Philip—in the promotion of "politically sensitive" South African writing at this time. Donker "made" the Soweto Poets, while Ravan, particularly via its Staffrider series of texts, introduced the new writing to an emerging black readership.
108. Mutloatse, *Forced Landing*, 2, 5.
109. Mtutuzeli Matshoba, *Seeds of War* (Johannesburg: Ravan, 1981).
110. Mbulelo Mzamane, *Mzala* (Johannesburg: Ravan, 1980); Mtutuzeli Matshoba, *Call Me Not a Man* (Johannesburg: Ravan, 1979).
111. See MacKenzie, *The Oral-Style South African Short Story in English*.
112. Matshoba, *Call Me Not a Man*, 161: "Arrival eNcobo. I had travelled a whole century backward in the South African Railways' time machine."
113. Achmat Dangor, *Waiting for Leila* (Johannesburg: Ravan, 1981). Although Dangor is better known for his later work, novels such as *Kafka's Curse* (Cape Town: Kwela Books, 1997) and *Bitter Fruit* (Cape Town: Kwela Books, 2001) are by comparison pretentious and overblown.
114. Albie Sachs, "Preparing Ourselves for Freedom," in *Spring Is Rebellious: Arguments About Cultural Freedom by Albie Sachs and Respondents*, ed. Ingrid de Kok and Karen Press (Cape Town: Buchu Books, 1990), 20.
115. Readers may be struck by the parallel with the Soviet program under Stalin and A. A. Zhdanov in Russia during the 1930s, though, to be fair, the formulations of Zhdanov and Malenkov were somewhat more sophisticated. See "Comments on Socialist Realism by Maxim Gorky and Others," in *Documents of Modern Literary Realism*, ed. George J. Becker (Princeton: Princeton University Press, 1963), 486–489.
116. For example, see Michael Vaughan, "The Stories of Mtutuzeli Matshoba: A Critique," *Staffrider* 4, no. 3 (1981): 45–47; revised and reprinted as "Can the Writer Become the Storyteller? A Critique of the Stories of Mtutuzeli Matshoba," *Ten Years of Staffrider 1978–1988*, ed. Andries Walter Oliphant and Ivan Vladislavić (Johannesburg: Ravan Press, 1988), 310–317. Blinkered Marxist rhetoric of this kind was widespread in South African university English departments in the 1980s, partly because the emphasis of dialectical materialism on the category of class

rather than race was for whites of conscience a politically respectable riposte to the exclusivity of Black Consciousness.

117. Njabulo S. Ndebele, "Turkish Tales, and Some Thoughts on SA Fiction" (review of Yashar Kemal, *Anatolian Tales*), *Staffrider* 6, no. 1 (1984): 24–25, 42–48; reprinted in Oliphant and Vladislavić, *Ten Years of Staffrider*, 318–340.
118. Ibid., 325.
119. Ibid., 333.
120. Njabulo S. Ndebele, "The Rediscovery of the Ordinary: Some New Writings in South Africa," *Journal of Southern African Studies* 12, no. 2 (1986): 143–157. Reprinted in Njabulo S. Ndebele, *The Rediscovery of the Ordinary: Essays on South African Literature and Culture* (Johannesburg: COSAW, 1991), 37–57.
121. Ibid., 149–150.
122. Njabulo S. Ndebele, *Fools and Other Stories* (Johannesburg: Ravan, 1983). "The Rediscovery of the Ordinary" was the keynote address at the conference New Writing in Africa: Continuity and Change, held at the Commonwealth Institute in November 1984.
123. Attwell, *Rewriting Modernity*, 181.
124. Ibid.
125. Njabulo S. Ndebele, *Fine Lines from the Box: Further Thoughts About Our Country* (Cape Town: Umuzi, 2007), 269.
126. Ndebele, *Fools*, 275.
127. Ibid. Is this scene not, ironically, the very epitome of what Ndebele condemns as the "spectacular" strain in South African writing?
128. Joël Matlou, *Life at Home and Other Stories* (Johannesburg: COSAW, 1991).
129. See, among others, *When Rain Clouds Gather* (London: Gollancz, 1968), *Maru* (London: Gollancz, 1971), and *A Question of Power* (London: Davis-Poynter, 1974).
130. Miriam Tlali, *Muriel at Metropolitan* (Johannesburg: Ravan, 1975). Bessie Head was a woman of mixed race; the black African Noni Jabavu had published two volumes of autobiography in the early 1960s.
131. Gordimer, preface to Ellen Kuzwayo, *Call Me Woman* (Johannesburg: Ravan, 1985), xi.
132. Ingoapele Madingoane, "Black Trial," *Africa My Beginning* (Johannesburg: Ravan, 1979), 1–32.
133. Alfred Temba Qabula, Mi S'dumo Hlatshwayo, and Nise Malange, *Black Mamba Rising: South African Worker Poets in Struggle*, ed. Ari Sitas (Durban: Worker Resistance and Culture Publications, 1986).
134. "Preparing Ourselves for Freedom" was run by the *Weekly Mail* newspaper in February 1990 and reprinted in de Kok and Press, *Spring Is Rebellious*, 19–29.
135. These are *Spring Is Rebellious*, which includes twenty-three written responses from a wide variety of contributors, and a collection of interviews, *Exchanges: South African Writing in Transition*, ed. Duncan Brown and Bruno van Dyk (Pietermaritzburg: University of Natal Press, 1991).
136. South Africans were making the difficult discovery that "liberation" was not an event but a contested and protracted process. Some of the worst violence in the entire conflict occurred in the years 1990–1994 (the Boipatong massacre, the Heidelberg Tavern shootings, and so on).
137. Sam Radithalo, "Assembling the Broken Gourds: An Appreciation," in Ndebele, *Fine Lines from the Box*, 258.
138. Sachs, "Preparing Ourselves," 27.
139. De Kock, "Does South African Literature Still Exist?" 80.
140. Barbara Masekela, "Culture in the New South Africa," *Akal*, October 1990, 16.
141. See, for example, Kelwyn Sole, "Democratizing Culture and Literature in a 'New South Africa': Organization and Theory," *Current Writing* 6, no. 2 (1994): 1–37.
142. André Brink, "Interrogating Silence: New Possibilities Faced by South African Literature," *Writing South Africa: Literature, Apartheid, and Democracy, 1970–1995*, ed. Derek Attridge and

Rosemary Jolly (Cambridge: Cambridge University Press, 1998), 24. In all fairness to Brink, and as he points out in this essay, this is a plea he had been making since as far back as 1979. See also Elleke Boehmer, "Endings and New Beginnings: South African Fiction in Transition," ibid., 43–56.

143. The novels of Mike Nicol and Brink himself deserve mention in this context: Mike Nicol, *The Powers That Be* (London: Bloomsbury, 1989), *This Day and Age* (Cape Town: David Philip, 1992), and *Horseman* (London: Bloomsbury, 1994); André Brink, *States of Emergency* (London: Faber, 1988), *The First Life of Adamastor* (London: Secker & Warburg, 1993), *Imaginings of Sand* (London: Secker & Warburg, 1996), *Devil's Valley* (London: Secker & Warburg, 1998), and *Praying Mantis* (London: Secker & Warburg, 2005).
144. Mandla Langa, *The Memory of Stones* (Cape Town: David Philip, 2000); Mongane Serote, *Scatter the Ashes and Go* (Johannesburg: Ravan, 2002); Lewis Nkosi, *Underground People* (Cape Town: Kwela Books, 2002).
145. Phaswane Mpe, *Welcome to Our Hillbrow* (Pietermaritzburg, South Africa: University of Natal Press, 2001); K. Sello Duiker, *Thirteen Cents* (Cape Town: David Philip, 2000). Sadly, Mpe died in 2004 and Duiker in 2005.
146. See Andrew Offenburger, "Duplicity and Plagiarism in Zakes Mda's The Heart of Redness," *Research in African Literatures* 39, no. 3 (2008): 164–199. Mda's defensive rejoinders fail to convince: Zakes Mda, "A Response to 'Duplicity and Plagiarism in Zakes Mda's The Heart of Redness' by Andrew Offenburger," *Research in African Literatures* 39, no. 3 (2008): 200–203; "A Charge Disputed," *Mail & Guardian*, October 18, 2008.
147. Mark Behr, *The Smell of Apples* (London: Abacus, 1995); Troy Blacklaws, *Karoo Boy* (Cape Town: Double Storey, 2004); Rachel Zadok, *Gem Squash Tokoloshe* (London: Macmillan, 2005).
148. Antjie Krog, *Country of My Skull* (London: Jonathan Cape, 1998), 42–43.
149. See Stephen Watson, "Annals of Plagiarism: Antjie Krog and the Bleek and Lloyd Collection," *New Contrast* 33, no. 2 (2005): 48–61; Colin Bower, "New Claims Against Krog," *Mail & Guardian*, March 3–9, 2006; Antjie Krog, "Stephen Watson in the Annals of Plagiarism," *New Contrast* 34, no. 5 (2006): 72–77.
150. A decade later, Jonny Steinberg produced a brilliant book about the murder of a white KwaZulu-Natal farmer, *Midlands* (Johannesburg: Jonathan Ball, 2002), in which the clash of Western and African ideas of justice, of social customs and ethical conventions, and of personal and public histories, produce a case history too dense and complicated for standard forensic analysis.
151. Compare with J. M. Coetzee: "If I look back over my own fiction, I see a simple (simple-minded?) standard erected. That standard is the body. Whatever else, the body is not 'that which is not,' and the proof that it is is the pain that it feels. . . . In South Africa it is not possible to deny the authority of suffering and therefore of the body" (*Doubling the Point*, 248).
152. J. M. Coetzee, *Disgrace* (London: Secker & Warburg), 124, 158.
153. These are the words of the protagonist in the William Plomer's novel *Turbott Wolfe* (London: Hogarth Press, 1925; rpt. Oxford: Oxford University Press, 1985), 117.
154. Crystal Warren, "South Africa," *Journal of Commonwealth Literature* 41 no. 4 (2006): 181.
155. Fredric Jameson, "Third-World Literature in the Era of Multinational Capitalism," *Social Text* 15 (1986): 65–88.

PART ONE

Authors A–Z

A

Abrahams, Lionel (1928–2004) Poet, short-story writer, critic, editor, publisher. Born in Johannesburg and schooled at Damelin College, he graduated from Witwatersrand University in 1955. He was a vigorous promoter of South African literature, both in his own writing and through his editing and publishing of the writings of others. From the 1970s through to the 1990s, at a time when traditional literary studies was energetically challenged on theoretical and political grounds, and in defiance of what he saw as the emergence of a normative practice of the cliché and the slogan, he remained committed to liberal-humanist values of literary research, tenaciously subscribing, in his many published articles, to a notion of the relative autonomy and the imaginative complexity of the literary work.

Abrahams published several volumes of poetry, including *Thresholds of Tolerance* (1975), *Journal of a New Man* (1984), *The Writer in Sand* (1988), *Hot News* (1994), and *A Dead Tree Full of Live Birds* (1995). He also published a sequence of stories, *The Celibacy of Felix Greenspan* (1977), which deals with the experience of physical disability. A sequel to this collection, the novel *The White Life of Felix Greenspan*, appeared in 2002. His selected stories, essays and poems, *Lionel Abrahams: A Reader*, appeared in 1988 to mark his sixtieth birthday. *A Writer in Stone* (1998), comprising contributions by various South African writers, honored his seventieth birthday.

It was as a poet that Abrahams secured his reputation as a writer. The volume *A Dead Tree Full of Live Birds*, in particular, reveals his characteristic concerns and strengths. The title of the volume underscores Abrahams's preoccupations with the paradoxes of life and death, writing and being, innocence and knowledge. Affirmation of the sensuous particularities of everyday experience, and an intimation of the hidden significance these reveal, are wrung from a physical and existential struggle for what is referred to as a "bare subsistence." Uncompromising and sharply intelligent, Abrahams's poems are unsentimental but celebratory, counterromantic rather than antiromantic, charged with the wonder of an existence enriched by the aesthetic imagination.

Abrahams edited and coedited several collections of South African writing, including *Twenty Stories* (1953) and *South African Writing Today* (1967). One of his most important contributions as an editor was to bring into print editions of the works of H. C. *Bosman, who was also his literary mentor for a short period. These include *A Cask of Jerepigo* (1957), *Unto Dust* (1963), *Bosman at His Best: A Choice of Stories and Sketches* (1965), *Jurie Steyn's Post Office* (1971), and *A Bekkersdal Marathon* (1971); a collection of Bosman's poetry, *The Earth Is Waiting* (1974); and *The Collected Works of Bosman* (1988). He is also editor of *Ruth Miller: Poems, Prose, Plays* (1990).

Abrahams cofounded the journal *The Bloody Horse*; founded and edited two literary journals, *The Purple Renoster* and *Sesame*; and coedited the literary journal *Quarry*. He was also cofounder of Bateleur Press and founder of Renoster Books. Abrahams was awarded the 1976 and 1987 Thomas Pringle Award (for the first of these he was a joint recipient, with Sipho *Sepamla), the 1986 Olive Schreiner Prize, and the 1992 English Academy Medal. He was also awarded two honorary doctorates.

Abrahams, Peter (b. 1919) Novelist, short-story writer, autobiographer, poet. Born in Vrededorp, Johannesburg, the son of an Ethiopian seaman and a woman of mixed race, Abrahams attended primary school in Vrededorp and received further education at St Peter's Secondary School in Rosettenville, Johannesburg, and the Anglican Diocesan Teachers' Training College near Pietersburg. He emerged from these institutions a socialist and an intellectual.

He left South Africa in 1939 and settled in England in 1941, where he worked as a journalist. He had a brief association with the British Communist Party, which ended when the party newspaper published scathing reviews of his early works after he refused to submit them for party approval prior to publication. This contributed to his realization that individual people were more important than causes, a belief that would act as a guiding principle in his life and work. In 1955 he was sent to Jamaica on Colonial Office business and began his *Jamaica: An Island Mosaic* (1957), an appreciative history of the island. He returned soon afterward and has lived there ever since, working as a journalist and editor.

His earliest work was a volume of poems, *A Black Man Speaks of Freedom* (1941), followed by *Dark Testament* (1942), a collection of reminiscences and stories. He then published four novels, *Song of the City* (1945), *Mine Boy* (1946), *The Path of Thunder* (1948), and *Wild Conquest* (1950), the last a historical novel set during the time of the Great Trek. *Mine Boy* stands out in this period. The tale of a black country boy who goes to Johannesburg and receives a rude education in the political and social realities of South African life, it is a famous example of the "Jim comes to Jo'burg" genre. The plight of the protagonist is poignantly captured, and the novel's protest against South African racial capitalism is acute and heartfelt.

A return visit to South Africa in 1952 on assignment for the London *Observer* resulted in *Return to Goli* (1953), which records Abrahams's dismay at the worsening conditions of life for black people in South Africa. His bitter experiences during this six-week visit also ensured that his exile from the country was to be permanent. *Tell Freedom* (1954) followed, an account of his life in South Africa up to the point of his departure for England on board a ship as a stoker in 1939. Told in a candid yet somewhat detached manner, the narrative recounts the hardships endured by the young Abrahams, his home circumstances, his early education, and his conversion to Marxism.

The next phase of Abrahams's writings is characterized by greater intellectual incisiveness and political awareness. In *A Wreath for Udomo* (1956) he turns his attention to the struggle for African independence, while *A Night of Their Own* (1965) deals with the resistance to apartheid and *This Island, Now* (1966; revised and enlarged edition 1985), set in the Caribbean, with issues of neocolonialism. *The View from Coyaba* (1985) is an epic work that begins and ends at Coyaba (near Kingston, Jamaica) and spans 150 years of oppression and exploitation of black people. In a series of episodes, a number of different locales are invoked: the southern states of America, Liberia (the state founded by freed slaves in Africa), Uganda and Kenya, and Jamaica again. The main character, Bishop Jacob Brown, a descendant of Jamaican slaves, works at a mission in Liberia and later Uganda and strives to redeem Africa from its history of slavery, oppression, and violence. Much of the novel is devoted to heated debates between Jacob and his son David, a medical doctor, about the efficacy of Christianity in a continent ravaged by colonial powers with which Christianity often colluded. The central argument of the novel is that it is time for people of African descent—with their experience of slavery and racial oppression—to show the West a new way of life. *The Coyaba Chronicles: Reflections on the Black Experience in the 20th Century* (2000) is Abrahams's most recent work. This work also appeared under the title *The Black Experience in the 20th Century: An Autobiography and Meditation.*

FURTHER READING

Michael Wade, *Peter Abrahams* (1972); Kolawole Ogungbesan, *The Writings of Peter Abrahams* (1979); Elleke Boehmer, *Colonial and Postcolonial Literature: Migrant Metaphors* (1995); Michael Green, *Novel Histories: Past, Present and Future in South African Fiction* (1997).

Adams, Peter Robert Charles (Perseus) (b. 1933) Poet and short-story writer. Born in Cape Town, he studied for a bachelor's degree and then traveled widely in Africa, Europe, and the Far East. He has worked mainly as an English teacher and now lives in London. His collections of poetry are *The Land at My Door* (1965), *A Single Leaf of the Baobab* (1966), and *Grass for the Unicorn* (1975). A selection of his poems appeared as *Cries and Silences* in 1996. His stories, including the well-known "A True Gruesome," have appeared in various anthologies over the years.

Afrika, Tatamkhulu (1920–2002) Poet and novelist. Born in Egypt of Egyptian and Turkish parents, he came to South Africa as a child and was raised by foster parents on a farm in North West Province. After matriculating, he served in World War II and subsequently worked for many years on the diamond mines of Namibia before moving to Cape Town in the 1960s, where, in a gesture of political solidarity with the oppressed black majority, he changed his racial classification to Coloured. He became actively involved in the political struggle as an armed militant and was given the name Tatamkhulu Afrika ("old man of Africa") by young township comrades. A convert to Islam, he was a founder member of the Al-Jihaad organization. He was banned in 1987 from writing and public speaking for five years.

After almost the entire print run of an early novel, *Broken Earth* (1940, published under the name John Charlton), was destroyed in a warehouse bombing in London during World War II, Afrika did not begin writing again until he was more than sixty years of age. He published several volumes of poetry, including *Nine Lives* (1991), *Dark Rider* (1992), *Maqabane* (1994), *Flesh and the Flame* (1995), *The Lemon Tree: Poems* (1995), *Turning Points* (1996), *The Angel and Other Poems* (1999), and *Mad Old Man Under the Morning Star: The Poet at Eighty* (2001). A posthumous selection of his poems appeared as *Nightrider* in 2003. Apart from his youthful venture into fiction, he published two other novels, *The Innocents* (1994) and *Bitter Eden* (2002), and a collection of four novellas, *Tightrope* (1996). His autobiography, *Mr Chameleon*, appeared posthumously in 2005.

In *Tightrope*, contemporary (and, in one case, future) South African society is laid bare to Afrika's penetrating gaze. There is no room for finer human sentiment, no sense that human empathy and support will somehow win out. The thin veneer of human decency has worn off in this fin-de-siècle dystopia, and raw desire, malice, and self-interest have burst through. "The Vortex" and "The Treadmill," the first two novellas, are linked. They trace the descent of the hapless Johnny Jackson from disaffected stepson to matricide, convict, "wife" to a cell-boss, parolee, rape victim, and, finally, murderer once again. In his tumble into the vortex, the maw of self-destruction and the abasement of others, he leaves a bisexual, drug-dealing, rent-boy lover who dies of AIDS, and two prostitutes who suffer similar fates. "The Quarry," which concerns the narrator's encounter with a musician-poseur who momentarily captivates the women in a small mining town before falling foul of the local racists, and "The Trap," which explores the narrowing circle of life for a Cape Town *bergie* (tramp), are no less riveting.

Afrika's poetry in particular that is highly regarded. Although his style is direct and down-to-earth, it characteristically reaches toward the archetypal and the mystical. The poetry describes engagements with daily life in a way that renders these experiences concrete and precise even as they are pressed into providing an opening onto the unknown, the other, represented in one poem as "the shade that inhabits the familiar shadows." The poems are distillations of a life marked by austere frugality, passionate intensity, and spiritual striving. *Flesh and the Flame* is explicitly Islamic in its concerns.

Afrika received the 1990 Sydney Clouts Memorial Prize, the 1991 and 1993 Thomas Pringle Award, the 1992 Olive Schreiner Prize, the 1992 CNA Debut Award, and the 1994 and 2000 Sanlam Literary Award.

FURTHER READING

Cheryl Stobie, "Mother, Missus, Mate: Bisexuality in Tatamkhulu Afrika's *Mr Chameleon* and *Bitter Eden*," *English in Africa* 32, no. 2 (2005): 185–211.

Altman, Phyllis (1918–1999) Novelist and short story writer. Educated at Jeppe Girls' High and the University of the Witwatersrand, Altman qualified as a teacher and taught for three years before joining the trade-union movement. Banned under the Suppression of Communism Act, she went into exile in London. Altman wrote several stories in the 1950s for the left-wing periodical *Fighting Talk*, but she is known chiefly for her novel *The Law of the Vultures*

(1952), set in the period 1930–1946. This "Jim comes to Jo'burg" novel tells the story of Thabo Thaele, a Masotho who comes to the city and after seventeen years of work is unjustly arrested and convicted of theft. Upon his release, the embittered Thaele encounters David Nkosi, a soldier recently demobilized from the Native Military Corps who also has reason to be disillusioned with white society, and Dhlamini, a Marxist trade-union organizer. The novel anticipates the Sharpeville calamity in its focus on life in Sophiatown and the hardships black people had to endure under apartheid.

FURTHER READING

Sally-Ann Murray, "'The Law of the Vultures': A Story for an Altered State?" *Kunapipi* 13, nos. 1 & 2 (1991): 34–43.

Aron, Geraldine (b. 1941) Dramatist and short-story writer. Born in Galway, Ireland, she came to South Africa in 1965 and settled in Cape Town. *Bar and Ger* (1975), which takes the form of a verse dialogue, traces the relationship between a brother and sister up to the point of the brother's sudden death. Other plays include *Mr McConkey's Suitcase* (1977), *Mickey Kannis Caught My Eye* (1978; published in Stephen *Gray's 1981 anthology *Theatre Two*), *A Galway Girl* (1979), *Joggers* (1979), *The Spare Room* (1981), and *Spider* (1985). These works have been collected as *Seven Plays and Four Monologues* (1985). Her other plays are *Zombie* and *The Final Sting of the Dying Wasp* (1979; coauthored by Aron), and *Same Old Moon*, *The Guest Room*, *Why Strelitzias Cannot Fly* (1982).

FURTHER READING

Stephen Gray, "Interview with Geraldine Aron, London, 4 July 1989," *South African Theatre Journal* 4, no. 2 (1990): 30–49; Stephen Gray, "Women in South African Theatre," *South African Theatre Journal* 4, no. 1 (1990): 75–87.

Asvat, Farouk (b. 1952) Poet and critic. Qualified as a medical doctor, he has also worked as a part-time journalist. A cultural activist and supporter of the Black Consciousness movement, he was a founding member of the Black Thoughts poetry and drama group, involved himself in the New Dawn Ensemble, served as cultural coordinator of the Black People's Convention, and was a founding member of the Writers' Forum. In 1973 he was served with a five-year banning order.

Asvat has published two volumes of poetry: *The Time of Our Lives* (1982) and *A Celebration of Flames* (1987). He is also represented in the poetry anthologies *Exiles Within* (1986) and *Horses: Athlone* (1988). Critical, anguished, occasionally satirical, Asvat's poems employ a passionate voice capable at times of great lyrical tenderness, seeking to subvert what he sees as the false rhetoric and self-serving concerns of the ruling classes. Asvat was a recipient of the 1987 AA Mutual Life/Ad. Donker Award.

Autobiography
See Biography and Autobiography

B

Badal, Sean (b. 1965) Novelist. Born in South Africa and raised in the United Kingdom, Badal currently lives and works in Johannesburg. He is the author of three novels, *Dead Sanctities* (1999), *Seeds of Disorder* (2002), and *The Fall of the Black-eyed Night* (2008), all of which explore transnational themes in the mode of the thriller. *Dead Sanctities* tells the story of a journalist, a British citizen of Indian descent, who takes up a position at a newspaper in Bombay and becomes involved with a corruption scandal that threatens to derail his career. *Seeds of Disorder* deals with corporate intrigues and competition around human genetic material arising out of the Human Genome Project. Set in Cape Town at the fictitious Bay Regal Hotel, *The Fall of the Blackeyed Night* deals with the return to his home country of a young Muslim man who is haunted by memories of London at the time of the July 2005 bombings, and who is drawninto events and relationships in the local Muslim community.

Baderoon, Gabeba (b. 1969) Poet. Born and raised in Cape Town, Baderoon has a doctorate from the University of Cape Town on representations of Islam in South African art, literature, and media. She has held fellowships at the African Gender Institute at the University of Cape Town, the Oxford Centre for Islamic Studies and Växjö University in Sweden, and teaches at Pennsylvania State University. In 2005 she received the Daimler-Chrysler Award for South African poetry. She is the author of three volumes of poetry, *The Dream in the Next Body* (2005), *The Museum of Ordinary Life* (2005), and *A Hundred Silences* (2006). Praised for its lucidity and grace, her poetry evinces a quiet intensity, characteristically addressing issues of identity, love, loss, and the unsaid or unsayable.

Bagley, Desmond (1923–1983) Novelist. Bagley became famous in the 1960s for his popular adventure novels. Born in Kendal, Westmoreland, in England's Lake District, he spent his childhood in Blackpool. In 1947 he undertook a long journey to South Africa by road. He lived in South Africa in the 1950s, working as a freelance journalist in Durban and Johannesburg. His first novel, *The Golden Keel* (1963), is apparently based on a story he heard in a Johannesburg bar. It concerns the mysterious disappearance of Mussolini's vast personal treasures during World War II. Bagley constructed a thriller around this anecdote: a successful Cape Town boatbuilder designs an oceangoing yacht, sails to the Mediterranean, and tries with his companion to get the treasure out of Italy. Bagley's other novels have non–South African settings, and this enabled him to achieve a truly international stature. Some of these are *Landslide* (1967), *The Tightrope Men* (1973), *The Snow Tiger* (1975), and *The Enemy* (1977).

Bailey, Brett (b. 1967) Dramatist. Bailey established Third World Bunfight in 1996 to promote the creation of an indigenous South African theater style. Using largely nonprofessional black performers drawn from the townships and rural areas, Bailey has staged some of the most innovative plays of the postapartheid period.

The early plays have been collected in *Plays of Miracle and Wonder: Ipi Zombi?, Imumbo Jumbo, and The Prophet* (2004). Drawing on Xhosa history and customs, they combine the ritual practices and iconography of traditional Xhosa culture with the spectacle of the musical to create a form of theater characterized by startling visual effects, closely choreographed sequences of movement and dance, and an atmosphere of the supernatural—a theater located at the interface of the sacred and the farcical, the solemn and the ironic. The plays take as point of departure events from South African history, witch-hunts in Kokstad, a Xhosa diviner in pursuit of King Hintsa's skull in Scotland, and the story of Nongqawuse and the cattle killing of the 1850s, presenting the viewer with a world of mythical creatures, ancestral spirits, and bewitched souls. Bailey has also produced *Big Dada: The Rise and Fall of Idi Amin* (2001), which uses archival television footage in reconstructing the spectacle of the dictator in the style of a media star; *Vodou Nation* (2004); and *Orfeus* (2007).

Bancroft, Francis (Frances Slater) *See* Writers Before 1945.

Banoobhai, Shabbir (b. 1949) Poet. Born in Durban and qualified as an accountant, Banoobhai has worked as a lecturer at the University of Durban-Westville and as consultant with the Small Business Development Corporation. He has published several volumes of poetry, including *Echoes of My Other Self* (1980), *Shadows of a Sun-Darkened Land* (1984), *Lightmail* (2002), *Inward Moon, Outward Sun* (2002), and *Book of Songs* (2004). Employing an Islamic perspective, the poems explore relationships with others, with society at large, and with God.

Barris, Ken (b. 1952) Novelist, short-story writer, and poet. Barris's poems have appeared regularly in the poetry journals *New Contrast*, *Carapace*, and *New Coin* and are gathered in *An Advertisement for Air* (1993) and *African Easter* (2005). His short stories have been collected as *Small Change* (1988). His most recent works are novels: *The Jailer's Book* (1996), *Evolution* (1998), *Summer Grammar* (2004), and *What Kind of Child* (2006). Set in the politically explosive period of the late 1980s, *The Jailer's Book* deals with the relationship between Dolf, a prison warden, and Grintz, a writer jailed for his political beliefs, exploring the power relationship between captor and captive, and exposing the dilemma of the white writer-intellectual committed to the black freedom struggle. *Evolution* focuses on two interracial relationships, one set in the 1930s and one in postapartheid South Africa, to explore the ambivalences that characterize relations between white and black. Engaged in research into her family as part of a project on oral history, Jessica, who is having an affair with her anthropology lecturer, Teboso, discovers that her grandfather might have been involved in a sexual relationship with his Coloured maid. *What Kind of Child* is a story of the intersecting lives of three characters: Bernal, a tattoo artist who, believing he is five hundred years old, wishes to record his experiences of the Spanish conquest of Mexico; Luke, who is obsessed with tattoos and serves as canvas for Bernal; and Malibongwe, a street child.

Beaumont, John Howland (1911–1979) Poet and short-story writer. Deaf from childhood, Beaumont composed poetry, gathered in *Poems* (1957), that shows sensitivity to the particularities of different settings. His second work, *The Tree of Igdrasil* (1971), is a collection of philosophical stories dealing with the habits and peculiarities of various creatures. Titles of some of the stories are "The Frogs That Came Back," "Horse," "The Three Wild Geese," and "Mantis." The volume was reissued in 1983 as *The Great Karoo*.

Becker, Jillian (b. 1932) Novelist. Born in Johannesburg, she left South Africa for England in 1961 and now lives in London. Her works about South Africa include *The Keep* (1967), *The Union* (1971), and *The Virgins* (1976), the last of which is a satirical treatment of affluent white South Africa and addresses the taboo topic of an interracial sexual liaison (between the main character, Annie Firman, and a Coloured man). Becker has also produced two works of nonfiction: *Hitler's Children: The Story of the Baader-Meinhof Terrorist Gang* (1978) and *The P.L.O.: The Rise and Fall of the Palestinian Liberation Organisation* (1984).

Beeton, Ridley (1929–1997) Academic, critic, poet, editor. Born in Zeerust, Transvaal (North West Province), and educated at the universities of Pretoria and South Africa, he was professor of English at the University of South Africa from 1963 to 1984 and is a past president of the English Academy of Southern Africa.

Beeton published two volumes of poetry: *The Landscape of Requirement* (1981) and *Tattoos* (1983). Focusing on interpersonal relationships, the poems exhibit a sensitivity of observation and a contemplative composure. Beeton also published a crime novel, *The Fatal Entrance* (1975), under the pseudonym Robert Barratt. He is the author of *Olive Schreiner: A Short Guide to Her Writings* (1974) and of *Facets of Olive Schreiner: A Manuscript Source Book* (1987). He also compiled *A Pilot Bibliography of South African English Literature* (1976).

Beeton edited *Four South African One-Act Plays* (1973), as well as *The Poetry Workshop 1985* and *The Poetry Workshop 1987*. He coedited *A Dictionary of English Usage in Southern Africa* (1975) and *Companion to South African Literature* (1986). He was the founding editor of the literary journal *UNISA English Studies*.

Behr, Mark (b. 1963) Novelist. Born in Tanzania, Behr moved with his family to South Africa as a child. He was educated in South Africa, Norway, and the United States. He currently lives in New Mexico, where he is associate professor of world literature and fiction writing at the College of Santa Fe. First published in Afrikaans as *Die Reuk van Appels* (1993), and later in English as *The Smell of Apples* (1995), Behr's debut novel won widespread critical and popular acclaim. Set in 1973, it tells the story of Marnus, an eleven-year-old Afrikaans boy who comes of age in a family that typifies the old South Africa. His father is a senior member of the armed forces and hosts a number of ranking officials from countries friendly with the apartheid regime. The corrupt heart of the regime is revealed in the distorted sexual relations the young boy shockingly discovers in his own family. Behr has written numerous articles for South African magazines—most notably *Fair Lady*—on various aspects of South African life and culture. His revelation that he served as a security police spy during his student years at the University of Stellenbosch has somewhat dampened the enthusiasm that greeted the appearance of his novel. *The Smell of Apples* has received numerous awards, including the CNA Literary Debut Award, the Eugène Marais Prize, the Betty Trask Award (UK), and the Boeke Prize. A second novel, *Embrace*, appeared in 2000.

Beiles, Sinclair (1930–2000) Poet, playwright, editor. Born in Kampala, Uganda, he graduated from the Witwatersrand University. In the 1950s and 1960s he lived in Paris, where he edited books for Olympia Press, and also lived in Athens and Malaga, making brief visits to South Africa. He returned to South Africa in the 1970s and lived in Johannesburg.

Beiles published eight volumes of poetry: *Ashes of Experience* (1969); *Tales* (1972); *Sacred Fix* (1976); *Ballets* (1978); *Dowsings* (1979), a book of prose poetry; *20 Poems* (1982), which was privately published; *The Crucifixion* (1984); and a volume of selected poems, *A South African Abroad* (1991). He also collaborated with William Burroughs, Brion Gysin, and Gregory Corso in *Minutes to Go* (1960), an experiment in cut-up poetry. In addition, he is the author of several unpublished plays, including "A Monologue by the Karate Kid," "Against Nature," "Bouzouki," "Chopin in Majorca," "Death in the Country," "Gauguin," "Lear in Los Angeles," "My Brother Frederico" (about Federico García Lorca), and "The Gay Young Things."

Beiles's first volume of poetry, *Ashes of Experience*, is generally regarded as his most accomplished. Portraying the bohemian lifestyle of the Mediterranean region in the 1960s, the poetry employs a surrealist style in yoking together disparate impressions and images.

Benson, Mary (1919–2000) Novelist, short-story writer, biographer, radio playwright, documentary writer, editor. Born in Pretoria, she was banned and placed under house arrest for her political activism. She lived in London from the 1960s onward, where she was closely associated with staging Athol *Fugard's plays. Throughout this period she continued to contribute to South Africa's political transformation through her writings and television documentaries.

Benson published one novel, *At the Still Point* (1969), edited Athol Fugard's *Notebooks* (1983), and wrote a memoir, *Athol Fugard and Barney Simon* (1997). She also wrote three political biographies: *Tshekedi Khama* (1960), *Chief Albert Luthuli of South Africa* (1963), and *Nelson Mandela* (1986; rev. ed. 1990). She produced several prose works on the South African political struggle, including *South Africa: The Struggle for a Birthright* (1966; rev. ed. 1985) and *The Sun Will Rise* (1981), and contributed the piece "Robben Island: A Dramatized Documentary Based on Historical Records and Testimonies of Prisoners" to *Voices from Robben Island* (Jürgen Schadeberg, 1994). In addition, she compiled two BBC documentaries: *Nelson Mandela and the Rivonia Trial* (1972) and *Robben Island* (1993). She also broadcast a radio play, *Sol Plaatje* (date unknown), and wrote an unpublished play, "The Thorn Tree." Her autobiography, *A Far Cry*, was published in 1989.

Dealing with the contradictions of her identity as a white person in South Africa, *A Far Cry* shows how this identity was reconstructed through a series of significant encounters: with, for instance, Alan *Paton's *Cry, the Beloved Country*, with the political activist Bram Fischer, and with the playwright Athol Fugard.

Berold, Robert (b. 1948) Poet and editor. Born in Johannesburg, he studied chemical engineering at Witwatersrand University. He started reading economics at Cambridge University but abandoned his studies and devoted himself to poetry instead. He has worked as a store manager, teacher, and journalist. Since settling on a farm near Grahamstown, he has worked with production cooperatives and has run regular writing workshops. He was editor of the poetry journal *New Coin Poetry* for ten years.

Berold has published three volumes of poetry: *The Door to the River* (1984), *The Fires of the Dead: Poems* (1989), and *Rain Across a Paper Field* (1999). Pursuing the image as a sign that seeks to close the gap between experience and meaning, the poetry seeks to suture the distances between self and other, whether ancestor or lover, landscape or community. The poems are lucid and sparing.

Berold is coeditor of the poetry anthologies *In the Land of Plenty* (1994) and *Parking Space: Poems from East Cape Schools* (1994). He also edited *Writing from Here* (2001), *It All Begins: Poems from Post-*

liberation South Africa (2002), and *South African Poets on Poetry: Interviews from New Coin 1992–2001* (2003).

Biography and Autobiography

BIOGRAPHY Several biographical works dealing with life at the Cape capture South Africa's early colonial history. An early example is Madeleine Masson's *Birds of Passage* (1950), an account of the lives of several prominent visitors to the Cape in the eighteenth and nineteenth centuries. The 1970s saw the appearance of Hymen Picard's biographical novel on the life of Simon van der Stel (1973) and his *Lords of Stalplein: Biographical Miniatures of the British Governors of the Cape of Good Hope* (1974). More recently, Peter Philip's *British Residents at the Cape 1795–1819: Biographical Records of 4800 Pioneers* (1981) appeared. The lives of some of the women at the Cape in early colonial times have been dealt with in Thelma Gutsche's *The Bishop's Lady* (1970), the life of Sophy Grey, wife of the first bishop of Cape Town; and Jose Burman's *In the Footsteps of Lady Anne Barnard* (1990), which reflects increasing interest in the women of this period. *Robert Jacob Gordon, 1743–1795: The Man and His Travels at the Cape* (1992), by the poet Patrick *Cullinan, is a recent example of the continuing interest in early Cape colonial figures.

A prominent feature of South African biographies is the abundance of writing about the lives of South African statesmen, and particularly Boer leaders. Marjorie Juta's *The Pace of the Ox: The Life of Paul Kruger* (1936), F. S. Crafford's *Jan Smuts: A Biography* (1946), and Eric Rosenthal's *General De Wet: A Biography* (1946) are three early examples. Johannes Meintjies dominated this subgenre with no fewer than four biographies of Boer leaders: General De la Rey (1966), President Steyn (1969), General Louis Botha (1970), and Paul Kruger (1974). Major South African writers have also shown an interest in the lives of political leaders: William *Plomer has written on Cecil John Rhodes (1934), Sarah Gertrude *Millin on Rhodes (1933) and Jan Smuts (1936), and Alan *Paton on the Afrikaner intellectual prodigy J. H. Hofmeyr (1964). Stuart *Cloete combined several biographies in his *African Portraits: A Biography of Paul Kruger, Cecil Rhodes and Lobengula, Last King of the Matabele* (1946; rev. ed. 1969), while Phyllis Lewsen's life of the statesman John X. Merriman (1982) and Jeff Guy's *The Heretic: A Study of the Life of John William Colenso 1814–1883* (1983) are two examples of more recent biographies on the lives of important and controversial colonial figures.

The lives of important African intellectuals and leaders have also received attention. Dan *Wylie's brilliant biography of the nineteenth-century Zulu king Shaka, *Myth of Iron*, appeared in 2006. Mary *Benson has published important works on the lives of Botswanan statesman Tshekedi Khama (1960) and ANC leaders Albert Luthuli (1963) and Nelson Mandela (1986). Peter Becker has treated the lives of Mzilikazi (1962), Dingane (1964), and Moshoeshoe (1969) in his series of biographical works. Donovan Williams's *Umfundisi: A Biography of Tiyo Soga 1829–1871* appeared in 1978 (appropriately enough in a Lovedale Press edition). Fatima Meer's authorized biography *Higher Than Hope, Mandela: The Biography of Nelson Mandela* (1989) perhaps caps the recuperation of the lives of important African leaders who have hitherto been denied full recognition. Her earlier *Apprenticeship of a Mahatma* (1970) dealt with the South African part of Mohandas Gandhi's life. More recently, Richard *Rive and Tim *Couzens have continued this trend in *Seme: The Founder of the ANC* (1991). As its title implies,

Diana Russell's *Lives of Courage: Women for a New South Africa* (1989) attempts to place the lives of some of the South African women in politics and public life more firmly on the map. Stephen Clingman's magisterial *Bram Fischer: Afrikaner Revolutionary* (1998) has provided a welcome appraisal of an Afrikaner dissident much maligned by the apartheid regime. One of the most outstanding examples of biographical writing that simultaneously constitutes a history of an era and a people is Charles van Onselen's masterly *The Seed Is Mine: The Life of Kas Maine, A South African Sharecropper, 1894–1985* (1996).

Biographical writing on South African authors has become an increasingly popular genre. However, before the 1970s few works in this genre had appeared. Margaret Lane's 1939 biography of the life of the journalist Edgar Wallace is an early example. And the life of Henry Rider *Haggard has been treated in a 1951 biography by his daughter, Lilias Rider Haggard.

The life and work of Olive *Schreiner has remained an area of fascination for biographers. No fewer than eight works on this pioneer woman writer have appeared over the years. The *Life of Olive Schreiner*, by her husband S. C. Cronwright Schreiner, appeared in 1924. Ruth First and Ann Scott's 1980 biography was widely acclaimed to be the most authoritative to date. However, three major new works have appeared recently: Joyce Avrech Berkman's *The Healing Imagination of Olive Schreiner: Beyond South African Colonialism* (1989), Karel Schoeman's *Olive Schreiner: 'n Lewe in Suid-Afrika 1855–1881* (1989) (translated into English in 1991 as *Olive Schreiner: A Woman in South Africa, 1855–1881*), and his more recent *Only An Anguish to Live Here: Olive Schreiner and the Anglo-Boer War, 1899–1902* (1992). Schoeman's painstaking research on Schreiner, coupled with his *Missionary Letters of Gottlob Schreiner, 1837–1846* (1991), provides a wealth of meticulously presented biographical information on this major South African writer.

The life of transport rider, prospector, statesman, and writer Sir Percy *FitzPatrick in many ways captures the ambience of late nineteenth-century colonial South Africa, and it has been treated in A. P. Cartwright's *The First South African: The Life and Times of Sir Percy FitzPatrick* (1971) and, more recently, by Andrew Duminy and Bill Guest in their authoritative *Interfering in Politics: A Biography of Sir Percy FitzPatrick* (1987).

The 1980s saw a spate of biographies of major South African writers following Valerie Rosenberg's *Sunflower to the Sun: The Life of Herman Charles Bosman* (1976; reissued in altered form as *The Life of Herman Charles Bosman* in 1991, and as *Between the Lines: Herman Charles Bosman* in 2005), and Martin Rubin's *Sarah Gertrude Millin: A South African Life* (1977). Rosenberg's own *Herman Charles Bosman: A Pictorial Biography* appeared in 1981 and was followed by Peter Alexander's *Roy Campbell: A Critical Biography* (1982), and his biographies of William *Plomer (1989) and Alan *Paton (1995). Noel Chabani Manganyi's *Exiles and Homecomings: A Biography of Es'kia Mphahlele* (1983), Brian Willan's definitive *Sol Plaatje: A Biography* (1984), and Tim *Couzens's thorough treatment of pioneer South African writer H. I. E. *Dhlomo in *The New African* (1985) are other major works of this period. Couzens has more recently written a highly acclaimed biographical study of Alfred Aloysius Horn, *Tramp Royal: The True Story of Trader Horn* (1992), winner of the 1993 CNA Literary Award. Gillian Stead Eilersen's *Bessie Head: Thunder Behind Her Ears: Her Life and Writing* (1995) was the first major biocritical study of this important writer. Among recent works must be mentioned two books by Stephen *Gray: *Beatrice Hastings: A Literary Life* (2004), and *Life Sentence: A Biography of Herman Charles Bosman* (2005).

Biographical writing in South Africa has been well served by several reference works in the genre. Some of these are the pioneering *The African Who's Who*, compiled by T. D. Mweli Skota and published in several editions beginning in 1930; *The South African Woman's Who's Who* (1938); Ken Donaldson's *South African Who's Who, 1951: An Illustrated Biographical Sketch Book of South Africans* (1951); M. E. Manjoo's *The Southern Africa Indian Who's Who* (1972); and, more recently, Mona de Beer's *Who Did What in South Africa* (1988). Eric Rosenthal's *Southern African Dictionary of National Biography* (1966) and the Human Sciences Research Council's *Dictionary of South African Biography*, which has appeared in several volumes between 1968 and 1977, remain the most comprehensive and useful works in the field.

AUTOBIOGRAPHY Early settler life in South Africa provided much memorable material for autobiographical accounts. These include the memoirs of the lieutenant governor of the Eastern Province of the Cape Colony, Sir Andries Stockenström, whose *Autobiography* appeared in two volumes in 1887. Thomas Pringle's experiences as an early settler during the turbulent period of the Frontier Wars are recorded in his *Narrative of a Residence in South Africa* (1835). H. H. Dugmore, another 1820 settler, wrote *The Reminiscences of an Albany Settler* (1871). More recent autobiographical work in this vein includes W. C. *Scully's *Reminiscences of a South African Pioneer* (1913) and Francis Carey *Slater's *Settler's Heritage* (1954).

The Second Boer War prompted many reminiscences, some of them very soon after the end of the war. These include *The Memoirs of Paul Kruger* (1902), the Boer general Ben Viljoen's frank but conciliatory *My Reminiscences of the Anglo-Boer War* (1902), and the ever-popular *Commando: A Boer Journal of the Boer War* (1929), by Deneys Reitz; later volumes in Reitz's autobiographical account include *Trekking On* (1933) and *No Outspan* (1943). J. C. Smuts's *Memoirs of the Boer War* (1966) has also enjoyed sustained popularity. On the other side, Edgar Wallace wrote his *Unofficial Dispatches of the Anglo-Boer War* (1901), while Major General Robert Baden-Powell's experiences of the siege of Mafeking and after are recorded in his *Sketches in Mafeking and East Africa* (1907). Sol *Plaatje was also trapped in Mafeking and his perspective is offered in *The Boer War Diary of Sol T. Plaatje* (1973), edited and published many years after Plaatje's death by John Comaroff.

Autobiographies by writers have also constituted a popular genre down the years. *The Autobiography of Kingsley Fairbridge* (1927), a minor classic of settler life, describes Fairbridge's youthful experiences of the Rhodesian bush, his visit to England in 1903 and his later entrance to Oxford as a Rhodes Scholar. The prolific Afrikaans writer C. Louis Leipoldt recorded his experiences as the first medical inspector of schools in the Transvaal from 1914 onward in the engrossing *Bushveld Doctor* (1937). Sarah Gertrude *Millin wrote two volumes of autobiography, *The Night Is Long* (1941) and *The Measure of My Days* (1955). Roy *Campbell's *Broken Record: Reminiscences* (1934) covers the author's boyhood in Natal, his experiences of setting up the controversial literary journal *Voorslag* with William *Plomer and Laurens *van der Post, and his departure for Europe, while *Light on a Dark Horse: An Autobiography 1901–1935* (1951) continues his account using a similar flamboyant mixture of fact and fiction. The more restrained William Plomer wrote *Double Lives* (1943) and *At Home* (1958); these were later revised and combined in the posthumously published *The Autobiography of William Plomer* (1975). Herman Charles *Bosman published his prison memoir as *Cold Stone Jug* (1949), while Es'kia *Mphahlele produced one of South Africa's best-known autobiographies, *Down Second Avenue* (1959). This was followed in 1984 by *Afrika My Music: An Autobiography 1957–1983*, which covers his years in exile and his return to South Africa in the tumultuous years after the Soweto uprising of 1976.

Many other black South Africans turned to the genre of literary autobiography in the 1950s and 1960s, including Peter *Abrahams, *Tell Freedom* (1954), Alfred *Hutchinson, *Road to Ghana* (1960) Todd *Matshikiza, *Chocolates for My Wife* (1961), and Bloke *Modisane, *Blame Me on History* (1963). Richard *Rive's *Writing Black* (1981) is a collection of essays dealing with his childhood in District Six, his later extensive travels in Africa and Europe, and his experiences as a visiting scholar in England and the United States.

Guy *Butler published three volumes of autobiography: *Karoo Morning: An Autobiography (1918–1935)* (1977), *Bursting World: An Autobiography (1936–45)* (1983), and *A Local Habitation: An Autobiography (1945–1990)* (1991). Another major South African literary figure, Alan *Paton, wrote two volumes of autobiography, *Towards the Mountain* (1980) and *Journey Continued* (1988), while his second wife, Anne Paton, told her side of the story in *Some Sort of Job: My Life with Alan Paton* (1992).

Autobiographical works in the 1990s by South African writers include Mary *Benson's *A Far Cry: The Making of a South African* (1989); Sindiwe *Magona's *To My Children's Children* (1990) and *Forced to Grow* (1992); a collection of Bessie *Head's autobiographical writings, *A Woman Alone* (1990); Breyten *Breytenbach's *Return to Paradise* (1993); Stephen *Gray's *Accident of Birth: An Autobiography* (1993); and Laurens *van der Post's *About Blady: A Pattern Out of Time* (1993). Accounts of the difficulties of growing up in racially divided and strife-torn South Africa include works like Rian *Malan's *My Traitor's Heart* (1990), Albie *Sachs's *The Soft Vengeance of a Freedom Fighter* (1990), and Marq de Villiers's *White Tribe Dreaming: Apartheid's Bitter Roots as Witnessed by Eight Generations of an Afrikaner Family* (1991).

Prominent figures in South African life who have written autobiographical works include Nelson Mandela, with *No Easy Walk to Freedom* (1965) and *Long Walk to Freedom* (1994); Father Trevor Huddlestone, with his *Naught for Your Comfort* (1956), and his later *Return to South Africa: The Ecstasy and the Agony* (1991); Chris Barnard, with *The Second Life: Memoirs* (1993); Ronnie Kasrils, with *"Armed and Dangerous": My Undercover Struggle Against Apartheid* (1993); and F. W. de Klerk, with *The Last Trek: A New Beginning* (1998). Less prominent persons who have nonetheless had momentous experiences include Naboth Mokgatle, with *The Autobiography of an Unknown South African* (1971); the journalist Tony Heard, with *The Cape of Storms: A Personal History of the Crisis in South Africa* (1991); Maggie Resha, with *"Mangoana Tsoara Thipa Ka Bohaleng": My Life in the Struggle* (1991); and the larger-than-life Sowetan Godfrey Moloi, with *My Life: Volumes 1 & 2* (1991; first part previously published in 1987).

Black, Stephen *See* Writers Before 1945

Blackburn, Douglas *See* Writers Before 1945

Blacklaws, Troy (b. 1965) Novelist. *Karoo Boy* (2004) is the best known of the three novels Blacklaws has written to date, the other two being *Blood Orange* (2005) and *Orange Sanguines* (2008). *Karoo Boy* tells the story of Douglas, a city boy who moves with his mother to a small town in the Karoo after the disintegration of the family following his twin brother's death. Here, in the context of the violence of South African politics of the 1970s, he befriends Marika, an adventurous girl with an oppressive father, and Moses, a garage worker who dreams of escape to metropolitan Cape Town.

Blignaut, Aegidius Jean (1899–1994) Short-story writer and biographer. Born in the Free State, he went to school in Kroonstad and later worked as a journalist in Johannesburg. In the 1930s he edited a number of satirical magazines with H. C. *Bosman (including *The Touleier*, 1930–31). He served with the RAF in World War II and remained in Britain thereafter. He is best remembered for his simple-seeming and yet complex "Hottentot Ruiter" narrator-figure, which influenced Bosman's "Schalk Lourens" character and which is part of a tradition of South African "oral-style" stories (Ernest *Glanville, Perceval *Gibbon, and F. C. *Slater are among the earlier users of the form). *The Hottentot's God* (1931), Blignaut's first collection of stories (introduced by Bosman), features Hottentot Ruiter. Few (if any) copies of this privately published volume have survived, however, and *Dead End Road* (1980) was issued to bring the stories back into print. The stories Ruiter narrates all deal with his picaresque exploits and in one of them Schalk Lourens himself makes an appearance.

Blignaut is also the author of the memoir *My Friend Herman Charles Bosman* (1981) and edited *Death Hath Eloquence* (1981), a selection of Bosman's poetry. *Talitha* (1984) is a further selection of Blignaut's stories.

FURTHER READING

Craig MacKenzie, *The Oral-Style South African Short Story in English* (1999).

Bloom, Harry (1913–1981) Novelist. He practiced as a lawyer in Johannesburg before moving to Cape Town, later leaving South Africa and going into exile in the late 1950s. He is best known for his novel *Transvaal Episode* (1959), originally published as *Episode in the Transvaal* (1955) and *Episode* (1956). Banned from 1955 until 1982, when it was rereleased, it has as its centerpiece a compelling evocation of a riot in the fictional town of Nelstroom during 1953, the year in which the Defiance Campaign came to an end. A collaborator on the hit musical, *King Kong: An African Jazz Opera* (1961), Bloom's other novels are *Sorrow Laughs* (1959) and *Whittaker's Wife* (1962).

FURTHER READING

J. A. Kearney, *Representing Dissension: Riot, Rebellion and Resistance in the South African English Novel* (2003).

Boehmer, Elleke (b. 1961) Novelist, editor, academic. Born in Durban, Elleke Boehmer studied at Rhodes University and Oxford, and she has taught at the universities of Exeter, Leeds, Nottingham Trent, and Royal Holloway, London. She currently teaches at Oxford University. She has published four novels, *Screens Against the Sky* (1990), *An Immaculate Figure* (1993), *Bloodlines* (2000), and *Nile Baby* (2008). She has also produced several critical works, including *Colonial and Postcolonial Literature: Migrant Metaphors* (1995), *Empire, the National, and the Postcolonial, 1980–1920: Resistance in Action* (2002), *Stories of Women: Gender and Narrative in the Postcolonial Nation* (2005), and *Nelson Mandela: A Very Short Introduction* (2008). She is the editor of *Altered State? Writing in South Africa* (1994) and *Empire Writing: An Anthology of Colonial Literature 1870–1918* (1998).

Screens Against the Sky and *An Immaculate Figure* are concerned with the politics of gender and race. *Bloodlines* weaves together two narrative strands. The first is about a journalist whose boyfriend is killed in a Durban bomb blast in the early 1990s, and the second is about the siege of Ladysmith during the Boer War. *Nile Baby* tells the story of two children who discover an ancient preserved fetus in the old laboratory attached to their school. In their journey to return the fetus to its original home, they discover the historical entanglement of Africa and Britain.

FURTHER READING

M. J. Daymond, "Bodies of Writing: Recovering the Past in Zoë Wicomb's *David's Story* and Elleke Boehmer's *Bloodlines*," *Kunapipi* 24, nos. 1–2 (2002): 25–38.

Boetie, Dugmore (1926–1966) Novelist/autobiographer. Born in Sophiatown, Boetie's short and eventful life as a tramp, con man, and jailbird is recounted in his autobiographical novel *Familiarity Is the Kingdom of the Lost* (1969), written in collaboration with Barney *Simon. (The 1970 American edition also contains a preface by Nadine Gordimer.) Extracts from this picaresque work first appeared in *The Classic* and *London Magazine*. Part of the first chapter of the novel has been anthologized under the novel's title and tells of the protagonist's struggle to survive as a young boy in Sophiatown and Cape Town. Another anthologized extract appeared as "Three Cons," which recounts later episodes in his life as a con man living by his wits on the streets of Johannesburg.

FURTHER READING

R. S. Edgecombe, "Dugmore Boetie's Picaresque Novel," *World Literature Written in English* 29, no. 2 (1989): 129–139.

Bosman, Herman Charles (1905–1951) Short-story writer, novelist, poet. Born in Kuils River near Cape Town, Bosman spent most of his life in the Transvaal, and it is the Transvaal milieu that permeates almost all of his writings. He was educated at Jeppe Boys' High School, the University of the Witwatersrand, and Normal College, where he qualified as a teacher. In January 1926 he received a posting as a newly qualified teacher to the Groot Marico in the remote Western Transvaal. The remarkable aspect of this stay was that, despite its short duration, it later inspired almost all of his 150 short stories. In July 1926, on the day he returned on vacation to the family home in Johannesburg, he became embroiled in a family quarrel and shot and killed his stepbrother, David Russell. In November he was tried and sentenced to death. This sentence was later commuted to imprisonment for ten years with hard labor. He eventually served four years of this sentence and was released on parole in August 1930.

Upon his release Bosman embarked on a series of journalistic ventures with Aegidius Jean *Blignaut. This began a relationship between the two men which was to last until 1934 (when Bosman left for London), a relationship that was to have important consequences for Bosman's development as a writer. Together the two men launched a series of short-lived periodicals, including *The Touleier* (1930), *The New L. S. D.* (1931), and *The New Sjambok* (1931). These journals carried some literary material, including, in the first edition of *The Touleier* (December 1930), Bosman's first major Oom Schalk Lourens story, "Makapan's Caves." Blignaut's stories written at this time used a fictional narrator, "Hottentot Ruiter," and this partly inspired Bosman's own famous storyteller.

In October 1932 Bosman married Ellaleen Manson, and the two departed for London in 1934. For the next six and a half years, Bosman contributed a steady stream of stories and sketches to South African magazines, including "In the Withaak's Shade," "The Music Maker," and perhaps his most famous story, "The Mafeking Road" (1935). In 1940 the Bosmans returned to South Africa, and in 1943 Bosman was appointed editor of a biweekly newspaper published in Pietersburg, in what was then Northern Transvaal. This milieu provided the fictional settings of Kalvyn in his first novel *Jacaranda in the Night* and Willemsdorp in the novel of the same name. In 1944, after divorcing Ella, Bosman married Helena Stegmann and began the most productive period of his career, producing some thirty bushveld stories and all of the nearly eighty "Voorkamer" conversation pieces. In 1947 two of the three works by Bosman to appear in his lifetime were published: *Jacaranda in the Night* and *Mafeking Road*. The third work, *Cold Stone Jug*, appeared in 1949. In 1950 Bosman commenced the "Voorkamer" series, which appeared regularly in the South African weekly *The Forum* until his sudden death of heart failure in October 1951.

Bosman has achieved a posthumous fame far greater than that won in his own lifetime. This is largely due to the efforts of his pupil and editor Lionel *Abrahams, who has over the years produced editions of Bosman's writings in the Human and Rousseau uniform series—a series that began in 1969 with *Mafeking Road* and *Cold Stone Jug*. The efforts of another notable Bosman scholar, Stephen *Gray, resulted in *Selected Stories* (1980), *Bosman's Johannesburg* (1986) and *Makapan's Caves and Other Stories* (1987), which has the distinction of being one of Bosman's rare successes on the overseas market.

Abrahams's editions of Bosman's selected essays and poems, *A Cask of Jerepigo* (1957, 1964) and *The Earth Is Waiting* (1974), gather together some of Bosman's better work in these genres, but it is unlikely that Bosman will be remembered for this aspect of his oeuvre. His early predilection for poetry, reflected in a series of mostly self-published slim volumes of poetry—*The Blue Princess* (1931); *Mara* (1932), which includes a one-act play; *Rust: A Poem*; and *Jesus: An Ode* (1933)—gave way to the more mature and refined vision that he achieved in his fiction, most notably his bushveld stories.

Mafeking Road was an instant success and has gone into numerous editions and impressions from 1947 to 1998, when a new edition appeared that attempted to restore the text to the form intended by the author. The significance of *Mafeking Road* to readers today is that it is the only selection of stories made by Bosman himself. All but one of the twenty-one stories in *Mafeking Road* feature the wily backveld raconteur Oom Schalk Lourens, through whom Bosman is able to reflect ironically on the prejudices and weaknesses of the Marico community, a community he nonetheless evokes with great sympathy and understanding. Memorable stories include "In the Withaak's Shade," "The Music Maker,"

"Mafeking Road," "Makapan's Caves" and "The Rooinek." It is clear, despite the regional setting and localized humor, that Bosman's concerns in these stories are not confined to the Groot Marico but touch upon wider issues that extend to the entire South African population and beyond.

Many of the stories contain references to events that are staple items in Boer folk history. These mainly concern the two Anglo-Boer wars and the various wranglings between the Boer community and the British authorities. Here again, however, Bosman's vision extends beyond sympathy only with the Boer cause. The opening passages of "The Rooinek" describe the Second Anglo-Boer War and the devastation caused to Boer farms in the course of hostilities. The concentration camps into which the British herded many Afrikaner women and children are also briefly alluded to. However, the bulk of the story concerns the actions of a young Englishman (the "rooinek" of the story's title) who comes to settle in the Marico in the midst of a community who are bitterly antipathetic to the English. He strikes up a friendship with a Boer couple to whose baby daughter he grows extremely attached. When the couple decides to trek to German West Africa after the *miltsiek* epidemic has laid waste to their cattle, he goes with them. The family dies in the Kalahari Desert, and the Englishman's body is discovered with them, clutching a bundle of rags he evidently believed in his feverish state was the little girl.

Unto Dust (1963) was the second collection of Bosman's bushveld stories to appear, and features Oom Schalk Lourens in all but four of the twenty-four stories. The title story about two dead men—one white, one black—whose bones become inextricably intermingled is a sustained piece of satire that targets Afrikaner prejudice against the black man. It is the subtle complexity of Bosman's style that enables him to carry off this indictment of racial prejudice with the most dexterous of touches.

The two collections of Bosman's "Voorkamer" pieces—*A Bekkersdal Marathon* and *Jurie Steyn's Post Office* (both published in 1971)—gather work written by Bosman in the last two years of his life. Numbering seventy-nine in all, these stories, which take place in Jurie Steyn's *voorkamer* (parlor), are conversation pieces: various characters, whom we get to know as the series unfolds, participate in desultory discussions on topics of current interest.

Cold Stone Jug is Bosman's chronicle of the four years he spent in Pretoria Central Prison, initially in the shadow of the gallows, until his sentence was commuted to ten years of imprisonment with hard labor. The story begins in a deceptively lighthearted manner that later disintegrates under the pressure of the narrator's descent into madness. In tone the work shifts from the jocular and sardonic to the anguished, desperate cry of a young man already half over the edge of insanity and hanging perilously on the precipice. In an important sense, the significance of *Cold Stone Jug* is that it is an early contribution to the corpus of "prison literature"—that all too populous genre in South Africa.

Bosman's ventures into longer fictional forms, principally represented by *Jacaranda in the Night* (1947) and *Willemsdorp* (which he was revising shortly before his death, but which only appeared in 1977 and then in an authoritative new edition in 1998), take him into an entirely different fictional terrain. While *Jacaranda* is very uneven in quality, *Willemsdorp* is an altogether more successful work. Critics have recognized its more mature vision, and its attempt to depict South African society against a broader historical backdrop. The reason that its impact on South African literature has been so muted is that it was incomplete at the time of Bosman's death, and it is only through the editorial efforts of Stephen Gray that the novel has begun to achieve due recognition.

Bosman's other works include an anthology of South African stories, *Veld-Trails and Pavements* (1949) and several collections of his stories published posthumously. These include *Bosman at His Best: A Choice of Stories and Sketches* (1965), *Almost Forgotten Stories* (1979), *The Bosman I Like* (1981), *The Illustrated Bosman* (1985), and *Ramoutsa Road* (1987). His *Collected Works* appeared in 1981.

In 1998, the Anniversary Edition of Bosman's works, which aimed to put the entire corpus into print in reliable, accurate editions, was launched under the general editorship of Stephen *Gray and Craig MacKenzie. The series began with a completely reedited *Mafeking Road and Other Stories* (1998) and *Willemsdorp* (1998). Other volumes in this series are *Cold Stone Jug* (1999), *Idle Talk: Voorkamer Stories (I)* (1999), which put into print for the first time the first half of Bosman's Voorkamer sequence, *Jacaranda in the Night* (2000) and *Old Transvaal Stories* (2000), which gathers together all the stories not written by Bosman in series—that is, non–Oom Schalk, non-Voorkamer stories. *Verborge Skatte* (2000, edited by Leon *de Kock) gathers all of the stories Bosman wrote in Afrikaans, together with his commentary on Afrikaans literature. *Seed-time and Harvest and Other Stories* (2001) and *Unto Dust and Other Stories* (2002) are two further Oom Schalk Lourens collections that feature the remaining stories in this sequence, while *A Cask of Jerepigo: Sketches and Essays* (2002) and *My Life and Opinions* (2003) are collections of Bosman's journalism—general and autobiographical, respectively. *Young Bosman* (2003) draws together Bosman's early writings, while *Wild Seed* (2004) is the most complete edition of Bosman's poetry to date. The Anniversary Edition concluded with *Homecoming: Voorkamer Stories (II)* (2005).

FURTHER READING

Valerie Rosenberg, *Sunflower to the Sun: The Life of Herman Charles Bosman* (1976); Aegidius Jean Blignaut, *My Friend Herman Charles Bosman* (1980); Stephen Gray, ed., *Herman Charles Bosman* (1986); Craig MacKenzie, *The Oral-Style South African Short Story in English* (1999); Stephen Gray, *Life Sentence: A Biography of Herman Charles Bosman* (2005).

Botha, W. P. B. (b. 1952) Novelist. Born in Johannesburg to working-class Afrikaans parents, he left South Africa in 1975 after graduating as a teacher and has taught in Papua New Guinea, Northern Ireland, and England. He is the author of three novels: *The Reluctant Playwright* (1993), *Wantok* (1995), and *A Duty of Memory* (1997), a harrowing tale about tensions that divide and ultimately destroy a family. Using an innovative style, which includes shifting narrative points of view and the epistolary mode, the novel explores the disturbing consequences for an entire family when, in the period immediately after World War II, an Afrikaans man brings home to the Eastern Transvaal an English bride and is branded a traitor by his community.

Breytenbach, Breyten (b. 1939) Poet, novelist, painter. Born in the Western Cape, he studied fine art at the University of Cape Town. He moved to Paris in 1960, where he cofounded an antiapartheid group called Okhela (Zulu for "ignite the flame"). On a clandestine visit to South Africa in 1975, he was arrested under the

Prevention of Terrorism Act and imprisoned for seven years, after which he returned to Paris, though he has made periodic visits to South Africa in later years.

Breytenbach writes primarily in Afrikaans, which he sometimes translates into English, though he has also tended increasingly to write in English. He has published several volumes of poetry in English: *Sinking Ship Blues* (1977), *And Death White as Words* (1978), *In Africa Even the Flies Are Happy* (1978), *Judas Eye and Self-Portrait / Deathwatch* (1988), and *Lady One* (2002). He has also published two novels in English, *Mouroir: Mirrornotes of a Novel* (1984) and *Memory of Snow and of Dust* (1989), as well as a prison autobiography, *The True Confessions of an Albino Terrorist* (1984). He has written four books of travel writing: *A Season in Paradise* (1980), *Return to Paradise* (1993), *Dog Heart: A Travel Memoir* (1998), and *A Veil of Footsteps: Memoir of a Nomadic Fictional Character* (2008). He has also published a work of literary-political commentary, *End Papers: Essays, Letters, Articles of Faith, Workbook Notes* (1986), and a book of essays, fiction and poetry, *The Memory of Birds in Times of Revolution* (1996). Breytenbach's visual art has been printed in works that combine image and text: *All One Horse* (1990) and *Painting the Eye* (1993). He has also held numerous exhibitions of his paintings.

His multiple forms of artistic expression are all centrally concerned with the elusive nature of identity. Using techniques that embrace surrealism, magical realism, and critical realism, he explores the effects of various forms of political and social coercion on human consciousness, seeking, through the artistic imagination, to create a space of freedom. That such freedom is only ever relative is evident in his account of political imprisonment, *The True Confessions of an Albino Terrorist*, which shows how prisoner and interrogator, captive self and the captivating other, are complicit in a system of relations that defines them in mutual rather than in exclusionary terms. The challenge, as Breytenbach describes it in *Return to Paradise*, is for the reader to traverse these borders of self in the act of reading, to become, as he puts it, a fellow "traveler" who is aware of the limits and possibilities of self.

Breytenbach is a recipient of the 1967, 1969, 1983, and 1990 CNA Literary Award, although he turned down the 1983 award, as well as the 1984 Hertzog Prize, on political grounds. He is also a recipient of the 1981 Poetry International Award, the 1984 Human Rights Award, the 1985 Pier Paolo Pasolini Prize, the 1986 Rapport Prize, the 1991 L'Ordre des Artes et Lettres, the 1994 Malaparte Prize, the 1994 *Sunday Times* Alan Paton Prize, and the 1996 Helgaard Steyn Prize.

FURTHER READING

Jack Cope, *The Adversary Within: Dissident Writers in Afrikaans* (1982); Kevin Goddard and Andries Wessels, eds., *Out of Exile: South African Writers Speak: Interviews with Albie Sachs, Lewis Nkosi, Mbulelo Mzamane, Breyten Breytenbach, Dennis Brutus, Keorapetse Kgositsile* (1992); Rosemary Jolly, *Colonization, Violence, and Narration in White South African Writing: André Brink, Breyten Breytenbach, and J. M. Coetzee* (1996); Paul Gready, *Writing as Resistance: Life Stories of Imprisonment, Exile, and Homecoming from Apartheid South Africa* (2003); Judith Lütge Coullie and J. U. Jacobs, eds., *A.K.A. Breyten Breytenbach: Critical Approaches to His Writings and Paintings* (2004).

Brink, André (Philippus) (b. 1935) Novelist, critic, translator. Born in Vrede, in the Free State, Brink was educated at Potchefstroom University and the Sorbonne. He lectured for thirty years in the Afrikaans and Nederlands Department at Rhodes University before joining the English Department at the University of Cape Town in 1991. He was a leading figure in the group of Afrikaans writers called the "Sestigers" (writers of the 1960s), who, influenced by writers like Albert Camus, introduced new styles and themes into traditional Afrikaans literature. The group's bold engagement with prohibited subjects such as sex, religion, and politics meant that the works of the Sestigers were often banned for periods of time.

Brink's early works in Afrikaans include *Die meul teen die hang* (1958), *Lobola vir die lewe* (1962; *Dowry for Life*) and *Die ambassadeur* (1963; *The Ambassador*, 1964). Although these works established Brink's reputation as a bold and inventive writer, it was with novels such as *Kennis van die aand* (1973; *Looking on Darkness*, 1974), *'n Oomblik in die wind* (1975; *An Instant in the Wind*, 1976), *Gerugte van reën* (1978; *Rumours of Rain*; winner of the CNA Award), and *'n Droë wit seisoen* (1979; *A Dry White Season*) that he became world-renowned.

Looking on Darkness, a story about a Coloured actor who has been sentenced to hang for the murder of his white lover, was his first novel to be banned in South Africa. From this point onward, Brink published his works simultaneously in English and Afrikaans, and this gave him a wider audience. Set in 1749, *An Instant in the Wind* tells the story of Adam Mantoor, a runaway black slave, and Elisabeth Larsson, wife of the Swedish explorer Erik Larsson, who dies during a journey into the interior of the Cape of Good Hope and leaves his wife stranded in the wilderness. Mantoor finds her, and the two have to undertake the grueling return journey to Cape Town. *Rumours of Rain*, like Nadine *Gordimer's *The Conservationist* (1974), explores the social effects of apartheid through the consciousness of a wealthy Afrikaans businessman. *A Dry White Season*, which takes its name from a line in a poem by Mongane Wally *Serote, concerns the investigation by schoolteacher Ben du Toit into the disappearance of the black janitor's son, who was taken into custody after the Soweto uprising. Du Toit's investigation begins innocuously enough—he merely seeks an official explanation for the mysterious disappearance—but his discovery of the brutality at the heart of the apartheid order draws him further and further into open rebellion.

A Chain of Voices (1982; winner of the CNA Award) is set in 1825 and concerns a slave rebellion at the Cape. It uses multiple narrators—slaves, masters, and other Europeans—in order to present the rebellion from divergent points of view. It also implicitly comments on the potentially explosive situation in the South Africa of the 1980s. In *The Wall of the Plague* (1984) Andrea, a Cape Coloured girl in exile in France, is sent to research the Great Plague of fourteenth-century Europe for a film script that is being written by her white South African lover, Paul. The Plague takes on an allegorical resonance for contemporary South Africa, and Andrea's research becomes a voyage into self-awareness. Other novels are *States of Emergency* (1988), *An Act of Terror* (1991), *The First Life of Adamastor* (1993), *On the Contrary* (1993), and *Imaginings of Sand* (1996). *Devil's Valley* (1998) is set in a valley based on Die Hel in the Little Karoo. It describes in a postmodernist vein the experiences of crime reporter Flip Lochner, who arrives in the region in order to write its history and discovers a world bizarre beyond his imaginings. Brink's novel *The Rights of Desire* (2000) is a text that engages with J. M.

*Coetzee's *Disgrace* (1999). Both novels deal with an aging white man in a rapidly changing South Africa. More recent novels include *The Other Side of Silence* (2002), *Before I Forget* (2004), *Praying Mantis* (2005), and the novella *The Blue Door* (2006).

A translator of various English, French, and German works into Afrikaans, Brink is also the author of several works of nonfiction, including *Mapmakers: Writing in a State of Siege* (1983), a set of essays dealing principally with the role of the writer in South Africa, *SA 27 April 1994: An Author's Diary* (1994), *Reinventing a Continent: Writing and Politics in South Africa, 1982–1995* (1996), *Destabilising Shakespeare* (1996), and *The Novel: Language and Narrative from Cervantes to Calvino* (1998). He has also coedited, with J. M. *Coetzee, *A Land Apart: A South African Reader* (1986). In 1993 Brink was awarded the rank of *commandeur* in the Ordre des Artes et Lettres, France's highest accolade for excellence in literature and the arts.

FURTHER READING

Rosemary Jane Jolly, *Colonization, Violence, and Narration in White South African Writing: André Brink, Breyten Breytenbach, and J. M. Coetzee* (1996); Sue Kossew, *Pen and Power: A Post-Colonial Reading of J. M. Coetzee and André Brink* (1996); Jochen Petzold, *Re-imagining White Identity by Exploring the Past: History in South African Novels of the 1990s* (2002).

Brown, Andrew (b. 1967) Novelist. Andrew Brown practices law in Cape Town. He has published two novels, *Coldsleep Lullaby* (2005) and *Inyenzi* (2007). Set in Stellenbosch, *Coldsleep Lullaby* alternates between two narratives, a contemporary story that focuses on police officer Februarie's investigation into the murder of a young student, Melanie, and a story that takes place during the early settlement of Stellenbosch and deals with viticulturist Van der Keesel's exploitative relationship with a slave woman and her young daughter. Themes of race, paternal care, and sexuality are presented in a way that each story mirrors the other. The novel won the *Sunday Times* Fiction Award in 2005. *Inyenzi* takes as subject the 1994 Rwandan genocide. Employing techniques of documentation and lyrical description to evoke both the political and the personal in events leading up to the killings, *Inyenzi* explores the interwoven fates of three characters, the Tutsi woman Selena, the Hutu priest Melchior, and his childhood friend Victor, a leader in the uprising against the Tutsi population.

Brown, James Ambrose (b. 1919) Playwright, novelist, and autobiographer. Born in Scotland and educated in Edinburgh and Kilmarnock, he came out to South Africa with his family in 1936. He worked as a journalist in Johannesburg and began writing plays. His *Governor of the Black Rock* (first performed in 1951) brought him critical attention; it was followed by several children's plays, including *The Three Wishes* (1954), *Circus Adventure* (1955), and *Mango Leaf Magic* (1956). Later work in theater includes *Lyndall: An Adaptation in Two Acts of Olive Schreiner's "The Story of an African Farm"* (1978).

His novels include *Splendid Sunday* (1956), *The Anthill* (1958), about the wartime experiences of South African soldiers in North Africa (adapted as the play *Seven Against the Sun* in 1962), *The Naked Blood* (1961), *The Return* (1971), *The Snare* (1975), *Adrift* (1981), *The White Locusts: A Saga of the Birth of Johannesburg* (1983), *Ridge of Gold* (1986), *Seeds of Anger* (1987), and *Whirlpool* (1990).

He also wrote a number of studies of the world wars, including *A Gathering of Eagles:*

The Campaigns of the South African Air Force in Italian East Africa, June 1940–November 1941, with an Introduction 1912–1939 (1970), *Eagles Strike: The Campaigns of the South African Air Force in Egypt, Cyrenaica, Libya, Tunisia, Tripolitania and Madagascar, 1941–1943* (1974), *The War of a Hundred Days: Springboks in Somalia and Abyssinia 1940–41* (1990), and *They Fought for King and Kaiser: South Africans in German East Africa 1916* (1991). His autobiography, *One Man's War: A Soldier's Diary*, appeared in 1980.

Brownlee, Frank *See* Writers Before 1945

Brownlee, Russel (b. 1966) Novelist. Resident in Cape Town, Brownlee is the author of the novel *Garden of the Plagues* (2005). Set in the early years of settlement at the Cape, and combining vivid realism of detail with magical reconstruction of the distant past, the novel tells the story of Adam Wijk, gardener and physician to the Dutch East India Company, and his involvement with a Malaysian girl, the surviving passenger of a ship that docks at the harbor and is rumored to be carrying the plague. The novel weaves together evocations of seventeenth-century life at the Cape with reflections on the emerging scientism of the age of enlightenment.

Brutus, Dennis (b. 1924) Poet, academic. Born in Rhodesia (now Zimbabwe), he studied at the Universities of Fort Hare and Witwatersrand before taking up a teaching post at Paterson High School in Port Elizabeth, where he taught the young Arthur *Nortje. As a result of his political opposition to the apartheid state, he was first served with a banning order and subsequently imprisoned on Robben Island. He went into exile in 1966, lived in London for several years, then settled in the United States, where he taught at the University of Denver before taking up the post of professor of poetry at Northwestern University. For many years he was banned under the Suppression of Communism Act (the Internal Security Act) and was prohibited from being quoted in South Africa. He was officially unbanned in 1990.

Brutus has published numerous volumes of poetry, including *Sirens, Knuckles, Boots* (1963), *Letters to Martha and Other Poems from a South African Prison* (1968), *Poems from Algiers* (1970), *Thoughts Abroad* (1970), *Denver Poems* (1971), *A Simple Lust: Selected Poems* (1973), *China Poems* (1975), *Strains* (1975), *The Ordeal: Poems of Anguish, Resistance and Hope* (1977), *Stubborn Hope* (1978; rev. ed. 1983), *Salutes and Censures* (1984), *Airs and Tributes* (1989), *Still the Sirens* (1993), *Remembering Soweto 1976* (2004), and *Leafdrift* (2005). A selection of his poems has been collected in the anthology *Seven South African Poets* (1971).

He is also the coeditor of *New Masks* (1988), *African Literatures: Retrospectives and Perspectives* (1990), and *New Writing from South and Southern Africa* (1998), collections of essays on African literature. *Poetry and Protest: A Dennis Brutus Reader* (2006), edited by Lee Sustar and Aisha Karim, is a collection of Brutus's essays, speeches, and letters.

Although Brutus has published numerous volumes of poetry since leaving South Africa on an exit visa, his early poems, particularly those collected in *Letters to Martha*, are especially memorable. Distinguished by an austere simplicity, at once analytical and lyrical, the poems trace the diminished circumstances of life in jail, describing the endurance and, unexpectedly, the awakening of the human spirit. The later poems continue to offer resistance to forms of social oppression.

Brutus is a joint recipient, with Arthur Nortje, of the 1962 Mbari Prize for Poetry, which he returned because the award was for nonwhites and thus discriminatory. He is also a recipient of two American literary awards, the 1987 Langston Hughes Award and the 1989 Paul Robeson Award.

FURTHER READING

Bernth Lindfors, *Palaver: Interviews with Five African Writers in Texas: Chinua Achebe, John Pepper Clark, Dennis Brutus, Ezekiel Mphahlele, Kofi Awoonor* (1972); Craig McLuckie and Patrick Colbert, eds., *Critical Perspectives on Dennis Brutus* (1995).

Bryden, H. A. *See* Writers Before 1945

Bryer, Lynne (1946–1994) Poet and historian. Bryer was born and educated in the Eastern Cape, completing her MA in English at Rhodes University in 1969. She worked in publishing in London and Cape Town before launching her own company, Chameleon Press, in 1985. She wrote two volumes of poetry, *A Time in the Country* (1991; jointly published with Fiona Zerbst) and the posthumously published *The Cancer Years* (1999), which deals with her illness in later life. She also wrote works of history: *The 1820 Settlers* (1984; with Keith Hunt) and *The Huguenot Heritage: The Story of the Huguenots at the Cape* (1987; with Francois Theron). In 1991 she received the AA Life Vita / Arthur Nortje Poetry Award.

Bryer, Sally (b. 1947) Poet. Born in Johannesburg, she studied languages and art history at the University of the Witwatersrand, after which she spent a year in Italy studying Italian and art before returning to South Africa to take a course in typology. She lives in Canada and has worked for a publishing house in Vancouver. Bryer has published one volume of poetry, *Sometimes Suddenly* (1973). Focusing on love, the poems evoke the nuances that characterize emotional life, often using images of nature as an index of inner experience. Bryer is the recipient of the 1973 Ingrid Jonker Prize and the 1978 Thomas Pringle Award.

Buchan, John *See* Writers Before 1945

Burgess, Yvonne (b. 1936) Novelist. Born in Pretoria and educated at Rhodes University, she worked as a reviewer and feature writer for the *Eastern Province Herald* in Port Elizabeth from 1960 to 1972. Since 1974 she has lived and worked as a writer in Nelspruit. Her first novel, *A Life to Live* (1973), tells the haunting story of an impoverished Afrikaner woman (a "poor-white") obliged to move from her rural home to take up menial employment in the city, where she settles into an existence of permanent disappointment. Most of Burgess's subsequent novels are similarly set in the squalor of white working-class Port Elizabeth. They include *The Strike* (1975), an apocalyptic novel about a general strike that precedes a revolution in South Africa; *Say a Little Mantra for Me* (1979), which explores the lives of three generations of white South African women; *Anna and the Colonel: An Alternative Love Story* (1997), and *Measure of the Night Wind* (2002). Her novel *A Larger Silence* (2000) won the 2001 Sanlam Literary Award for Fiction. *Two Kinds of Women* (2005) is a collection of short stories.

Butler, (Frederick) Guy (1918–2001) Poet, playwright, autobiographer. Born in the Karoo town of Cradock, where he went to school and spent his boyhood years, Butler was educated at Rhodes University and Oxford. He served with the Allies in North Africa and Italy from 1940 to 1945. After the war he attended Oxford and then taught for a short while at the University of the Witwatersrand before joining Rhodes University in 1951, where he became professor and head of the English Department in 1952, a position he held until his retirement in 1984. As an advocate of English-speaking South African cultural values, Butler's influence on South African English literary culture has been considerable.

His first collection of poems was *Stranger to Europe: Poems 1939–1949* (1952), which includes poems dealing with his war experiences. This collection was republished in expanded form in 1960. His next collection, *South of the Zambesi: Poems from South Africa*, appeared in 1966 and was followed by *On First Seeing Florence* (1968). His *Selected Poems* (winner of the CNA Award) appeared in 1975; this volume was reprinted with additional poems in 1989. In 1978 *Songs and Ballads* appeared, a volume of poems by Butler and Patrick *Cullinan, followed by *Pilgrimage to Dias Cross: A Narrative Poem* (1987). In 1998 his *Collected Poems* appeared. It contains a full range of poetry from the various periods of Butler's writing, as well as several previously unpublished poems.

His best-known poems deal with war experiences and a culturally dislocated sensibility seeking to come to terms with how Europe and Africa are, in different ways, both alien and familiar. In "Karoo Town, 1939" the speaker evokes the textures of a small farming community disrupted by a drummer with his call to arms. In "Cape Coloured Batman," an officer comes upon his servant in a state of drunken oblivion and pauses to reflect humorously on the various strands of the man's mixed racial heritage ("This is the man the Empires made") before concluding that the man also embodies "the pathos of the human race." "Stranger to Europe" explores the speaker's sense of alienation from Europe, exemplified in the foreign names of trees and flowers. In "Myths" a converse case of alienation is described, with the speaker located in Africa and pondering whether European culture can have any purchase on a hostile African terrain. "Tourist Insight Into Things" again takes up the theme of cultural disparity, centering on the different ways in which Europeans and Africans kill their cattle. The poem concludes that to regard as "barbarous" the ritualistic manner in which the latter slaughter cattle evinces a lack of imagination and understanding.

Butler has also been an important editor of South African poetry. In 1965 he founded the poetry journal *New Coin Poetry*. His Oxford *Book of South African Verse* appeared in 1959 and was revised as *A New Book of South African Verse in English* in 1979 (coedited with Chris *Mann). He has also edited (together with his son, David) a collection of African animal poems and sketches, *Out of the African Ark* (1988), and *The Magic Tree: South African Stories in Verse* (1989).

Guy Butler was a prolific playwright. His plays include *The Dam* (1953), *The Dove Returns* (1956), *Judith: A Tragedy* (1957; broadcast by the SABC), *Cape Charade or Kaatjie Kekkelbek* (1968), *A Scattering of Seed* (1968; broadcast by the SABC), *Take Root or Die* (1970), *Richard Gush of Salem* (1982), and *Demea* (1990). He has also published three well-received volumes of autobiography: *Karoo Morning: An Autobiography (1918–1935)* (1977), *Bursting World: An Autobiography (1936–45)* (1983), and *A Local Habitation: An Autobiography (1945–1990)* (1991). His fiction includes *A Rackety Colt: The Adventures of Thomas Stubbs* (1989) and *Tales from the Old Karoo* (1989). Among his other publications are a selection of extracts from South African diaries, *When Boys Were Men* (1969), *The 1820 Settlers: An Illustrated Commentary* (1974), and *The Re-Interment on Buffelskop: S. C. Cronwright-Schreiner's Diary 7–15 June and 8–29 August 1921*, coedited with Nick Visser. *His Essays and Lectures: 1949–1991*, edited by Stephen *Watson, appeared in 1994. His last work was *The Prophetic Nun* (2000).

Butler was influential in promoting English South African literature over the years. He established the Institute for the Study of English in Africa in 1964 and was its chairman until 1972. He was elected president of the English Academy of Southern Africa in 1966 and served in this position until 1969. He was a member of the Council of the 1820 Settlers Foundation from 1967 onwards and was Honorary Life Vice-President of the National Arts Festival of Grahamstown. He founded the Thomas Pringle Collection in 1972, an archive that formed the nucleus of the National English Literary Museum in Grahamstown. He was elected first president of the Shakespeare Society of Southern Africa in 1985, a position he held until 1991, then served as life president of the Shakespeare Society and of the English Academy of South Africa.

FURTHER READING

John Read, *Guy Butler: A Bibliography* (1992); Michael Chapman et al., eds., *Perspectives on South African Literature* (1992); Jeanette Eve, *Guy Butler: Fifty Years of Press-clippings (1944–1994)* (1994); Don Maclennan, "The Poetry of Guy Butler," *English in Africa* 32, no. 2 (2005): 39–52.

C

Camoëns, Luis de *See* Writers Before 1945.

Campbell, Roy (Ignatius Royston Dunnachie) (1901–1957) Poet. Born in Durban to a family of Scottish and Irish descent, Campbell attended Durban High School and spent a year at Oxford, where he made contact with T. S. Eliot, the Sitwells, and other writers. He became part of the literary society of London and published his first long poem, *The Flaming Terrapin*, in 1924. Returning to South Africa for an extended visit, in 1926 he cofounded, with William *Plomer and Laurens *van der Post, the short-lived literary magazine *Voorslag*, which carried satirical pieces by Campbell and Plomer attacking the complacency and insularity of white society at the time, and provoked a strong backlash. Campbell's left-wing posturing at this time is ironic in view of his later admiration for figures such as Franco and Mussolini. Throughout his life, Campbell liked to adopt the minority view and to buck the establishment.

His scathing view of conventional white South Africa is conveyed in *The Wayzgoose* (1928), published after his return to England. It is a long, satirical poem that lampoons journalists, critics, and writers to whom he took exception. After settling in the south of France in 1928, he published *Adamastor* (1930), the collection for which he is best known, which includes "Rounding the Cape," "The Serf," "The Zulu Girl," "The Zebras," and "Horses on the Camargue." The title of the collection refers to the mythical spirit of the Cape of Storms, an anthropomorphic "spirit of Africa" invented by the Portuguese Renaissance poet Luis de *Camoëns. This threatening figure features in "Rounding the Cape," a poem in which Campbell registers his deeply ambivalent response to the continent of Africa and to South Africa in particular ("all that I have hated or adored"). "The Serf" and "The Zulu Girl" contain a similar sense of

Africa's threat to the European intruder. In the former, the surly, patient figure of the peasant tilling the soil "ploughs down palaces, and thrones, and towers." In the latter, the Zulu girl holds an infant to her breast and is perceived to be nurturing a "coming harvest" of social and political revolution.

In *The Georgiad* (1931), Campbell returned to the genre of the long verse satire, this time attacking contemporary English literary figures, including Vita Sackville-West, who is reputed to have had an affair with his wife. In 1932 Campbell moved to Spain, and in 1933 he published the more contemplative *Flowering Reeds*. *Mithraic Emblems* (1936) contains a noteworthy sequence of sonnets probing issues of faith and mysticism. The poems also contain images of bullfighting, a sport with which Campbell was much taken. With the outbreak of the Spanish Civil War in 1936 he returned to England, serving subsequently as a news correspondent in Spain in 1937 before settling in Portugal. Upon the outbreak of World War II he joined an African regiment deployed in Kenya.

After the war, *Talking Bronco* (1946), his last collection of poems, appeared. At this time Campbell was living in London and working with the radio service of the BBC, where he was instrumental in getting several of Herman Charles *Bosman's *Mafeking Road* stories read on air. He settled once again in Portugal in 1952, where he lived until his death in a car accident.

His poems have been collected in three volumes (1949–1960), and in 1985 his *Collected Works* appeared. His *Selected Poems* (2001) was edited by Joseph Pearce (a new edition, edited by Michael Chapman, appeared in 2004). An energetic translator of poetry (he translated works by Baudelaire, Rimbaud, and Lorca), his other works include two volumes of autobiography, *Broken Record* (1934) and *Light on a Dark Horse* (1951); two critical studies, *Wyndham Lewis* (1931; first published 1985) and *Lorca* (1952); two travel books, *Taurine Provence* (1932) and *Portugal* (1957); and a children's adventure story, *The Mamba's Precipice* (1953).

FURTHER READING

David Wright, *Roy Campbell* (1961); Rowland Smith, *Lyric and Polemic: The Literary Personality of Roy Campbell* (1972); John Povey, *Roy Campbell* (1977); Peter Alexander, *Roy Campbell: A Critical Biography* (1982); Joseph Pearce, *Bloomsbury and Beyond: The Friends and Enemies of Roy Campbell* (2001).

Cartwright, Justin (b. 1945) Novelist. Born in South Africa and educated at Oxford University, Justin Cartwright currently lives in London.

He is the author of numerous novels, including *Fighting Men* (1977), *The Horse of Darius* (1980), *Freedom for the Wolves* (1983), *Interior* (1988), *Look at It This Way* (1990), *Masai Dreaming* (1993), *In Every Face I Meet* (1995), *Leading the Cheers* (1998), *Half in Love* (2001), *White Lightning* (2002), *The Promise of Happiness* (2004), and *The Song Before It Is Sung* (2007). *The Promise of Happiness* won both the British Hawthornden Prize and the South African *Sunday Times* Fiction Award.

He has written about South Africa in *Not Yet Home: A South African Journey* (1996), and while novels such as *In Every Face I Meet* and *Half in Love* invoke South Africa in some way, *White Lightning*, short-listed for the 2002 Whitbread Award, engages directly with the country of his birth. Set in postapartheid South Africa, the novel describes the return from England of a young man whose inheritance enables him to purchase a small farm on the slopes of the Helderberg near Cape Town, where he tries to recreate a pastoral retreat. The protagonist's involvement with a pet baboon, a local white woman, and an African family of squatters draws him into an encounter with the countryside that attracts with the promise of a more elemental life and repels with the brutality of its apartheid legacy.

Case, Maxine (b. 1976) Novelist. A resident of Cape Town, Case works for a publishing company. She has written one novel, *All We Have Left Unsaid* (2006), winner of the 2007 Commonwealth Writers' Prize for Best First Book: Africa, and joint winner of the Herman Charles Bosman Prize 2007. While keeping vigil at her mother's hospital bed, Danika recalls her childhood in 1980s South Africa, during the State of Emergency when armed soldiers patrolled the streets of the Cape Flats, reliving the confusing political and familial contexts from the point of view of the seven-year-old observer.

Christiansë, Yvette (b. 1954) Poet and novelist. Born in Johannesburg, Christiansë lived in Cape Town and Mbabane, Swaziland, before moving to Australia with her parents. She holds a doctorate from the University of Sydney and currently lives in New York, where she teaches literature at Fordham University.

She has published a volume of poetry, *Castaway* (1999), and the novel *Unconfessed* (2006), which was finalist for the 2007 Hemingway/PEN International Prize for First Fiction and recipient of the 2007 ForeWord Magazine BEA Award. Both the poetry and the novel draw on colonial histories of conquest, slavery, and exile, using archival documents to reconstruct the dispossessed and silenced voices of the past. *Unconfessed* tells the story of Sila van den Kaap, a slave woman who is banished to hard labor on Robben Island for the murder of her son. While negotiating the daily humiliations and dangers as female prisoner, she reconstructs in a dreamlike fashion the events of the past, returning repeatedly to moments of trauma: her capture as a child in Mozambique, her life as a slave on a Cape farm, the fleeting promise of freedom offered by her former owner, and the bitterness of betrayal by the son when the mistress dies.

Cloete, Stuart (Edward Fairlie Stuart Graham) (1897–1976) Novelist and short-story writer. Born in Paris and educated in Britain, he served in the British army during and after World War I and retired as a result of war wounds in 1922. Of Dutch extraction (his forebears being among the first settlers at the Cape in 1652), he first came to South Africa in 1927 and attempted to establish himself as a cattle rancher and farmer. In 1935 he returned to England and began a writing career, over the years publishing some eight volumes of short stories and fourteen novels, many of them with a South African historical backdrop.

His collections of stories include *The Soldiers' Peaches and Other African Stories* (1959), *The Silver Trumpet and Other African Stories* (1961), *The Looking Glass and Other African Stories* (1963), *The Honey Bird and Other African Stories* (1964), and *The Writing on the Wall and Other African Stories* (1968). His first novel, *Turning Wheels* (1937), dealt somewhat controversially with the Boer Trekkers and was banned until 1974. Later novels include *Watch for the Dawn* (1939), *The Hill of Doves* (1942), *The Curve and the Tusk* (1952), *The Mask* (1958), *The Fiercest Heart* (1960), *Rags of Glory* (1963; about the Boer War), and *How Young They Died* (1969).

Other works include a volume of poetry, *The Young Men and the Old* (1941), and two autobiographies: *A Victorian Son: An Autobiography, 1897–1922* (1972) and

The Gambler: An Autobiography, 1920–1939 (1973).

FURTHER READING

Frederick Hale, "Stuart Cloete's Construction of Voortrekker Religion in *Turning Wheels*," *Acta Theologica* 21, no. 1 (2001): 24–40.

Clouts, Sydney (David) (1926–1982) Poet. Born in Cape Town to a South African mother and a Scottish father, Clouts was educated at the University of Cape Town and Rhodes University. In 1961 he left South Africa for London, where—with the exception of a return visit as research fellow at Rhodes University from 1969 to 1971, when he completed a dissertation on the poetry of Thomas Pringle, Francis Carey Slater, and Roy Campbell —he lived for the remaining twenty years of his life.

Clouts's poetry began appearing in South African literary magazines in the late 1940s and early 1950s and was broadcast on the SABC in 1955. The only volume to appear in his lifetime, *One Life*, appeared in 1966 and won the Olive Schreiner and the Ingrid Jonker Poetry Awards. His substantial reputation as a poet is based on this one volume. Arranged in three parts, the poems are characterized by striking images and an austere style. Clouts's poetic concerns are starkly elemental: stones, flowers, trees, stars, and rivers recur in his work and are carefully weighed for their semantic and symbolic value. In the smallest of elements he saw the universe reflected.

Another characteristic of his poetry is its relentless probing at the nature of poetry itself. Often difficult to access, the poems are carefully honed and linguistically taut. They are complete in themselves, and yet reveal a poetic sensibility restless in its search for a more comprehensive statement about poetry and life.

In "After the Poem," nature resists containment, with the coastline described in the poem "toughly disputing the right of a poem to possess it." This poem adumbrates one of Clouts's principal themes, the relationship between the percipient subject and the object of poetic treatment. He persistently shows his concern with the "thisness" and irreducible "otherness" of things.

One of his best-known poems, "The Sleeper," describes with great sensitivity a sleeping woman and explores ideas of human consciousness and the contrasting unselfconsciousness of nature; of ultimate human aloneness and the inexorable approach of death. "Earth, Sky" describes the speaker's engagement with nature, emblematically captured in the image of a flower he sticks in his coat, while he ponders the birth of his child. His three poems dealing with Prince Henry the Navigator attempt to inhabit the consciousness of an early explorer of Africa and probe at the mystery of what drew him on. Strikingly different in style are his two "Hotknife" poems, which deploy a Cape Coloured patois.

While Clouts's poetry concerns itself with the much-worked dilemma of the European consciousness in Africa, he brings to this preoccupation a modern, radically skeptical sensibility and an expressive vehicle of highly compressed, elusive and metaphorically rich phrasings.

Clouts's poetry was collected posthumously in *Collected Poems* (1984). This volume contains all of the poems from *One Life*, poems published individually, and several previously unpublished poems.

FURTHER READING

Guy Butler and Ruth Harnett, eds., *English in Africa* (Sydney Clouts memorial issue) (1984); Ian Glenn, "Sydney Clouts—Our Peninsular Poet," *English Academy Review* 3 (1985): 127–

134; Michael Chapman et al., eds., *Perspectives on South African Literature* (1992); Stephen Watson, *Selected Essays 1980 –1990* (1990); Kevin Goddard, "Sydney Clouts's Poetry," *English in Africa* 19, no. 2 (1992): 15–34.

Coetzee, J. M. (John Maxwell) (b. 1940) Novelist and literary critic. Born in Cape Town, Coetzee was educated at the University of Cape Town and the University of Texas, where he was teaching assistant and later fellow. He worked as a computer programmer for several years in England and taught at the State University of New York at Buffalo. From 1972 until retirement he taught English at the University of Cape Town, where he was professor of general literature. In 2002 he emigrated to Australia.

Coetzee's impact on literary studies in South Africa has been considerable. His fiction is highly self-conscious and innovative: it constructs compelling fictional landscapes and characters while simultaneously probing at the philosophical and linguistic foundations of the fictional enterprise itself.

His first work, *Dusklands* (1974), introduced a new postmodernist strain to South African fiction. It is a two-part work that explores the worlds of two men obsessed with power and technology. As their stories unfold it becomes apparent that the two parts of the book are connected by their focus on the mentality of colonialism. The first part, "The Vietnam Project," is narrated by Eugene Dawn, who is writing an analysis of the psychological war in Vietnam for the U.S. Department of Defense under the eye of a superior by the name of Coetzee. We witness the mental collapse of the protagonist, who stabs his son and is taken into custody. The second part, "The Narrative of Jacobus Coetzee," purports to be the translation by J. M. Coetzee of the eighteenth-century South African explorer Jacobus Coetzee's adventure into the African interior. The narrative begins with a detailing of the most efficient methods for slaughtering the "Bushman" and progresses to a description of Coetzee's journey into Namaqualand, where he descends into the kind of savagery he earlier professed to deplore. He is deserted by his "Hottentot" companions, who join the Namaqua tribespeople among whom the party has been living and subject him to humiliation. Eventually released, he returns some months later with a military expedition, wreaks genocidal revenge on the tribe, and executes the deserters. The two stories are emblematic instances of Western colonial intrusion and violence, of a desire to master the "other," the unknown and unknowable colonial subject.

Like the two narratives in *Dusklands*, *In the Heart of the Country* (1977) is a first-person narrative, the extended interior monologue of Magda, who lives in isolation on a sheep farm with her widowed father and their two servants, Hendrik and Klein-Anna. The novel consists of 266 numbered passages suggestive of diary entries (although this is not made explicit). Magda relates how she kills her father, then attempts to take over the farm and the servants, fails to assert her mastery over them, attempts a relationship of equality with them, is raped by Hendrik, and is then abandoned and left at the end with her father's corpse, communing with "sky-gods" who leave cryptic messages in the sky. It becomes clear that Magda is not a reliable narrator (she murders her father twice, for example) and the whole narrative becomes a metafictional game in which the very notion of psychological realism (which conventionally underpins an interior monologue of this sort) is subverted. *Inthe Heart of the Country*, as its title ironically suggests, is also a subversion of the conventions of the *plaasroman* (the farm or pastoral novel): the farm, by Magda's testimony, is not a quiet rural retreat where one can live a life of simple plenitude; it is a dark, disturbing world of patriarchal and racial domination, of murder, rape, and insanity.

Waiting for the Barbarians (1980) is probably Coetzee's most widely read work. It is narrated by a magistrate who has for years been the law enforcer in a remote village of "the Empire." A humane and rational man, his tranquility is disturbed by the arrival of the sinister Colonel Joll, sent out by the authorities to quell a rumored barbarian rebellion in the isolated frontier region. No actual enemies come to light, and the rebellion appears increasingly to be a phantom in Joll's obsessive mind. However, this does not prevent him from torturing an old man and his young nephew, who have come to the village to seek medical help. In the process, it becomes clear that the barbarian is already within the gates of the village. The magistrate is appalled at Joll's calculated brutality and his inability to "see" the truth of things: Joll's peculiarly opaque glasses, noted at the outset by the magistrate, suggest a blindness, a lack of moral vision, and this becomes a central theme in the novel. The novel's precise setting in time and place is deliberately obscure so that it becomes an exploration of the archetypal mindset of colonial repression.

Coetzee's fourth novel, *Life & Times of Michael K* (1983), centers on the experiences of Michael K, a young gardener (presumed to be of mixed-race origin, although this is deliberately suppressed in the novel) who, in part one of the novel, flees war-torn Cape Town with his mother to seek refuge in the countryside on a farm where his mother grew up. En route his mother dies; he buries her ashes on the farm and begins to live off the land. He is arrested and detained in a resettlement camp, where a military medical officer, who narrates the second part of the novel, takes an interest in him. K escapes from the camp, and the third part finds him back in Cape Town, where he lives amid the rubble and destruction wrought by the war. Like the first three novels, *Michael K* is concerned with the entrapment of human subjects in circumstances not of their own making. Unlike the other characters, however, Michael K attempts to live in his own "life and times," and outside those of his disintegrating society.

Foe (1986) is a reflexive retelling of Defoe's story of Robinson Crusoe. The castaway-narrator this time, however, is a resourceful and resilient woman by the name of Susan Barton. She relates how she had embarked on a journey to Bahia (Brazil) in a vain search for her only daughter. Two years later she sets sail for Lisbon; a mutiny breaks out on the ship, however, and she ends up being cast adrift with the mortally wounded captain, her former lover. He dies, and she swims to an island where she encounters Cruso—Coetzee's version of Defoe's hero Crusoe—and Friday. Coetzee's Cruso is a parody of the Protestant industriousness of Defoe's character, while the mute Friday (his tongue has been cut out) is Coetzee's inarticulate Caliban. He is compliant with his master's wishes, but he offers nothing but a blank, silent inaccessibility to Barton and to the reader. All attention, therefore, reverts to the other two characters. A passing ship rescues the three, but Cruso dies three days before it arrives in Bristol. Barton is encouraged by the captain of the ship to tell her story, and the reader discovers at this point (the end of part 1) that what he or she has read thus far is Barton's journal, addressed to "Mr Foe," the man who will turn her tale into a saleable book. Part 2 takes the form of a series of (unanswered) letters Barton addresses to the absent Foe in which we see her becoming increasingly assailed by self-doubt as to the veracity of her experiences. In the bizarre last part of the novel, she locates Foe, and together they attempt to supply Friday with a plausible story to fill the hole in the narrative that he represents. As this synopsis suggests, *Foe* is above all concerned with the practice of writing itself.

In *Age of Iron* (1990), the central character, Elizabeth Curren, is told that she is terminally ill with cancer. She returns home to find that a vagrant is living in her garden. This is the mysterious Mr. Vercueil, her guardian angel, messenger, and confidant—and reluctant witness to her last two months on earth. The strife and chaos of South Africa in a state of emergency erupts into her life when she goes in search of her maid's son, lost in the melee of factional strife on the Cape Flats. The novel is a bleak but compelling chronicle of Elizabeth Curren's descent into death, written as a series of letters to her daughter in exile in the United States. In its pellucid, deceptively simple style, its felicitous narrative structure and trenchancy of observation, the novel bears all the marks of Coetzee's hand. Where it diverges sharply from his previous works is in its historical specificity.

Set in 1869, *The Master of Petersburg* (1994) describes Dostoevsky's journey from Germany to St. Petersburg, where he attempts to resolve the mysteries surrounding the death of his stepson (it is unclear whether he has committed suicide or been killed by the local police). As with *Age of Iron*, *The Master of Petersburg* engages with historical personages and events. The Dostoevsky figure is repeatedly adjured by the nihilist Sergei Nechaev to use his writing to expose state violence (it is asserted that his stepson was in fact a victim of this violence) but is reluctant to do so, since this would involve entering the terms of the debate as predetermined by the repressive Czarist forces. The key issue raised by these novels, then, is how the writer can engage with urgent historical events without reinstating the customary privileging of history over fiction.

In 1999 Coetzee produced three books. *The Novel in Africa* is the text of a lecture presented in Berkeley, California, in November 1998. *The Lives of Animals* is the text of two lectures that Coetzee presented as the 1997–98 Tanner Lectures in the Humanities at Princeton University. However, this text is more of a story, purporting to be a lecture on animal rights presented by an elderly novelist, Elizabeth Costello. Members of her audience comment on her lecture. The rest of the book is devoted to responses by actual academics in the fields of bioethics and anthropology.

Disgrace is Coetzee's major work of 1999, and it won him his second Booker Prize. The novel's central character, David Lurie, is a fifty-two-year-old professor of English at the Technical University of Cape Town. A specialist in the Romantics, he deplores the decline of his discipline into the teaching of "communication" in the pursuit of a "technical education." He has a brief affair with a young student, Melanie, whose feelings for him are ambiguous. When the affair is made known to the university authorities, Lurie is brought before a disciplinary committee and told to apologize and undergo counseling. He refuses to do so, rankling at the political correctness of the committee's decision, and accepts dismissal.

He leaves the university and goes to visit his lesbian daughter Lucy, who lives on an isolated farm outside Grahamstown in the Eastern Cape. Through Lucy he meets Bev, a middle-aged woman who runs a voluntary clinic for abandoned and abused animals. Although initially dismissive of her and her activities, he eventually has an affair with her, but more importantly, through helping her at the clinic, he develops a keen empathy with the unwanted animals. By the end of the novel we see that there is more than a casual resemblance between Lurie, disgraced and unwanted by society, and the animals he cares for.

Lucy's smallholding is invaded by three men who beat Lurie and rape Lucy (she falls pregnant in the process) before making off in Lurie's car with looted goods. The disjunction between Lurie's and his daughter's understanding of the rape is marked. Lurie takes a conventional, conservative South Africa view, and he urges Lucy to have an abortion. Lucy interprets the act as a form of historical retribution, is prepared to have the baby, and even makes peace with her attacker, who is the nephew of Petrus, the neighboring black farmer. Lurie himself comes to a greater acceptance of the event by the end of the novel, and he is able to see more clearly his culpability in having taken advantage of—and perhaps even raped—the student Melanie.

The character Elizabeth Costello features in *Elizabeth Costello: Eight Lessons* (2005), a curious volume that gathers together several narratives that Coetzee had earlier delivered from the lecture podium. Coetzee appears to use Costello to explore issues and ideas without committing himself to a single perspective or conclusion (in the chapter "At the Gate," Costello confesses, "I have beliefs but I do not believe in them"). Through its demonstration of the ethical power of narrative as a medium for the staging of important human challenges and dilemmas, *Elizabeth Costello* is a compelling defense of Coetzee's conception of his role as a novelist.

Set in Australia, the novel *Slow Man* (2005) deals with a cyclist who loses a leg after being hit by a car, and who then attempts to engage in a love relationship with a Croatian immigrant home-care worker. Elizabeth Costello makes a reappearance, and the novel takes a characteristic postmodernist turn, in which the artifice and contrivances of writing are foregrounded.

The novel *Diary of a Bad Year* (2007) deals with a seventy-two-year-old Australian writer who is invited to contribute to a book entitled *Strong Opinions*. A set of essays on a range of urgent concerns ensues, together with the story of the writer's involvement with the young woman he employs as a secretary. The threads of the narrative—the essays, events as seen from his point of view and events as seen from her point of view—literally unfurl alongside each other, with the text on the page being divided into three parallel sections. The work thus presents a whole new challenge to Coetzee's readers.

Coetzee's critical works include a study of colonial writing in South Africa, *White Writing: On the Culture of Letters in South Africa* (1988), *Giving Offense: Essays on Censorship* (1996), *Doubling the Point: Essays and Interviews* (1992), edited by David Attwell, *Stranger Shores: Essays 1986–1999* (2001), and *Inner Workings: Essays 2000–2005* (2007). He coedited (with André *Brink) *A Land Apart: A South African Reader* (1986) and has translated Marcellus Emants's *A Posthumous Confession* (1975) and Wilma Stockenström's *The Expedition to the Baobab Tree* (1983). Another work of translation is his *Landscape with Rowers: Poetry from the Netherlands* (2004).

His *Boyhood: Scenes from Provincial Life* (1997), is a memoir of childhood artfully told in the third person. It recounts the young narrator's childhood in provincial Worcester and lower-middle-class Cape Town, the torments and travails he experiences at school and in his troubled home, and his youthful yearning for the sense of rootedness that the family farm in the Karoo seems to hold out to him. *Youth* (2002) is a continuation of this memoir, and also uses the third-person point of view. It details the narrator's experiences as a young student in Cape Town and an immigrant in London, where he seeks romance and fulfillment as a poet. Instead, he finds a job as a computer programmer, settles into a drab daily routine, and has to endure the misery of London's cold indifference to his artistic aspirations. The tone of both memoirs is wry and humorous, with the narrator in both cases invariably the target of the memoirs' brutal frankness.

Coetzee has been awarded numerous literary prizes, including: for *Dusklands*, the Mofolo-Plomer Prize; for *In the Heart of the Country*, the CNA Award; for *Waiting for the Barbarians*, the Geoffrey Faber Prize, the James Tait Black Memorial Prize, and the CNA Award; for *Life & Times of Michael K*, the Booker-McConnell Prize, the Jerusalem Prize, and the CNA Award; for *Age of Iron*, the *Sunday Express* Book of the Year Award; for *The Master of Petersburg* a Commonwealth Writers Prize; and for *Disgrace*, the Booker-McConnell Prize. In 1988 he was elected a fellow of the Royal Society of Literature and, in 1990, was made an honorary fellow of the Modern Languages Association of America. He holds honorary doctorates from the University of Adelaide, La Trobe University, the University of Natal, the University of Oxford, Rhodes University, Skidmore College, the State University of New York at Buffalo, the University of Strathclyde, and the University of Technology, Sydney. In 2003 he was awarded the Nobel Prize in literature.

FURTHER READING

Teresa Dovey, *The Novels of J. M. Coetzee: Lacanian Allegories* (1988); Dick Penner, *Countries of the Mind: The Fiction of J. M. Coetzee* (1989); Kevin Goddard and John Read, *J. M. Coetzee: A Bibliography* (1990); Susan VanZanten Gallagher, *A Story of South Africa: J. M. Coetzee's Fiction in Context* (1991); David Attwell, *J. M. Coetzee: South Africa and the Politics of Writing* (1993); Graham Huggan and Stephen Watson, eds., *Critical Perspectives on J. M. Coetzee* (1996); Rosemary Jolly, *Colonization, Violence, and Narration in White South African Writing: André Brink, Breyten Breytenbach, and J. M. Coetzee* (1996); Sue Kossew, *Pen and Power: A Post-Colonial Reading of J. M. Coetzee and André Brink* (1996); Dominic Head, *J. M. Coetzee* (1997); Stefan Helgesson, *Writing in Crisis: Ethics and History in Gordimer, Ndebele and Coetzee* (2004); Derek Attridge, *J. M. Coetzee and the Ethics of Reading: Literature in the Event* (2004); Jane Poyner, ed., *J. M. Coetzee and the Idea of the Public Intellectual* (2006).

Colenso, Frances Ellen *See* Writers Before 1945

Conyngham, John (b. 1954) Novelist. Conyngham grew up on a sugar farm on the Natal North Coast. He is now editor of the *Natal Witness* newspaper in Pietermaritzburg. His first novel, *The Arrowing of the Cane* (1986), joint winner of the 1985 AA Mutual Life / Ad. Donker Literary award and winner of the 1988 Olive Schreiner Prize, is set in the politically turbulent mid-1980s, and centers on Natal sugar farmer James Colville, who fears the imminent assumption of power by the black majority. Deciding not to emigrate to Europe, he instead writes a chronicle of this phase in South African history and it is through his self-reflexive diary that we come to learn about his life. He becomes haunted by the prospect of being disemboweled by rampaging Zulus, and eventually chooses to commit suicide rather than suffer this fate. Through the character of James Colville, Conyngham interrogates the legacy of colonialism and white liberalism in South Africa.

The Desecration of the Graves (1990) is another first-person narrative that also takes place against the backdrop of the politically turbulent 1980s. Jeremy Cranwell is an amateur biographer researching the life of a British general. He travels to the northeastern Cape, where this general reportedly fell from grace during a skirmish in the Anglo-Boer War. Part of the novel concerns the help that Cranwell offers to a black political activist, and through this subplot Conyngham appears to be exploring a more positive response to the political crisis in South Africa than was demonstrated by the protagonist of his previous novel. However, by the end of the novel we see Cranwell retreating from an engagement with the political realities of the country.

Set in the fictionalized Natal Midlands town of Bushmansburg, *The Lostness of Alice* (1998) takes place in the period immediately preceding South Africa's first democratic elections of 1994. The narrator is a dairy farmer, his wife a journalist on a local newspaper. She takes up the case of Alice Walker, a sixteen-year-old girl who mysteriously disappears from the town. The case is never solved, but the event provides the catalyst for the narrator's own wanderings through Europe and Africa. Part travelogue, part detective story, the novel continues Conyngham's probing of the complex inheritance of the European colonial settlement of Africa.

FURTHER READING

Peter Blair, "Of Lostness and Belonging: Interview with John Conyngham," *Current Writing* 15, no. 1 (2003): 74–90; J. A. Kearney, "Haunted by Dispossession: A Study of John Conyngham's Novels," *English in Africa* 19, no. 1 (1992): 67–87.

Coovadia, Imraan (b. 1970) Novelist. Born in Durban, Coovadia studied at Harvard University and lived for a time in New York. He currently lectures at the University of Cape Town. He has published two novels, *The Wedding* (2001), which was runner-up for the *Sunday Times* Literary Award, and *Green-Eyed Thieves* (2006). Drawing on the history of his own family, *The Wedding* spans India and South Africa in narrating the courtship and marriage of Ismet, a clerk from Bombay, and Khateja, a village beauty with a sharp tongue who is scornful of her husband and determined to make his life as miserable as she can. Told from the point of view of their grandson, the story is a comic and poignant portrayal of love and the vagaries of fortune.

Cope, Jack (Robert Knox) (1913–1991) Novelist, short-story writer, poet, editor. Born and educated in Natal (now KwaZulu-Natal), he trained as a journalist on the *Natal Mercury*, subsequently becoming political correspondent in London for South African newspapers. At the outbreak of World War II he returned to South Africa to farm and began, at this stage, to devote himself fully to creative writing and the promotion of South African literature. As editor, he has had a pervasive and lasting influence. He relocated to England in 1980.

Cope published eight novels: *The Fair House* (1955), *The Golden Oriole* (1958), *The Road to Ysterburg* (1959), *Albino* (1964), *The Dawn Comes Twice* (1969), *The Rain-Maker* (1971), *The Student of Zend* (1972), and *My Son Max* (1978). He also published four volumes of short stories, *The Tame Ox* (1960), *The Man Who Doubted and Other*

Stories (1967), *Alley Cat and Other Stories* (1973), and *Selected Stories* (1986), and three volumes of poetry, *Lyrics and Diatribes* (1948), *Marie: A South African Satire* (1948), and *Recorded in Sun* (1979). He is also author of the literary-critical study *The Adversary Within* (1982), dealing with Afrikaans dissident writers, and a historical work, *King of the Hottentots* (1967).

Cope addresses the racial and political conditions prevalent in South Africa. Although his novels have a topical interest, it is as a short-story writer that he has particularly distinguished himself. Praised for their fine craftsmanship, their absence of didacticism, and their emblematic simplicity, the stories explore the interaction between the individual and nature and the individual and society. The stories characteristically employ suggestion rather than narrative closure.

Cope was founding editor of the literary journal *Contrast* (now *New Contrast*), and of the *Mantis Poets* series. He edited *Seismograph* (1970), a selection of writings from *Contrast*, coedited, with Uys *Krige, *The Penguin Book of South African Verse* (1968), and translated, with William *Plomer, Ingrid *Jonker's *Selected Poems* (1988). He is also editor of *Under the Horizon: Collected Poems of Charles Eglington* (1977). Cope was winner of the 1971 CNA Literary Award and the 1972 Argus Literary Award.

FURTHER READING

Sheila Roberts, "Character and Meaning in Four Contemporary South African Novels," *World Literature Written in English* 19, no. 1 (1980): 19–36; David Maughan-Brown, "The Image of the Crowd in South African Fiction," *English in Africa* 14, no. 1 (1987): 1–20; Paul A. Scanlon, "The Short Stories of Jack Cope," *World Literature Written in English* 36, no. 1 (1997): 86–92.

Cope, Michael (b. 1952) Poet and novelist. Son of Jack *Cope, Michael Cope trained as a jeweler and lives and works in Cape Town. He has published several volumes of poetry, including *Scenes and Visions* (1991), *Birds of a Different Feather* (1992), *Crossing the Desert* (1993), *Back View* (1996), and *Ghaap: Sonnets from the Northern Cape* (2005). His works of fiction include the novels *Spiral of Fire* (1986) and *Goldin: A Tale* (2005), a work that deploys myth and fairy tale to arrive at ecological and spiritual understanding. *Intricacy: A Meditational Memory* (2005) is a portrait of the author's family, with his artist mother as focus. Cope's poetry frequently focuses on the minute and the particular, and features "portrait sketches" of characters and events. It is also informed by ecological concerns and evinces a strong sense of the interconnectedness of humanity, nature, and the biosphere. Several of his poems take the form of humorous ballads, portraying characters and situations in a lighthearted yet incisive way.

Cornell, Fred *See* Writers Before 1945

Cotton, Roy Joseph (1953–1985) Poet and playwright. Born and raised in Cape Town, he worked as a pharmacist. Cotton published several volumes of poetry, including *Comforts Frighten Me* (1981), *Everything Is Saycred Boere-Orkestra: Salvayshin Is Coming* (1984), which was privately issued, and *Ag, Man: Selected Poems* (1986). A further selection of his poems appeared under the editorship of Lionel Abrahams as *My Conveyerquick Eagles* (1995). He is also the author of many unpublished plays, including three play cycles: *The Blackmoon Cycle*, *The Bluewindow Cycle*, and *The Gingergreen Cycle*. Cotton's poetry is characterized by an experimental form and style and by a voice that fluctuates with the mood and themes. By turns hallucinatory and lucid, the verse tends toward verbal playfulness.

Couzens, Tim (b. 1944) Literary critic and biographer. Born in Durban, he was educated at Rhodes University and Oxford. He lectured in the English Department at the University of the Witwatersrand until 1976, when he joined the African Studies Institute at Wits, where he was professor until his retirement. A pioneer of literary-historical research into South African English literature, Couzens is known particularly for his research into early black South African writing, and has published extensively on such writers as Sol T. *Plaatje and the *Dhlomo brothers. He coedited (with Nick Visser) the *Collected Works of H. I. E. Dhlomo* (1985) and is the author of *The New African* (1985), a study of the life and work of H. I. E. Dhlomo. He collected the stories of R. R. R. Dhlomo in a special edition of *English in Africa* (March 1975), a selection that was republished as *20 Short Stories* (1996). He is also coeditor (with Essop Patel) of an anthology of black South African writing, *The Return of the Amasi Bird* (1982), and with Landeg White he edited a volume of essays, *Literature and Society in South Africa* (1984). He is coauthor (with Richard *Rive) of *Seme: The Founder of the ANC* (1991), while his highly acclaimed biographical study of Alfred Aloysius Horn, *Tramp Royal: The True Story of Trader Horn* (1992) won the 1993 CNA Literary Award. His new edition of Sol *Plaatje's *Mhudi* appeared in 1996.

Couzens's more recent work in social history includes the lighthearted *Pees and Queues: The Complete Loo Companion* (1999), while his *Murder at Morija* (2003) is a magisterial piece of investigative research. Its centerpiece is the murder by poisoning in 1920 of the French missionary Edouard Jacottet in Lesotho, but, in order to tell the story fully, the entire sweep of the missionary endeavor in nineteenth-century Lesotho is brought into view. Using devices more commonly associated with detective fiction, but nonetheless remaining faithful to historical fact, Couzens weaves a compelling tale that is both a story about a single family's tragedy and the history of an entire nation.

Drawing on both oral and written sources, his *Battles of South Africa* (2004) is a lively recounting of a series of military clashes in South Africa ranging in date from 1724 to 1927.

FURTHER READING

Isabel Hofmeyr and Catherine Woeber, eds., "Tim Couzens: A Festschrift," *English in Africa* 30, no. 2 (2003).

Couzyn, Jeni (b. 1942) Poet. Born in South Africa and educated at Natal University, Durban, she left the country in 1966 for London, where she has worked widely in the arts. Founder member of the Poets' Conference and Poets' Union, she was also the first chairperson of the National Poetry Secretariat, founded in 1973. She subsequently divided her time between England and Canada, where she was employed as a writing instructor in the Department of Creative Writing at the University of Victoria, British Columbia. She has done work for films and art festivals and has appeared on radio and television.

Couzyn has published several volumes of poetry, including *Flying* (1970); *Monkey's Wedding* (1972); *Christmas in Africa* (1975); *House of Changes* (1978); *Life by Drowning: Selected Poems* (1985; rev. ed. 1990); *Singing Down the Bones* (1989); and *In the Skinhouse* (1993). *Homecoming* (1998) records a personal journey through contemporary South Africa, and *A Time to Be Born* (1999) celebrates childbirth. Frequently unsettling in the somberness of its vision, the poetry ranges between a portrayal of the deep interiority of the self and the way the self relates to a larger natural world.

Couzyn is represented in *The Bloodaxe Book of Contemporary Women Poets: Eleven British Writers* (1985), and *The Selected Poems of Jeni Couzyn* appeared in 2000. She is also the author of the unpublished play "Getting There."

Cronin, Jeremy (b. 1949) Poet and critic. Born in the Western Cape, he spent his childhood in various naval bases, including Simonstown, moving later to Rondebosch, where he attended school and graduated from the University of Cape Town. He lectured in philosophy and politics before he was arrested and convicted in 1976 under the Terrorism Act for underground ANC activities. He served a seven-year prison sentence. Since his release he has worked in the labor movement and is an office holder in the South African Communist Party.

Cronin has published several volumes of poetry, including *Inside* (1983; reissued 1987) and *Even the Dead: Poems, Parables and a Jeremiad* (1997). These collections have since been published in a single volume called *Inside and Out* (1999). A more recent collection is *More Than a Casual Contact* (2006). He also coauthored *Thirty Years of the Freedom Charter* (1986) with fellow political detainee Raymond Suttner.

Inside was one of the most influential volumes of poetry of the 1980s. Together with Cronin's literary-critical articles, it helped define a resistance aesthetic in South Africa that diverged from the Black Consciousness philosophy so influential in the 1970s. Cronin's poetry locates political oppression not in race only, nor exclusively in class, but in diverse contexts of social interaction and intimates that the only viable basis for social coexistence is the individual's recognition of the humanity of others. *Inside* contains several poems addressed to Cronin's wife, who died while he was incarcerated, as well as the much-anthologized "To Learn How to Speak," in which the poet articulates a desire to create an authentic South African poetic idiom that expresses "the voices of this land."

Cronin was a recipient of the 1983 Ingrid Jonker Prize and the 1996 Sydney Clouts Memorial Prize.

FURTHER READING

Peter Anderson, "Essential Gestures: Gordimer, Cronin and Identity Paradigms in White South African Writing," *English in Africa* 17, no. 2 (1990): 37–57; David Schalkwyk, "Confession and Solidarity in the Prison Writing of Breyten Breytenbach and Jeremy Cronin," *Research in African Literatures* 25, no. 1 (1994): 23–45; Barbara Harlow et al., "A Chapter in South African Verse: Interview with Jeremy Cronin," *Alif* 21 (2001): 252–267; Rita Barnard, "Speaking Places: Prison, Poetry, and the South African Nation," *Research in African Literatures* 32, no. 3 (2001): 155–176.

Cullinan, Patrick (b. 1932) Poet, editor, publisher. Born in Pretoria and educated at Magdalen College, Oxford, Cullinan has pursued various occupations, including that of lecturer at the University of the Western Cape.

He has published several volumes of poetry. *The Horizon Forty Miles Away* (1973) was followed by *Today Is Not Different* (1978), *The White Hail in the Orchard and Other Poems* (versions from the poetry of Eugenio Montale, 1984), *I Sing Where I Stand* (versions from the Afrikaans poetry of Phil du Plessis, 1985), *Selected Poems* (1991; rev. ed. 1994), and *Transformations* (1999). A selection of his poems has appeared under the title *Escarpments: Poems 1973–2007* (2008). He is also the author of the biography *Robert Jacob Gordon, 1743–1795: The*

Man and His Travels at the Cape (1992), has edited *Lionel Abrahams: A Reader* (1988), and has written a novel, *Matrix* (2002). His memoir of Bessie Head, *Imaginative Trespasser: Letters Between Bessie Head, Patrick and Wendy Cullinan 1963–1977* (2005) is a carefully constructed work that presents an unparalleled insight into a troubled and yet productive phase of Head's life.

Cullinan's poems offer vivid descriptions, sometimes sharply imagistic, often simply registering the imprint of landscape on the imagination. Concerned with the life of the senses, his poems seek to convey not so much the meaning of a given encounter as the experience itself. This experience exists in time but is also out of time, framed by the poem like a photograph or video recording, a residue of experience which, like memory, is a ghostly remainder of what no longer exists—like the dead father in one of his poems, who haunts the upstairs snooker room, his footsteps falling heavily on the floorboards.

Cullinan cofounded Bateleur Press and the literary journal *The Bloody Horse*. He received the 1980 Olive Schreiner Award for Literature; the 1983, 1985, and 1990 Thomas Pringle Awards; the 1989 Sanlam Literary Award; and the 1992 and 1997 Eleanor Anderson Awards.

FURTHER READING

Dirk Klopper, "Native from the Start," *Current Writing* 7, no. 1 (1995): 125–138.

Currey, R. N. (Ralph Nixon) (1907–2001)
Poet. Born in Mafeking (now Mafikeng), Currey left for the United Kingdom when he was fourteen. He studied at Wadham College, Oxford, and taught at the Royal Grammar School, Colchester. He became a fellow of the Royal Society of Literature in 1970.

Currey published several volumes of poetry, including *Tiresias and Other Poems* (1940), *This Other Planet* (1945), *Indian Landscape: A Book of Descriptive Poems* (1947), *Formal Spring: Translations of French Renaissance Poems* (1950), and *The Africa We Knew* (1973). He also wrote the radio poem *Between Two Worlds* (1947) and the radio feature *Early Morning in Vaaldorp* (1961). He published one prose work, *Vinnicombe's Trek: Son of Natal, Stepson of Transvaal, 1854–1932* (1989), and edited *Letters and Other Writings of a Natal Sheriff, Thomas Phipson, 1815–1876* (1968).

Currey's poetry characteristically addresses the problematic of being caught between two worlds and the abiding sense of alienation this induces. The specific circumstance is generalized to address the exilic status of the human condition, from which, he suggests, there is only ever temporary relief. The poetry has been praised for its accurate observation of both the detail of landscape and its larger design. Currey received the 1945 Viceroy's Poetry Prize and the 1959 South Africa Poetry Prize. His *Collected Poems* appeared in 2001.

D

Dangor, Achmat (Achmed) (b. 1948)
Poet, short-story writer, novelist. Born in Newclare, Johannesburg, Dangor lived in many South African cities and towns after leaving school. His compelling portrayal of outsider characters in his fiction is a product of these early years. He has worked in business and various development organizations, including the funding agency Kagiso Trust and the Independent Development Trust. Banned for five years from 1973, Dangor abandoned his first language, Afrikaans, after the 1976 Soweto uprising, which was sparked by resistance to its use

in schools. He was active for many years on various cultural bodies, including the group Black Thoughts, the Writers' Forum, and the Congress of South African Writers (COSAW), on which he served as vice president. He has also been director of the Nelson Mandela Children's Fund.

Dangor's early writing centered on the effects of racial segregation and forced removals, and these themes bulk large in his award-winning prose collection *Waiting for Leila* (1981) and many of the poems in *Bulldozer* (1983). One of Dangor's major achievements is the title piece in *Waiting for Leila*, which focuses on the anguish of the dropout Samad as he drunkenly reels through a series of personal mishaps and disasters that take place against the backdrop of the demolition of District Six.

Juxtaposing different linguistic registers—*skollietaal* (a kind of underworld argot) exists alongside literary English and classical allusions—Dangor plumbs the depths of his characters' private lives while taking cognizance of the weight of public events that falls upon them. The story "Jobman" (which was later made into a film) reveals his preoccupation with characters who have been marginalized by society. In this instance Jobman, a mute Karoo farmworker, comes back to reclaim his wife but falls afoul of the farm foreman and its owner. He is hunted down and eventually shot dead on the veld.

Dangor has published a play, *Majiet* (1986), and another collection of poetry, *Private Voices* (1992). This collection received the Book Award of the BBC Prize for African poetry, and it reveals a poet unafraid of voicing the intensely personal while addressing the contradictory demands of political commitment with a wry and sardonic wit. Dangor's poetry has appeared alongside that of several other South African poets as *Exiles Within: An Anthology of Poetry* (1986). He has also collaborated with Michael Chapman in compiling *Voices from Within* (1982), an anthology of southern African poetry.

Other work in prose includes *The Z-Town Trilogy* (1990), *Kafka's Curse* (1997), and *Bitter Fruit* (2001). *Kafka's Curse* consists of a novella and three short stories. The main piece tells the story of Oscar Kahn (born Omar Khan), a Coloured Muslim architect who passes himself off as a Jewish man and is married to a white woman. He ultimately experiences an inexplicable physical transformation. The story, which uses multiple voices and narrative points of view, is a retelling of an Arabic legend about a gardener who falls in love with a princess and is punished for this transgression by being transformed into a tree.

Bitter Fruit, short-listed for the Man Booker Prize, is set at a key moment in South Africa's transition. Nelson Mandela is about to leave office, and the Truth and Reconciliation Commission's report is about to be finalized. Lieutenant du Boise, a retired security policeman, comes back into the lives of Silas Ali, a former political activist, and his wife Lydia, a nursing sister. She had been raped by Du Boise twenty years earlier, and the couple's son, Mikey, is the progeny of this act. His discovery of the truth of his paternity and the unwelcome reactivation of the past shatter the lives of all three characters. Dangor's recent work has won him acclaim and established him as a major South African writer.

FURTHER READING

Elaine Young, "Cursing and Celebrating Metamorphosis: Achmat Dangor's *Kafka's Curse*," *Current Writing* 12, no. 1 (2000): 17–30; Wendy Woodward, "Beyond Fixed Geographies of the Self: Counterhegemonic Selves and Symbolic Spaces in Achmat Dangor's *Kafka's Curse* and Anne Landsman's *The Devil's Chimney*," *Current Writing* 12, no. 2 (2000): 21–37; Loren Kruger, "Black

Atlantics, White Indians and Jews: Locations, Locutions, and Syncretic Identities in the Fiction of Achmat Dangor and Others," *South Atlantic Quarterly* 100, no. 1 (2001): 111–143; Ato Quayson, "Symbolization Compulsion: Testing a Psychoanalytical Category on Postcolonial African Literature," *University of Toronto Quarterly* 73, no. 2 (2004): 754–772; Jack Kearney, "Representations of Islamic Belief and Practice in a South African Context: Reflections on the Fictional Work of Ahmed Essop, Aziz Hassim, Achmat Dangor and Rayda Jacobs," *Journal of Literary Studies* 22, nos. 1–2 (2006): 138–157.

De Kock, Leon (b. 1956) Poet, critic, translator. Born in Mayfair, Johannesburg, he studied at the Rand Afrikaans University and the University of Leeds. After working as a journalist for several years, he joined the English Department of the University of South Africa, where he was professor until 2006. He is now head of the School of Literature and Language Studies at the University of the Witwatersrand. Author of *Civilizing Barbarians: Missionary Narrative and African Textual Response in Nineteenth-Century South Africa* (1996), he compiled (with Ian Tromp) the anthology *The Heart in Exile: South African Poetry in English, 1990–1995* (1996) and was founding editor of the English studies journal *Scrutiny2*. His first collection of poems, *Bloodsong* (1997), is a set of deeply personal poems that probe childhood experiences and grapple with understanding life in contemporary South Africa. Poems from this collection won him the 1995 Thomas Pringle Poetry Award. He is also the translator into English of the Afrikaans novel *Triomf* (1994, trans. 1999), by Marlene *van Niekerk. His articles on cultural politics in South Africa have introduced new dimensions to debates on postcoloniality. A second volume of poetry, *Gone to the Edges*, appeared in 2006.

De Kok, Ingrid (b. 1951) Poet and editor. Born and raised in Stilfontein, a mining town in North West Province, she was educated at the universities of the Witwatersrand, Cape Town, and Queen's in Canada. She has worked at Khanya College, Johannesburg, and is currently employed in the Department of Adult Education and Extra-Mural Studies at the University of Cape Town.

De Kok has published several volumes of poetry, including *Familiar Ground* (1988), *Transfer* (1997), *Terrestrial Things* (2002), and *Seasonal Fires* (2006), a collection of new and selected poems. She has also coedited a collection of literary-theoretical essays, *Spring Is Rebellious: Arguments About Cultural Freedom* (1990).

De Kok's poetry has both personal and political dimensions, and it is crafted from a language of memories and dreams. The familiar is rendered unfamiliar and transformed through highly original inflections of language and meaning. Her poems often record domestic epiphanies, occurring in the midst of play or of lovemaking, political protest or mourning, and they confer metaphoric patterns of significance on a life sensitively and imaginatively embraced.

De Kok's poetry has been widely anthologized and is a staple of many university readers. She appears in *The Paperbook of South African English Poetry* (1984), *Ten South African Poets* (1999), *City in Words: An Anthology of Cape Town Poems* (2001), and *Crossings: Three Cape Town Poets* (2001), among others.

De Waal, Shaun (b. 1965) Short-story writer, critic. Born in Johannesburg, he holds a master's degree in English from the University of the Witwatersrand. He lived abroad for a short while to avoid the draft, returned in 1988, and began work as a journalist. In 1989 he joined *The Weekly*

Mail (from 1995 the *Mail & Guardian*) and became books editor in 1991. His work as a literary journalist won him a Thomas Pringle Award in 1997.

His stories are collected in the volume *These Things Happen* (1996). A remarkable quality of intimacy is achieved in the opening story "Jacaranda Street," about a young boy's fraught relationship with his older brother and his fascination with an old man who lives nearby. "X and I," where De Waal pieces together his recollections of encounters with the writer Koos Prinsloo, is skilful and absorbing. "Stalwart," another story from the collection, won him the 1992 Sanlam Literary Award.

He is editor of the *Mail & Guardian Bedside Book* (1998), a selection of pieces from the newspaper. Further gatherings under this title appeared in 2002 and 2003. Another such collection edited by De Waal is *Mirth of a Nation: 15 Years of Humour in the Mail & Guardian* (2000). He also coedited (with Anthony Manion) *Pride: Protest and Celebration* (2006), a collection of material that draws on the Gay and Lesbian Archives at the University of the Witwatersrand.

Delius, Anthony (1916–1989) Poet, editor, broadcaster. Born in Simonstown, Western Province, and a graduate of Rhodes University, he was employed as parliamentary correspondent and leader writer on the *Cape Times* before emigrating to England, where he worked as a broadcaster on the BBC.

Delius published four volumes of poetry, *An Unknown Border* (1954), *The Last Division* (1959), *A Corner of the World* (1962), and *Black South Easter* (1965). He is the author of two books of travel, *The Young Traveller in South Africa* (1947; rev. ed. 1959) and *The Long Way Round* (1956). He published a play, *The Fall: A Play About Rhodes* (1960), and scripted an unpublished play, "The Day of the Ancestors" (1967). His prose works include a satirical piece, *The Day Natal Took Off* (1963), and a novel, *Border* (1976), which employs the form of a Settler Diary.

Written at a time of increasing political repression under post–World War II National Party rule, the "unknown border" of the first volume, the poetry evokes a country whose physical and climatic features offer lucid metaphors of discontent and sudden reprisal. The poetry uses past and present to indict a future fraught with uncertainty. Delius received the 1959 Roy Campbell Prize for Poetry, the 1976 Thomas Pringle Award, and the 1976 CNA Literary Award.

Dhlomo, H. I. E. (Herbert Isaac Ernest) *See* Writers Before 1945

Dhlomo, R. R. R. (Rolfes Reginald Raymond) *See* Writers Before 1945

Dike, Fatima (b. 1948) Playwright. Born in Langa, Cape Town, she went to school in Cape Town and Rustenburg and worked in a number of positions at shops and restaurants until appointed stage manager at the Space Theatre (later The People's Space Theatre) in 1975.

Dike has published three plays: *The Sacrifice of Kreli* (1976), *The First South African* (1977), and *So What's New* (1996). The last deals with the lives of four Sowetan women, portraying their solidarity in the face of suffering and showing how their acts of survival are also acts of self-destruction. Dike is the author of an unpublished play, "The Glass House" (1979), and is also represented in *Black South African Women: An Anthology of Plays* (1999).

FURTHER READING

Stephen Gray, "The Theatre of Fatima Dike," *English Academy Review* 2 (1984): 55–60; Ian

Steadman, "Stages in the Revolution: Black South African Theatre Since 1976," *Research in African Literatures* 19, no. 1 (1988): 24–33; Geoffrey V. Davis and Anne Fuchs, eds., *Theatre and Change in South Africa* (1996); Marcia Blumberg and Dennis Walder, eds., *South African Theatre as/and Intervention* (1999); Miki Flockemann, "On Not Giving Up: An Interview with Fatima Dike," *Contemporary Theatre Review* 9, no. 1 (1999): 17–26; Michael Picardie, "A Comparative Perspective on Two Plays by South African Women," *Contemporary Theatre Review* 9, no. 2 (1999): 39–50; Martin Banham et al., eds., *African Theatre: Women* (2002); Stephen Gray, *Indaba: Interviews with African Writers* (2005).

Dikeni, Sandile (b. 1966) Poet. Dikeni lives in Cape Town and has published three volumes of poetry, *Guava Juice* (1992), *Telegraph to the Sky* (2000), and *Planting Water: Collected Poems* (2007). The writing combines a cosmopolitan frame of reference with a sensibility finely attuned to the local, using both English and Afrikaans to project a hybrid cultural identity.

Dikobe, Modikwe (Marks Ramitloa) (b. 1913) Novelist, poet. Born in Seambe, Northern Province, and schooled in Johannesburg, he worked as vegetable hawker, newspaper vendor, security guard, and clerk. Prominent in the Alexandra Squatters movement of the 1940s and active in the trade union movement, he was banned in the early 1960s and, as a "listed" person, was prevented from publishing under his own name (Marks Ramitloa). He retired from his job at the Johannesburg city council in 1977 and returned to Seambe to farm.

Dikobe has published one novel, *The Marabi Dance* (1973), and one volume of poetry, *Dispossessed* (1983). *The Marabi Dance* describes life in the black townships of the 1930s. It juxtaposes the values of an aspirant black middle class with those of a shebeen culture characterized by *marabi* music, which is seen as subversive of values derived from the white oppressor. The volume of poetry, *Dispossessed*, is even more incisive in its critique of colonial and apartheid oppression. Focusing on black dispossession and deprivation, the poetry records experiences both recounted by tribal elders and personally undergone by the poet. The volume is a noteworthy historical and cultural as well as literary document.

Dixon, Isobel (b. 1969) Poet. Born and raised in South Africa, Isobel Dixon now lives in London. She is the author of two volumes of poetry, *Weather Eye* (2002) and *A Fold in the Map* (2008). The latter volume deals with the idea of the journey, exploring, in the first section, the experience of leaving the home country to settle abroad, along with the sense of displacement, ambiguity and longing this entails, and, in the second section, the experience of coming to terms with the illness and death of a father.

Dowling, Finuala (b. 1962) Poet and novelist. Born and raised in Kalk Bay, Cape Town, Dowling graduated from the University of Cape Town and taught at the University of South Africa before returning to the Cape, where she is currently a full-time writer and contract lecturer and developer of educational materials. With her sisters Tessa and Cara she runs an entertainment company, Dowling Sisters Productions, which stages cabaret, readings, and music.

She is the author of three volumes of poetry: *I Flying* (2001), winner of the Ingrid Jonker Prize; *Doo-Wop Girls of the Universe* (2006), joint winner of the Sanlam Award; and *Notes from the Dementia Ward* (2008), all three of which are characterized by what she calls her favored tragic-comic mode. She is also author of two novels, *What Poets Need* (2005) and *Flyleaf* (2007), the latter short-listed for the Commonwealth Writers' Prize Best Book Africa 2008. *What Poets Need* tells the story of John, a poet who lives with his sister and niece in a house on the coast, attending to the everyday domestic necessities while pursuing a love affair, conducted largely in written correspondence, with a married woman whose inaccessibility may bring anguish but nevertheless fuels his romantic longing and poetic fervor. Like the first novel, *Flyleaf* provides a textured sense of the specificities of place and the idiosyncrasies of character. It describes Violet's recovery of her life following the collapse of her marriage, the relationship she develops with the friends of her eccentric housemate, the rapport she generates with students at the college where she engages in unorthodox teaching methods, and the decision she makes under the influence of a colleague to start a bookshop called Flyleaf.

Drayson, A. W. *See* Writers Before 1945

Driver, C. J. (Charles Jonathan) (b. 1939) Poet and novelist. Born in Cape Town and educated at St Andrew's College, Grahamstown, and at the University of Cape Town, he was detained on grounds of political activism as a student. He subsequently left South Africa for England, where he resumed his studies at Trinity College, Oxford. He taught in Hong Kong before returning to England, where he was for many years headmaster of Wellington College.

Driver has published several volumes of poetry, including *Occasional Light* (1979), *I Live Here Now* (1979), *Hong Kong Portraits* (1986), *In the Water-Margins* (1994), *Holiday Haiku: July–August 1996* (1997), and *Requiem* (1997). *So Far: Selected Poems 1960–2004* appeared in 2005. He has also published several novels, including *Elegy for a Revolutionary* (1969), *Send War in Our Time, O Lord* (1970), *Death of Fathers* (1972), *A Messiah of the Last Days* (1974), and *Shades of Darkness* (2004). He is the author of a political biographical study, *Patrick Duncan: South African and Pan-African* (1980).

The novels are political and deal with themes of guilt and betrayal. The first two concern revolutionary groups in South Africa, the third describes relations among masters, pupils and parents at a British school, and the fourth portrays a revolutionary movement in Britain. *Shades of Darkness* deals with an exile's return to South Africa to visit his dying brother. In the course of events, old memories are evoked, and the horror of the apartheid past is recalled.

Drum The first issue of *Drum* appeared in March 1951 in Cape Town under the title *African Drum*. In this first issue Jim Bailey, the magazine's proprietor, anticipated that the magazine would be pan-African in its appeal: it would be aimed at the "150,000,000 Bantu and Negro inhabitants of the continent whom we will attempt to reach for the first time in history with words that will express their thoughts, their impulses, their endeavors and, ultimately, their souls." This ambition was never realized, although the magazine did later have editions in other parts of the continent, including Nigeria, Ghana, and East and Central Africa.

The main reason that the early issues of the magazine failed was that the proprietor and editor misjudged the tastes of potential buyers. The first few issues contained articles on tribal music and history, famous chiefs, religion, and sport.

Its fiction pages were devoted to translated African folktales and stories about life in traditional rural settings. The magazine relocated to Johannesburg and became *Drum*. Its focus became distinctly urban, the earlier rural idiom being abandoned in favor of a sophisticated township feel. Anthony Sampson became the magazine's editor and attracted an extraordinary array of emerging black writing talent, including, at various points, Es'kia *Mphahlele, Nat *Nakasa, Henry Nxumalo, Casey *Motsisi, Can *Themba, Bloke *Modisane, Arthur *Maimane, Lewis *Nkosi, Todd *Matshikiza, Richard *Rive, Alex *La Guma, and James *Matthews.

The heyday of the magazine was the 1950s. It was in this era that it established its reputation as nurturing and publishing writing of quality while retaining a popular, exciting character. Serious fiction was run alongside startling exposés of conditions of life for black people under apartheid—the latter including articles on forced labor on white farms, prison conditions, and apartheid practices in religion.

It was the heady mixture of quality fiction, humorous columns and journalism of both an investigative and sensationalistic sort that enabled *Drum* to make such an impact during this era. This apparently contradictory blend of populism and serious journalism is also reflected in the ideology of the magazine: it demonstrated a keen understanding of the needs and aspirations of the new black proletariat while feeding it glamorous images of American life and culture. For example, it ran love stories, "true confessions," and pinup photographs of local beauties alongside serious fiction and articles on the politics of the day.

This ideological mélange aside, perhaps the most important and enduring contribution of *Drum* is that it provided a literary outlet for emergent black writers whose work would not be considered by the mainstream white press and magazine industry of the day. The unprecedented interest among black writers in finding a venue for publication is demonstrated by the "Great African International Short Story Contest" *Drum* ran in April 1951. It offered £50 to the winning entry and £4 for each story deemed worthy of publication. Can Themba was the first winner of this competition. The competition continued for several years and attracted 1,683 entries in its peak year of 1957.

The shift from a traditional African focus to a modern, urban one was reflected in the kind of stories *Drum* carried. Early stories, like the translations of African oral tales that appeared in the first editions, were supplanted by stories by writers like Modisane and Themba, and these were racy and exciting in both style and content. The township argot that was current in Sophiatown and like places in the 1950s was deployed to great effect. The style of the writing published in *Drum* in the 1950s—the reviews of Todd Matshikiza and the columns of Casey Motsisi are good examples—broke the mould of the earlier, more conservative writing by mission-educated writers like *Plaatje and the *Dhlomo brothers, and opened up exciting new possibilities for young black writers. *Drum*'s bold innovativeness also had a political edge: it implicitly rejected the role that was increasingly assigned to black South Africans by the newly elected National Party government and carved out a space for independent-minded black intellectuals.

Sophiatown, the racially mixed "location" northwest of Johannesburg, symbolized the *Drum* era in its defiance of the newly promulgated race laws of the government, in its cutting across class and race boundaries, its vibrant jazz and shebeen culture (so memorably described by Themba), and its vitality and resilience. With its destruction in 1957 came the end of this era. Many of the writers who lived there and wrote for *Drum* went into exile in the 1960s, and this broke the back of the literary movement that sprang up around the magazine and Sophiatown.

The *Drum* era marks an important phase in the development of a distinctive South African literary culture. The writers of the period were not products of the Bantu Education system that was introduced in the course of the 1950s. They grew up in a freer, more nuanced society, and their access to a better (mission-school) education gave them a command of English and a cultural reach that would be denied the writers who came after them. The hardening of political attitudes in the late 1950s and early 1960s would give rise to a greater militancy in black writers of the 1960s and 1970s, and the *Drum* era therefore represents a brief but very productive interregnum in the relentless drive toward the politicization of South Africa life and culture in the latter half of the twentieth century.

FURTHER READING

Michael Chapman, *The 'Drum' Decade: Stories from the 1950s* (1989); Paul Gready, "The Sophiatown Writers of the Fifties: The Unreal Reality of Their World," *Journal of Southern African Studies* 16, no. 1 (1990): 139–165; Bernth Lindfors, *Loaded Vehicles: Studies in African Literary Media* (1996); Sylvester Stein, *Who Killed Mr Drum?* (1999); Anthony Sampson, *Drum: The Making of a Magazine* (2004).

Duiker, K. Sello (1974–2005) Novelist. Born and raised in Soweto, Duiker studied journalism at Rhodes University and lived for a while in Cape Town before moving back to Johannesburg.

He is the author of three novels: *Thirteen Cents* (2000), winner of the 2001 Commonwealth Writer's Prize Best First Book (African); *The Quiet Violence of Dreams* (2001); and *The Hidden Star* (2006), published posthumously. Set in the world of the street children of Cape Town, *Thirteen Cents* is a harrowing account of the coming of age of young Azure as he attempts to transform the conditions of his life, having to deal with drugs and prostitution and corrupt adults who exploit him in numerous ways. *The Quiet Violence of Dreams* is similarly set on the dark side of South African life, and tells the story of Tshepo, a university student who is hospitalized for drug-induced psychosis and turns eventually to prostitution. Both novels explore issues of race, sexuality, and psychic instability, offering a trenchant indictment of the way in which society fails to protect those who are most vulnerable. *The Hidden Star*, written in the style of a folktale, combines the fantastical and the realistic in showing a concern also with forms of innocence in circumstances of corruption.

FURTHER READING

Shaun Viljoen, "Non-Racialism Remains a Fiction: Richard Rive's *'Buckingham Palace,' District Six* and K. Sello Duiker's *The Quiet Violence of Dreams*," *English Academy Review* 18 (2001): 46–53; Cheryl Stobie, *Somewhere in the Double Rainbow: Representations of Bisexuality in Post-Apartheid Novels* (2007).

Du Plessis, Menán (b. 1952) Novelist. Born and educated in Cape Town, Du Plessis was active in student politics and the United Democratic Front while pursuing her studies in linguistics at the University of Cape Town. Her first novel, *A State of Fear* (1983; winner of the 1985 Olive Schreiner Prize and the 1986 Sanlam Literary Prize), focuses on Anna Roussouw, a white schoolteacher at a Coloured school during the school boycotts and disruptions of 1980. She takes two of her students into her care when they are threatened by the police, and her experiences during this turbulent time cause her to ponder the contradictions of her own racial and social inheritance. The title refers to the nationwide condition of paranoia as well as of insecurity.

Longlive! (1989) is also set in Cape Town, during the period leading up to the declaration of a national State of Emergency in 1986. The action of the novel covers the events of a single day, from sunrise to nightfall, and explores the lives of a group of young people: an academic, an opera singer, a trade union activist, and an actress. Their experiences and musings on the past are set against the broader social canvas of riots, boycotts, police detentions and brutality, and a township funeral. In both novels, Du Plessis probes at the contradictions and tensions of daily life in South Africa in the 1980s, in which private need is weighed up against the demand for public redress.

FURTHER READING

M. J. Daymond, "The Reader's Role in the Fiction of Menán du Plessis," *Literator* 31, no. 1 (1992): 101–109; Eva Hunter and Craig MacKenzie, eds., *Between the Lines II: Interview with Nadine Gordimer, Menán du Plessis, Zoë Wicomb, Lauretta Ngcobo* (1993).

Du Toit, Basil (b. 1951) Poet. Born in Cape Town, he studied at Rhodes University and lectured at the universities of Fort Hare, Zimbabwe, Witwatersrand, and Cape Town. He currently lives in Edinburgh, Scotland, with his wife and daughter.

Du Toit has published two volumes of poetry, *Home Truths: Poems* (1988) and *Older Women* (1996). Exhibiting casual erudition and unobtrusive technical accomplishment, and delighting in playful sophistry, the first volume of poetry is notable for its use of irony and restrained, detached passion. These characteristics are also evident in the second volume, which extends the concerns of the first to embrace satirical and self-deprecatory ruminations on the physiology of experience. The poetry relates sensation and thought, biology and psychology, in unexpected and surprising ways. Du Toit was awarded the 1988 Sanlam Literary Award.

E

Ebersohn, Wessel (b. 1940) Novelist. Ebersohn has established a reputation for himself as a writer of compelling thrillers with serious undertones. His first novel, *A Lonely Place to Die* (1979), centers on the activities of a Jewish psychologist employed by the Department of Prisons in Pretoria. *The Centurion* (1980) shifts in setting between the Middle East and South Africa and has a similar gripping and disquieting quality, while *Store up the Anger* (1980) focuses on the oppressive South African regime as seen through the eyes of a detainee and his interrogators. His later novels include *Divide the Night* (1981), *Klara's Visitors* (1987), and *Closed Circle* (1990). He has also written a story for children, *The Otter and Mister Ogilvie* (1988), and an autobiography, *In Touching Distance* (2004).

Eglington, Charles (1918–1971) Poet, biographer, journalist, editor. Born in Johannesburg and educated at Diocesan College, Cape Town, he subsequently studied at the University of the Witwatersrand, where he obtained a bachelor's degree. Principally a journalist and editor, he also worked as a linguist, broadcaster, and translator. In the latter role, he translated some of the novels of the Afrikaans writer Etienne le Roux.

Eglington's one volume of poetry, *Under the Horizon: Collected Poems of Charles Eglington* (1977), was published posthumously under the editorship of Jack *Cope. Widely read and admired for their disciplined craftsmanship and elegant deployment of poetic conventions, his poems on African landscapes and wildlife have a clarity and monumentality that belie the disturbing emotional currents beneath their surface.

Eppel, John (b. 1947) Poet and novelist. Born in Lydenburg, South Africa, he was raised in Zimbabwe and studied at the universities of Natal and Zimbabwe. He has worked in various jobs and has taught at a number of schools, including the Girls' College in Bulawayo.

Eppel has published several volumes of poetry. *Four Voices* (1982) was followed by *Spoils of War* (1989) and *Sonata for Matabeleland* (1995). *Selected Poems, 1965–1995* appeared in 2001, and *Songs That My Country Taught Me: Collected Poems 1965–2005* in 2005. He has also published several novels, among them *D. G. G. Berry's 'The Great North Road'* (1992), *Hatchings* (1993), *The Giraffe Man* (1994), and *The Holy Innocents* (2002), a satirical novel about the white community in Bulawayo. *The Caruso of Colleen Bawn* (2004) gathers his shorter writings.

Sonata for Matabeleland adopts a tripartite chronological framework that seeks to locate experience in terms of a colonial childhood, a youthful period of personal and political liberation, and an adult present characterized by wry disenchantment. Within this framework, which correlates the private with the public spheres, the poems are sensitively alert to natural phenomena and seasonal changes, using these as points of reference in exploring the vicissitudes of human life. The novels, by contrast, are (often very funny) satirical farces directed against the colonial nostalgia of white settlers, the corruption of postindependence political systems, and the senseless destruction of the fragile African ecology. Eppel is the recipient of the 1990 Ingrid Jonker Prize, the 1991 AA Life/Arthur Nortje Award, and the 1993 M-Net Book Prize.

Eprile, Tony (b. 1955) Short-story writer and novelist. Born and raised in South Africa, Eprile has taught at Northwestern University, Williams College, Bennington College, Lesley University, and at the Iowa Writers' Workshop. He currently lives in Vermont. He has published two books, *Temporary Sojourner and Other South African Stories* (1989) and *The Persistence of Memory* (2004), both nominated New York Times Notable Books of the Year. The stories in *Temporary Sojourner* explore a range of South African characters and situations, portraying the lives of liberal whites and dispossessed blacks, parochial jailers and transnational immigrants. *The Persistence of Memory* returns to the theme of the cynical and detached liberal white observer, focusing on a young man whose ironic, postmodern take on South African life fails to protect him from having to appear before a Truth and Reconciliation Commission hearing for his involvement in a border war atrocity.

Essop, Ahmed (b. 1931) Short-story writer, novelist, biographer. Born in India, Essop came to South Africa as a child in 1934. He later studied at the University of South Africa and took postgraduate degrees at Essex and Stanford. He taught at various schools in and around Johannesburg, but left the Education Department responsible for "Indian Affairs" in 1974 after a dispute. He worked in commerce for several years before resuming teaching in Eldorado Park, southwest of Johannesburg, in 1980. He has since retired and devoted himself full-time to writing.

His collection *The Hajji and Other Stories* (1978) was widely acclaimed and was awarded the Olive Schreiner Prize in 1979. It is set mainly in the largely Indian community of Fordsburg, a suburb west of Johannesburg. The memorable title story concerns the relationship between Hajji Hassen and his brother, Karim. The latter, who is estranged from his brother and the Indian community and is living with his white girlfriend in the city, sends word to Hassen that he is dying and pleads for reconciliation. On his way to see Karim, Hassen is insulted by three white youths in the lift of the block of flats in which his brother lives, and this provokes him to abandon Karim to his fate. Inevitably, a deep sense of remorse ensues when Karim dies without being reconciled with Hassen. Like many of the other stories in this collection, "The Hajji" deals with the theme of human relationships distorted by the intrusion of artificial racial-social categories.

In his novel *The Visitation* (1980), Essop satirizes the main character, Emir Sufi, a wealthy property owner who falls prey to a villainous gangster. Sufi's affairs become increasingly entangled with those of the gangster and this ultimately leads to his undoing. Essop's second novel, *The Emperor* (1984), concerns the travails of the headmaster of an Indian school, whose fall is occasioned by the authoritarian policies of the apartheid education system.

Another collection of stories, *Noorjehan and Other Stories* (1990), covers the same social terrain as the earlier collection. The lives of the characters are now centered in the apartheid-created township of Lenasia rather than Fordsburg, but the themes are very similar: Noorjehan is a young girl who leaves home to escape an arranged marriage; Hussein crosses a local thug to protect the honor of a young woman and has to take the consequences; Sultan cannot decide whether he wants to keep his wife or not, and he encounters aspects of Islamic law that complicate matters; Hafez Effendi is a religious instructor at an Islamic seminary who has to swallow his pride when it is discovered that his flamboyant wife invites the attentions of other men in the community.

The issues that Essop explores in all of his works are those that beset the day-to-day life of a community squeezed by the interests of the dominant racial groups in South Africa. His work as a whole testifies to the resilience and vitality of the individuals who make up this beleaguered community. Essop's more recent work includes *The King of Hearts and Other Stories* (1997), which continues his gently satirical probings of the follies and pretensions of South African society, *Narcissus and Other Stories* (2002) and the novel *The Third Prophecy* (2004). He has also written a biography, *Suleiman M. Nana: A Biographical and Historical Record of His Life and Times* (2002).

FURTHER READING

Eugenie R. Freed, "Mr. Sufi Climbs the Stairs: The Quest and the Ideal in Ahmed Essop's *The Visitation*," *Theoria* 71 (1988): 1–13; Antje Hagena, "Straightforward Politics and Ironic Playfulness: The Aesthetic Possibilities of Ahmed Essop's *The Emperor*," *English in Africa* 17, no. 2 (1990): 59–69; Christopher Hope (interviewed by Robyn English), "Good Books: Ahmed Essop's *The Visitation*," *English in Africa* 25, no. 1 (1998): 99–103; Rajendra Chetty, "A Community Bard: Interview with Ahmed Essop," *Alternation* 6, no. 1 (1999): 272–278; Jack Kearney, "Representations of Islamic Belief and Practice in a South African Context: Reflections on the Fictional Work of Ahmed Essop, Aziz Hassim, Achmat Dangor and Rayda Jacobs," *Journal of Literary Studies* 22, no. 2 (2006): 138–157.

F

Fairbridge, Dorothea Ann *See* Writers Before 1945

Fairbridge, Kingsley *See* Writers Before 1945

Faller, Francis (b. 1946) Poet. Born in Cape Town, Faller taught in Cape Town and Johannesburg and has been a lecturer in English and head of the department at the Johannesburg College of Education. His interest in writing poetry is closely related to his professional involvement, through teaching and research, with the relations between language acquisition and the development of the poetic imagination. A prolific contributor of poetry and reviews to various journals over the years, his poetry has appeared in *Weather Words* (1986; winner of the AA Vita Poetry Award) and *Verse-Over* (1992; winner of the Sanlam Poetry Award). He has also been an editor of poetry publications, a judge of a number of national competitions, and has contributed several articles on South African poetry to literary journals.

Ferguson, Gus (b. 1940) Poet, editor, publisher. A pharmacist by profession, Ferguson runs the publishing firm Snail Press from Cape Town. He has published numerous volumes of poetry, including *The Herding of the Snail* (1978), *Snail Morning* (1979), *Doggerel Day* (1982), *Carpe Diem* (1992), *Versions of Jacques Prevert's "The Song of the Snails Who Went to a Funeral"* (with Barend Toerien, Uys Krige, Winifred Thomson, and Marc Glaser, 1993), *Icarus Rising: Selected Poems* (1994), *In a Borrowed Tent: Ninety Nine Haiku* (1994), *An Alphabet of Small Poems* (1995), *Light Verse at the End of the Tunnel* (1996), *Love Amongst the Middle-Aged and Other Cartoons* (1997), *On the See-Saw* (1997), and *Mad Rains* (1998). A selection of his poems and drawings appeared as *Stressed-Unstressed* (2000). He is also a contributor to *City in Words: An Anthology of Cape Town Poems* (2001) and has published volumes of poetry for young readers, including *The Land of Pong* (2002) and *In the Land of Upper-Ping* (2002).

The poems are illustrated with line sketches, and the volumes are at once whimsical and insightful, wryly humorous, and cleverly erudite. Ferguson has created a fantastical mythology around, incongruously, the image of the lowly snail, the common garden mollusk whose whorled shell is seen to mirror the spiral nebula of the universe.

Ferguson has edited several works of other poets, including *Mokum: Poems* (Richard Jurgens, 1994), *Ag Man* (Roy Joseph Cotton, 1986), *All Blues: Selected Works* (Peter Kantey, 2004), and *Ghaap: Sonnets from the Northern Cape* (Michael Cope, 2005). His collection *Arse Poetica: Musings on Muse Abuse: Prose, Poems, Drawings, Intertextualities* appeared in 2003, and he has coedited (with Tony Morphet) *Birds in Words: The Twitchers' Guide to South African Poetry* (2006, with illustrations by Willem Jordaan), a collection of fifty-five South African poems on birds. As a publisher, Ferguson can be said to have kept South African poetry alive when established firms ceased to consider poetry manuscripts. He is the recipient of the 1990 AA Life / Arthur Nortje Prize.

Fitzpatrick, J. P. *See* Writers Before 1945

Fugard, Athol (Harold Lannigan) (b. 1932) Playwright. Born in Middelburg in the Karoo to an Afrikaans mother and an English-speaking father of Irish descent,

Fugard moved with his family at the age of three to Port Elizabeth, which was his home for the bulk of his life and the setting for many of his plays. His father was ill in the last years of his life and the family was poor. Fugard's mother ran a boardinghouse and later managed the St George's Park tearoom, a period of his childhood explored in the play *'Master Harold' . . . and the Boys* (1982).

Fugard was educated at Port Elizabeth Technical College and the University of Cape Town, where he studied anthropology and philosophy. He left without completing his degree and hitchhiked through Africa to Port Sudan, where he joined the crew of a tramp steamer bound for the Far East. He worked for two years with people of all races, and this early experience laid the foundation for the antiracist, humanistic views that were later to be expressed in his plays.

Upon returning to South Africa in 1955, he became involved in experimental drama. In 1958 he and his wife Sheila *Fugard (later to become a poet and novelist in her own right) moved to Johannesburg, where he worked as a clerk in a Native Commissioner's Court for six months—an experience that was later worked into *Sizwe Bansi Is Dead* (1972). During his stay in Johannesburg, Fugard began his association with aspirant black actors. *No-Good Friday* (1958) and *Nongogo* (1959) were the result. These plays were "fringe" performances and used black actors such as Bloke Modisane and Zakes Mokae (who was to perform in many of Fugard's later plays).

After a short stay in Europe (1960–61), where he gained experience in drama, Fugard returned to South Africa and met up again with Zakes Mokae. The pair acted the parts of two brothers, one light-skinned and the other darker-skinned, in the two-hander *The Blood Knot* (1961). Other plays using a sparse setting and small cast followed. In 1963 Fugard was approached by several men and women from New Brighton Township in Port Elizabeth with the idea of starting a drama group. Thus the theater group the Serpent Players was formed (so named because the members performed in an abandoned snake pit at Port Elizabeth's Snake Park).

The next decade saw the production of plays like *Hello and Goodbye* (1965), *People Are Living There* (1968), and *Boesman and Lena* (1969), which all focus on dysfunctional family relationships in impoverished and demeaning settings (boardinghouses and squatter settlements). They also use local dialects and accents (an important feature also of *The Blood Knot*), and they infused much-needed vitality into South African theater. *Sizwe Bansi Is Dead* was devised by Fugard in collaboration with John Kani and Winston Ntshona. First performed in Cape Town in 1972, the play went on to have premieres in London in 1973 and New York in 1974. It was Fugard's first major international success, and effectively launched his career as a world-acclaimed playwright.

As a direct consequence of the highly constrained circumstances in which he and his early collaborators worked, Fugard became interested in what he called "pure theater," which he conceptualized as theater stripped down to its bare essentials: "the actor and the stage, the actor on the stage." Although Fugard first expressed such ideas as early as 1961, they were to find fuller expression in the dramatic theories of the Polish experimental playwright Jerzy Grotowski (in his *Toward a Poor Theatre*, 1969), an important influence on Fugard. These principles are applied in a play like *Sizwe Bansi Is Dead*. Very few props and other theatrical devices are used and the focus therefore falls on the actors themselves. In addition, the notion of single authorship is foregone in favor of collaborative effort. These principles informed most of Fugard's plays of this period.

In *Sizwe Bansi*, the title character, who has been "endorsed" out of Port Elizabeth, is forced to adopt a dead man's identity in order to remain and work in the city. The play is concerned with how human beings cling to a sense of self, of dignity and self-respect, under conditions that conspire to rob them of these feelings. The play's principal protest is against the Pass Laws and the human consequences of such laws. Under these laws people were forced to treat each other with callous disregard in order to survive, and this, the play suggests, deprives us all of our humanity.

The Island (1973), about Robben Island prisoners, and *Statements after an Arrest under the Immorality Act* (1974) were two further collaborations with Kani and Ntshona that protested against uniquely South African forms of cruelty. The more conventional *Dimetos* (1975) was commissioned for the Edinburgh Festival and was followed by the filming of *The Guest* (1977), based on the life of the Afrikaans author Eugène Marais. At this time *Hello and Goodbye* was filmed for the SABC, to be followed by a documentary on *A Lesson from Aloes* for the BBC (1979) and the film *Marigolds in August* (1980). *A Lesson from Aloes* (1978) centers on the dilemma of Piet Bezuidenhout, an aloe-collecting Afrikaner with left-wing sympathies whose Coloured friends have come to suspect him of being a police informer.

Fugard's forgotten novel *Tsotsi* appeared in 1980, the year in which he accepted a fellowship at Yale University. This began Fugard's special relationship with Yale, and his *'Master Harold' . . . and the Boys*, an award-winning exploration of childhood memories of his ill, alcoholic father and his friendship with two black employees at his mother's tearoom, premiered at the Yale Repertory Theatre in 1982. This was also the venue for the premiere of his next play *The Road to Mecca* (1984), about the life of the eccentric artist Helen Martins, whose concrete sculptures and worldview threatened the people of Nieu-Bethesda, the remote Karoo village in which she lived (and in which Fugard has also established a home).

His more recent work includes *A Place with the Pigs* (1987), based on the story of a Russian army deserter who hid in a pigsty for forty-one years, *My Children! My Africa!* (1989), about two children who meet across the color bar and establish a friendship in the face of social obstacles, and *Valley Song* (1996), about the relationship of an old Coloured man with his granddaughter and their attempts to achieve an understanding that bridges the gulf between her desire for release from "the Valley" and his struggle to hold on to his land in the face of threats by a white man to appropriate it.

Fugard's plays are collected as *Statements: Three Plays* (1974; *Sizwe Bansi Is Dead, The Island, Statements After an Arrest Under the Immorality Act*); *Three Port Elizabeth Plays* (1974; *The Blood Knot, Hello and Goodbye, Boesman and Lena*); *Boesman and Lena and Other Plays* (1978; *The Blood Knot, People Are Living There, Hello and Goodbye*); *Selected Plays* (1987; *'Master Harold' . . . and the Boys, Blood Knot* [new version], *Hello and Goodbye, Boesman and Lena*); *My Children! My Africa! and Selected Shorter Plays* (1990; *The Occupation, The Coat, Mille Miglia, Orestes, The Drummer*); *The Township Plays* (1993; *No-Good Friday, Nongogo, The Coat, Sizwe Bansi Is Dead, The Island*); *Plays One* (1998; *The Road to Mecca, A Place with the Pigs, My*

Children! My Africa! Playland, Valley Song); and *Interior Plays* (2000; *People Are Living There, Statements, Dimetos, The Guest, A Lesson from Aloes*).

Fugard's *Notebooks: 1960–1977* appeared in 1983, and his autobiography *Cousins: A Memoir* in 1994. *Sorrows and Rejoicings* (2002) is a play about an activist writer who returns from exile to die on the family's Karoo farm; while *Karoo and Other Stories* (2005) is a collection of stories in two parts: the stories in the first are based on characters associated with Nieu-Bethesda, while the second part has a more contemporary, harrowing urban focus. *Exits and Entrances* is a semiautobiographical play that features the great South African actor André Huguenet as its centerpiece (2005).

Fugard has received numerous accolades and awards, including a Tony Award (1981) and the New York Drama Critics Award (1981) for *A Lesson from Aloes*; London's Evening Standard Award (1983) for *Master Harold*; the New York Drama Critics Award (1988) for *The Road to Mecca*; and an Obie Award (1992) and the FNB / Vita National Theatre Award (1994) for his contribution to theater. His only novel, *Tsotsi* (1980), was turned into a major film directed by Gavin Hood, and it received an Oscar for best foreign-language film in 2006.

FURTHER READING

Stephen Gray, ed., *Athol Fugard* (1982); Temple Hauptfleisch, ed., *Athol Fugard: A Source Guide* (1982); Dennis Walder, *Athol Fugard* (1984); Russell Vandenbroucke, *Truths the Hand Can Touch: The Theatre of Athol Fugard* (1985); Margarete Seidenspinner, *Exploring the Labyrinth: Athol Fugard's Approach to South African Drama* (1986); John Read, *Athol Fugard: A Bibliography* (1991); Stephen Gray, *File on Fugard* (1991); Mary Benson, *Athol Fugard and Barney Simon: Bare Stage, a Few Props, Great Theatre* (1997); Marcia Blumberg and Dennis Walder, eds., *South African Theatre as / and Intervention* (1999); Albert Wertheim, *The Dramatic Art of Athol Fugard: From South Africa to the World* (2000); Dennis Walder, *Athol Fugard* (2002); Loren Kruger, *Post-Imperial Brecht: Politics and Performance, East and South* (2004).

Fugard, Lisa (b. 1961) Novelist. Born in South Africa, the daughter of Athol and Sheila Fugard, she moved to the United States in 1980, where she worked in the theater, performing in New York, London, and South Africa. Fugard has since turned her attention to writing, publishing short stories in various literary magazines, and travel articles, essays, and book reviews in the *New York Times*. She now lives in California. Her novel *Skinner's Drift* (2007) tells of Eva's return to South Africa from New York after an absence of ten years, having heard news of her father's ill health. On the family farm on the banks of the Limpopo River, working through her late mother's journal, she recovers repressed memories of her apartheid-era childhood. She is led to confront her family history as the country works through its national history, prompted by the Truth and Reconciliation Commission hearings.

Fugard, Sheila (b. 1932) Novelist, poet, short-story writer. Born in Birmingham, England, her parents immigrated to South Africa when she was five years old. She studied drama at the University of Cape Town and married playwright Athol *Fugard.

Fugard has published three novels: *The Castaways* (1972), winner of the 1972 CNA Prize and the 1973 Olive Schreiner Award for Literature, *Rite of Passage* (1976), and *A Revolutionary Woman* (1983). She has also published three volumes of poetry: *Thresholds* (1975), *Mythic Things* (1981), and *Reclaiming Desert Places* (1992). While showing a strong interest in the history of South Africa, her writings also embrace the mysterious and the mythical. *Rite of Passage* deals with the relationship between a doctor and a young boy traumatized by a tribal circumcision ceremony. *A Revolutionary Woman*, set in the Karoo of the 1920s, tells the story of a woman, a follower of Gandhi, who gets entangled in a rape case involving a Coloured boy and a retarded Boer girl.

G

Galgut, Damon (b. 1965) Novelist and playwright. Born in Pretoria, Damon Galgut studied drama at the University of Cape Town. He currently lives in Cape Town, where he writes full-time. He has published two plays, gathered into one volume as *Echoes of Anger and No. 1 Utopia Lane* (1983); a film script, *The Red Dress* (1994); and two short-story collections, *Small Circle of Beings* (1988) and *Strategy and Siege* (2005). He is also author of five novels: *A Sinless Season* (1982); *The Beautiful Screaming of Pigs* (1992), winner of the 1992 CNA Literary Award; *The Quarry* (1995); *The Good Doctor* (2003), which won the 2003 Commonwealth Writers Prize Best Book: Africa and was short-listed for the 2003 Man Booker Prize for Fiction and the 2005 International IMPAC Dublin Literary Award; and *The Impostor* (2008).

A Sinless Season is set in a reformatory for boys situated on a deserted stretch of coastline and explores the intense relationships that develop among the young inmates. The novella *Small Circle of Beings* persuasively evokes the tensions and frustrations among members of a family living somewhere in rural KwaZulu-Natal. The prose is limpid and pared down and far removed from the exuberant but overheated writing of the first novel. *The Beautiful Screaming of Pigs* focuses on a young white army conscript who suffers a nervous breakdown while doing military duty on the Namibian border. *The Quarry* tells the story of a man who murders a minister who is on his way to assume pastoral office in a small town. He takes the minister's place, and finds that his first duty is to bury the man he has murdered.

Set in postapartheid South Africa in a remote rural hospital, *The Good Doctor* (2003) pits idealism against cynicism, exploring the uneasy friendship between two men of diametrically opposed outlooks. The novel's bleak take on the ethical heritage of the "new" South Africa invites comparison with J. M. *Coetzee's *Disgrace*. *The Impostor* (2008) tells the story of a young white man who, suddenly out of a job, makes a temporary move to a dusty Karoo town, where he intends to take inspiration from nature and devote himself to poetry but finds himself embroiled, instead, in a corrupt deal that sees a game farm transformed into a golf course. Assuming a cynical stance toward "development" in postapartheid South Africa, the novel simultaneously questions the romantic impulses that inform the pastoral ideal.

FURTHER READING

María Jesús Cabarcos-Traseira, "'Dire Situations and Bad Prospects': Damon Galgut's Glance at South Africa's Past and Present in *The Good Doctor*," *Current Writing* 17, no. 2 (2005): 42–55; Ken Barris, "Realism, Absence and the Man Booker Short-list: Damon Galgut's *The Good Doctor*," *Current Writing* 17, no. 2 (2005): 24–41; Andie Miller, "Ambiguous Territory: Damon Galgut Interviewed," *Journal of Commonwealth Literature* 41, no. 2 (2006): 139–145.

Gibbon, Perceval *See* Writers Before 1945

Glanville, Ernest *See* Writers Before 1945

Gordimer, Nadine (b. 1923) Novelist, short-story writer, and essayist. Born in Springs to a mother of British descent and a Jewish Lithuanian father, Gordimer grew up in this East Rand mining town (which provided the setting for her first novel, *The Lying Days*, 1953). She has spent most of her adult life in Johannesburg. She began writing at an early age, her first published story, "The Quest for Seen Gold," appearing in the *Sunday Express* in 1937, when she was just thirteen years old. Her adult fiction began appearing in publications like *The Forum* two years later. She attended the University of the Witwatersrand, but left after one year.

Her first collection of stories, *Face to Face*, appeared in 1949. It was republished in expanded form as *The Soft Voice of the Serpent and Other Stories* in 1952. The well-known "Train from Rhodesia," about a misunderstanding that arises between a young married couple who acquire an item of African art at a station platform, appeared in both of these early collections. The title story of her next collection, *Six Feet of the Country* (1956), is equally well known. Gordimer's skill at capturing the many nuances in human relationships—whether these be master-servant, husband-wife, or black-white—is brought sharply into focus in this story. A young black man, who has illegally entered South Africa from Rhodesia, dies on the farm of a white farming couple. Tension develops between them when they vainly attempt to recover the body from the authorities.

Gordimer's early novel *The Lying Days* was followed by *A World of Strangers* (1958), which was banned in South Africa until 1970; *Occasion for Loving* (1963); *The Late Bourgeois World* (1966); and *A Guest of Honour* (1970). These novels are an acute examination of the peculiarly South African forms of master-servant relationships, and the kinds of mindsets and attitudes espoused by privileged white people in a neocolonial situation. The novels also reveal an increasingly sophisticated political outlook, which is especially evident in *A Guest of Honour* (winner of the CNA Prize), about a central African state struggling to throw off its colonial legacy and secure independence.

Several story collections were interspersed among these novels. *Friday's Footprint and Other Stories* (1960) won the W. H. Smith Literary Award. It contains the story "The Bridegroom," a tale about a young road construction foreman, his relationship with his servant, his musings about his impending marriage and his concern about whether his young wife could endure the isolated and crude lifestyle he is forced to lead. This collection was followed by *Not for Publication* (1965), which contains the story "A Chip of Glass Ruby" about the effects on a family of the mother's political activism, and *Livingstone's Companions* (1971).

The period of the mid-1970s saw the appearance of Gordimer's classic, *The Conservationist* (1974), winner of the CNA Prize and joint winner of the Booker Prize, and her *Selected Stories* (1975), published in shorter form as *Some Monday for Sure* (1976). *The Conservationist* is the story of Meiring, a successful businessman who buys a plot of land on the outskirts of Johannesburg and indulges his fantasies about returning to the land. His successful initial attempts take a turn for the worse when a dead black man is discovered on his farm, is summarily (and irregularly) buried there by the inept police, and is then disinterred by flooding. This harrowing tale about the moral and psychic disintegration of a man (and, by implication, of his race and class) is made all the more powerful by the modernist stream-of-consciousness narrative style employed by Gordimer.

Critics have argued that this novel marks Gordimer's transition from her "liberal" to her "radical" phase, a phase characterized by highly politicized works like *Burger's Daughter* (1979), which won the CNA Prize, *July's People* (1981), and the novella and short-story collection *Something Out There* (1984). *Burger's Daughter*, set in the turbulent years after the Soweto uprisings of 1976, is narrated by Rosa Burger, daughter of Lionel Burger, a fictional version of the political activist Bram Fischer, jailed for life for subversive activities against the state. Rosa initially moves away from her father's political views and goes in search of personal freedom in Europe, but returns to take up the cause he espoused and ends up incarcerated in the same cell that he occupied.

July's People is set in an imaginary future South Africa torn apart by civil war. Maureen Smales flees war-ravaged Johannesburg with her husband and two children and seeks refuge in the countryside at the home of her longtime servant, July. The balance of power shifts in this new setting, and July gradually takes over the symbols of white, male South African power: the gun and the car. The end of the novel sees Maureen fleeing once again, this time toward a helicopter whose occupants represent either "saviors or murderers," an ambivalence that suggests something about the uncertainty of South Africa's future. *A Sport of Nature* (1987), which follows the somewhat picaresque career of its protagonist from the 1950s to a future postliberation South Africa, also has a predictive dimension.

Other works of the 1980s include the story collection *A Soldier's Embrace* (1980), which includes the well-known "Town and Country Lovers," and a new version of *Six Feet of the Country* (1982), a set of stories that were produced as six one-hour films and televised in Europe in the early 1980s. The films were not initially shown in South Africa, owing to their sensitive political nature, but were eventually screened in 1983 (with the exception of "A Chip of Glass Ruby," which remained banned). A collection of essays, *The Essential Gesture: Writing, Politics and Places* appeared in 1988.

In *My Son's Story* (1990), a truant schoolboy encounters his father emerging from a cinema with a woman. The father, a Coloured man, is a teacher turned political activist and has been detained; while in detention, he strikes up a relationship with a white woman who represents an international human rights organization. The event of the son's encountering them is the catalyst to an anguished reappraisal by the teenage boy—the son of the novel's title—of himself, his father, his father's relationship to his family, and political activism, with its corrosive effects on family life.

Other works of this period include *Crimes of Conscience* (1991), a selection of stories from the 1980s, *Jump and Other Stories* (1991), a collection of new stories, and *Why Haven't You Written? Selected Stories 1950–1972* (1992). *Jump* includes the story "Teraloyna," a fictionalized account of the checkered history of an island off the southern African coast, and "The Ultimate Safari," a story narrated by an orphaned Mozambican girl who treks with her grandparents and siblings across the Kruger Park in a desperate bid for survival. Gordimer's achievements as a writer up to this point culminated in her being awarding the Nobel Prize in literature in 1991.

Her more recent work includes two novels with rather different concerns. *None to Accompany Me* (1994) has a dual focus: it is an analysis of the "new" South Africa, with a particular focus on a black family of returnees; and it also explores the interior life of sixty-year-old Vera Stark, a leftist white lawyer, as she looks back on a life of failed marriages and personal defeats. In both cases, life in an evolving new society proves to be difficult. *The House Gun* (1998) moves away from the explicitly political to examine the lives of Harald and Claudia Lindgard, whose son and only child, Duncan, is arrested and charged with murder. The house gun of the novel's title (a ubiquitous feature of suburban South African life) has been used to kill Duncan's male former lover. Duncan's erstwhile homosexuality (he has since taken up with a female lover) thus emerges as the second of two unwelcome revelations to his parents. The novel deals with the parents' attempting to come to terms with what their son has done and concludes with the trial and its aftermath. Other works of the past decade include *Living in Hope and History: Notes from Our Century* (1999)—a collection of essays that spans her writing career and includes discussions of South African politics, African and international writers and the role of writers in society—the novels *The Pickup* (2001) and *Get a Life* (2005), and the short-story collections *Loot and Other Stories* (2003), and *Beethoven Was One-Sixteenth Black and Other Stories* (2007).

Gordimer's recent work represents a pronounced move away from the political sphere that has dominated her oeuvre, and this suggests that the normalization of South Africa's political and social life has allowed her to move back to an exploration of the private lives of her protagonists—an aspect of her early writing that became overlaid with the urgent political themes and messages of the day.

FURTHER READING

Robert F. Haugh, *Nadine Gordimer* (1974); Michael Wade, *Nadine Gordimer* (1978); Christopher Heywood, *Nadine Gordimer* (1983); John Cooke, *The Novels of Nadine Gordimer: Private Lives/Public Landscapes* (1985); Stephen Clingman, *The Novels of Nadine Gordimer: History from the Inside* (1986); Judie Newman, *Nadine Gordimer* (1988); Rowland Smith, ed., *Critical Essays on Nadine Gordimer* (1990); Dorothy Driver et al., *Nadine Gordimer: A Bibliography* (1993, 1994); Kathrin Wagner, *Rereading Nadine Gordimer: Text and Subtext in the Novels* (1994); Andries Walter Oliphant, ed., *A Writing Life: Celebrating Nadine Gordimer* (1998); Louise Yelin, *From the Margins of Empire: Christina Stead, Doris Lessing, Nadine Gordimer* (1998); Barbara Temple-Thurston, *Nadine Gordimer Revisited* (1999); Ileana Sora Dimitriu, *Art of Conscience: Re-reading Nadine Gordimer* (2000); Brighton J. Uledi Kamanga, *Nadine Gordimer's Fiction and the Irony of Apartheid* (2000); Judie Newman, *Nadine Gordimer's "Burger's Daughter": A Casebook* (2003); Stefan Helgesson, *Writing in Crisis: Ethics and History in Gordimer, Ndebele and Coetzee* (2004); Ronald Suresh Roberts, *No Cold Kitchen: A Biography of Nadine Gordimer* (2005).

Gordin, Jeremy (b. 1952) Poet. Gordin has published three volumes of poetry: *With My Tongue in My Hand* (1981); *Hard On* (1987), winner of the Vita Poetry Award; and *Pomegranates for My Son* (1998). Conversational in style and calculated to shock, the poetry reveals a raw energy in its preoccupation with drugs and sex. In 1992 Gordin received the Vita/Arthur Nortje Memorial Award for Poetry. He also coauthored Bob Aldworth's *The Infernal Tower* (1996) and ghostwrote Eugene de Kock's *A Long Night's Damage: Working for the Apartheid State* (1998).

Goudvis, Bertha *See* Writers Before 1945

Govender, Ronnie (b. 1934) Playwright, short-story writer, novelist. Born in Cato Manor, Durban, Govender devoted much of his early creative life to developing forms of community theater that chronicle political events and address community concerns. His best-known play, *At the Edge*, won Vita nominations for Best South African Playwright and Best Actor. Govender was appointed marketing manager of the Baxter Theatre in Cape Town in 1991 and director of Durban's Playhouse Theatre in 1993. Some of his thirteen plays have been published in *Inter-play: A Collection of Plays (*2007). In 2008 he was awarded the Order of Ikhamanga for his contribution to democracy, peace and justice through the medium of theater. The stories collected in *At the Edge and Other Cato Manor Stories* (1996) describe the 1949 riots in Cato Manor, Durban, and the volume was awarded the Commonwealth Writers' Prize for the Africa region. His novel *Song of the Atman* (2006) tells of an Indian family and its community, focusing on the son who returns home to Cato Manor in the 1940s with a story that covers several generations and multiple political landscapes. Govender is also author of the memoir *In the Manure* (2008).

Gray, Stephen (b. 1941) Novelist, poet, dramatist, critic. Born in Cape Town, Gray was educated at the universities of Cape Town, Cambridge, and Iowa, where he was a member of the Iowa Writers Workshop. He edited *Granta* while at Cambridge and taught in France for some years before taking up a position in 1969 at the Rand Afrikaans University, where he became a professor and chair of the English Department. He took early retirement in 1991 and has since then worked as a freelance writer, notably for the *Mail & Guardian* newspaper. The author of several works of poetry, drama, and fiction, Gray is also South Africa's foremost anthologist and literary historiographer.

His early novels are the satirical *Local Colour* (1975) and *Invisible People* (1977), and the historical *Caltrop's Desire* (1980). His fascination with history is also reflected in *John Ross: The True Story* (1987), a fictionalized treatment of the life of Charles Maclean ("John Ross"), a ship's boy who survived a shipwreck off the Natal coast in 1825 and spent several years at the court of King Shaka. Later novels include *Time of Our Darkness* (1988), *Born of Man* (1989), and the semiautobiographical *War Child* (1991). His autobiography, *Accident of Birth*, appeared in 1993.

He edited the 1970s poetry journal *Izwi*. His own poetry is collected as *It's About Time* (1974); *The Assassination of Shaka* (1974), with woodcuts by Cecil Skotnes; *Hottentot Venus and Other Poems* (1979); and *Love Poems: Hate Poems* (1982). Later collections are *Apollo Café* (1990) and *Season of Violence* (1992). His *Selected Poems (1960–92)* appeared in 1993 and was followed by the engaging and innovative *Gabriel's Exhibition* (1998) and *Shelley Cinema and Other Poems* (2006).

His work in drama includes a script based on the prison experiences of Herman Charles Bosman, *Cold Stone Jug: The Play* (1982) (coproduced with Barney Simon), and the acclaimed *Schreiner: A One-Woman Play* (1983). He has made available the work of several out-of-print dramatists, from Stephen *Black to Geraldine *Aron in collections such as *Theatre One* (1978), *Theatre Two* (1981) and *Stephen Black: Three Plays* (1984).

As an anthologist, he has produced many influential collections, including the very successful selection of southern African prose *Writers' Territory* (1973;

rev. ed. 1999); *On the Edge of the World* (1974), updated as *Modern South African Stories* (1980; rev. ed. 2002); *The Penguin Book of Southern African Stories* (1985); *The Penguin Book of Contemporary South African Short Stories* (1993); and *The Picador Book of African Stories* (2000). His own collection of short prose, *Human Interest and Other Pieces* (1993), includes "Letters to Pratt," a piece about the would-be assassin of H. F. Verwoerd, David Pratt, which includes the text of letters sent to him by relatives and admirers. A later collection of stories is *My Serial Killer and Other Stories* (2005). His anthologies of South African poetry, which have been influential in shaping the canon, include *A World of Their Own: Southern African Poets of the Seventies* (1976), *Modern South African Poetry* (1984), and *The Penguin Book of Southern African Verse* (1989).

His doctoral dissertation was published as *Southern African Literature: An Introduction* (1979), a seminal series of historiographical essays on the formation of South African English literature, and he has edited two volumes in the McGraw-Hill casebook series: *Athol Fugard* (1982), and *Herman Charles Bosman* (1986). His most recent work includes a set of essays on important South African writers, *Freelancers and Literary Biography in South Africa* (1999), and new editions of the works of Herman Charles Bosman and C. Louis Leipoldt. He is also the author of the biographies *Beatrice Hastings: A Literary Life* (2004) and *Life Sentence: A Biography of Herman Charles Bosman* (2005).

FURTHER READING

Louise Shabat Bethlehem, "Under the Proteatree, at Daggaboersnek: Stephen Gray, Literary Historiography and the Limit Trope of the Local," *English in Africa* 24, no. 2 (1997): 27–50; Robert W. Gray, "Black Mirrors and Young Boy Friends: Colonization, Sublimation, and Sadomasochism in Stephen Gray's *Time of Our Darkness*," *Ariel* 30, no. 2 (1999): 77–98; Chris Dunton, "Stephen Gray at Sixty: An Interview and Bibliography of Primary Works," *English in Africa* 28, no. 2 (2001): 49–64.

Green, Michael Cawood (b. 1954) Poet and novelist. Born and raised in Durban, Green studied at the University of Natal, and has a master's degree from Stanford University and a doctoral degree from the University of York. He is one of the founders of the Poetry Africa and Time of the Writer Festival held annually in Durban, where he taught at the University of KwaZulu-Natal. He is the author of *Sinking: A Verse Novella* (1997) and *For the Sake of Silence* (2008). The latter deals with Franz Pfanner, a Trappist monk who, in the late nineteenth century, leaves Europe for South Africa, where he establishes the monastery at Mariannhill. Narrated by Father Joseph Cupertino, the story is at once a chronicle of the Abbot's life and a silencing of its darker aspects, where faith borders on possession.

Gwala, Mafika Pascal (b. 1946) Poet and critic. Born in Verulam outside Durban, Gwala attended school in Vryheid, Natal, and worked as a legal clerk, secondary-school teacher, factory hand, and publications researcher. He edited *Black Review* (1973) and began publishing articles and poems in various literary periodicals in the early 1970s. His poetry has appeared in two volumes, *Jol'iinkomo* (1977) and *No More Lullabies* (1982). Like other black poets of the seventies including *Serote and *Sepamla, Gwala used Black Consciousness rhetoric, jazz rhythms, and elements of African oral culture to provoke political change under apartheid rule. The author of several critical articles on South African arts and culture (with a particular emphasis on the influence of orality) he coedited (with Liz Gunner) *Musho: Zulu Popular Praises* (1994). Some of his poems are also included in the anthologies *Exiles Within* (1986) and *Ten South African Poets* (1999).

FURTHER READING

Jacques Alvarez-Pereyre, *The Poetry of Commitment in South Africa* (1984); Colin Gardner, "Catharsis: From Aristotle to Mafika Gwala," *Theoria* 64 (1985): 29–41; Anne McClintock, "'Azikwelwa': We Will Not Ride: Politics and Value in Black South African Poetry," *Critical Inquiry* 13, no. 3 (1987): 597–623; Ari Sitas, "Traditions of Poetry in Natal," *Journal of Southern African Studies* 16, no. 2 (1990): 307–326.

H

Haarhoff, Dorian (b. 1944) Poet, dramatist, children's story writer. Born in Kimberley, he has lived in Windhoek since 1979, where he lectures at the University of Namibia. He has taught creative writing in Namibia, South Africa, and Canada.

Haarhoff has published four volumes of poetry: *Wrist and Rib* (1978), *Stickman* (1981), *Bordering* (1991), and *Aquifers and Dust* (1994). He has also written several plays, three of which are gathered as *Goats, Oranges and Skeletons: A Trilogy of Namibian Independence Plays* (2000). He is the author of the literary critical study *The Wild South-West: Frontier Myths and Metaphors in Literature Set in Namibia, 1760–1988* (1991), and editor of *Personal Memories: Namibian Texts in Process* (1996). He has written several children's books, including *Desert December* (1991), *Water from the Rock* (1992), *Legs, Bones and Eyes: A Children's Trilogy* (1994), *Big, Red and Dangerous* (1996), and *Grandpa Enoch's Pipe* (2002), and coauthored (with Ivan *Vladislavić) *The Writer's Voice: A Workbook for Writers in Africa* (1998). Active in various creative writing initiatives, he has edited two volumes of *Once Upon a Life* (2002, 2003), subtitled *Stories from a Creative Writing Workshop*.

Sharply evocative, and adroitly self-reflexive about the linguistic medium it employs, *Aquifers and Dust* sifts through the sands of memory, dream, and experience in search of hidden sources of sustenance.

Haarhoff was the winner of the 1987 English Association of Southern Africa Annual Literary Competition.

Haggard, Sir Henry Rider *See* Writers Before 1945

Haresnape, Geoffrey Lawrence (b. 1939) Poet, novelist, critic, and short-story writer. Born in Durban, Haresnape was educated at the University of Cape Town, where he taught for many years and retired as professor of English. He edited a collection of South African pioneering prose entitled *The Great Hunters* (1974), and was for many years editor of the literary journal *Contrast*. He wrote the first critical biography of Pauline *Smith (1969) and has published several collections of poetry, including *Drive of the Tide* (1976), *New-Born Images* (1991), and *Mulberries in Autumn* (1996). His book *The Living and the Dead: Selected and New Poems 1976–2005* appeared in 2005. He is also the author of *African Tales from Shakespeare: Ten Narratives Based Upon His Poetry and Plays* (1999). His novel *Testimony* (1992; joint winner of the 1990 *Weekly Mail*–Heinemann Literary Award) is a contemporary retelling of the story of Mary Magdalene. Set in South Africa, with distinctively South African themes, it concerns a young woman's struggle to survive and to raise her son. Haresnape has been awarded *The Classic* prize for short story contributions, the Arthur Nortje Memorial Prize for poetry, and the Sanlam Prize for fiction.

Harries, Ann (b. 1942) Novelist. Born and educated in Cape Town, Ann Harries divides her time between England and South Africa.

She is the author of three novels, *The Sound of the Gora* (1980), *Manly Pursuits* (1999), and *No Place for a Lady* (2005), all concerned with events in South Africa's troubled history. Set toward the end of nineteenth-century South Africa, *Manly Pursuits* evokes a country on the brink of the Anglo-Boer War, deploying as motif British songbirds that have been imported to South Africa by Cecil Rhodes in the belief that they will restore his life, which he believes is nearing its end. Confused by the changed coordinates of the southern hemisphere, the birds are unable to sing. *No Place for a Lady* is set during the war itself, and focuses on the attempt made by a few Englishwomen, the campaigner Emily Hobhouse among others, to bring relief to those women and children who were interned in the belief that this would force Boer soldiers to surrender. The novels are notable for the author's careful historical research and vivid characterization.

Head, Bessie Amelia (1937–1986) Novelist and short-story and nonfiction writer. Born in Pietermaritzburg's Fort Napier Mental Institution, her white mother Bessie Amelia Emery (née Birch) having unexpectedly fallen pregnant and having had a history of mental illness, Head grew up in foster care until the age of thirteen, after which the welfare authorities placed her in an Anglican mission orphanage in Durban. (The identity of Head's black father has never been discovered.) At the orphanage she received a secondary-school education and trained as a teacher. Finding out very soon that teaching did not suit her temperament, Head moved into the world of journalism, working in Cape Town and Johannesburg in the early 1960s for the *Golden City Post*, a newspaper in the famous *Drum* stable. In 1961 in Cape Town she met and married fellow journalist Harold Head; their only child, Howard, was born in 1962. After the breakup of her marriage in 1964 she relinquished South African citizenship and took up a teaching post in Serowe, Botswana. She soon lost this job, was declared a refugee, and turned to market gardening and writing in order to survive. Having been turned down before, Head was granted Botswanan citizenship in 1979. Plagued by ill health and mental instability, she died in Serowe with six published works to her name and an international reputation.

Head's first work, *When Rain Clouds Gather* (1968), deals with the flight from South Africa of a young black political activist, Makhaya Maseko, his resettlement in Botswana and marriage to a Batswana woman. With an underlying tone of romance, it describes the efforts of Makhaya and Gilbert Balfour, a young English agricultural expert, to establish cooperative farming in a village in southeastern Botswana. Despite its naive, naturalistic style and clumsy characterization, Head's first work contains some of the innovative qualities that would characterize her later writings. It eschews a simplistic paradigm of racial conflict in southern Africa by constructing the possibility of interracial cooperation and friendship, and tackles issues very real to an independent and developing Africa in a challenging and forceful way.

Head's second novel, *Maru* (1971), which derives its name from its eponymous central character, is an altogether more complex work. It has a surface realism that describes the conflicts that arise between Maru and Moleka in their love for the same woman. They are both in line for the chieftaincy of their tribe. Margaret is a "Masarwa," a member of the despised Bushman (San) people who for generations had been the slaves of the Batswana. By scheming and manipulating, Maru eventually succeeds in winning Margaret from her first love, Moleka, and marries her. This act throws time-honored Batswana prejudices into disarray. Beneath the novel's surface realism there is an allegorical struggle between human character types that assume godlike proportions. The energy of the novel is located at this level: Margaret's racial oppression achieves a universal resonance, and Maru and Moleka become human archetypes whose natures draw them into an unavoidable conflict. The resolution of the novel is therefore both a sociopolitical statement and an authorial comment on a universal pattern that inexorably controls human events.

A Question of Power (1973) is Head's most unusual and perplexing novel, and it is also the work that has received the most critical attention. Although all four of Head's novels have an autobiographical dimension, elements of *A Question of Power* are most conspicuously drawn from the life experience of the author. After a disastrous early life in South Africa, the protagonist Elizabeth leaves on an exit permit for Motabeng village in Botswana, where she engages in cooperative gardening ventures with the local Batswana and an international group of volunteer workers. It is in this context that Elizabeth's mental breakdown occurs. The narrative constantly switches between her tormented consciousness and the "real world" of the novel—the bustling village life, communal gardening, and daily activities of Elizabeth and her son, so tangibly evoked as to suggest a re-creation of the realism of *Rain Clouds*. Elizabeth confronts in her consciousness universal powers of good and evil and struggles to attain a sense of human value amidst her mental confusion. The novel charts the terrifying course of her breakdown and recovery, and it ultimately affirms the primary human values of decency, generosity, and compassion.

Head's first collection of short stories, *The Collector of Treasures and Other Botswana Village Tales* (1977), is remarkable for its skilful evocation of aspects of Botswanan village life: tribal history, the influence of the missionaries, religious conflict, witchcraft, rising illegitimacy and, most importantly, problems that women in the society encounter. Her social history *Serowe: Village of the Rain Wind* (1981) is composed of a series of transcribed interviews edited and prefaced by the author to constitute a portrait of Serowe village. The historical novel *A Bewitched Crossroad: An African Saga* (1984) simultaneously describes the process toward the establishment of the British Protectorate of Bechuanaland, and tells the story of Sebina, the leader of a clan which is eventually absorbed into the Bamangwato nation.

Four texts have appeared posthumously. *Tales of Tenderness and Power* (1989) is a collection of mostly fictional short writings and contains the widely anthologized story "The Prisoner Who Wore Glasses." *A Woman Alone: Autobiographical Writings* (1990) collects miscellaneous pieces Head wrote in both South Africa and Botswana. Randolph Vigne's *A Gesture of Belonging: Letters from Bessie Head, 1965–1979* (1991) is an important collection of letters interspersed with commentary, while *The Cardinals: With Meditations and Stories* (1993) is a previously unpublished novella (which

Head wrote in Cape Town in the early 1960s) and a set of seven shorter pieces. The themes which the novella takes up are familiar: the girl protagonist, Mouse, is abandoned by her mother when the family forces her to give her illegitimate baby to a poor domestic worker (we discover later that Mouse is the issue of a relationship that crosses class and race boundaries); Mouse enters the world of journalism and encounters Johnny, with whom she begins a relationship, unaware that he is her own father. The reader now knows what neither Mouse nor Johnny knows: that, with the increasing closeness of their relationship, they are in danger of committing incest.

Head has achieved a posthumous fame that places her in the forefront of African literature. Doggedly individualistic and courageous, she has been a pioneering, inspirational figure for African writers in general, and for African woman writers in particular.

FURTHER READING

Cecil Abrahams, ed., *The Tragic Life: Bessie Head and Literature in Southern Africa* (1990); Craig MacKenzie and Catherine Woeber, *Bessie Head: A Bibliography* (1992); Gillian Stead Eilersen, *Bessie Head: Thunder Behind Her Ears: Her Life and Writing* (1995); Huma Ibrahim, *Bessie Head: Subversive Identities in Exile* (1996); Craig MacKenzie, *Bessie Head* (1999); Maxine J. Cornish Sample, ed., *Critical Essays on Bessie Head* (2003); Coreen Brown, *The Creative Vision of Bessie Head* (2003); Huma Ibrahim, ed., *Emerging Perspectives on Bessie Head* (2004); Patrick Cullinan, ed., *Imaginative Trespasser: Letters Between Bessie Head and Patrick and Wendy Cullinan, 1963–1977* (2005); Desiree Lewis, *Living on a Horizon: The Writings of Bessie Head* (2007).

Herbstein, Manu (b. 1936) Novelist. Born in Muizenberg, near Cape Town, Herbstein studied engineering at the University of Cape Town before leaving for West Africa. He has since lived in Accra, Ghana, returning for the first time to South Africa during the end of apartheid. His novel *Ama, A Story of the Atlantic Slave Trade* (2001), follows the narrative of Ama, who is captured as slave by a Dagomba raiding party in West Africa in the late eighteenth century, and is sold to Asante, Dutch, and British traders before ending up on a sugar estate in Bahia, Brazil. Through the events of Ama's life, the novel depicts the historical and cultural circumstances of slavery and its varied practices in Africa and in the European colonies. It skillfully shows the interrelationship of contradictory human impulses and the complexities of moral dilemmas. The novel was a 2002 Commonwealth Prize winner.

Heyns, Michiel (b. 1943) Novelist. Raised in Thaba Nchu, Kimberley, Grahamstown, and Cape Town, Heyns studied at the Universities of Stellenbosch and Cambridge and subsequently taught at Stellenbosch University. He is now a full-time writer.

He is the author of four novels, *The Children's Day* (2002), *The Reluctant Passenger* (2003), *The Typewriter's Tale* (2005), and *Bodies Politic* (2008). *The Children's Day* describes a boy's coming of age in Verkeerdespruit, a small town in the Free State. The young protagonist, astute and innocent, grapples with questions of identity in the oppressive apartheid era, coming to terms with his sexuality in the conservative community. Extending the satiric reach of the first novel, *The Reluctant Passenger* tells the story of a man who is drawn out of the routine existence and middle-class comforts of his suburban life when he becomes involved in a case to save the chacma baboons of Cape Point. The subsequent novels have taken historical subjects and themes as their material. *The Typewriter's Tale* offers a fictional portrait of writer Henry James, observed from the perspective of his secretary. *Bodies Politic* focuses on events surrounding the death of Harry, son of the suffragette Emmeline Pankhurst, and explores, through three interlinked narratives, the private lives of these public figures.

Higginson, Craig (b. 1971) Novelist and dramatist. Born in Zimbabwe, Higginson grew up and was educated in South Africa, graduating from the University of the Witwatersrand with a degree in literary studies. He worked at the Market Theater for a year before moving to London in 1996, where he worked as a theater director, dramatist, and assistant director for theater companies such as the Royal Shakespeare Company, the Young Vic, the Hampstead Theatre, the Almeida, and the Oxford School of Drama. He returned to South Africa in 2004, and he currently works as literary editor and teaches writing at the University of the Witwatersrand. He is the author of three published plays, *Laughter in the Dark* (2000), *Dream of the Dog* (2007), and *Truth in Translation* (second author, 2008), and two novels, *Embodied Laughter* (1998) and *The Hill* (2005). Both novels deal with the unsavory aspects of boarding school experience concealed under a surface of discipline and order. Set in an isolated school in the Drakensberg, a region formerly occupied by hunter-gatherers, *The Hill* tells the story of a teacher's abuse of a boy whose close bond with nature is framed by San mythology.

Hirson, Denis (b. 1951) Novelist, translator, anthologist. Born in South Africa, he left the country in 1973 with his family when his father, Baruch Hirson, a political prisoner for nine years, was released and went into exile. He has lived in France since 1975 and has worked as an actor and English teacher. His autobiographical novel, *The House Next Door to Africa* (1986), is an episodic series of memories of a South African childhood narrated in a witty and idiosyncratic manner. Further works in an autobiographical vein have followed: *I Remember King Kong (the Boxer)* (2004), *We Walk Straight So You Better Get out of the Way* (2005), and *White Scars: On Reading and Rites of Passage* (2006). He is the translator of a selection of Breyten *Breytenbach's poetry, *In Africa Even the Flies Are Happy* (1978), and of Antjie *Krog's *Down to My Last Skin* (2000). He is also coeditor (with Martin Trump) of *The Heinemann Book of South African Short Stories* (1994) and has edited *The Lava of This Land: South African Poetry, 1960–1996* (1997).

Hobbs, Jenny (b. 1937) Novelist and journalist. Hobbs has published several novels, including *Darling Blossom* (1979), *Thoughts in a Makeshift Mortuary* (1989), *The Sweet-Smelling Jasmine* (1993), *Video Dreams* (1995), and *The Telling of Angus Quain* (1997). Popular rather than highbrow, the novels are said to reveal a sound ear for dialogue and a convincing portrayal of the emotional life of the characters. *The Sweet-Smelling Jasmine* deals with adolescent experience and middle-aged love. Hobbs has also compiled *Paper Prophets: A Treasury of Quotations About Writers and Writing* (1998) and collaborated with Tim *Couzens in *Pees & Queues: The Complete Loo Companion* (1999).

Hope, Christopher (David Tully) (b. 1944) Novelist, poet, short-story writer. Born in Johannesburg and educated at the Universities of the Witwatersrand and Natal, Hope worked as a journalist in Durban for some years, where he edited a literary review, *Bolt* (1972–73), in which some of his first poems appeared. He settled in London in 1975, where he now lives and works as a writer. One of the most significant and prolific authors to have emerged from South Africa in recent times, Hope has a wry and distinctive style of satirical humor that he has used to good effect in his poetry, short stories, novels, and autobiographical and documentary writing.

His early publications were two volumes of poetry: *Whitewashes* (1971, with Mike Kirkwood), and *Cape Drives* (1974), which deals principally with his dislocated South African origins. His work of this period received the Thomas Pringle Award (1971) and the 1974 Cholmondeley Award for Poetry. Later collections of poetry are *In the Country of the Black Pig* (1981) and *Englishmen* (1985), a long poem dealing satirically with colonialism in South Africa.

His first novel, *A Separate Development* (1980), which received the David Higham Prize for Fiction, was banned in South Africa. The title, which is a play on the obfuscatory jargon used by the National Party to make its apartheid strategies more palatable, is an indication of the novel's content. The novel takes the form of a supposed confession by Harry Moto, a black security police detainee, writing from his police cell, in which he details the events preceding his arrest. In the course of these revelations, the absurd structure of South African society is laid bare.

Hope's collection of short stories *Private Parts and Other Tales* (1981, 1982), later rereleased with changes as *Learning to Fly and Other Tales* (1990), continues in this satirical vein. The much-anthologized title story, subtitled "An African Fairy Tale," provides an indication of the kind of stories Hope writes. It is set in an imaginary postapartheid period (the story was written in the mid-1970s), and details the career of Captain "Window-jumpin'" du Preez, a security policeman renowned for his capacity to induce his prisoners to talk—or, as his nickname suggests, to commit suicide by leaping from the window of his thirteenth-story office. One of his captives, Jake Mphahlele, turns the tables on him, however, and Du Preez ends up on the pavement below. Mphahlele (henceforth Colonel Jake "Dancin'" Mphahlele) then takes his former captor's place and achieves notoriety himself by inducing his uncooperative white prisoners to hang themselves. In its dark and ironic way, the story both exposes the follies and crimes perpetrated by the apartheid regime and warns against the kind of regime that may succeed it.

Kruger's Alp (1984), winner of the Whitbread Literary Award, is widely considered to be one of Hope's most accomplished works. The novel is another work of satire, this time playing off against the story of the "Kruger Millions"—the treasure reputedly taken into exile in Switzerland by President Kruger after the British defeat of the Boer Republic. In a parody of Bunyan's *Pilgrim's Progress*, the protagonist, a failed priest, travels to Switzerland to investigate the whereabouts of this fortune and on the way there encounters the endemic corruption at the dark heart of the apartheid system. Hope's surrealistic style offers the reader kaleidoscopic glimpses of absurd facets of South African society, presented with a savage wit that simultaneously amuses and horrifies.

Hope's next novel, *The Hottentot Room* (1986), centers on the lives of the South African political exiles who frequent the London club after which the novel is named. The complex ironies of the situation are explored through a portrayal of the protagonist, Caleb Looper, a left-wing journalist in the employ of the South African regime, and Frau Katie, the German Jewish woman who runs the club and who was once married to a Nazi. The parallels between Nazi Germany and apartheid South Africa are implicitly established and contribute to the general sense of insecurity felt by the Hottentot Room's habitués.

Hope's novella, *Black Swan*, appeared in 1987 and was followed by his autobiographical work *White Boy Running* (1988), which both records his impressions of the all-white 1987 elections in South Africa and explores his childhood experiences in relation to the South Africa of the day and his own identity as a writer. His more recent work moves away from his country of origin, although *My Chocolate Redeemer* (1989), while set in France, has as one of its main characters an exiled African leader who once styled himself his country's savior. The novel is a skilful examination of the relationship that develops between the young girl protagonist, Bella Dresseur, and the deposed African leader who runs the gauntlet of French provincial xenophobia.

Hope's *Moscow! Moscow!* (1990), a collection of journalistic writings, was followed by *Serenity House* (1992), in which the Englishman Max Montfalcon is put into the ironically named retirement home of the novel's title, where his identity as Maximilian von Falkenberg, a Nazi war criminal, emerges. He is exposed, but not before most of the old people in the home have met grotesque fates at the hands of Jack, a young Nazi-worshipping thug. *The Love Songs of Nathan J. Swirsky* (1994) sees Hope returning to a South African setting—a 1950s housing estate outside Johannesburg. Narrated by a young boy called Martin, the series of sketches that make up the book feature Swirsky, who opens up a pharmacy and has to endure racist attacks, a black house servant who "came with the house," and an array of whites displaying attitudes distinctively and hilariously South African. And in *Darkest England* (1996), David Mungo Booi, a man of Khoi extraction, goes on a mission to England to see the Queen (the "Great She-Elephant") in order to solicit her sympathy for the plight of his tribe, still suffering under the Boers. Hope's most recent works include *Me, the Moon and Elvis Presley* (1997); *Signs of the Heart: Love and Death in Languedoc* (1999); *Heaven Forbid* (2002), a powerful novel about coming of age in the watershed year of 1948, when the National Party was swept to power; and *My Mother's Lovers* (2006).

Hope's place in South African literature is unique. His bizarre flights of imagination, anchored in fragments of reality all too tellingly South African, have afforded him a platform for satire that strikes at the heart of South Africa's unique set of prejudices without forgoing an appreciation of the country's less repellent aspects. He has become a truly international writer while retaining a hold on his South African roots.

FURTHER READING

Felicity Wood, "An Interview with Christopher Hope," *English Academy Review* 15 (1998): 59–66; Felicity Wood, "Beyond the Walls of the Lunatic Asylum: Christopher Hope's Early Fiction," *Literator* 25, no. 2 (2004): 45–62.

Horn, Peter (b. 1934) Poet, short-story writer, critic, editor. Born in Czechoslovakia, Horn emigrated to South Africa in 1955 and taught for many years in the Department of German at the University of Cape Town.

He has published numerous volumes of poetry, including *Voices from the Gallows Tree* (1968), *Walking Through Our Sleep* (1974), *Silence in Jail* (1979), *The Civil War Cantos* (1987), *Selected Poems 1964–1989* (1991), *Under Lansdowne Bridge* (1991), *Under Lansdowne Bridge 2* (1992), *An Axe in the Ice* (1992), *Emergency Poems* (with Keith Gottschalk, 1992), *Under Lansdowne Bridge 3* (1995), and *The Rivers that Connect Us to the Past* (1996). He has also published a collection of short stories, *My Voice Is Under Control Now* (1999, winner of the Herman Charles Bosman Prize 2000), and a collection of literary-critical essays, *Writing My Reading: Essays on Literary Politics in South Africa* (1994).

Ranging from the symbolic and the lyrical to the rhetorical and the exhortatory, Horn's poetry has consistently sought to expose the ways in which racism and political repression, and the commoditization of culture, brutalize the imagination. Two groups of poems stand out. In the sequence *The Plumstead Elegies*, Horn attempts to create an aesthetic that would connect the personal and the public. In *The Civil War Cantos*, he attempts to forge an aesthetic that would speak more directly to the elementary needs of an exploited humanity in a time of civil war.

Horn is cofounder of the literary journal *Ophir*. He has coedited *It's Gettin' Late and Other Poems from Ophir* (1973), as well as *Kap der Guten Hoffnung: Gedichte aus dem sudafrikanischer Widerstand* (1980), a collection of "freedom" poems. He is recipient of the 1974 Thomas Pringle Award, the 1992 Noma Award for Publishing in Africa, and the 1993 Bessie Head/Alex La Guma Fiction Award.

FURTHER READING

Dirk Klopper, "Death, Resistance and Liberation in Peter Horn's *The Plumstead Elegies*," *Journal of Literary Studies* 21, nos. 1–2 (1996): 171–186; Priya Narismulu, "'Here Be Dragons': Challenging 'Liberal' Constructions of Protest Poetry," *Alternation* 5, no. 1 (1998): 191–214; Geoffrey Haresnape, "'No Instant Amnesia': Short Stories by Peter Horn and Gertrude Strauss," *English Academy Review* 18 (2001): 100–111; Ulrike Ernst, *From Antiapartheid to African Renaissance: Interviews with South African Writers and Critics on Cultural Politics Beyond the Cultural Struggle* (2002).

Howarth, Anna
See Writers Before 1945

Hutchinson, Alfred (1924–1980)
Autobiographer and playwright. Born in the Eastern Transvaal (now Mpumalanga), the grandson of a Swazi chief, Hutchinson studied at the University of Fort Hare, where he graduated with a bachelor's degree and a diploma in education. He went into exile in the late 1950s, an experience reflected in the autobiographical *Road to Ghana* (1960), which was banned for many years in South Africa. It was reissued in 2006, with an afterword by Es'kia Mphahlele. Hutchinson's plays include *The Rain-Killers: A Play in Four Acts* (1964) and *Fusane's Trial* (1968). The latter was reprinted in Cosmo Pieterse's *Ten One-Act Plays* (1968).

FURTHER READING

James Olney, *Tell Me Africa: An Approach to African Literature* (1973).

I

Ingram, Joseph Forsyth *See* Writers Before 1945

J

Jabavu, Helen Nontando (Noni) (b. 1919)
Autobiographer. Born into a distinguished family (her mother was a teacher at Lovedale College, and her father, D. D. T. Jabavu, was a professor of African languages and Latin at the University of Fort Hare),

Jabavu married an Englishman and has spent most of her adult life in England. She first went to England at the age of fourteen and was educated at Mount School in York and at the Royal Academy of Music until the outbreak of World War II. After the war she traveled extensively in Africa and spent five years in Uganda, where her director husband established a film unit.

Her two works of autobiography record her experiences of growing up in South Africa, a country with repellent social and political policies, but with great physical beauty and human vitality. *Drawn in Colour: African Contrasts* (1960) records her emotions and experiences upon returning to South Africa for her brother's funeral; later chapters describe her travels in East Africa. *The Ochre People: Scenes from a South African Life* (1963) focuses more squarely on Xhosa life and is clearly intended to capture aspects of an African culture changing inexorably under the influence of colonialism.

FURTHER READING

James Olney, *Tell Me Africa: An Approach to African Literature* (1973); Jane Watts, *Black Writers from South Africa: Towards a Discourse of Liberation* (1989); Susan VanZanten Gallagher, *Truth and Reconciliation: The Confessional Mode in South African Literature* (2002).

Jacobs, Rayda (b. 1950) Short-story writer, autobiographer, novelist. Born and raised in Cape Town, Rayda Jacobs left South Africa at the age of twenty-one during the apartheid years and returned after a twenty-seven-year absence. She currently lives in Cape Town, where she works as writer and documentary filmmaker.

She has published *The Middle Children* (1994), *Eyes of the Sky* (1996), *The Slave Book* (1998), *Sachs Street* (2001), *Confessions of a Gambler* (2003), *Postcards from South Africa* (2004), *The Mecca Diaries* (2005), *My Father's Orchid* (2006), and *Masquerade* (2008). The short-story collections *The Middle Children* and *Postcards from South Africa* combine autobiography and fiction. Many of these stories are interlinked in narrating events in the life of Sabah, a Coloured girl who, at the age of sixteen, decides to pass as white until she is found out and forced to emigrate, returning many years later to a South Africa that has undergone fundamental political change. The question of identity in respect of mixed-race offspring is taken up also in the novels *Eyes of the Sky* (recipient of the Herman Charles Bosman Prize for English Literature) and *The Slave Book*, which narrate life on a Cape farm of the late eighteenth and early nineteenth centuries, describing in well-researched detail the material and social conditions that governed the lives of masters and slaves, and the blurring of racial and cultural boundaries on the periphery of settlement. The significance of Islam in South African communal life, particularly in the Cape, evident throughout the short story collections and the novels, is addressed directly in *The Mecca Diaries*, which records the author's experience of pilgrimage to the holy site.

Jacobs, Steve (b. 1955) Short-story writer and novelist. Having practiced as an advocate in Johannesburg, Jacobs now lives in Cape Town. His collection of stories, *Light in a Stark Age* (1984), deploys a number of modes, including science fiction, social realism and fantasy. His novels include *Diary of an Exile and Crystal Night* (1986), *Under the Lion* (1988), and *The Enemy Within* (1996).

Jacobson, Dan (b. 1929)
Born in Johannesburg, Jacobson spent his school days in Kimberley and later studied at the University of the Witwatersrand,

gaining a bachelor's degree in 1949. Soon afterward he left for Israel, where he spent two years on a kibbutz. Thereafter he went to London and started writing. Coming back to South Africa in 1951, he spent the next three years working in business and journalism. In 1954 he returned to London and has lived there ever since, making his living as a writer and university lecturer.

The Trap (1955) and *A Dance in the Sun* (1956) marked Jacobson early as a writer of ability, and are still the works for which he is best known (new combined editions of these novels were rereleased by several publishers in the 1980s). Both novels concern life on a South African farm and engage with problems in the relationship between white employer and black employee in which tension and violence cannot be contained.

In *The Trap*, the farmer Van Schoor discovers that his trusted "boy" Willem is stealing his sheep. In an attempt to purge himself of this betrayal, he pounds his fists into Willem's badly beaten face. Ironically, he later drinks coffee with Willem's accomplice, a white man who betrayed Willem to the police. In *A Dance in the Sun* the young narrator and his companion bear witness for the black servant Joseph against his employer Fletcher, who is guilty of crimes against Joseph's family. In a peculiarly South African twist, Joseph uses their testimony to blackmail Fletcher into taking him back into employment. At the end, the demented Fletcher is left dancing like a madman at the knowledge that his whole life will be fashioned by the power that Joseph now exerts over him. An allegorical dimension is discernible in these novels: the implication is that the whole of South Africa is trapped in relationships of dominance and subordination and is destined to act out a ritualistic "dance in the sun."

Jacobson's third novel, *The Price of Diamonds* (1957), is set in Lyndhurst, a fictionalized Kimberley. As the title implies, the story concerns the temptations of acquiring wealth by illicit means—in this case illegal diamonds. His novel *The Evidence of Love* (1960) deals with miscegenation, a recurring theme in South African literature. The fair-skinned Kenneth Makeer, who is officially classified as Coloured, dates and later marries a white woman. The consequence is a prison sentence for the couple. *The Beginners* (1966) is an autobiographical novel that deals with the lives of members of a South African Jewish family.

The Rape of Tamar (1970), which retells the Old Testament story of an incestuous rape, marks a departure from overtly South African themes. This and later novels by Jacobson, including *The Wonder-Worker* (1973) and *The Confessions of Josef Baisz* (1977), evince the author's increasing fascination with the creative process itself, and these later works have distinctively postmodernist, reflexive qualities. *The Confessions of Josef Baisz* invites comparisons with J. M. *Coetzee's *Waiting for the Barbarians* (1981) in that it is set in an indeterminate region (middle Europe or, obliquely, South Africa) and is a recounting of the life of a servile state functionary in a totalitarian country.

Jacobson's abilities as a novelist are matched by his expertise in the short-story genre. His stories have appeared in several collections over the years, including *A Long Way from London* (1958), *Beggar My Neighbour* (1964), *Through the Wilderness and Other Stories* (1968), *A Way of Life and Other Stories* (1971), and *Inklings: Selected Stories* (1973). One of Jacobson's best-known stories, "Beggar My Neighbor," is the story of a young white boy who befriends two black children and later has to come to terms with the harsh implications of rigid racial segregation, which consigns the children to disparate futures largely determined by race.

Jacobson's more recent work includes *Time and Time Again: Autobiographies* (1985), *Adult Pleasures: Essays on Writers and Readers* (1988), and the novels *Her Story* (1987), *Hidden in the Heart* (1991), *The God-Fearer* (1992), and *All for Love* (2005). His account of a return trip to Southern Africa is recounted in *The Electronic Elephant: A Southern African Journey* (1994), while *Heshel's Kingdom* (1998) is a partly autobiographical account of his Lithuanian family's history. He has received numerous literary awards, including the Rhys Memorial Prize (1959), the Somerset Maugham Award (1964), and the H. H. Wingate Award (1978).

FURTHER READING

Sheila Roberts, *Dan Jacobson* (1984); Richard Peck, *A Morbid Fascination: White Prose and Politics in Apartheid South Africa* (1997); Ann Blake et al., *England Through Colonial Eyes in Twentieth Century Fiction* (2001); Ian Hamilton, *Ian Hamilton in Conversation with Dan Jacobson* (2002).

James, Alan (b. 1947)

Poet and editor. He emigrated to Australia in 1992. James has published several volumes of poetry. The first two, *The Dictator* (1972) and *From Bitterfontein* (1974), were published privately. These were followed by *At a Rail Halt* (1981), *Producing the Landscape* (1987), *Morning Near Genadendal* (1992), and *Ferry to Robben Island* (1996). Noteworthy for their detailed evocations of place, the poems characteristically infuse landscape with a sense of history, combining the spatial and the temporal dimensions of experience. They deal with arrivals and departures, movements toward and away from, into and out of places, leave-takings and exile, creating a restlessness, a rootlessness even, that seems obliquely to describe a peculiarly modern condition.

James is founding editor of the poetry magazine *Upstream* and is coeditor of Roy Joseph *Cotton's posthumous selection of poems *Ag, Man* (1986). He is also the author of *The First Bushman's Path: Stories, Songs and Testimonies of the /Xam of the Northern Cape: Versions, with Commentary* (2001). He received the 1995 Olive Schreiner Prize for Poetry.

Jenkins, Geoffrey (Ernest) (1920–2001)

Novelist. Born in Port Elizabeth, he was educated in Potchefstroom and wrote his first book, *A Century of History: The Story of Potchefstroom* (1939; 2nd ed. 1971; foreword by Jan Smuts), while still at school. He worked as a journalist in South Africa and London, where he met Ian Fleming. He lived for most of his life in Pretoria with his wife, the writer Eve Palmer (author of *The Plains of Camdeboo*).

His first novel, *A Twist of Sand* (1959), set on the Skeleton Coast, was a commercial success and was followed by other novels in a popular thriller vein: *The Watering Place of Good Peace* (1960), *A Grue of Ice* (1962), *The River of Diamonds* (1964), *Hunter-Killer* (1966), and *Scend of the Sea* (1971). Later works include *Southtrap* (1979), *A Ravel of Waters* (1981), *The Unripe Gold* (1983), *Fireprint* (1984), *Harm's Way* (1986), and *A Hive of Dead Men* (1991). He is also the author of *The Companion Guide to South Africa* (1978).

FURTHER READING

Coleman Dick, *Geoffrey Jenkins: The Man Who Always Writes Best Sellers* (1972).

Jensma, Wopko (b. 1939)

Sculptor, painter, poet. Born in Middelburg, Western Cape, he pursued a career as artist in Botswana before returning to

South Africa in 1971, after which he led a homeless existence. Jensma has published three volumes of poetry: *Sing for Our Execution* (1971, reissued with woodcuts by the author in 1973), *Where White Is the Colour, Where Black Is the Number* (1974), and *I Must Show You My Clippings* (1977). Speaking on behalf of society's outcasts, those marginalized by a culture of bureaucracy and commercialization, the poetry uses colloquial and fractured speech to resist the grammar of modern, middle-class existence. Jensma received the 1983 Ad Donker Creative Writing Award.

FURTHER READING

Michael Gardiner, "Funking the Jive: The Poetry of Wopko Jensma," *English Academy Review* 3 (1985): 109–125; Michael Gardiner, "Self and Circumstance: A Note on Wopko Jensma's Poetry," *Theoria* 69 (1987): 53–57; Michael Gardiner, "The Real Substance of Nightmare: The Struggle of Poetry with History," *Alternation* 5, no. 2 (1998): 177–191; Ayub Sheik: "'I Feel Like Hollerin but the Town Is Too Small': A Biographical Study of Wopko Jensma," *Alternation* 9, no. 2 (2002): 236–276; Stefan Helgesson, "Sing for Our Metropolis: Self, Place and Media in the Poetry of Rui Knopfli and Wopko Jensma," *English in Africa* 33, no. 1 (2006): 71–92.

Johnson, Shaun (b. 1959) Novelist and journalist. Johnson lives and works in Cape Town and is the author of *Strange Days Indeed* (1994), which chronicles the decade between revolution and settlement in South Africa, and *The Native Commissioner* (2007), which tells the story of how Sam comes to piece together his deceased father's life from papers left behind at his death some forty years previously. Sam discovers that a life of forced compromise in South Africa's bureaucratic apartheid system was responsible for destroying this well-meaning man whose despair eventually overtook him. *The Native Commissioner* was winner of the Best Book in Africa Commonwealth Writer's Prize 2007, the M-Net Literary Award 2007 for English, and The Nielsen Booksellers' Choice Award 2007, and was short-listed for the *Sunday Times* Fiction Prize 2007.

Jonker, Ingrid (1933–1965) Poet. Born on a farm near Kimberley, Jonker led a troubled life. That, and her introspective poems, have resulted in her being identified with confessional poets such as Anne Sexton and Sylvia Plath.

Written in Afrikaans, her poems have appeared in English translation, the most recent publication being *Black Butterflies: Selected Poems* (2007). Among the first poems in Afrikaans to register the human tragedy of apartheid politics and deal frankly with the experience of female desire, they project an existential sense of dread and anguish illuminated by moments of sudden joy. Invoking the immanence of loss and loneliness even in moments of intimacy and love, the poems address themselves to questions of relationship, repeatedly raising the possibility of restoring, but never achieving, an imagined integrity.

Jooste, Pamela (b. 1946) Novelist. Born and educated in Cape Town, where she still lives, Jooste worked for some years in publishing and public relations. She has written radio and film scripts and several short stories. Her first novel, *Dance with a Poor Man's Daughter* (1998), dealing with the impact of forced removals on a Cape Town family, won the Sanlam Literary Award and the Commonwealth Best First Book Award. Her second novel, *Frieda and Min* (1999), is set in 1964 and tells the story of two girls thrown together by circumstance. Min, raised in the bush by her doctor father, is foisted on Frieda's family because Min's mother wants to go off with her new husband. The friendship between the girls is tested in the years of apartheid that follow. *Like Water in Wild Places* (2000), Jooste's third novel, tells the story of Conrad, a young man deeply influenced by Bushman mythology. The novel traces his formative years: his relationship with his reactionary father, his young adulthood, and his experience of border warfare. Recent novels include *People Like Ourselves* (2003) and *Star of the Morning* (2007), which tells the story of two orphaned Coloured girls and their struggle to survive and make a life for themselves in apartheid-era Cape Town.

FURTHER READING

Devi Sarinjeive, "Transgressions/Transitions in Three Post-1994 South African Texts: Pamela Jooste's *Dance with a Poor Man's Daughter*, Bridget Pitt's *Unbroken Wing* and Achmat Dangor's *Kafka's Curse*," *Journal of Literary Studies* 16, nos. 3–4 (2002): 259–274.

Jordan, A. C. (Archibald Campbell) (1906–1968) Novelist, short-story writer, critic. Born at the Mbokothwana mission station in the Transkei, the son of an Anglican minister, Jordan worked as a schoolteacher and lecturer before leaving South Africa on an exit permit in 1961 to take up a Carnegie fellowship. He worked for the rest of his life as an academic and was professor of African languages and literature at the University of Wisconsin, Madison, at the time of his death. A dedicated scholar of the Xhosa language, Jordan published a novel in Xhosa, *Ingqumbo Yeminyanya* (1940; translated and published as *The Wrath of the Ancestors* in 1980), and the critical study *Towards an African Literature: The Emergence of Literary Form in Xhosa* (1973). *The Wrath of the Ancestors* is a classic story of the clash between tradition and modernity that wisely counsels that to embrace the latter does not necessitate repudiating the former. The posthumously published *Tales from Southern Africa* (1973) is an anthology of thirteen Xhosa folktales (*iintsomi*) that Jordan collected both in rural areas, where he sought out old women who were renowned as storytellers, and in Cape Town's District Six, where people from the Tsolo and Qumbu districts of the Transkei lived. These tales, translated and retold by Jordan, are a sustained attempt by a black South African writer to render oral tales in the written form. "The Turban," probably the best-known of Jordan's tales, traces very economically and with well-controlled dramatic tension the fate of its central character, Nyengebule, who kills his favorite wife in a momentary fit of rage and is forced to submit himself to ritual execution by members of her family.

FURTHER READING

Craig MacKenzie, "The Use of Orality in the Short Stories of A. C. Jordan, Mtutuzeli Matshoba, Njabulo Ndebele, and Bessie Head," *Journal of Southern African Studies* 28, no. 3 (2002): 347–358.

Joubert, Elsa (b. 1922) Novelist. Born and raised in Paarl, Joubert was educated at the universities of Stellenbosch and Cape Town.

Written in Afrikaans, her books have appeared in English translation, and include *The Long Journey of Poppie Nongena* (1980), *To Die at Sunset* (1982), *The Four Friends and Other Tales from Africa* (1987), *The Last Sunday* (1989), and *Isobelle's Journey* (2002). Covering the story of a family over three generations, *The Long Journey of Poppie Nongena* describes the struggle of a Xhosa woman living in Cape Town to keep together a family threatened with relocation and separation by apartheid pass laws. *The Last Sunday* portrays a remote community of farmers cut off from contemporary events and tells the story of the pastor around whose church their lives revolve.

K

Kaganof, Aryan (b. 1964) Filmmaker, artist, poet, and novelist. Having made films under the name of Ian Kerkhof, Kaganof changed his name in 1999 to draw attention to his mixed Jewish and gentile origins, creating a deliberate provocation characteristic also of his work. Referred to as a counterculture revolutionary, Kaganof is the author of several volumes of poetry, including *Drive Through Funeral* (2003), *The Freedom Fighter* (2004), *Jou Ma Se Poems* (2005), and *The Ballad of Sugar Moon and Coffin Deadly* (2007), and the novels *Hectic!* (2002), *Uselessly* (2006), and *12shooters* (2007). The novels offer irreverent glimpses into the dearth of culture in South Africa. *Hectic!* is a satiric portrayal of the subculture of pool halls in white South Africa, focusing on a young Jewish male who wants to be a Nazi to fit in with his peers, while *Uselessly* purports to offer letters to and from the author's father, God, and the Devil.

Kani, John (b. 1943) Actor, director, and playwright. Born in New Brighton, South Africa, Kani is executive trustee of the Market Theatre Foundation, founder and director of the Market Theatre Laboratory, and chairman of the National Arts Council of South Africa. He rose to prominence in the early 1970s through plays such as *Sizwe Bansi Is Dead* (1972) and *The Island* (1973) and *Statements After an Arrest Under the Immorality Act* (1974), cowritten with Athol Fugard and Winston Ntshona. He is also the author of *Nothing but the Truth* (2002), in which the Truth and Reconciliation Commission serves as backdrop to a story of betrayal and falsehood within a family torn apart by the conflict between two brothers, one who stayed in South Africa under apartheid oppression and the other who left for exile as a hero of the struggle. The return of the remains of the latter to his home country precipitates the exposure of the truth of the past. The play won the 2003 Fleur du Cap Awards for best actor and best new South African play.

Karodia, Farida (b. 1942) Short-story writer and novelist. Born and raised in Aliwal North, Karodia trained as a teacher and taught in Johannesburg and later in Zambia. She emigrated to Canada in 1969 and returned to South Africa in 1994. She is the author of three novels. Her first, *Daughters of the Twilight* (1986), reworked into the more expansive *Other Secrets* (2000), is set in a small rural town in South Africa and concerns the struggle of a family of Indian descent to resist the racist legislation that threatens their livelihood. The events are seen through the eyes of the two young daughters, who witnesses the inevitable disintegration of the family. The novel *A Shattering of Silence* (1993) concerns the kidnapping and enslavement of children in Mozambique. It was followed by *Boundaries* (2003).

She is also the author of two collections of short stories. The title piece in *Coming Home and Other Stories* (1988) explores life on a Cape wine farm, while the other stories take in a wide range of settings and themes, including a portrait of white Zimbabwean society ("The World According to Mrs Angela Ramsbotham") and black township life ("The Necklace").

Farodia's second collection of short stories is *Against an African Sky and Other Stories* (1995). The long title story describes the reunion of childhood friends separated for years largely on account of their different races. "Crossmatch," about a nonconformist Indian girl and a young engineer whose parents are desperate to make what they consider to be an ideal match, is a deft, ironic piece: Sushi, it turns out, has a live-in lover in her apartment in London, and Dilip has a gay lover awaiting his return in Stanford, California. Both children have traveled far from their cloistered, traditional home environments, and both sets of parents are blissfully unaware of this until the story's conclusion. "In the Name of Love," the long story that closes the collection, is a compelling account of the fraught relationships within a family brought about largely by the questionable business transactions conducted by the father.

FURTHER READING

Miki Flockemann, "'Not-Quite Insiders and Not-Quite Outsiders': The 'Process of Womanhood' in *Beka Lamb*, *Nervous Conditions* and *Daughters of the Twilight*," *Journal of Commonwealth Literature* 27, no. 1 (1992): 37–47; Wendy Woodward, "The Powers of Discourse: The Identity of Subaltern Women Under Colonial Law in *Nervous Conditions* and *Daughters of the Twilight*," *Journal of Literary Studies* 9, no. 1 (1993): 80–91; Ronit Fainman-Frenkel, "Ordinary Secrets and the Bounds of Memory: Traversing the Truth and Reconciliation Commission in Farida Karodia's *Other Secrets* and Beverley Naidoo's *Out of Bounds*," *Research in African Literatures* 35, no. 4 (2004): 52–65.

Kente, Gibson (1932–2004) Playwright. Born in the Eastern Cape and educated at Lovedale College and Bethal College, he started writing songs and scripts for amateur theater productions at a young age. He is a founding member of the musical groups The Symphonic Five and The Kente Choristers, has served as director for Union Artists, Dorkay House, and is a founding member of the Federated Union of Black Arts (FUBA).

Kente has published one play, *Too Late*, in *South African People's Plays* (1981). Written in 1973, it was originally called *How Long?* and was filmed under this title in 1976. He is also author of many unpublished plays and musicals which have enjoyed considerable popularity in South Africa's black townships, including *Manana, the Jazz Prophet* (1963), *Sikhalo* (musical, 1966), *Life* (musical, 1968), *Zwi* (musical, 1970), *I Believe* (1974), *Beyond a Song* (1975), *Can You Take It?* (1977), *Taximan and the Schoolgirl* (1978), *La Duma* (1978), *Mama and the Load* (1979), and *Mfowethu/My Brother* (1993).

In his earlier work, Kente depicted stereotypical situations and characters from township life and avoided direct political commentary. When he did venture into producing politicized work (*How Long?*), he was detained from 1976 to 1977. Thereafter he vacillated between pure entertainment (*Can You Take It?*) and social commentary (*La Duma*). He is credited with having developed a theatrical style that captures black township experience.

Kente received a 1993 Moyra Fine Award and the 1997 Woza Africa Award.

FURTHER READING

Maishe Maponya and Carola Luther, "Problems and Possibilities: A Discussion on the Making of Alternative Theatre in South Africa," *English Academy Review* 2 (1984): 19–32; Andrew Horn, "South African Theater: Ideology and Rebellion," *Research in African Literatures* 17, no. 2 (1986): 211–233; Ian Steadman, "Stages in the Revolution: Black South African Theatre Since 1976," *Research in African Literatures* 19, no. 1 (1988): 24–33; Bhekizizwe Peterson, "Apartheid and the Political Imagination in Black South African Theatre," *Journal of Southern African Studies* 16, no. 2 (1990): 229–245; Ian Steadman, "Towards

Popular Theatre in South Africa," *Journal of Southern African Studies* 16, no. 2 (1990): 208–228; Ian Steadman, "Theatre Beyond Apartheid," *Research in African Literatures* 22, no. 3 (1991): 77–90.

Kentridge, William (b. 1955) Artist and dramatist. Born and raised in Johannesburg, William Kentridge studied at the University of the Witwatersrand, the Johannesburg Art Foundation, and the Ecole Jacques Lecoq in Paris. Although he is considered a visual artist and filmmaker, he was actor and director in Johannesburg's Junction Avenue Theatre Company in the 1970s and 1980s, and more recently has collaborated with the Handspring Puppet Company in staging multimedia productions that allude to classical European theater in exploring apartheid and postapartheid landscapes.

His productions include *Woyzek in the Highveld* (1992), *Ubu and the Truth Commission* (1998), and *Faustus in Africa* (2002). Adapted from Büchner's play about an individual's struggle against an indifferent and brutal society, *Woyzek in the Highveld* tells the story of a black migrant worker in the bleak industrial environment of 1950s Johannesburg. Inspired by Alfred Jarry's *Ubu Roi* and drawing on actual recordings of the Truth and Reconciliation Commission hearings, *Ubu and the Truth Commission*, by Jane Taylor, provides a portrait of a policeman with a bestial appetite for murder and torture, sex and food. *Faustus in Africa* is an adaptation of Goethe's famous play about an astrologer's pact with the devil. The combination of puppetry, animated film, and song in his productions creates a powerfully multifaceted experience.

Kgositsile, William Keorapetse (b. 1938) Poet, writing instructor, journalist. Born in Johannesburg, he wrote for the Cape Town journal *New Age* before going into exile in 1962, first to Tanzania, were he worked for *Spearhead* magazine, and then to the United States, where he was employed on the staff of New York's *Black Dialogue Magazine*. He has been writing instructor at Lincoln University, University of New Hampshire, Columbia University, the University of Dar Es Salaam, the University of Nairobi, and the University of Gaborone, appointments that reflect his nomadic academic existence in the United States and Africa.

Kgotsitsile has published numerous volumes of poetry, including *Spirits Unchained: Paeans* (1969), *For Melba* (1969, reissued 1970), *My Name Is Afrika* (1971), *Places and Bloodstains* (1975), *The Present Is a Dangerous Place to Live* (1993), *When Rain Clouds Clear* (1990), and *To the Bitter End* (1995). A volume of his collected poems was published in 1980 as *Heartprints*, and two editions of his selected poems have appeared, *If I Could Sing* (2002) and *This Way I Salute You* (2004). Drawing on Black Consciousness philosophy, the poems are uncompromising in their denunciation of white rule and their promotion of black resistance.

Kgotsitsile is editor of *The Word Is Here: Poetry from Modern Africa* (1973) and is the author of *Approaches to Poetry Writing* (1994). He was a recipient of the National Endowment for the Arts grant in 1969 and has served as poet-in-residence at the North Carolina Agricultural and Technical State University.

FURTHER READING

John F. Povey, "I Am the Voice: Three South Africa Poets: Dennis Brutus, Keorapetse Kgositsile and Oswald Mbuyiseni Mtshali," *World Literature Written in English* 16, no. 2 (1977): 263–280; Charles H. Rowell, "'With Bloodstains to Testify': An Interview with Keorapetse Kgositsile," *Callaloo* 2 (1978): 23–42; Kevin Goddard and Charles Wessels, eds., *Out of Exile: South African Writers Speak: Interviews with Albie Sachs, Lewis Nkosi, Mbulelo Mzamane, Breyten Breytenbach, Dennis Brutus, Keorapetse Kgositsile* (1992).

Khumalo, Fred (b. 1966) Novelist, biographer, and autobiographer. Editor of the *Sunday Times* Insight & Opinion section, Khumalo has produced four books to date. Two are life stories: the autobiography *Touch My Blood* (2006), short-listed for the Alan Paton Prize, and *Zuma: The Biography of Jacob Zuma* (2007). He has also written the novels *Bitches' Brew* (2006), joint winner of the European Union literary award in 2005, and *Seven Steps to Heaven* (2007). Set in the KwaZulu-Natal Midlands, *Bitches' Brew* re-creates the life and times of gang leader Zakes and his shebeen queen lover Lettie. The story is resumed by the son Kokoroshe in *Seven Steps to Heaven*. The racy style of the novels is reminiscent of the *Drum* writers of the 1950s.

Kirkwood, Mike (Robert Michael) (b. 1943) Poet, editor, publisher. Born in the West Indies, he graduated from the University of Natal, Durban, where he lectured before venturing into publishing as director of the influential left-wing Ravan Press. Kirkwood has published two volumes of poetry, *Whitewashes* (with Christopher *Hope, 1971) and *Between Islands* (1975). The latter employs a deliberately prosaic voice, which one poem terms "post-lyrical," in offering vignettes of scenes and characters from the Durban environment. Kirkwood was joint founder of *Staffrider* and editor of *Bolt*.

Kozain, Rustum (b. 1966) Poet. Born and raised in Paarl, Kozain studied at the University of Cape Town and spent a year in the United States on a Fulbright scholarship. He has taught at the University of Cape Town and currently works as freelance writer and editor.

He has published one volume of poetry, *This Carting Life* (2005), which was awarded the Ingrid Jonker Prize in 2006 and the Olive Schreiner Prize in 2007. Finely attuned to the interweaving of the personal and the political, and seeking to transform mundane experiences and bleak landscapes into sites of hard-won beauty, the poems explore themes of memory and loss.

Kraak, Gerald (b. 1956) Novelist. Born in South Africa and educated at the University of Cape Town, Kraak is Programme Executive of Reconciliation and Human Rights in the Johannesburg office of Atlantic Philanthropies. He has published two books on South African politics and has directed a film on gay conscripts. His novel *Ice in the Lungs* (2006) is set just before the political uprising of 1976, which inaugurated a period of sustained struggle against apartheid. It deals with the political and sexual awakening of Matthew, a second-year student at the University of Cape Town who is drawn in to the turbulent history of his times through his friendship with Pru and his homosexual involvement with Paul. The group of students meets regularly in The Kalamata, a Greek bar whose immigrant owner recounts his own experience of political oppression under military rule in Greece. The novel was joint winner of the European Union literary award.

Krige, Uys (1910–1991) Playwright, short-story writer, poet. Born in the Western Cape and educated at Stellenbosch University, he spent a number of years in France and Spain, immersing himself in the Romance languages and assimilating the culture of Mediterranean Europe. Better known as an Afrikaans writer, he has published extensively in that language.

Krige has published, in English, autobiographical sketches in *The Way Out* (1946). Translations from Afrikaans include the collections of stories, *The Dream and the Desert* (1953) and *Orphan of the Desert* (1967). He has also published two collections of plays, *The Sniper and Other One-Act Plays* (1962) and *The Two Lamps and The Big Shot* (1964). Krige is the editor of *Poems of Roy Campbell* (1962) and of *Olive Schreiner: A Selection* (1968), and coeditor of *The Penguin Book of South African Verse* (1968).

Krog, Antjie (b. 1952) Poet and journalist. Born in Kroonstad, she studied at the universities of the Orange Free State and Pretoria. She has worked as a radio and print journalist and is a prolific Afrikaans writer. Two works translated into English have brought her international fame. *Country of My Skull* (1998) is an intensely personal response to the hearings of the Truth and Reconciliation Commission in which private history and political history are interwoven. A similar structure is evident in *A Change of Tongue* (2003), which explores the political and personal landscapes of postindependence in South Africa. Krog returns to her place of birth on the farm and recounts events of family history, depicts her aspirations and struggle as a writer, provides a harrowing account of the impact of AIDS in a rural hospital, and describes a poetry caravan to the legendary Timbuktu. Her poetry has appeared in English translation as *Down to My Last Skin* (2000) and *Body Bereft* (2006). She has coauthored (with Sandile Dikeni) *Soul Fire: Writing the Transition* (2002), a collection of essays dealing with the Truth and Reconciliation Commission and postapartheid South Africa. She is also the coeditor of *Birds of a Different Feather: Poems for Children* (1992), and has produced a selection of San poetry entitled *The Stars Say 'Tsau': /Xam Poetry* (2004).

FURTHER READING

P. P. van der Merwe, "A Poet's Commitment: Antjie Krog's *Lady Anne*," *Current Writing* 2, no. 1 (1990): 131–146; Mary K. Deshazer, *A Poetics of Resistance: Women Writing in El Salvador, South Africa and the United States* (1994); Zoë Wicomb, "Five Afrikaner Texts and the Rehabilitation of Whiteness," *Social Identities* 4, no. 3 (1998): 363–384; Kim Wallmach, "'Seizing the Surge of Language by Its Soft, Bare Skull': Simultaneous Interpreting, the Truth Commission and *Country of My Skull*," *Current Writing* 14, no. 2 (2002): 64–82; Susan VanZanten Gallagher, *Truth and Reconciliation: The Confessional Mode in South African Literature* (2002); Meg Samuelson, "Cracked Vases and Untidy Seams: Narrative Structure and Closure in the Truth and Reconciliation Commission and South African Fiction," *Current Writing* 15, no. 2 (2003): 63–76; Shane Graham, "The Truth and Reconciliation Commission and Postapartheid Literature in South Africa," *Research in African Literatures* 34, no. 1 (2003): 11–30; Judith Lütge Coullie, "Translating Narrative in the New South Africa: Transition and Transformation in *A Change of Tongue*," *English Academy Review* 22 (2005): 1–21; Ashleigh Harris, "Accountability, Acknowledgement and the Ethics of 'Quilting' in Antjie Krog's *Country of My Skull*," *Journal of Literary Studies* 22, nos. 1–2 (2006): 27–53; Anthea Garman, "Confession and Public Life in Postapartheid South Africa: A Foucauldian Reading of Antjie Krog's *Country of My Skull*," *Journal of Literary Studies* 22, nos. 1–2 (2006): 324–346; Kay Schaffer and Sidonie Smith, "Human Rights, Storytelling, and the Position of the Beneficiary: Antjie Krog's *Country of My Skull*," *PMLA* 121, no. 5 (2006): 1577–1584.

Kunene, Daniel P. (b. 1923) Poet, short-story writer, critic. Born in Edenville, Free State, he studied at the University of South Africa and subsequently took his master's and doctoral degrees at the University of Cape Town before leaving South Africa in 1964 for the United States. In 1986 he became a professor of African languages and literature at the University of Wisconsin, Madison, where he is now professor emeritus.

Kunene has published two collections of poetry, *Pirates Have Become Our Kings* (1979) and *A Seed Must Seem to Die* (1981). He has also published one volume of short stories, *From the Pit of Hell to the Spring of Life* (1986). He is the author of several works on African language and literature, including *The Beginning of South African Vernacular Literature* (1967), *The Works of Thomas Mofolo: Summaries and Critiques* (1967), *From Oral to What: Some Problems of Transition from Spoken to Written Art* (1971), *Heroic Poetry of the Basotho* (1971), *The Ideophone in Southern Sotho* (1978), *Thomas Mofolo and the Emergence of Written Sotho Prose* (1989), and *The Zulu Novels of C. L. S. Nyembezi: A Critical Appraisal* (2007).

Kunene's poems and stories focus on the struggle against apartheid rule in the 1970s and 1980s. Denouncing oppression, they celebrate communality and a vision of freedom. *A Seed Must Seem to Die* offers a vivid account of the events that triggered this phase of the liberation struggle. Locating itself as a voice from within the context of the Soweto uprisings, the poems both mourn the cruelties inflicted on the children and urge an intensification of the war, claiming that new life will emerge from the carnage. Insurrectionary in intent, the poetry employs a variety of voices and rhythms in its endeavor to recover the inspiration of ancestral Africa.

FURTHER READING

Reginald Gibbons, *Writers from South Africa: Fourteen Writers on Culture, Politics and Literary Theory and Activity in South Africa Today* (1989); Michael Chapman et al., eds., *Perspectives on South African English Literature* (1992).

Kunene, Mazisi (1930–2006) Poet. Born in Durban and a graduate of the University of Natal, Durban, he left South Africa in 1959 to pursue his studies in England. He ran the London office of the ANC and served as director of education for the South African United Front and director of finance for the ANC. He subsequently left England for Lesotho, where he taught at what is now the National University. Thereafter he went to the United States, where he taught at the University of Iowa and Stanford University and served as professor of African literature and language at the University of California, Los Angeles. He returned to South Africa to take up a professorship at the University of KwaZulu-Natal, Durban, where he worked until his retirement.

Kunene published four volumes of poetry in English: *Zulu Poems* (1970), *Emperor Shaka the Great: A Zulu Epic* (1979), *Anthem of the Decades: A Zulu Epic Dedicated to the Women of Africa* (1981), and *The Ancestors and the Sacred Mountain* (1982). His more recent publications are in Zulu.

Seeking to portray and preserve Zulu history and culture, and intent on emphasizing African spiritual beliefs and values, the poems, particularly those in the volume *The Ancestors and the Sacred Mountain*, characteristically employ a symbolist style to convey mystical experiences associated with nature and with the shadowy presence of the ancestors. Kunene received the 1956 Bantu Literary Competition Award.

FURTHER READING

Kenneth L. Goodwin, *Understanding African Poetry: A Study of Ten Poets* (1982); John

Haynes, *African Poetry and the English Language* (1987); Reginald Gibbons, *Writers from South Africa: Fourteen Writers on Culture, Politics and Literary Theory and Activity in South Africa Today* (1989); Emmanuel Ngara, *Ideology and Form in African Poetry: Implications for Communication* (1990); Jane Wilkinson, ed., *Talking with African Writers: Interviews with African Poets, Playwrights and Novelists* (1992); Rolf Solberg and Malcolm Hacksley, eds., *Reflections: Perspectives on Writing in Postapartheid South Africa* (1996); Duncan Brown, *To Speak This Land: Identity and Belonging in South Africa and Beyond* (2006).

Kuzwayo, Ellen (1914–2006) Autobiographer and short-story writer. Born in Thaba Patchoa in the Free State, she trained as a teacher at Adams College, Amanzimtoti, and later at Lovedale College. After her marriage in 1941, she lived in Rustenburg, and had two sons. The breakdown of her marriage resulted in her moving to Johannesburg, where she became secretary of the Youth League of the ANC in 1946. She trained as a social worker (with Winnie Mandela) at the Jan Hofmeyr School of Social Work, University of the Witwatersrand, and afterwards worked for the School and for the YWCA. After the Soweto 1976 clashes she became a member of the Committee of Ten, and a founder Board member of the Urban Foundation. In 1977–78 she was detained for five months at the Johannesburg Fort, but she was released without being charged.

Kuzwayo's autobiography, *Call Me Woman* (1985; winner of the CNA Prize), tells the story of her life as a member of a "privileged," Christian, land-owning family, a life that inevitably became intertwined with the political history of South Africa, with its legacy of laws depriving blacks of their land, family rights, and political voice. The book is a lucid political and social document as well as a history of one woman's life.

Her collection of stories *Sit Down and Listen* (1990) is divided into five parts, each of which tackles a particular theme: "The Meaning of Cowardice," "Waiting at the Altar," "What Is a Family?" "How Much Does a Rood Cost?" and "A Person Is a Person Because of Another Person." Kuzwayo's method is to juxtapose stories that invite comparison. The two stories concerning marriage, for example, overturn conventional expectations: in the first story, an untraditional suitor who does not conform to the norms of society makes an excellent husband, while in the second story a wedding meeting all of the society's requirements is aborted when the would-be groom is surprised by the arrival at the ceremony of his first wife and is summarily exposed as a bigamist. In the process of telling her stories, Kuzwayo is concerned to impart knowledge of traditional African custom.

She also collaborated in the making of two films, *Awake from Mourning* (1981), and *Tsiamelo: A Place of Goodness* (1984), about the forced removal of her family from their rural home, and compiled *African Wisdom: A Personal Collection of Setswana Proverbs* (1998).

FURTHER READING

Craig MacKenzie and Cherry Clayton, eds., *Between the Lines: Interviews with Bessie Head, Sheila Roberts, Ellen Kuzwayo, Miriam Tlali* (1989).

L

La Guma, Alexander (Alex) (1925–1985) Novelist and short-story writer. Born in District Six and educated in Cape Town, La Guma worked as a factory hand, clerk, and journalist. He joined the Communist

Party in 1948 (which was banned under the Nationalist government's Suppression of Communism Act of 1950), and became a committee member of the South African Coloured People's Organization (SACPO). This political activity led to increasing harassment by the regime. A successful defendant in the Treason Trial (1956–61), he was detained and placed under house arrest several times for suspected underground activity before he went into exile with his family to London in 1966. From 1978 until his death he lived in Cuba, where he represented the ANC.

La Guma began writing fiction in the 1950s as a columnist for the leftist weekly *New Age*. *A Walk in the Night* (1962), his first novel, was republished together with a selection of short stories in 1968. Set in District Six, the novel focuses on an eventful few hours in the lives of a small group of characters. As with his later fiction, these characters are portrayed as subject to socio-historical forces. *And a Threefold Cord* (1964), which also deals with slum life, shows the gradual realization of its main character that establishing links with other people in similar oppressive circumstances is essential both for personal survival and for successful collective resistance to the status quo. *The Stone Country* (1967), La Guma's third novel, was also the last to be written in South Africa before his departure into exile. Set in a Cape Town jail, a metonymy for the imprisoned state of South Africa at large, the novel describes an inmate's success at politicizing his fellow prisoners.

Two further novels followed. *In the Fog of the Seasons' End* (1972) focuses on the plight of two resistance fighters who are on the run from the authorities. One manages to smuggle three young men over the border for military training, while the other dies at the hands of the security police. In *Time of the Butcher Bird* (1979), the protagonist, Shilling Murile, avenges a personal wrong by killing a white man. The suggestion is that a similar fate awaits all the perpetrators of apartheid repression.

La Guma's fiction is informed by his socialist convictions and traces the process of increasing radicalization among oppressed communities under apartheid. Some of his stories are collected in *Quartet: Four Voices from South Africa* (1964), edited by Richard *Rive. His travel book, *A Soviet Journey*, appeared in 1978.

FURTHER READING

Dennis Duerden and Cosmo Pieterse, eds., *African Writers Talking: A Collection of Interviews* (1972); Gerald Moore, *Twelve African Writers* (1980); Abdul R. JanMohamed, *Manichean Aesthetics: The Politics of Literature in Colonial Africa* (1983); Emmanuel Ngara, *Art and Ideology in the African Novel: A Study of the Influence of Marxism on African Writing* (1985); Cecil A. Abrahams, *Alex La Guma* (1985); Simon Gikandi, *Reading the African Novel* (1987); Kathleen M. Balutansky, *The Novels of Alex La Guma: The Representation of a Political Conflict* (1990); André Odendaal and Roger Field, *Liberation Chabalala: The World of Alex La Guma* (1993); Nahem Yousaf, *Alex La Guma: Politics and Resistance* (2001); Gareth Cornwell, "*And a Threefold Cord*: La Guma's Neglected Masterpiece?" *Literator* 23, no. 3 (2002): 63–80.

Landsman, Anne (b. 1959) Novelist. Born and raised in the Western Cape, Landsman studied at the University of Cape Town before leaving in 1981 for the United States, where she obtained an MFA in screenwriting and directing from Columbia University. She currently lives in New York City.

Landsman has published two novels to date, *The Devil's Chimney* (1997) and *The Rowing Lesson* (2008). Set in the Oudtshoorn region and employing techniques of magical realism, *The Devil's Chimney* interweaves the stories of two women trying to salvage their respective lives. The alcoholic narrator, Connie, becomes absorbed with the story of an aristocratic Englishwoman, Beatrice. When her husband disappears one day on the veld, Beatrice takes over the responsibilities of the ostrich farm and is drawn into a world charged with erotic energy in which reality and fantasy increasingly blur. In the course of elaborating Beatrice's story from the museum items of this early-twentieth-century life, Connie encounters the complex entanglements of South Africa's past and present. In *The Rowing Lesson*, the narrator, Betsy, is called from her home in New York to the hospital bed of her father, Harold, in Cape Town. While keeping vigil over him as he lies in a coma, she addresses him and reconstructs his life in her imagination, transforming their fraught relationship into an elegy of remembrance.

Lang, Graham (b. 1956) Artist and novelist. Born in Bulawayo, Zimbabwe, Lang obtained an MFA degree from Rhodes University before leaving South Africa in 1990 to settle in Australia, where he currently teaches Fine Art at the University of Newcastle.

He has published two novels to date, *Clouds Like Black Dogs* (2003) and *A Place of Birth* (2006). Set in the period leading up to the democratic election of 1994, *Clouds Like Black Dogs* explores the difficult three-way relationship between the narrator, Manas, a young Coloured man assisted by a white benefactor to study art at Rhodes University; Zelda, a fellow art student who is descended from an old Eastern Cape farming family; and her brother, who is an officer conscript in the army, patrolling the black townships and finding it difficult to reconcile himself to the changing political landscape. The novel raises issues of guilt and accountability in the context of treacherous student politics and ambiguous familial obligations.

Langa, Mandla (b. 1950) Novelist and editor. Born in Durban and educated at Fort Hare University without completing his degree, Mandla Langa left South Africa in 1976 for Botswana and subsequently went to London, where he studied journalism and edited *Rixaka*, a journal of South African culture. Since 1994 he has been involved in public broadcasting in South Africa. He has published four novels, *Tenderness of Blood* (1987), *A Rainbow on the Paper Sky* (1989), *The Memory of Stones* (2000), and *The Lost Colors of the Chameleon* (2008), which was awarded the Commonwealth Prize for Best Book: Africa. He has also published a collection of short stories, *The Naked Song* (1996).

FURTHER READING

Jabulani Mkhize, "'The Human Face of the Movement': Mandla Langa's *A Rainbow on the Paper Sky*," *Research in African Literatures* 26, no. 1 (1995): 53–60; Annie Gagiano, "Adapting the National Imaginary: Shifting Identities in Three Post-1994 South African Novels," *Journal of Southern African Studies* 30, no. 4 (2004): 811–824.

Leipoldt, C. Louis *See* Writers Before 1945

Leroux, Etienne (1922–1989) Novelist. A graduate of Stellenbosch University, where he studied law, Leroux worked briefly in the profession before turning his attention to running a sheep farm in the Free State.

He is the author of several Afrikaans novels, four of which have appeared in English translation, the trilogy *To a Dubi-*

ous Salvation (1972), which comprises *Seven Days at the Silbersteins*, winner of the Hertzog Prize, *One for the Devil* and *The Third Eye*, and the novel *Magersfontein, O Magersfontein* (1983), winner of the CNA Literary Award and the Hertzog Prize. Also known as the Welgevonden Trilogy after the fictional setting, *To a Dubious Salvation* comprises a series of linked narratives that explore the dilemma of modern Afrikanerdom. Employing a mix of mythical allusion, philosophical speculation, and political satire, it opens with a social gathering spanning seven days on a wealthy country farm, mutates into a detective novel, and ends with a journey into a contemporary underworld. *Magersfontein, O Magersfontein* engages more directly with Afrikaner history in describing, with satiric relish and ironic effect, the events around the recreation of a Boer War battle by a film and television crew stranded when nearby rivers overflow their banks.

Leshoai, Bob (Benjamin Letholoa) (1920–1996) Folklorist, short-story writer, and playwright. Born in Bloemfontein and educated at the University of Fort Hare, he taught in various southern African states and retired as professor of literature at the University of Bophuthatswana. His lifelong interest in African folklore is reflected in his collections of tales *Masilo's Adventures and Other Stories* (1968) and *Iso le Nkhono: African Folk-tales for Children* (1983). His plays include *The Wake* (1968) and *Wrath of the Ancestors and Other Plays* (1972).

Lessing, Doris (May) (b. 1919) Novelist and short-story writer. Born in Persia (Iran) to British parents, in 1925 she moved with her family to Southern Rhodesia (now Zimbabwe), where her father was allocated a farm northeast of Salisbury (Harare). Lessing went to a convent school in Salisbury, but left early and educated herself while working as an au pair, telephone operator, and clerk. During the war years she joined left-wing groups such as the Left Book Club and the Current Affairs Group, which had a lobby in the Southern Rhodesian Labour Party, and began publishing poems and stories in left-wing periodicals. She divorced her first husband in 1943 and devoted herself to Communist politics. In 1945 she married Gottfried Lessing, a Communist German exile. A year later, while working as a Hansard typist in Parliament, she began work on *The Grass Is Singing* (1950). Her second marriage did not last and in 1949 she divorced Lessing and left for England via Cape Town, where she spent a short time working as a journalist and publishing poems and stories in South African literary periodicals.

Lessing arrived in London in 1950 and found a publisher for *The Grass Is Singing*, which appeared in the same year. It was an instant success, and Lessing was able to give up her secretarial job and become a full-time writer. Regarded by some as her most powerful and accomplished work, the novel traces the fate of Mary Turner, who marries a white Rhodesian farmer and settles into the routine of being a conventional farmer's wife on a remote farmstead. Under the stress of her isolation, her husband's well-meaning but frustratingly conventional responses to her, and the heat, dirt, and unfamiliarity of rural life she begins to disintegrate. In violation of the most entrenched of codes in this racially divided society, she begins a sexual relationship with her black servant, Moses, who eventually murders her. The novel thus tackles the familiar theme of miscegenation, but it brings to this theme a keen sense of the injustice perpetrated by the colonial regime and a measure of sympathy for the avenging Moses.

Lessing's first collection of stories, *This Was the Old Chief's Country*, appeared in 1951, and was followed by *Martha Quest* (1952), the first of a semiautobiographical five-part saga of Rhodesian life collectively entitled *Children of Violence*. The series traces the fortunes of Martha Quest in her attempt to gain sexual and intellectual freedom in a conservative settler society, describing her life from her childhood in colonial Rhodesia to her resettlement in England. The other volumes are *A Proper Marriage* (1954), *A Ripple from the Storm* (1958), *Landlocked* (1965), and *The Four-Gated City* (1969). Other works followed, including *Five: Short Novels* (1953), winner of the Somerset Maugham Award in 1954.

In 1956, Lessing made a return trip to Rhodesia to write a series of articles, which appeared in book form as *Going Home* (1957). She received a hostile reception both in South Africa and Rhodesia and was declared a "prohibited immigrant." At this time her romantic novel *Retreat to Innocence* (1956) appeared, to be followed by *The Habit of Loving* (1957), a collection of stories mainly English in setting and preoccupation. The next year saw the premiere of her play *Each His Own Wilderness* about the life of a radical woman (collected in *New English Dramatists 1*, ed. E. Martin Browne, 1959). A second play, *Mr Dollinger*, about a Rhodesian tobacco farmer, also opened in 1958. Lessing's other plays include *Play with a Tiger* (1962) and *The Singing Door*, collected in *Second Playbill Two* (1973; ed. Alan Durband). A collection of her poems, *Fourteen Poems*, appeared in a limited edition in 1959.

Another of Lessing's major works, *The Golden Notebook* (1962), appeared at this time. A narrative in two parts, one of which consists of a series of four "notebooks" which document the fragmented experiences of the woman writer Anna Wulf, this novel has been hailed as a classic feminist text. Two experimental novels followed: *Briefing for a Descent Into Hell* (1971) and *The Memoirs of a Survivor* (1974). Lessing's venture into science fiction is represented by her *Canopus in Argos: Archives* series, consisting of *Re: Colonised Planet 5, Shikista* (1979), *The Marriages Between Zones Three, Four, and Five* (1980), *The Sirian Experiments* (1981), *The Making of the Representative for Planet 8* (1982), and *Documents Relating to the Sentimental Agents in the Volyen Empire* (1982). Her return to narrative realism was marked by *The Diary of a Good Neighbour* (1983) and *If the Old Could . . .* (1984), both published under the pseudonym Jane Somers. Other novels of the 1980s include *The Good Terrorist* (1985) and *The Fifth Child* (1988).

Lessing's stories have been collected in several editions. *African Stories* (1964) is a selection which includes her well-known "The Old Chief Mshlanga," "A Sunrise on the Veld," "No Witchcraft for Sale," and "The De Wets Come to Kloof Grange." Most of the stories in this selection also appeared in two separate editions: *The Black Madonna* and *Winter in July* (both 1966). Her *Nine African Stories* (1968) was followed by *The Story of a Non-Marrying Man and Other Stories* (1972) (published in America as *The Temptation of Jack Orkney and Other Stories*). *Collected African Stories*, which includes all of the stories from *This Was the Old Chief's Country* as well as several others, appeared in two volumes: *This Was the Old Chief's Country* and *The Sun Between Their Feet* (both 1973). *Collected Stories* also appeared in two volumes: *To Room Nineteen* and *The Temptation of Jack Orkney* (both 1978).

Lessing is also the author of several autobiographical and travel books, including *In Pursuit of the English* (1960) and *Particularly Cats* (1967). *A Small Personal Voice: Essays, Reviews, Interviews*, edited by Paul Schlueter, appeared in 1974. Her recollections of Zimbabwe have appeared as *African Laughter: Four Visits to Zimbabwe* (1992). Her autobiography has appeared in two volumes: *Under My Skin: Volume One of My Autobiography, to 1949* (1994), and *Walking in the Shade: Volume Two of My Autobiography, 1949–1962* (1997). Her considerable literary achievements over a long and very productive career were crowned by her being awarded the Nobel Prize in literature in 2007.

FURTHER READING

Dorothy Brewster, *Doris Lessing* (1965); Paul Schlueter, ed., *The Fiction of Doris Lessing* (1971); Annis Pratt and L. S. Dembo, eds., *Doris Lessing: Critical Studies* (1974); Michael Thorpe, *Doris Lessing's Africa* (1978); Roberta Rubenstein, *The Novelistic Vision of Doris Lessing* (1979); Jenny Taylor, ed., *Notebooks/Memoirs/Archives: Reading and Rereading Doris Lessing* (1982); Lorna Sage, *Doris Lessing* (1983); Mona Knapp, *Doris Lessing* (1984); Eve Bertelsen, ed., *Doris Lessing* (1985); Judith Kegan Gardiner, *Rhys, Stead, Lessing and the Politics of Empathy* (1989); Carey Kaplan and Ellen Cronan Rose, *Approaches to Teaching Lessing's "The Golden Notebook"* (1989); Jeannette King, *Doris Lessing* (1989); Jean Pickering, *Understanding Doris Lessing* (1990); Antonia Fraser, *The Pleasure of Reading* (1992); Louise Yelin, *From the Margins of Empire: Christina Stead, Doris Lessing, Nadine Gordimer* (1998); Carole Klein, *Doris Lessing: A Biography* (2000); Harold Bloom, ed., *Doris Lessing* (2003).

Lewin, Hugh (b. 1939) Autobiographer and journalist. Born in the Eastern Transvaal (now Mpumalanga) and educated at Rhodes University, Lewin served a seven-year term of imprisonment for sabotage during the political struggle. Thereafter he left for London, where he worked as information officer of the International Defence and Aid Fund and as journalist on *The Observer* and *The Guardian*. Since his return to South Africa, he has headed the School of Journalism in Johannesburg and founded Baobab Press.

Lewin is the author of the prison autobiography, *Bandiet: Seven Years in a South African Prison* (1974), which is admired for its unsensational, honest, and straightforward account of the harrowing circumstances of political imprisonment in South Africa's apartheid jails. He has also published several children's books: *Jafta: My Mother* (1981), *Jafta* (1981, reissued 1982), *Jafta: The Town* (1983), *Jafta and Jafta's Mother* (1992), and *The Picture That Came Alive* (1992). Lewin is winner of the 1993 Alan Paton Literary Competition.

Lewis, Ethelreda *See* Writers Before 1945

Lindsay, Kathleen (1903–1973) Novelist. Born in Aldershot, England, Lindsay settled in South Africa in 1930. A prolific popular novelist, Lindsay wrote some nine hundred books under her own name as well as eight pseudonyms. Her stories that have a historical background were written under the name Margaret Cameron; Mary Richard and June Darnley were the names she used for love stories; Betty Manvers for doctor-nurse romances; Molly Waring for adventure stories; Elizabeth Fenton for stories with a South African setting; Hugh Desmond for thrillers and crime fiction; and Nigel MacKenzie for science fiction. She traveled widely and was married four times. She died in Somerset West.

Livingstone, Douglas (James) (1932–1996) Poet. Born in Kuala Lumpur to Scottish parents, Livingstone came to South Africa in 1942 after the Japanese invasion of Malaya. He attended Kearsney College, near Durban, and worked as a laboratory technician in Durban and as a commercial diver on the Kariba Dam project in Rhodesia. He later qualified as a microbiologist at the Pasteur Institute in Salisbury (Harare) and worked as a marine bacteriologist for the rest of his life, mainly monitoring water pollution for the Council for Scientific and Industrial Research (CSIR) in the greater Durban area. He received a doctorate in science for his work in this field.

His early slim collection *The Skull in the Mud* appeared in 1960. The grimly humorous title poem records his bizarre encounter with a skull at the bottom of Kariba Dam. At this time he published numerous poems in various literary periodicals, notably *London Magazine* and *Contrast*. *Sjambok and Other Poems from Africa* (1964), his first important collection, includes the ironic "Sunstrike," about a solitary prospector driven to delirium by sun and thirst who comes upon a dry river bed and shovels aside priceless gems in a last despairing search for water. Other poems deal with African wildlife and reveal Livingstone's considerable skill at capturing the distinctiveness of various animals while imposing wry anthropomorphisms upon them. Notable characteristics of his poetry, evident even at this early stage, are tautness of structure, sparseness of style, and an astringent, antiheroic tone. *Poems*, which appeared in 1968, contains a selection of Livingstone's poems alongside some by the Irish poet Thomas Kinsella and the American poet Anne Sexton.

Eyes Closed Against the Sun (1970) is more urban in focus, although it does contain the moving "Gentling a Wildcat," in which the speaker describes coming upon a wildcat mauled by jackals and easing her passage to death. Another memorable poem, "Vanderdecken," deftly evokes the myth of the "Flying Dutchman," a spectral ship reputed to haunt the seas around the Cape coast and lure other vessels to their destruction. *A Rosary of Bone* (1975; enlarged edition 1983) introduced the voice of Livingstone's poetic persona "Giovanni Jacopo" (the first names of the libertine Casanova), which he uses to comment on social mores, fads, and fashions.

In *The Anvil's Undertone* (1978) Livingstone's startling use of imagery begins to have a surreal edge. "Under Capricorn," one of his best-known poems, describes a motorist's chance encounter with a herd of goats that take on demonic qualities, while the head-dressed goatherd, hands raised in a greeting or a curse, becomes a latter-day Moses with Lucifer-like undertones. In its juxtaposing of the weirdly disparate worlds occupied by the motorist and the goatherd, the poem also subtly questions the place of each in Africa. "The Zoo Affair" is a poetic rendering of a real incident in which an insane man stole into a tiger's cage one night and was discovered a bloody pulp the next morning. In its imaginative re-creation of the motives of the man, the poem provides the bizarre incident with a surreal logic. In "Sonatina of Peter Govinda, Beached" the subject is an old fisherman, sometime busdriver and father of five, now "beached" and holding within himself the lesson learnt from a life of hardship: "Contempt for death is the hard won / ultimate, the only freedom."

A Littoral Zone appeared in 1991. As its title suggests, this collection probes at metaphysical questions: the notion of an area along the seashore between the low and high water marks adumbrates ultimate questions about life and death, and about the indeterminate zone that lies between the two. In "The Wall Beyond Station X," the speaker recounts his increasingly perilous adventure along a wall that extends out into the sea, pointing "straightly to some promised land." Considering it safe, he "foolishly" advances. Hours later, the sky turns overcast and the sea stormy, but still the adventurer presses on, until he finds that he has traveled too far to return. Glancing back, he finds that the wall behind him is "dissolving" as he passes. The metaphorical dimensions of this solitary walk become increasingly clear as the poem progresses, leaving the reader with a strong sense of the bleak power of Livingstone's poetic vision.

Livingstone's *Selected Poems* appeared in 1984 and received the 1985 CNA Award. His collected poems have appeared as *A Ruthless Fidelity* (2004), edited by Malcolm Hacksley and Don *Maclennan. Other awards include the Cholmondely Poetry Prize (1970) and the Olive Schreiner Prize (1975) for his radio play *A Rhino for the Boardroom* (1974). His earlier radio verse play, *The Sea My Winding Sheet* (1963; pub. 1971; rev. 1978), is a mock-heroic treatment of the Adamastor myth, now degraded and reduced to the persona of "Mr Adam Astor." Livingstone's sudden death of stomach cancer robbed South Africa of a writer regarded by many as the country's leading contemporary poet.

FURTHER READING

A. G. Ullyatt, *Douglas Livingstone: A Bibliography* (1979); Michael Chapman, *Douglas Livingstone: A Critical Study of His Poetry* (1981); Michael Chapman et al., eds., *Perspectives on South African English Literature* (1992); Don Maclennan, "Life Triumphs Even on No Longer Trusted Planets: The Poetry of Douglas Livingstone," *English Academy Review* 12 (1995): 8–10; Tony Morphet, "Littorally: A Note on Douglas Livingstone," *Pretexts* 6, no. 2 (1997): 205–211; Tony Voss, "A Cellular Universe: Douglas Livingstone's Collected Poems, *A Ruthless Fidelity*," *Current Writing* 17, no. 2 (2005): 125–143; Ian Glenn and Ed Rybicki, "Douglas Livingstone's Two Cultures," *Current Writing* 18, no. 1 (2006): 78–89.

M

Maclennan, Don (Donald Alasdair Calum) (1929–2009) Poet, literary critic, dramatist. Born in London, Maclennan came to South Africa in 1938 and was educated at the Universities of the Witwatersrand and Edinburgh. He taught for nearly thirty years at Rhodes University in Grahamstown, where he retired as professor of English in 1994.

Maclennan's friendship with the playwright Athol *Fugard gave rise to several plays, including *The Third Degree* (1971) and *The Voyage of the Santiago* (1977). The author of several short stories, Maclennan has also published works of criticism, most notably *Perspectives on South African Fiction* (1980), coauthored with Sarah Christie and Geoffrey Hutchings. He also coedited (with Malvern van Wyk Smith) *Olive Schreiner and After: Essays in Southern African Literature* (1983). It is for his poetry, however, that he is best known.

His first collection, entitled "Life Songs," appeared together with the work of four other South African poets in the volume *Bateleur Poets* (1977). This collection of personal lyrics followed *In Memoriam Oskar Wolberheim* (1971), a collaborative work combining Maclennan's poetry and the music of Norbert Nowotny.

In *Reckonings* (1983), Maclennan engages with the subject matter and themes that reappear in his subsequent collections: the nature of being, the limits of human understanding, and the rhythms and cycles of the natural world. As its title suggests, the collection also contains musings on mortality and death and ponders whether human existence has any lasting significance in the face of nature's impersonal, inexorable processes. Maclennan brings to these traditional poetic preoccupations a wry whimsicality that personalizes the issues with which he deals.

The tendency in Maclennan's oeuvre toward shorter, highly compressed poems finds further expression in his next collection, *Collecting Darkness* (1988). These poems are again characterized by ironic musings on natural phenomena: the sun, drought, winter, death, and the ineluctable passage of time. Again, a wry humor leavens the somberness of the subject matter, usually by way of witty alternating rhymes at the ends of poems.

Letters (1992) employs the device of an address to absent parties: family members, friends, lovers, and the poet himself become recipients of these poetic missives. Haunted as ever by the inconsequentiality of human endeavor (and of his own, in particular), the poet tests the capacity of language to signify. The various musings on the enigma of writing, of placing abstract notation on the blank page and attempting to derive significance from this, bind the poems in this collection into a thematic unity.

In *The Poetry Lesson* (1995), Maclennan hones the wry, deeply personal voice developed in earlier collections in a series of pared-down lyric poems. Bleak honesty, expressed in pellucid and minutely worked phrasings, is the defining characteristic of this collection. He returns to the themes and concerns of his earlier work, but with an even greater commitment to clarity of expression. The title poem captures in its whimsical nuances and spare style the simultaneous "being and nothingness" that is poetry's paradoxical nature. The speaker in the poem is a teacher of English who ponders the purpose of poetry and why young people bother with it at all, while admiring "their courage that they / at this unnerving time in history / still want to know / the purpose and meaning of poetry."

A similar probing at metaphysical questions is in evidence in *Solstice* (1997), winner of the Sanlam Literary Award. He was subsequently astonishingly prolific, publishing *Of Women and Some Men* (1998), with charcoal drawings by Grahamstown artist George Coutouvides, *Rock Paintings at Salem* (2001), *Notes from a Rhenish Mission* (2001), *The Dinner Party* (2002), *The Road to Kromdraai* (2002), *Under Compassberg* (2003), *Excavations* (2004), *Reading the Signs* (2005), *The Necessary Salt* (2006), *The Owl of Minerva* (2007), and *Through a Glass Darkly* (2008). Maclennan's recent work sees him finding a mature poetic voice. The relative obscurity of his earlier poems gives way to a poetic style that is limpid and terse. In an era in which poets in South Africa increasingly adopted a public voice to give expression to social themes, Maclennan spoke in an intensely private voice and grappled with deeply personal concerns that nevertheless resonate beyond the private poetic space he created.

Macnab, Roy (1923–2004) Poet, novelist, editor. Born in Durban and a graduate of Oxford University with a degree in history, he served as diplomat in South Africa's Public Service and as London director of the South African Foundation. Macnab published three volumes of poetry: *Testament of a South African* (1947), *The Man of Grass and Other Poems* (1960), and *Winged Quagga* (1981). He published one novel, *The Cherbourg Circles* (1994), and one biographical study, *The French Colonel: Villebois-Mareuil and the Boers 1899–1900*

(1975). He is also author of two historical works, *Journey Into Yesterday: South African Milestones in Europe* (1962) and *For Honour Alone: The Cadets of Samur in the Defence of the Cavalry School, France, June 1940* (1988).

While the early poetry deals frequently with the dilemma of being both of Africa and of Europe, the later poetry seeks to integrate this divided heritage into a whole, of which the "winged quagga" is proffered as a visionary symbol.

Macnab edited and coedited several literary anthologies, namely, *South African Poetry* (1948), *Towards the Sun* (1950), an anthology of poetry and prose, and *Poets in South Africa* (1958). He also edited *George Seferis: South African Diaries, Poems and Letters* (1990).

Macphail, E. M. (Ella Mary) (b. 1922) Novelist and short-story writer. Macphail's first novel was *The Story of Westcliff: A Chronicle of a Kind* (1986; new edition 1997). Her collection of stories, *Falling Upstairs* (1982), brought her critical acclaim, and was followed by *Phoebe & Nio: A Novel* (1987). Her third novel, *Mrs Chud's Place* (1992) won the 1993 Sanlam Literary Award. She has since produced *Ugogo and Other Stories from South Africa* (1994) and has edited two volumes, *Hippogriff New Writing* (1990) and (with Peter Esterhuysen) *Some Roses, a Hamburger, the AK47 and a Puddle: New South African Writing* (1993).

Magona, Sindiwe (b. 1945) Autobiographer, short-story writer, novelist. Born in a small village in rural Transkei, Magona grew up in the townships around Cape Town. After experiencing motherhood and life as a domestic worker, she studied part-time through UNISA and took a postgraduate degree at Columbia University in New York. She has for many years worked for the United Nations in New York.

The first volume of her autobiography, *To My Children's Children* (1990; translated by the author into Xhosa as *Kubantwana babantwana bam*, 1995), is written in the form of a letter "from a Xhosa grandmother to her grandchildren." Covering the first twenty-three years of her life, it charts her rite of passage from rural Transkei to periurban Cape Town. After an idyllic childhood, she qualifies as a teacher, falls pregnant six months later, gets employment as a domestic worker and is then deserted by her husband—four months after which she gives birth to their third child. *Forced to Grow* (1992) takes up the narrative from this point and traces Magona's struggle to gain an education, her involvement in women's organizations, and her stressful journeyings between Guguletu (Cape Town) and New York. Her autobiographies are remarkable for their humor, linguistic playfulness, and complete absence of self-pity.

Magona is also the author of two volumes of short stories. *Living, Loving and Lying Awake at Night* (1991) focuses principally on the experiences of women in South Africa, especially in their work environments (a sequence of stories is entitled "Women at Work"), but there are also stories of childhood and old age. All are told with the wit and humor evident in her autobiographies. The stories in *Push-Push! and Other Stories* (1996) have a diversity of settings—from the rural Eastern Cape to the ghettoes around Cape Town and to metropolitan New York. Less conspicuously autobiographical than her first collection, these stories explore the lives of black South Africans in the pre-1994 era. Magona's first novel, *Mother to Mother*, a fictionalized account of the Amy

Biehl killing, appeared in 1998. Her second novel, *Beauty's Gift (2009),* takes up the issue of HIV/AIDS, telling the story of how the lives of four women are changed when their friend dies as a result of her husband's sexual indiscretions.

FURTHER READING

Margaret Daymond, "Class in the Discourses of Sindiwe Magona's Autobiography and Fiction," *Journal of Southern African Studies* 21, no. 4 (1995): 561–572; Sarah Nuttall, "Reading and Recognition in Three South African Women's Autobiographies," *Current Writing* 8, no. 1 (1996): 1–18; Stephen Meyer, "Interview with Sindiwe Magona," *Current Writing* 11, no. 1 (1999): 79–90; J. U. Jacobs, "Cross-Cultural Translation in South African Autobiographical Writing: The Case of Sindiwe Magona," *Alternation* 7, no. 1 (2000): 41–61; Siphokazi Koyana and Rosemary Gray, "An Electronic Interview with Sindiwe Magona," *English in Africa* 29, no. 1 (2002): 99–107; Margaret J. Daymond, "Complementary Oral and Written Narrative Conventions: Sindiwe Magona's Autobiography and Short Story Sequence, *Women at Work*," *Journal of Southern African Studies* 28, no. 2 (2002): 331–346; Siphokazi Koyana, ed., *Sindiwe Magona: The First Decade* (2004).

Mahola, Mzi (b. 1949) Poet. Born in the Eastern Cape and educated in Port Elizabeth, Lovedale, and Healdtown, he works as educational officer at the Port Elizabeth Museum. He has published three volumes of poetry, *Strange Things* (1994), *When Rains Come* (2000), and *Dancing in the Rain* (2006). Written from the perspective of traditional rural society, and seeking to integrate the rural and the urban, the traditional and the political, the poems display a persuasive simplicity and directness.

Maimane, Arthur (1932–2005) Playwright, novelist, journalist. Having matriculated at St Peter's Secondary School, Rosettenville, he worked as journalist on several South African newspapers, including *Drum* magazine. He went into exile in 1958 and worked for Reuters, first as correspondent for East and Central Africa, based in Dar es Salaam, and then in the London news offices. He joined the BBC in 1964 as commentator on current affairs.

Maimane published two novels, *Victims* (1976) and *Hate No More* (2000), and produced two radio plays for the BBC, *Where the Sun Shines* and *The Opportunity*, the latter being published in *Ten One-Act Plays* (1968).

Malan, Rian (b. 1954) Autobiographer. Born in Vereeniging, Malan worked as a journalist on *The Star* in Johannesburg until he went into exile in 1977. After traveling in Europe, he settled in the United States in 1979 and worked as a freelance journalist, returning in 1985 to settle in Cape Town. *My Traitor's Heart* (1990) is his best-selling autobiographical account of his familial origins and life in South Africa in the 1980s. Subtitled "Blood and Bad Dreams: A South African Explores the Madness in His Country, His Tribe, and Himself," it is a harrowing confessional work that explores the story of modern South Africa in a synchronic fashion. Book 1, "Life in This Strange Place," traces the advent of the white man in Africa, the follies committed by Malan's forebears, his childhood and early adulthood in Johannesburg and his departure into exile after the Soweto uprising in 1976. Book 2, "Tales of Ordinary Murder," documents the bleak contemporary scenario of bloodshed and mayhem, while book 3, "A Root in Arid Ground," focuses on a white couple who settle in the strife-torn region of Masinga in KwaZulu-Natal and attempt to right some of the wrongs of apartheid. Malan also published *The New South Africa: Will It Work?* (1994), a special issue of the *Sunday Times Magazine.*

FURTHER READING

Paul Gready, "The Witness: Rian Malan's *My Traitor's Heart* and Elsa Joubert's *Poppie*," *Current Writing* 7, no. 1 (1995): 88–104; Sarah Ruden, "Country of My Skull: Guilt and Sorrow and the Limits of Forgiveness in the New South Africa," *Ariel* 30, no. 1 (1999): 165–179.

Manaka, Matsemela (1956–1998) Playwright. Born in Alexandra, near Johannesburg, Manaka was a product of the post-1976 era. Having trained as a teacher, he became involved in politicized black drama, founding the Soyikwa African Theater group, which produced workshopped rather than scripted plays, mainly in response to the political events of the day. This style of drama characterizes Manaka's own published plays, which include *Egoli: City of Gold* (1979), *Blues Afrika Café* (1980), *Vuka* (1981), *Mbumba* (1984), *Domba, the Last Prince* (1986), *Pula* (published in *Market Plays*, edited by Stephen *Gray, 1986), *Size* (1987), *Toro: The African Dream* (1987), *Koma* (1988), *Ekhaya: Coming Home* (1991), and *Yamina* (1993). With Motsumi Makhene and Peter Boroto he wrote the musical *Gorée* (1989). In South Africa his plays contributed substantially to the promotion of Black Consciousness and the general politicization of township audiences in the 1980s, but they have also been staged successfully at festivals abroad, notably in Edinburgh and Berlin. He is also the author of *Echoes of African Art: A Century of Art in South Africa* (1987). Some of his plays have been collected in *Beyond the Echoes of Soweto: Five Plays* (1997), edited by Geoffrey V. Davis. This volume also contains essays by Manaka on South African drama.

FURTHER READING

Ian Steadman, "Black South African Theatre After Nationalism," *English Academy Review* 17, no. 2 (1986): 9–18; Ian Steadman, "Stages in the Revolution: Black South African Theater Since 1976," *Research in African Literatures* 19, no. 1 (1988): 24–33; M. T. Bindella and Geoffrey V. Davis, eds., *Imagination and the Creative Impulse in the New Literatures in English* (1993).

Mann, Christopher Zithulele (b. 1948) Poet, editor, playwright. Born in Port Elizabeth and educated at the Universities of the Witwatersrand and Oxford, he has taught in Swaziland, lectured at Rhodes University, and worked for the Natal Valley Trust. He is currently professor of poetry at Rhodes University and employed by the Institute for the Study of English in Africa in Grahamstown to organize the annual Wordstock literary festival.

Mann has published several volumes of poetry, including *First Poems* (1977), *New Shades* (1982), *Kites and Other Poems* (1990), *Mann Alive!* (1992), *South Africans: A Set of Portrait-Poems* (1996), *The Horn of Plenty: A Series of Painting-Poems* (with illustrations by his wife Julia Skeen, 1997), *Heartlands* (2002), and *Lifelines* (2006), a collection of animal poems with illustrations by Julia Skeen. He has published several verse plays, including *The Sand Labyrinth* (1980) and *Thuthula: Heart of the Labyrinth* (2004), a love story based on Xhosa history. He also coedited, with Guy *Butler, *A New Book of South African Verse in English* (1979).

The poems in *The Horn of Plenty* rejoice in the cornucopia of life, finding in everyday experience, and particularly in natural phenomena, intimations of a deeper, more mysterious existence beyond the apprehension of rational thought, and supplementing the scientist's penetrating eye with the poet's lyrical vision. Employing a plain idiom that aims at disclosing reality, the poetry finds inspiration in such diverse cultural traditions as Zulu folklore, Romantic poetry, and a beer-swilling, sport-loving, South African way of life. The democratic impulse that informs the work is most evident in the portrait-poems that make up *South Africans*, which seeks to embrace a tumultuous humanity, carefully delineating its desires and fears.

Mann is a recipient of the 1973 Sir Roger Newdigate Prize for English Verse, the 1979 Roy Campbell Prize for Poetry, the 1983 Olive Schreiner Award for Literature, and the 1984/1985 SACPAC Drama Prize. In 1995 he was awarded second place in the Soundscapes Radio Playwriting Competition.

FURTHER READING

Colin Gardner, "A Rediscovery of the Ordinary: A Reading of Three Recent Poems by Chris Mann," *English Academy Review* 12 (1995): 99–107.

Maponya, Maishe (b. 1951) Dramatist. Born in Alexandra Township, Johannesburg, Maponya's family was forcibly removed to Diepkloof, Soweto, when he was eleven. He has been a semiprofessional soccer player and worked for a time as a clerk with an insurance company before taking up a position lecturing in the history and theory of African performance at the University of the Witwatersrand. He began by writing poetry and was a member of the Allah Poets, a group of performance poets. Some of his poems appeared in *Staffrider* in the early 1980s, but it is as a Black Consciousness–oriented playwright that he is best known. With his Bahumutsi Theatre Group, he produced plays that tackled sociopolitical issues in South Africa and became the target of harassment by the state in the 1970s and early 1980s. His plays include *The Hungry Earth* (1979), concerned with the exploitation of labor in South African industries, *Umongikazi: The Nurse* (1982), which deals with the conditions of workers in the health service, and *Gangsters* (1984), which focuses on the harassment of writers by the state. *The Hungry Earth*, *Gangsters*, *Umongikazi: The Nurse*, *Jika*, and *Dirty Work* appear in Maponya's *Doing Plays for a Change: Five Works* (1995).

FURTHER READING

Matsemela Manaka, "Some Thoughts on Black Theatre," *English Academy Review* 2 (1984): 33–39; Ian Steadman, "Black South African Theatre After Nationalism," *English Academy Review* 2 (1984): 9–18; Ian Steadman, "Stages in the Revolution: Black South African Theater Since 1976," *Research in African Literatures* 19, no. 1 (1988): 24–33; Bhekizizwe Peterson, "Apartheid and the Political Imagination in Black South African Theatre," *Journal of Southern African Studies* 16, no. 2 (1990): 229–245; Sikhumbuzo Mngadi, "The Antinomies and Possibilities of 'Radical' Historical Consciousness: The Case of Three South African Playtexts in English," *Alternation* 3, no. 1 (1996): 30–55.

Marais, Eugène *See* Writers Before 1945

Maseko, Bheki (b. 1951) Short-story writer. Born in Newcastle, he attended school in Soweto and has worked as a driver and laboratory assistant. His stories first appeared in *Staffrider* in the early 1980s and were collected as *Mamlambo and Other Stories* (1991; with an introduction by Njabulo Ndebele). These stories explore aspects of daily life for black South Africans in the 1970s and 1980s: "Finder Finder" traces the fate of a black server after she succumbs to the exploitative sexual advances of the restaurant owner; "Some Breeders for Sure" describes the brutality of a farmer who murders the relative of one of his farmhands after some goats go missing; while in "The Prophets" an elderly woman is duped by confidence tricksters posing as priests. Other stories deal with sinister aspects of the "muti" (traditional medicine) trade, prison life, the iniquities of the pass-law system, and the problem of the mentally infirm in a society without the infrastructure to deal with the problem. The title story is a departure from the realist mode of the other stories and deals wittily with a snake with magical powers ("Mamlambo") that suddenly appears under the pillow of a lovesick young girl who has consulted a traditional doctor.

FURTHER READING

Njabulo S. Ndebele, "The Rediscovery of the Ordinary: Some New Writings in South Africa," *Journal of Southern African Studies* 12, no. 2 (1986): 143–157.

Mashile, Lebogang (b. 1979) Poet. Born in the United States, Mashile returned to her home country when she was sixteen years old. She currently lives in Johannesburg, where she works as television presenter and producer, as well as appearing in various performance contexts. She was recipient of the Noma award in 2006. Cofounder of the "Feel a Sistah!" Spoken Word Collective, she has produced an album, *Lebo Mashile Live*, that combines performance poetry and hip-hop, and she has published two volumes of poetry, *In a Ribbon of Rhythm* (2007) and *Flying Above the Sky* (2008). Her work characteristically addresses sociopolitical conditions and violence from the perspective of gender and identity, presenting transformation as an inner creative process.

Matlou, Joël (b. 1953) Short-story writer. Matlou's stories, which first appeared in *Staffrider* in the 1980s, are gathered in *Life at Home and Other Stories* (1991), an unusual mix of autobiographical reminiscence and fictional contrivance. An important aspect of Matlou's stories is their continuity with a rich oral tradition of storytelling. This is evident in his concern with tribal, familial and personal origins, in the way the main narrative is frequently interrupted to allow for digression, and in the way an oral mode of delivery sometimes obtrudes. In his best-known stories, "Carelessman Was a Madman" and "My Ugly Face," the fantastic and the commonplace are combined to offer a powerful portrait of deprivation and oppression.

FURTHER READING

Njabulo S. Ndebele, "The Rediscovery of the Ordinary: Some New Writings in South Africa," *Journal of Southern African Studies* 12, no. 2 (1986): 143–157; Johan Geertsema, "Homelessness, Irony and Suffering: Ndebele and Matlou's *Life at Home*," *Journal of Commonwealth Literature* 36, no. 1 (2001): 91–106.

Matlwa, Kopano (b. 1986) Novelist. Written while Matlwa was a medical student at the University of Cape Town, *Coconut* (2007) tells the story of two young black women struggling with questions of identity in contemporary postapartheid society. The privileged Ofilwe, who lives in a predominantly white neighborhood and attends a private school, is thoroughly urban and middle-class but is driven to recover her African culture to fill the vacuum created by a dysfunctional family life and a racist social structure that persists at school. Fiks, on the other hand, has grown up in poverty in the black township, and seeks to escape her blackness by embracing whiteness. The contrast between the two protagonists and the positions they occupy in contemporary black South African society brings into sharp focus the dilemmas currently addressed by urban black identity politics.

Matshikiza, Todd (1922–1968) Playwright, novelist, jazz critic, radio broadcaster, journalist. Born in Queenstown and educated at Lovedale College, he worked as teacher and as journalist for the SABC and the *Sunday Post*. He wrote the column "With the Lid Off" for *Drum* magazine in the 1950s. Banned under the Suppression of Communism Act, he emigrated to London in 1960 and worked subsequently in Malawi and Zambia. He was an accomplished jazz musician.

Matshikiza composed the music for the stage show *King Kong* (1959) and collaborated with Alan *Paton on the musical *Mkhumbhane* (1965). He also published one autobiographical novel, *Chocolates for My Wife* (1961). His *Drum* columns have been collected and published together with the *Mail & Guardian* columns of his son, John Matshikiza, as *With the Lid Off* (2000).

FURTHER READING

James Olney, *Tell Me Africa: An Approach to African Literature* (1973); N. W. Visser, "South Africa: The Renaissance That Failed," *Journal of Commonwealth Literature* 11, no. 1 (1976): 42–57; Bob Gosani and Jürgen Schadeberg, *The Fifties People of South Africa* (1987); Paul Gready, "The Sophiatown Writers of the Fifties: The Unreal Reality of their World," *Journal of Southern African Studies* 16, no. 1 (1990): 139–164; Anthony Sampson, *Drum: The Making of a Magazine* (2005).

Matshoba, Mtutuzeli (b. 1950) Short-story writer and playwright. Born in Orlando, he attended primary school in Soweto, received his secondary schooling at Lovedale College, and attended the University of Fort Hare. After publishing several pieces in *Staffrider*, his collection of stories, *Call Me Not a Man*, appeared in 1979 and was promptly banned. The seven stories that make up the volume are strident in tone and take issue with the oppressive policies of the apartheid regime and the hardships they engender. "My Friend, the Outcast," for example, concerns the unjust eviction of a township family from their rented home; the title story deals with the corruption and brutality of township policemen; "A Glimpse of Slavery" describes the protagonist's harsh experiences as a convict laborer on a white farm; "A Pilgrimage to the Isle of Makana" describes the protagonist's journey to Robben Island to see a relative imprisoned there. All of the stories are narrated in the first person, and the shared narrator adopts a style strongly reminiscent of an oral storyteller. An accomplished painter, Matshoba is also the author of the play *Seeds of War* (1981), about the devastating effects on a family of forced removal, and of another collection of short stories, *Majola's Ancestors* (1996).

FURTHER READING

Michael Vaughan, "Literature and Politics: Currents in South African Writing in the Seventies," *Journal of Southern African Studies* 9, no. 1 (1982): 118–138; Jenny Williams, "'A New Act of Meditation': The Screenplays of Mtutuzeli Matshoba," *Current Writing* 4, no. 1 (1992): 25–39; Derek Wright, ed., *Contemporary African Fiction* (1997); Michael Chapman, "African Popular Fiction: Consideration of a Category," *English in Africa* 26, no. 2 (1999): 113–123; Nahem Yousaf, ed., *Apartheid Narratives* (2001); Kelwyn Sole, "Political Fiction, Representation and the Canon: The Case of Mtutuzeli Matshoba," *English in Africa* 28, no. 2 (2001): 101–121; Craig MacKenzie, "The Use of Orality in the Short Stories of A. C. Jordan, Mtutuzeli Matshoba, Njabulo Ndebele, and Bessie Head," *Journal of Southern African Studies* 28, no. 2 (2002): 347–358.

Mattera, Don (b. 1935) Poet, short-story writer, autobiographer, journalist. Born in Sophiatown, his paternal grandfather was an Italian sailor who married a Griqua woman, while his mother is Tswana. At school he was leader of the Vultures Gang, but the forced removals of the 1950s, when black residents were removed from designated white areas, led to his subsequent involvement in political organizations, including the Western Areas Student Organization. He was a founding member of the Black Consciousness Movement (BCM) and the Congress of South African Writers (COSAW), founder of the Union of Black Journalists, and an executive member of the National Forum after the banning of the BCM.

Mattera has published three volumes of poetry: *Azanian Love Song* (1983), *Memory Is the Weapon* (1987), and *Inside the Heart of Love* (1997). He is coeditor of *Exiles Within: An Anthology of Poetry* (1986). He has written two collections of stories, *The Storyteller* (1991) and *The Five Magic Pebbles and Other Stories* (1992). He has also published an autobiography, *Gone with the Twilight: A Story of Sophiatown* (1987), issued in the United States as *Sophiatown: Coming of Age in South Africa* (1989).

Vigorous in its opposition to white rule and graphic in its description of the psychological and physical impact of oppression, Mattera's writing tempers indignation with human warmth and empathy.

Mattera has received the 1983 PEN Award, the 1992 Bookchat Awards, and the 1993 Noma Award for Publishing in Africa. He also appeared on the 1988 and the 1990 Kwanzaa Honours List.

FURTHER READING

Jacques Alvarez-Pereyre, *The Poetry of Commitment in South Africa* (1984); Rolf Solberg and Malcolm Hacksley, eds., *Reflections: Perspectives on Writing in Postapartheid South Africa* (1996).

Matthee, Dalene (1938–2005) Novelist. Born in Riversdale in the Cape, Matthee began by writing children's stories and then moved on to short stories and fiction for adults. Her Knysna Trilogy—*Circles in the Forest* (1984), *Fiela's Child* (1986), and *The Mulberry Forest* (1989)—established her reputation as a best-selling novelist. Perhaps the best known of her works is *Fiela's Child*, which deals with a boy who goes missing in the Knysna Forest, is raised by a Coloured family, and is then forcibly returned to his original white family, to the great distress of his adoptive mother, Fiela. Matthee publishes her novels in Afrikaans and translates them herself into English. Her more recent work includes the novels *The Day the Swallows Spoke* (1993), *Dreamforest* (2004), and *Driftwood* (2005).

Matthews, James David (b. 1929) Short-story writer and poet. Born in Athlone, near Cape Town, Matthews worked as a journalist before establishing Blac Publishing House. A detainee during the period of the 1976 Soweto uprising, his work is characterized by strong political messages and has often been banned as a result.

He is best known for his 1950s story "The Park," about a young black boy who yearns to play in a whites-only park and who defies the authorities by returning to the park at night to play on the swings. At the end of the story, he swings higher and higher in the face of threats by the park attendant, his state of exultation suggesting a serene transcendence of the pettiness of apartheid legislation. The story appeared in *The Park and Other Stories* (1974; reissued in an expanded edition in 1983). Four of Matthews's stories earlier appeared in *Quartet: Four Voices from South Africa* (1964), edited by Richard *Rive.

Matthews's earlier poetry is collected in *Cry Rage!* (1972; coauthored with Gladys Thomas), a volume banned for its strident protest against racism and call for justice.

A similar uncompromising message is conveyed in his later poetry collections *Pass Me a Meatball, Jones* (1977; banned), *No Time for Dreams* (1981), *Flames & Flowers* (2000), and *Poems from a Prison Cell* (2001). His poetry has been collected as *Cry Rage: Odyssey of a Dissident Poet* (2006). He also edited the anthology *Black Voices Shout!* (1974) and is the author of the novel *The Party Is Over* (1997), which is set in the arty circles of Cape Town in the 1960s.

FURTHER READING

Gareth Cornwell, "Evaluating Protest Fiction," *English in Africa* 7, no. 1 (1980): 51–70; Jacques Alvarez-Pereyre, *The Poetry of Commitment in South Africa* (1984); Hein Willemse, *More Than Brothers: Peter Clarke and James Matthews at Seventy* (2000); Mohamed Adhikari, "From Manenberg to Soweto: Race and Coloured Identity in the Black Consciousness Poetry of James Matthews," *African Studies* 62, no. 2 (2003): 171–186.

Mbuli, Mzwakhe (b. 1959) Performance poet. Born in Sophiatown, as a youngster he would accompany his father, a traditional harmonic singer, to performances at migrant workers' hostels. Involved in dramatic and musical groups during the politically volatile 1970s, he subsequently achieved popularity during the struggle years of the 1980s with his recitation of his poetry at public gatherings. Detained for six months under Section 29 of the Internal Security Act, he was elected media officer for the United Democratic Front and helped establish its Cultural Desk in 1986.

Mbuli has released several recordings of his poetry, including *Change Is Pain* (1986), *Unbroken Spirit* (1989), *Resistance and Defence* (1992), and *Africa* (1993). He has also published one book of poetry, *Before Dawn* (1989).

Aimed at mobilizing mass resistance to apartheid rule, the performances are delivered in a resonant bass voice and draw on a variety of influences, including traditional oral poetry, dub poetry, political invective, and an apocalyptic rhetoric derived from the cadences and the imagery of the Old Testament prophets.

FURTHER READING

Steve Kromberg, "Worker Izibongo and Ethnic Identities in Durban," *Journal of Literary Studies* 10, no. 1 (1994): 57–74; Michael Drewett, "Battling Over Borders: Narratives of Resistance to the South African Border War Voiced Through Popular Music," *Social Dynamics* 29, no. 1 (2003): 78–98.

McClure, James (b. 1940) Novelist. Born in Johannesburg, McClure worked as a crime reporter in Pietermaritzburg, an experience that provided him with material for most of his books that have a South African setting. His dislike of the intensifying apartheid in the 1960s prompted his emigration to the United Kingdom and also colors his fiction. Although his novels can be classified as popular mysteries, their implicit stance on social and racial issues has caused critics to consider him a "progressive" mystery writer.

Beginning with *The Steam Pig* in 1971, McClure embarked on a series of detective mysteries featuring the Afrikaans Lieutenant Tromp Kramer and the Zulu Detective Sergeant Michael Zondi of the Trekkersburg (Pietermaritzburg) Murder and Robbery Squad: *The Caterpillar Cop* (1972), *The Gooseberry Fool* (1974), *Snake* (1975), *The Sunday Hangman* (1977), *The Blood of an Englishman* (1980), and *The Artful Egg* (1984). A prequel to this historical sequence, *The Song Dog*, appeared in 1991. His other novel with a southern African setting is *Rogue Eagle* (1976).

FURTHER READING

Bert B. Lockwood, "A Study in Black and White: The South Africa of James McClure," *Human Rights Quarterly* 5, no. 4 (1983): 440–466; Richard Peck, "The Mystery of McClure's Trekkersburg Mysteries: Text and Reception in South Africa," *English in Africa* 22, no. 1 (1995): 48–71; Richard Peck, *A Morbid Fascination: White Prose and Politics in Apartheid South Africa* (1997).

Mda, Zakes (b. 1948) Playwright, novelist, poet, critic, painter, journalist. Born in the Eastern Cape, reared in Soweto, and schooled in Lesotho, where he joined his father in exile, he was educated at universities in Switzerland and the United States, obtaining a master's degree in theater from Ohio University and, in 1989, a doctoral degree in drama from the University of Cape Town. In 1984 he took up a lecturing post in the Department of English at the University of Lesotho. In the early 1990s he was writer-in-residence at the University of Durham and research fellow at Yale University before returning to South Africa as visiting professor at the University of Witwatersrand. He currently works fulltime as a writer, painter, and director of theater and film.

Mda has published three collections of plays. The first collection, *The Plays of Zakes Mda* (1990), contains *Dead End*, *We Shall Sing for the Fatherland*, *Dark Voices Ring*, *The Hill*, and *The Road*. The second collection, *And the Girls in Their Sunday Dresses: Four Works* (1993), contains *And the Girls in Their Sunday Dresses*, *Banned*, *The Final Dance*, and *Joys of War*. The third collection, *Four Plays* (1996), contains, among other items, *The Nun's Romantic Story* and *You Fool, How Can the Sky Fall?* Mda has also published one volume of poetry, *Bits of Debris* (1986).

He is the author of several novels, *She Plays With the Darkness* (1995), *Ways of Dying* (1995), *Ululants* (1999), *The Heart of Redness* (2000), *The Madonna of Excelsior* (2002), *The Whale Caller* (2005), and *Cion* (2007). Combining social commentary and magical realism, the compassionate and the brutal, and spanning rural and urban contexts, Mda's writings are admired for their sensitive characterizations and inventive story lines. *Ways of Dying* concerns a professional mourner in the townships of the Cape peninsula, the relationship he develops with a home girl, and the imaginative ways in which they are able to recreate their lives. *The Heart of Redness* has two interwoven narratives, the one dealing with the cattle killings in Xhosaland in the 1850s, and the other showing how the past continues to impact on the present.

Among other awards, Mda has received the 1978 and the 1979 Amstel Playwright of the Year Award, the 1984 Christina Crawford Award of the American Theatre Association, the 1995 Sanlam Literary Award, the 1996 Olive Schreiner Prize, and the 1997 M-Net Book Prize.

FURTHER READING

Myles Holloway, "Social Commentary and Artistic Mediation in Zakes Mda's Early Plays," *English Academy Review* 6 (1989): 28–41; Jan Gorak, "Nothing to Root for: Zakes Mda and South Africa Resistance Theatre," *Theatre Journal* 41, no. 4 (1989): 478–491; Geoffrey V. Davis and Anne Fuchs, eds., *Theatre and Change in South Africa* (1996); Johan van Wyk, "Catastrophe and Beauty: *Ways of Dying*, Zakes Mda's Novel of the Transition," *Literator* 18, no. 3 (1997): 79–90; André Brink, "Challenge and Response: The Changing Face of Theater in South Africa," *Twentieth Century Literature* 43, no. 2 (1997): 162–176; Martin Banham et al., eds., *African Theatre in Development* (1999); J. U. Jacobs, "Zakes Mda and the (South) African Renaissance: Reading *She Plays with the Darkness*," *English in Africa* 27, no. 1 (2000): 55–74; Myles Holloway et al. *Love, Power and Meaning*

(2001); Wendy Woodward, "'Jim Comes from Jo'burg': Regionalized Identities and Social Comedy in Zakes Mda's *The Heart of Redness*," *Current Writing* 15, no. 2 (2003): 173–185; Ralph Goodman, "Describing the Centre: Satiric and Postcolonial Strategies in *The Madonna of Excelsior*," *Journal of Literary Studies* 20, nos. 1–2 (2004): 62–70; Rita Barnard, "On Laughter, the Grotesque, and the South African Transition: Zakes Mda's *Ways of Dying*," *Novel: A Forum on Fiction* 37, no. 3 (2004): 277–302; Sikhumbuzo Mngadi, "Some Thoughts on Black Male Homosexualities in South African Writing: Zakes Mda's 'The Hill' and Kaizer Nyatsumba's 'In Happiness and in Sorrow,'" *English in Africa* 32, no. 2 (2005): 155–168.

Medalie, David (b. 1963) Short-story writer and novelist. Born and raised in South Africa, Medalie is professor of English at the University of Pretoria. He has published a collection of stories, *The Shooting of the Christmas Cows* (1990), and a novel, *The Shadow Follows* (2006), which portrays the interconnecting lives of a group of South Africans. Incorporating the mythical tales of Pandora's box and the Ten Plagues of Egypt, the novel touches on contemporary issues of HIV, crime, and white supremacism.

Metelerkamp, Joan (b. 1956) Poet. Born and raised in the midlands of Natal (now KwaZulu-Natal), she graduated at the University of Natal, Pietermaritzburg, was involved in educational theater, and lectured at the University of Natal before taking up a lecturing post at the University of the Western Cape.

She has published four volumes of poetry, *Towing the Line* (1992), *Stone No More* (1995), *Into the Day Breaking* (2000), and *Requiem* (2004). Pursuing love and meaning in the midst of the everyday, and exhibiting a clarity and precision of expression, the poems seek to connect with others and with nature. The vehicle of such connection is seen to be the poetic word itself. Metelerkamp is recipient of the 1991 Sanlam Literary Award.

Mhlongo, Niq (b. 1973) Novelist, short-story writer, scriptwriter. Born in Soweto, Mhlongo is a graduate of the University of the Witwatersrand and works as a journalist. He has published two novels, *Dog Eat Dog* (2004) and *After Tears* (2007), referred to by reviewers as representations in style and content of the "kwaito generation" (kwaito is a harshly rhythmical contemporary musical form that blends township pop with Western house music and hip-hop). Where *Dog Eat Dog* deals with the difficulty university student Dingz has in juggling his studies with his social life, *After Tears* describes the dilemma university dropout Bafana faces when he returns home to the demands made by family and friends on his imagined expertise and influence as a newly qualified lawyer.

Mhlophe, Gcina (b. 1958) Dramatist and short-story writer. Born in Hammarsdale near Durban, Mhlophe went to school in the Transkei. She was raised by her grandmother, who made a lasting impression on her, not least because she passed on to her granddaughter a wealth of traditional tales. She was later taken back by her mother. Some of these experiences are worked into her play *Have You Seen Zandile?* (1989). Her well-known autobiographical short story "The Toilet," first published in the anthology *Sometimes When It Rains* (1987), recounts the protagonist's struggle to find her feet in the working world of Johannesburg. With no place to gain privacy, she resorts to holing up in a whites-only public toilet, where she begins writing, an experience that opens up a world of creativity and self-expression. "Nokulunga's Wedding," first published in *LIP from South African Women* (1983), deploys an oral storytelling style to reflect critically on patriarchal practices in African society. Mhlophe has devised many stage productions, most notably for the Market Theatre in Johannesburg, including the popular *Inyanga: About Women in Africa* (staged in 1989). She has presented numerous traditional stories on stage and has written several children's books, including *The Snake with Seven Heads* (1989), *Queen of the Tortoises* (1990), *The Singing Dog* (1992), *A Mother's Search for Stories* (1995), *Nalohima, the Deaf Tortoise* (1999), *Fudukaz's Magic: A Traditional Southern African Tale* (1999), and *Nozincwadi, Mother of Birds* (2001). Story collections include *Stories from Africa* (1997), *An African Mother Christmas* (2002), *Stories from Africa* (2003), *Songs and Stories of Africa* (2006), and *Love Child, Our Story Magic* (2006). Mhlophe was awarded an honorary doctorate by the University of Natal in 1998.

FURTHER READING

Tyrone August, "Interview with Gcina Mhlophe," *Journal of Southern African Studies* 16, no. 2 (1990): 329–335; Cherry Clayton, "Radical Transformations: Emergent Women's Voices in South Africa," *English in Africa* 17, no. 2 (1990): 25–36; Pamela Ryan, "Black Women Do Not Have Time to Dream: The Politics of Time and Space," *Tulsa Studies in Women's Literature* 11, no. 1 (1992): 95–102; Zoë Wicomb, "Reading, Writing, and Visual Production in the New South Africa," *Journal of Commonwealth Literature* 30, no. 2 (1995): 1–15; Rolf Solberg and Malcolm Hacksley, eds., *Reflections: Perspectives on Writing in Postapartheid South Africa* (1996); Miki Flockemann and Thuli Mazibuko, "Between Women: An Interview with Gcina Mhlophe," *Contemporary Theatre Review* 9, no. 1 (1999): 41–51; Dennis Walder, "The Number of Girls Is Growing: An Interview with Gcina Mhlophe," *Contemporary Theatre Review* 9, no. 1 (1999): 27–39; Michael Picardie, "A Comparative Perspective on Two Plays by South African Women," *Contemporary Theatre Review* 9, no. 2 (1999): 39–50; Haike Frank, *Role-Play in South African Theatre* (2004); Jennifer Delisle, "Finding the Future in the Past: Nostalgia and Community-Building in Mhlophe's *Have You Seen Zandile?*" *Journal of Southern African Studies* 32, no. 2 (2006): 387–401.

Miller, Kirsten (b. 1973) Novelist. A graduate of the University of KwaZulu-Natal, Miller has worked as a university lecturer, creativity teacher, and dolphin trainer. She lives in Durban and currently works with autistic children. Miller has published the nonfiction study *Children on the Bridge: A Story of Autism in South Africa* (2006) and the novel *All Is Fish* (2007). The latter concerns the relationship of twins Jonathan and Sarah, as narrated by Simon, a childhood friend who returns to rural Mtunzini to confront his past.

Miller, Ruth (1919–1969) Poet, short-story writer, radio playwright. Born in Uitenhage, Eastern Cape, and raised in Pietersburg (now Polokwane), she worked as typist and later as English teacher in Johannesburg.

Miller published two volumes of poetry, *Floating Island* (1965) and *Selected Poems* (1968). She also wrote two verse plays for the radio, *The Finches* (date unknown) and *Ice* (date unknown), as well as a play, *Fact* (date unknown). Her collected works, *Ruth Miller: Poems, Prose, Plays*, edited by Lionel *Abrahams, was published in 1990.

Miller's poems offer brooding and frequently dark reflections on mortality and violence, often in the context of the elemental forces of nature. With pain described in one poem as the speaker's "daily bread," the poems evince a lyrical introspection that edges, at times, toward the melancholic. Morbidity is held at bay by clarity of imagery and a sure control of tone, with the result that the poems resolutely resist self-indulgence and self-pity. Miller was the recipient of the 1965 Ingrid Jonker Memorial Prize.

FURTHER READING

Michael Chapman, *South African English Poetry: A Modern Perspective* (1984); Michael Chapman et al., eds., *Perspectives on South African English Literature* (1992); Michael Chapman, "Ruth Miller: Breaking Silences?" *English Academy Review* 7 (1990): 13-23; Joan Metelerkamp, "Ruth Miller: Father's Law or Mother's Lore," *Current Writing* 4, no. 1 (1992): 57–71; Wendy Woodward, "Dog(s) of the Heart: Encounters Between Humans and Other Animals in the Poetry of Ruth Miller," *English Academy Review* 18 (2001): 73–86.

Millin, Sarah Gertrude *See* Writers Before 1945

Modisane, (William) Bloke (1923–1986) Short-story writer, autobiographer, journalist, broadcaster. Born in Sophiatown, where he was reared amid township poverty and violence, with his father murdered and his mother running a shebeen to make ends meet, he worked at the Vanguard bookshop before becoming a journalist with *Drum* magazine and a jazz critic for the *Golden City Post*. Associated with the vibrant cultural life of 1950s Sophiatown, a culture strongly influenced by American gangster films and jazz music, he published his short stories in *Drum*, and acted in the first performance of Athol *Fugard's play *No Good Friday* and also in the film *Come Back Africa*. In 1959 he went into exile in London, where he worked as broadcaster for the BBC, acted in Jean Genet's *The Blacks*, and appeared in *Waiting for Wenda* on the BBC. He was banned under the Suppression of Communism Act in 1966.

Modisane published an autobiography, *Blame Me on History* (1963). The book is a frank portrayal of life in the Sophiatown of his youth, simultaneously exposing the brutality of apartheid rule and evincing nostalgia for a culture that had been destroyed by the state's policy of forced removals.

FURTHER READING

Jean Coste, "The Masks of Modisane," *World Literature Written in English* 19 (1971): 45–54; Thengani H. Ngwenya, "The Ontological Status of Self in Autobiography: The Case of Bloke Modisane's *Blame Me on History*," *Current Writing* 1, no. 1 (1989): 67–76; Paul Gready, "The Sophiatown Writers of the Fifties: The Unreal Reality of Their World," *Journal of Southern African Studies* 16, no. 1 (1990): 139–164; Mark Sanders, "Responding to the 'Situation' of Modisane's *Blame Me on History*: Towards an Ethics of Reading in South Africa," *Research in African Literatures* 25, no. 4 (1994): 51–67; Liz Gunner, "Exile and the Diasporic Voice: Bloke Modisane's BBC Radio Plays 1969–1987," *Current Writing* 15, no. 2 (2003): 49–62.

Moele, Kgebetli (b. 1978) Novelist. A student in Johannesburg, Moele made his debut with *Room 207* (2006), which portrays the lives of six young men who share a room in a derelict block of flats in Hillbrow, Johannesburg, living by their wits to survive in a harsh environment where criminality, xenophobia and sexism are the norm and dreams edge on despair.

Moolman, Kobus (b. 1964) Poet, short-story writer, radio playwright. Previously education officer at the Tatham Art Gallery, he teaches creative writing at the University of KwaZulu-Natal in Durban. He has published two volumes of poetry, *Time Like Stone* (2000), which won the Ingrid Jonker Prize for 2001, and *Separating the Seas* (2007), both of which are distinguished by finely honed poems of clarity and stillness. He has also published *Blind Voices: A Collection of Radio Plays* (2007).

Morojele, Morabo (b. 1960) Novelist. Born in Lesotho and raised in Ethiopia, Morojele studied at the London School of Economics and the Institute of Social Sciences at The Hague, has been employed in various international organizations and consulting firms, and has performed in several jazz groups. He is the author of the novel *How We Buried Puso* (2006), which describes an exile's return to his hometown after a seven-year absence, where the burial of his brother reawakens childhood memories and obliges him to confront the displacements and alienation of his diasporic identity.

Motsisi, Casey (Karabo Moses) (1932–1977) Short-story writer and columnist. Born in Western Native Township, Motsisi attended school at Madibane High and trained as a teacher at Pretoria Normal College. He interrupted his studies to become a journalist with *Drum* in the mid-1950s and also worked on *The World* for a short period. Writing as "The Kid," he achieved renown for his column "On the Beat," which he wrote for *Drum* magazine between 1958 and 1977. His style is lively and inventive in the Damon Runyon mould. "Kid Playboy," for example, describes a wedding ceremony that goes awry when a girl arrives and interrupts proceedings by presenting a baby to the groom, claiming that he is the infant's father. Other stories describe life in Sophiatown shebeens and various picaresque escapades in which Motsisi and his colorful characters engage. Motsisi is also known for his poem "The Efficacy of Prayer," which in its free structure and rhythms anticipates the new wave of black poetry in the 1970s. A selection of his prose pieces appeared as *Casey & Co.: Selected Writings of Casey 'Kid' Motsisi* (1978), edited by Mothobi *Mutloatse.

FURTHER READING

Es'kia Mphahlele, "The Language of African Literature," *Harvard Educational Review* 34, no. 2 (1964): 298–305; Paul Gready, "The Sophiatown Writers of the Fifties: The Unreal Reality of their World," *Journal of Southern African Studies* 16, no. 1 (1990): 139–164.

Mpe, Phaswane (1970–2004) Novelist. Born in Polokwane, Phaswane Mpe studied at the University of the Witwatersrand, where he subsequently lectured in African literature as well as working in the South African publishing industry.

He is the author of two books, the novel *Welcome to Our Hillbrow* (2001), short-listed for the Sanlam Literary Award 2001 and the *Sunday Times* Literary Award for Fiction 2002, and the posthumous collection of short stories and poems *Brooding Clouds* (2007). Written as a prequel to the novel, the thematically linked stories and poems in *Brooding Clouds* anticipate the subsequent concerns with rural, urban and cosmopolitan life in *Welcome to Our Hillbrow*. The latter evokes new forms of communality evolving in the high-density urban landscape of a city that is host to migrants from across Africa, exploring themes of modernization, sexuality, xenophobia, and violence in the context of changing notions of African culture and identity. Mpe received the South African Posthumous Literary Award 2007.

FURTHER READING

Ralph Goodman, "Textuality and Transformation in South African Parodic-Travestying Texts: *Welcome to Our Hillbrow*," *English Academy Review* 20 (2003): 88–97; Rob Gaylard, "'Welcome to the World of Our Humanity': (African) Humanism, Ubuntu and Black South African Writing," *Journal of Literary Studies* 20, nos. 3–4 (2004): 265–282; Michael Green, "Translating the Nation: Phaswane Mpe and the Fiction of Post-Apartheid," *Scrutiny2* 10, no. 1 (2005): 3–16; Lizzy Attree, "Healing with Words: Phaswane Mpe Interviewed," *Journal of Commonwealth Literature* 40, no. 3 (2005): 139–148; Mbulelo

Vizikhungo Mzamane, ed., *Words Gone Two Soon: A Tribute to Phaswane Mpe & K. Sello Duiker* (2005).

Mphahlele, Ezekiel (later, Es'kia) (1919–2008) Short-story writer, novelist, autobiographer. Born in Pretoria, Mphahlele spent his childhood in a village in the Pietersburg area and in the township of Marabastad, outside Pretoria. He was educated at schools in Marabastad and at St. Peter's, Johannesburg. Between 1939 and 1940 he trained as a teacher at Adams College, near Durban, and taught at schools in the Johannesburg area while taking degrees part-time at the University of South Africa. In 1946 his first collection of stories, *Man Must Live and Other Stories*, appeared. Banned from teaching at government schools in 1952 because of his opposition to the introduction of Bantu Education (a government policy of separate and "special" education for blacks), he taught at private schools before joining *Drum* magazine in 1956 as a fiction editor and political reporter. At this time he was awarded a master's degree in English by the University of South Africa for a study entitled "The Non-European Character in South African English Fiction."

In 1957 he went into exile in Nigeria and taught English at the University of Ibadan. Two years later, his autobiography *Down Second Avenue* appeared, describing his life from childhood up to his departure into exile. Perhaps his best-known work, it impressionistically charts the protagonist's passage from country to city, from rural goatherd to educated political exile, from a state of ignorance to one of political awareness. In 1961 his second collection of stories, *The Living and Dead and Other Stories*, appeared, and was followed a year later by a critical work based on his master's thesis, *The African Image* (1962). Between 1962 and 1963 he worked in Uganda, Congo, and Senegal, and settled briefly in Kenya before leaving for the United States to study for a doctorate in creative writing at the University of Denver (1966–68). In 1967 his third collection of stories, *In Corner B and Other Stories*, was published. It contained his classic and much-anthologized "Mrs Plum," an acute and subtle interrogation of white liberalism in South Africa by a black narrator whose steady growth in knowledge and understanding allows her to pry open the liberal ideology of her employer and expose the hypocrisy and injustice that it contains. In 1968 he was awarded a doctorate for the novel *The Wanderers*, which was published in 1971. In 1972, *Voices in the Whirlwind and Other Essays* appeared. After a brief spell of teaching in Zambia, he returned to the United States and taught at the universities of Denver and Pennsylvania. A revised edition of *The African Image* appeared in 1974.

In 1977, Mphahlele returned permanently to South Africa. He was appointed research fellow at the Institute for the Study of English in Africa at Rhodes University in 1979 and later became senior research fellow at the University of the Witwatersrand. His second novel, *Chirundu* (1979), appeared at this time, followed by *The Unbroken Song: Selected Writings* (1981), which contains some of his poetry. In 1983 the Department of African Literature was established at the University of the Witwatersrand, and Mphahlele was appointed to its chair, a position he held until his retirement in 1987. *Afrika My Music: An Autobiography 1957–1983* appeared in 1984, as did his story for teenagers, *Father Come Home*. *Bury Me at the Marketplace: Selected Letters of Es'kia Mphahlele 1943–1980* was also published in 1984. A selection of his stories, *Renewal Time*, appeared in 1988.

As an editor, Mphahlele produced *Modern African Stories* (1964; with Ellis Ayitey Komey); *Thought, Ideology and Literature in Africa* (1970), which contains chapters on African literature and oral tradition by Mphahlele; *The Voice of the Black Writer in Africa* (1980; with Tim *Couzens); *Perspectives on South African English Literature* (1992; with Michael Chapman and Colin Gardner); and *Seasons Come to Pass: A Poetry Anthology for Southern African Students* (1994; with Helen Moffat). A collection of his essays, edited by James Ogude, appeared in 2002 as *Es'kia: Education, African Humanism and Culture, Social Consciousness, Literary Appreciation*, and was followed in 2005 by *Es'kia Continued*.

FURTHER READING

Gerald Moore, *Seven African Writers* (1962); Dennis Duerden and Cosmo Pieterse, *African Writers Talking: A Collection of Interviews* (1972); Bernth Lindfors, *Palaver: Interviews with Five African Writers in Texas* (1972); Ursula Barnett, *Ezekiel Mphahlele* (1976); Adrian Roscoe, *Uhuru's Fire: African Literature East to South* (1977); N. Chabani Manganyi, *Exiles and Homecomings: A Biography of Es'kia Mphahlele* (1983); Catherine Woeber and John Read, *Es'kia Mphahlele: A Bibliography* (1989); Ruth Obee, *Es'kia Mphahlele: Themes of Alienation and African Humanism* (1999); David Attwell, *Rewriting Modernity: Studies in Black South African Literary History* (2005).

Mtshali, Mbuyiseni Oswald Joseph (b. 1940) Poet. Born in Vryheid, Natal, Mtshali worked as a messenger in Johannesburg and began publishing poems in the late 1960s in various literary periodicals. His volume of poems *Sounds of a Cowhide Drum* (1971) introduced the voice of the modern black poet in South Africa, exposing the hardships and injustices suffered by black township residents. Mtshali became known as one of the Soweto Poets (the others were Mafika *Gwala, Sipho *Sepamla, and Mongane *Serote). He spent four years at Columbia University in the late 1970s and returned to work for the Johannesburg daily *The Star*. Thereafter he taught at a private college in Soweto. His second volume of poetry, *Fireflames* (1980), was more radical in tone and was banned. It was not as successful as his first, due possibly to its less nuanced and innovative style. Mtshali also edited *Give Us a Break: Diaries of a Group of Soweto Children: A Collection of Anecdotes, Episodes, Incidents, Events and Experiences of a Group of School Children from Pace College, Soweto* (1988). He was awarded the Olive Schreiner Prize for his poetry in 1975.

FURTHER READING

Ursula Barnett, "Interview with Oswald Mbuyiseni Mtshali," *World Literature Written in English* 12, no. 1 (1973): 26–35; John F. Povey, "I Am the Voice: Three South African Poets: Dennis Brutus, Keorapetse Kgositsile, and Oswald Mbuyiseni Mtshali," *World Literature Written in English* 16, no. 2 (1977): 263–280; Michael Chapman, ed., *Soweto Poetry* (1982); Colin Gardner, "Irony and Militancy in Recent Black Poetry," *English Academy Review* 3 (1985): 81–88.

Mutloatse, Mothobi (b. 1952) Short-story writer, playwright, editor, journalist. Born in Western Township, Johannesburg, he has worked as journalist at the *Golden City Post*, *Weekend World*, and *The Voice*. He founded the cultural movement Medupe in 1976 and is founder of the publishing house Skotaville.

Mutloatse has published a collection of stories, *Mama Ndiyalila* (1982), and one children's book, *The Boy Who Could Fly* (1990). He has also written two unpublished plays, "Lakutshou'ilanga" (1989) and "Baby Come Duze" (1990). The novella *Mama Ndiyalila* describes the impact of political events on black middle-class aspirations.

As editor, Mutloatse has endeavored to document and preserve black writing. He has edited *Casey and Co.: Selected Writings of Casey 'Kid' Motsisi* (1978) and what he calls an "Azanian Trilogy," comprising *Forced Landing: Africa South Contemporary Writing* (1980), *Reconstruction: 90 Years of Black Historical Literature* (1981), and *Umhlaba Wethu: A Historical Indictment* (1984). Africanist in intent, the first book in the trilogy is a collection of recent writings in various genres; the second is a historical profile of black writing in South Africa; and the third, aimed at providing an alternative people's history, features diverse reflections ranging from the autobiographical to subjects such as African music. He has also edited *Hope and Suffering: Sermons and Speeches* by Desmond Tutu (1983), *Tauza: Bob Gosani's People* (2005; with Jacqui Masiza and Lesley Hay-Whitton), *Soweto '76: Reflections on the Liberation Struggles* (2006; with Ali Khangela Hlongwane and Sifiso Ndlovu) and *The Women's Freedom March of 1956* (2006; with Marie Human and Jacqui Masiza).

FURTHER READING

Dieter Welz, ed., *Writing Against Apartheid: South African Writers Interviewed* (1987); Horst Zander, "Prose-poem-drama: 'Proemdra': 'Black Aesthetics' Versus 'White Aesthetics' in South Africa," *Research in African Literatures* 30, no. 1 (1999): 12–33.

Mutwa, Credo (Vusa'mazulu) (b. 1921)

Short-story writer and dramatist. Born in Natal (now KwaZulu-Natal), he was raised for a while by his grandfather, a *sangoma*, when his parents parted shortly after his birth. Subsequently reclaimed by his father, he moved to a rural area outside Potchefstroom in 1928. He trained as a *sangoma* and worked for many years in a Johannesburg curio shop. His tales, drawn from African oral tradition but published in English, appeared under the titles *Indaba My Children* (1966; new edition 1998) and *Africa Is My Witness* (1966). A selection from the latter was published as *My People: Writings of a Zulu Witchdoctor* (1969). His play *u Nosilimela* appeared in *South African People's Plays* (1981), edited by Robert Kavanagh. In the 1990s his stories about African animals and folklore were published in serial form in *Drum*. Recent collections of his tales include *Isilwane: The Animal—Tales and Fables of Africa* (1996) and *African Signs of the Zodiac* (1997). Other books by Mutwa include *African Symbols of Goodwill* (1997), *African Proverbs* (1997), and *Zulu Shaman: Dreams, Prophecies, and Mysteries* (2003).

FURTHER READING

Bhekizizwe Peterson, "Apartheid and the Political Imagination in Black South African Theatre," *Journal of Southern African Studies* 16, no. 2 (1990): 229–245; Sikhumbuzo Mngadi, "'Popular Memory' and Social Change in South African Historical Drama of the Seventies in English: The Case of Credo Mutwa's *Unosilimela*," *Alternation* 1, no. 1 (1994): 37–41; Sikhumbuzo Mngadi, "The Antinomies and Possibilities of 'Radical' Historical Consciousness: The Case of Three South African Playtexts in English," *Alternation* 3, no. 1 (1996): 30–55; David Chidester, "Credo Mutwa, Zulu Shaman: The Invention and Appropriation of Indigenous Authenticity in African Folk Religion," *Journal for the Study of Religion* 15, no. 2 (2002): 65–86.

Mzamane, Mbulelo (b. 1948)

Short-story writer, novelist, poet. Born in Brakpan and raised in Soweto, he received his secondary schooling in Swaziland and his tertiary education at the University of Botswana, Lesotho and Swaziland, where he also taught for many years at the Botswana and Lesotho campuses. He left for the United Kingdom in 1979 and completed a doctorate at the University of Sheffield. He has taught at the University of Sheffield and at the universities of Georgia and Vermont in the United States, and served as vice chancellor of Fort Hare University, Eastern Cape.

Mzamane has published two collections of short stories, *Mzala* (1980), reissued as *My Cousin Comes to Jo'burg and Other Stories* (1981), and *The Children of the Diaspora and Other Stories of Exile* (1996). He has also published one novel, *The Children of Soweto* (1982).

The early stories are notable for their depiction of township life, offering a vibrant and often humorous account of ordinary people in typical situations. The later stories deal with Mzamane's experience of exile. The novel, *Children of Soweto*, focuses on the response of the township community to the political events around the Soweto uprising of 1976. Mzamane is also editor of *Selected Poems* by Mongane *Serote (1982) and Sipho *Sepamla (1984) and edited *Hungry Flames and Other Black South African Short Stories* (1986). His recent work includes the critical study *Words Gone Two Soon: A Tribute to Phaswane Mpe and K. Sello Duiker* (2005). He was the joint recipient, with Achmat *Dangor, of the 1979 Mofolo-Plomer Prize.

FURTHER READING

Jane Watts, *Black Writers from South Africa: Towards a Discourse of Liberation* (1989); Kevin Goddard and Andries Wessels, ed., *Out of Exile: South African Writers Speak: Interviews with Albie Sachs, Lewis Nkosi, Mbulelo Mzamane, Breyten Breytenbach, Dennis Brutus, Keorapetse Kgositsile* (1992); Rolf Solberg and Malcolm Hacksley, eds., *Reflections: Perspectives on Writing in Postapartheid South Africa* (1996).

N

Naidoo, Beverley (b. 1943) Novelist and children's author. Born Beverley Trewhela in Johannesburg of English and Russian descent, she grew up as a white child in apartheid South Africa, and witnessed the hardening political realities and racial divisions in the country from 1948 onward. She studied for the BA degree at Wits University from 1961 to 1963, in the wake of the Sharpeville massacre of March 1960, became involved in the antiapartheid movements that sprang up at South Africa universities at this time, and was imprisoned in 1964 under the ninety-day detention law. Released after eight weeks, she soon afterwards went into exile, traveling by ship to London in March 1965. She studied at the University of York, meeting the activist Nandha Naidoo in 1968 and marrying him six months later.

Naidoo began writing in 1980, and the realities of apartheid South Africa formed the subject matter of her work from the start. Naidoo's works are chiefly intended for a young adult readership. *Journey to Jo'burg: A South African Story* (1985) was her first book, and was followed by *Chain of Fire* (1989) (both books were banned in South Africa until 1991). Other works include *No Turning Back* (1995), *Out of Bounds: Stories of Conflict and Hope* (2001), *The Other Side of Truth* (2000) and its sequel *Web of Lies* (2004), and *Burn My Heart* (2007).

One of her plays was included in *New South African Plays* (2006), edited by Charles Fourie, and she has published children's stories, including *Trouble for Letang and Julie* (1994), *Letang and Julie Save the Day* (1994), *Letang's New Friend* (1994), *Where Is Zami?* (1998), *The Great Tug-of-War and Other Stories* (2003), *Baba's Gift*

(2004), and *King Lion in Love and Other Stories* (2004). She has also published a book of critical essays, *Through Whose Eyes? Exploring Racism: Readers, Text and Context* (1992). Naidoo returned to South Africa for the first time in 1991, but now lives in England.

FURTHER READING

Graeme Harper, "As if by Magic: World Creation in Postcolonial Children's Literature," *Ariel* 28, no. 1 (1997): 39–52; Ronit Fainman-Frenkel, "Ordinary Secrets and the Bounds of Memory: Traversing the Truth and Reconciliation Commission in Farida Karodia's *Other Secrets* and Beverley Naidoo's *Out of Bounds*," *Research in African Literatures* 35, no. 4 (2004): 52–65.

Nakasa, Nat (Nathaniel Ndazana) (1937–1965) Columnist. Born in Durban, Nakasa settled in Johannesburg and pursued a career in journalism. He was a regular contributor to *Drum* and *Golden City Post*, and became the first black journalist on the *Rand Daily Mail*, for which he wrote a regular column. In 1963 he founded and edited the literary magazine *The Classic*, which sought to provide a publishing outlet for emerging black writers while promoting the principles of artistic freedom and multiracialism. He collaborated with white writers (including Nadine *Gordimer) in his work on the magazine and for newspapers, and his writing insistently rejected the hardening racial attitudes in the South Africa of the late 1950s and early 1960s.

In 1964 Nakasa was awarded a Nieman Fellowship to study journalism at Harvard. When his application for a passport was rejected he was forced to leave South Africa on an exit permit. He recorded his experiences of America in "Mr Nakasa Goes to Harlem," commissioned by the *New York Times* in 1965. Here he wryly describes the mixed reception he was accorded as an African in black American society. Nakasa died after a fall from a high-rise building in New York. A selection of his writings has been posthumously collected by Essop *Patel as *The World of Nat Nakasa* (1975; expanded edition 1985).

FURTHER READING

Janheinz Jahn, Ulla Schild, and Almut Nordmann, "Two African Writers: Nathaniel Nakasa and Issa Traore," *Research in African Literatures* 5, no. 1 (1974): 66–69; Vernon February, "A Long Way from Home: Reflections on Three Writers: Henry Dumas (1934–1968), Dobru (Robin Ravales, 1935–1983), Nat Nakasa (1937–1965)," *Black American Literature Forum* 22, no. 2 (1988): 227–231.

Ndebele, Njabulo Simakahle (b. 1948) Short-story writer and critic. Born in Western Native Township near Johannesburg, Ndebele moved with his family in 1954 to Charterston Location near Nigel, a small mining town south of Johannesburg. He attended high school in Swaziland, studied at the University of Botswana, Lesotho and Swaziland and between 1973 and 1974 read for a master's degree at Cambridge. In 1975 he joined the teaching staff of the University of Lesotho, where, after completing his doctorate at the University of Denver, he became professor of English and, later, vice chancellor. In 1991 he was appointed professor of African literature at the University of the Witwatersrand. Shortly thereafter he moved to the University of the Western Cape, where he took up the post of vice rector. From 1993 until 1998 he was rector of the University of the North. He then served as vice chancellor of the University of Cape Town until his retirement.

Ndebele is known principally for his collection of short stories *Fools and Other Stories* (1983), which won the 1984 Noma Award, and for his seminal contribution to literary debate in South Africa in the 1980s.

Although his output has been relatively slight in volume, especially in the case of his fiction, his influence on South African literature has been significant. This is due in large measure to his work's divergence from much of the politicized black fiction of the 1970s and 1980s. In some ways Ndebele's writing constitutes a return to more traditional concerns with narrative complexity and literary quality.

Many of Ndebele's most influential postulations are contained in his "Turkish Tales, and Some Thoughts on South African Fiction" (1984). Rejecting protest fiction as an impoverishment of South African writing, Ndebele calls for "storytelling" in the place of "case-making" and praises writers who "give African readers the opportunity to experience themselves as makers of culture." He uses the example of the figure of the oral storyteller on the buses or trains who tells stories of a largely "apolitical" nature as tacit support for his own style of "rediscovering the ordinary."

Fools and Other Stories shows Ndebele attempting to put his theoretical postulates into fictional form. The first story of the collection, entitled "The Test," sees the protagonist taking up a schoolboy challenge to run home in the rain without a shirt on. "The Prophetess" describes a young boy's anxiety in his efforts to procure "holy water" from the local medicine woman for his mother and to get it home safely while running the gauntlet of local street kids. In "The Music of the Violin," a young boy struggles to fend off the values and lifestyle that his overbearing middle-class parents attempt to impose on him.

The longer title story "Fools" describes an intense and troubled relationship that develops between a disgraced schoolteacher and a young, idealistic activist who represents the potential for new life and a new society. It is the most overtly political of the stories and yet the political content is embedded in a complex story line that includes troubled relationships, drunkenness, misunderstandings, and personal defeats.

In the story "Uncle" can be discerned much of what Ndebele expounds in theory. Like the three shorter pieces, the story focuses on the consciousness of a sensitive young boy. The boy's father has died and he is the only child. He has a close, warm relationship with his mother, who is a nurse by profession and a churchgoer with strong principles and a sense of dignity. Into this protected environment arrives the proverbial black sheep of the family, the mother's younger brother, a man in his late twenties but rich in experience of life. His arrival is the catalyst to a number of events that have a profound effect on the impressionable young boy. "Uncle" sows the seeds of social consciousness in his young nephew's mind and provides him with a personal history imbued with traditional African cultural values.

The character "Uncle" in effect redraws the white man's map of South Africa and charges it with the significance that rises out of a uniquely African perspective. His young nephew will begin to experience himself, his family and his people (the black majority at large) as—to use Ndebele's own phrase—"makers of culture;" in other words, as people capable of appropriating the white man's landscape for their own social and political ends.

Ndebele's other fiction includes the children's story *Bonolo and the Peach Tree* (1991) and the novel *The Cry of Winnie Mandela* (2003). His poetry is contained in *To Whom It May Concern: An Anthology of Black South African Poetry* (1973), edited by Robert Royston. His essays have appeared as *Rediscovery of the Ordinary: Essays on South African Literature and Culture* (1991), and in *Fine Lines from the Box: Further Thoughts on Our Country* (2007).

FURTHER READING

Raoul Granqvist and John A. Stotesbury, eds., *African Voices: Interviews with Thirteen African Writers* (1989); Bernth Lindfors, ed., *Kulankula: Interviews with Writers from Malawi and Lesotho* (1989); Jane Wilkinson, ed., *Talking with African Writers: Interviews with African Poets, Playwrights and Novelists* (1992); Emmanuel Ngara, *New Writing from Southern Africa: Authors Who Have Become Prominent Since 1980* (1996); Derek Wright, ed., *Contemporary African Fiction* (1997); Anthony O'Brien, *Against Normalization: Writing Radical Democracy in South Africa* (2001); Stefan Helgesson, *Writing in Crisis: Ethics and History in Gordimer, Ndebele and Coetzee* (2004).

Ngcobo, Lauretta (b. 1932) Novelist and short-story writer. Raised in the Ixopo district of Natal (now KwaZulu-Natal), she received her bachelor's degree from Fort Hare University in 1953. Exiled in 1963 after the political turmoil occasioned by the Sharpeville uprising, she lived in several African countries before settling in London. She returned from exile in 1994.

Ngcobo has published two novels, *Cross of Gold* (1981) and *And They Didn't Die* (1990). She is also the author of the children's book *Fiki Learns to Like Other People* (1993). The novels are both concerned with political events of the 1950s and 1960s in South Africa. *And They Didn't Die* focuses on the rebellion of black women in the late 1950s. Set in rural Natal, it portrays the suffering of women whose husbands are migrant workers and celebrates the solidarity they create in order to survive. *Cross of Gold* focuses on the freedom struggle of the 1960s. It tells a story of oppression and revolt, tracing the fortunes of a young Zulu man who survives the brutalities of hard labor and imprisonment only to meet a violent end as a freedom fighter. Ngcobo is also the editor of *Let It Be Told: Essays by Black Women in Britain* (1988).

FURTHER READING

Raoul Granqvist and John A. Stotesbury, eds., *African Voices: Interviews with Thirteen African Writers* (1989); Eva Hunter and Craig MacKenzie, eds., *Between the Lines II: Interviews with Nadine Gordimer, Menán du Plessis, Zoë Wicomb, Lauretta Ngcobo* (1993); Elleke Boehmer et al., eds., *Altered State?: Writing and South Africa* (1993); Erhard Reckwitz et al., eds., *The African Past and Contemporary Culture* (1993); Ernest N. Emenyonu and Patricia T. Emenyonu, eds., *New Women's Writing in African Literature: A Review* (2004).

Nicol, Mike (b. 1951) Novelist, poet, journalist. Born in Cape Town, Mike Nicol was educated at the University of the Witwatersrand and has worked as a journalist on *The Star*, *African Wildlife Magazine*, and *Leadership*.

He has published two volumes of poetry, *Among the Souvenirs* (1978), winner of the 1979 Ingrid Jonker Prize, and *This Sad Place* (1993). He is the author of the prose work for children *Africana Animals* (1982) and the biographical works *A Good-Looking Corpse* (1991), which describes the lives and times of the *Drum* journalists of the 1950s, and *Bra Henry* (1997), about *Drum* magazine's Henry Nxumalo. He has published an autobiography, *The Waiting Country: A South African Witness* (1995), and an autobiographical travel book, *Sea-Mountain, Fire City: Living in Cape Town* (2001). He collaborated in *Mandela: The Authorised Portrait* (2005), and has also edited several books, including *The Invisible Line: The Life and Photography of Ken Oosterbroek 1962–1994* (1998).

It is as a novelist that Nicol is best known. *The Powers That Be* (1989), *This*

Day and Age (1992), *Horseman* (1994), and *The Ibis Tapestry* (1998) eschew familiar frameworks of time and place in favor of indeterminate settings, but nevertheless draw, even if only obliquely, on South African history. They evoke a violent and apocalyptic world in which fantasy and myth are interwoven with realistic description to create works of what one critic refers to as visionary lyricism. In his most recent novels, *Out to Score* (2006; with Joanne Hichens) and *Payback* (2008), he has turned to the detective thriller, invoking a world of smugglers, drugs, and protection rackets where crime has become the norm and the protagonists are tasked with upholding law and civility.

FURTHER READING

Zelia Roelofse-Campbell, "Enlightened State Versus Millenarian Vision: A Comparison Between Two Historical Novels," *Literator* 18, no. 1 (1997): 83–92; Devi Sarinjeive, "A Magisterial Weave," *English Academy Review* 15 (1998): 303–310; Sandra Chait, "Mythology, Magic Realism, and White Writing After Apartheid," *Research in African Literatures* 31, no. 2 (2000): 17–28; Ralph Pordzik, "Nationalism, Cross-Culturalism, and Utopian Vision in South African Utopian and Dystopian Writing 1972–92," *Research in African Literatures* 32, no. 3 (2001): 177–197; Meg Samuelson, "Cracked Vases and Untidy Seams: Narrative Structure and Closure in the Truth and Reconciliation Commission and South African Fiction," *Current Writing* 15, no. 2 (2003): 63–76; Michael Titlestad and Mike Kissack, "The Secularization of South Africa's Truth and Reconciliation Commission in Mike Nicol's *The Ibis Tapestry*," *Research in African Literatures* 37, no. 4 (2006): 48–67.

Nkosi, Lewis (b. 1936) Novelist, critic, journalist. Born in Durban, he worked for *Ilanga lase Natal, Drum*, and *Golden City Post*. He left South Africa in 1961 on a Nieman Fellowship Award to study journalism at Harvard University, and was barred from returning to South Africa. In 1966 he was banned under the Suppression of Communism Act. Based in London for a long period, he wrote for several newspapers and journals. Subsequently he became a professor of English at the University of Wyoming and thereafter held other academic positions in the United States and Europe.

Nkosi has published one play, *The Rhythm of Violence* (1964), and three novels: *Mating Birds* (1986), which was awarded the 1987 Macmillan PEN Prize for Fiction, *Underground People* (1993), and *Mandela's Ego* (2006). *The Rhythm of Violence* was written shortly after the first bombing campaign by the ANC and PAC in the early 1960s. Focusing on the relationship between a black activist and a white Afrikaner girl, the play deals with issues of multiracialism and violence. *Mating Birds* provides a controversial perspective on the politics of sexual obsession across racial lines with its portrait of a black man imprisoned for the rape of a white woman. *Mandela's Ego* offers a satirical take on the consequences of hero worship, describing how the protagonist, a young Zulu boy, loses his potency when Mandela is imprisoned.

Nkosi is also author of three collections of literary-critical essays: *Home and Exile* (1965), *The Transplanted Heart* (1975), and *Tasks and Masks: Themes and Styles in African Literature* (1981). Characterized by wide reading and subtle argumentation, his essays attempt to articulate an African aesthetic that is cognizant of but not slavishly dependent on European literary tradition.

FURTHER READING

Dennis Duerden and Cosmo Pieterse, eds., *African Writers Talking: A Collection of Interviews* (1972); David Cook, *African Literature: A Critical View* (1977); Stewart Brown,

Writers from Africa (1989); Jane Watts, *Black Writers from South Africa: Towards a Discourse of Liberation* (1989); Mike Nicol, *A Good-Looking Corpse* (1991); Kevin Goddard and Andries Wessels, eds., *Out of Exile: South African Writers Speak: Interviews with Albie Sachs, Lewis Nkosi, Mbulelo Mzamane, Breyten Breytenbach, Dennis Brutus, Keorapetse Kgositsile* (1992); Lindy Stiebel and Liz Gunner, eds., *Still Beating the Drum: Critical Perspectives on Lewis Nkosi* (2005).

Nortje, Arthur Kenneth (1942–1970) Poet. Born in Oudtshoorn and raised in Port Elizabeth, Eastern Cape, he attended Paterson High School, where he was taught by Dennis *Brutus, and graduated from Bellville College (which subsequently became the University of the Western Cape) in 1964. In 1965, after a brief spell of teaching, he took up a scholarship to study at Jesus College, Oxford, and obtained a bachelor's degree. He emigrated to Canada in 1967, where he taught in Hope and Toronto before returning to Oxford in 1970 to continue his studies. He died unexpectedly in December of the same year.

Nortje's poetry has appeared in two posthumous volumes, *Dead Roots* (1973) and *Lonely Against the Light* (1973). A complete edition of his poems, *Anatomy of Dark*, was published in 2000.

The poems deal with themes of exile, alienation, and loss. Intimate in tone and confessional in style, they explore the nature of identity from the vantage point of one whose identity as Coloured is permanently in question in a society polarized along racial lines. Through rigorous self-interrogation, the poems put identity on hold, exposing its contingency and tenuousness, particularly in relation to the "love experience" which acts as basis of the self. The poems are distinguished by their incisiveness and lyricism.

Nortje was joint recipient, with Dennis *Brutus, of the 1962 MBARI Prize for Poetry, and was named on the 1989 Kwanzaa Honors List.

FURTHER READING

Jacques Alvarez-Pereyre, *The Poetry of Commitment in South Africa* (1984); Grant Farred, *Midfielder's Moment: Coloured Literature and Culture in Contemporary South Africa* (2000); Anthony O'Brien, *Against Normalization: Writing Radical Democracy in South Africa* (2001); Craig McLuckie and Ross Tynan, eds., *Arthur Nortje: Poet and South African* (2004).

Novel The South African novel in English is usually dated to Olive Schreiner's *The Story of an African Farm* (1883), although there is at least one earlier work of some consequence. In 1880 Frances Colenso (daughter of Bishop John Willam Colenso) published her fictionalized account of the Langalibalele uprising against the British colonial authorities in Natal in 1873 under the title *My Chief and I*. Although it achieved some fame in its day, it was soon out of print and was only reissued more than one hundred years later in Margaret Daymond's edition, along with its previous unpublished sequel, *Five Years Later*, in 1994.

The Story of an African Farm, however, is justifiably considered South Africa's founding work in the genre of the novel. In its exploration of life on a remote South African farm from a predominantly female (and protofeminist) point of view, Schreiner engaged with many of the issues that were to preoccupy later South African novelists: the harshness of life on the land; the rigid roles prescribed to individuals on the basis of gender; and the interaction of the different races—especially, at this time, Boer and Briton. More universal issues were also tackled: the helplessness of children in the face of adult venality, the crass expediency of individuals in their desire to advance narrow personal ambition, the contingency and fragility of human consciousness in the context of the inexorable forces of nature. Underlying these thematic concerns were considerations of a formal nature that Schreiner was forced to negotiate, chief among them the issue of how one goes about writing a novel that employs a linguistic style appropriate to an African landscape.

In the early years of the twentieth century, Douglas *Blackburn established his reputation in his novelistic portrayals of small-town South African life. His Sarel Erasmus trilogy—*Prinsloo of Prinsloodorp* (1899), *A Burger Quixote* (1903), and *I Came and Saw* (1908)—deal partly with the Boer War and its aftermath, while *Leaven: A Black and White Story* (1908) is an early treatment of the "Jim comes to Jo'burg" theme—the drift to the cities of rural black people and the often disastrous social consequences. Perceval *Gibbon's *Margaret Harding* is another noteworthy novel of the early twentieth century. In its perspicacious and sympathetic treatment of race issues on a Karoo farm, Gibbon takes up many of Schreiner's concerns regarding relations between Boer and Briton, but places a black man at the center of the novel and thus anticipates a theme—miscegenation—that would preoccupy South African novelists for the next half-century.

William *Plomer's *Turbott Wolfe* (1926) dealt squarely and—for the time—challengingly with the theme of love across the racial divide, and it caused a sensation when it was first published. The novel has the fractured style and form of literary modernism (it was first published, significantly, by Leonard and Virginia Woolf's Hogarth Press), and is structured as a series of reminiscences by the protagonist, Turbott Wolfe, as told to one "William Plomer," a former classmate. It deals with a group of people—white and black—who band together to oppose the colonial order in rural Natal by establishing an association called "Young Africa—for the regeneration of our country." Sarah Gertrude *Millin had earlier dealt with the theme of miscegenation in *God's Step-Children* (1924), although in a significantly more conservative manner. Later novels in Millin's "trilogy of the Coloured Race" are *King of the Bastards* (1949) and *The Burning Man* (1952). Pauline Smith's *The Beadle* (1926) is another important novel of this period. Vastly different from the work of both Plomer and Millin in both setting and the thematic concern, Smith's work harks back to the relatively untainted rural world of the nineteenth century, and portrays with great poignancy the personal tragedy of Andrina, the novel's young protagonist, who falls pregnant after a brief affair with a feckless Englishman.

Pioneering novels by black writers appeared in the first few decades of the twentieth century. Thomas Mofolo's *Chaka* (1925), which first appeared in Sesotho, is a narrative based on the life of the Zulu king Shaka. It was translated into English and French in the 1930s and this did much to establish Mofolo's status as one of the most important African writers of the first half of the twentieth century. Commonly considered a historical novel, it is more accurately described as a romance, a blend of folktale, fable, legend, and myth. In its mixing of historical fact and literary imagination it anticipated Sol *Plaatje's *Mhudi: An Epic of South African Life a Hundred Years Ago* (1930). Like Mofolo, Plaatje used South Africa's rich history as the background for his work. The *mfecane* (the dispersion of tribes following the Matabele king Mzilikazi's incursions into the hinterland after his clash with Shaka) provides the larger historical canvas on which Plaatje locates the love story of his principal characters—Mhudi and Ra-Thaga. *Chaka* and *Mhudi* both contain an eclectic blend of literary genres and styles, and this above all marks them off as pioneering works in the genre of the novel. R. R. R. *Dhlomo's novella *An African Tragedy* (1928), noteworthy principally for the fact that it is the first extended work of prose fiction in English by a black South African writer, turns to more contemporary themes in its somber depiction of life in black urban slums.

Alan *Paton's *Cry, the Beloved Country* (1948) is probably South Africa's best-known and most enduring novel. Published in the watershed year of the National Party's accession to power, it sounded a poignant lament for the decline of rural life and social order, and prophesied ominously about the dire consequences for South African society if harmony between the races—and between humankind and nature—was not established. It also signaled a decisive midcentury shift in literary attention from the countryside to the city.

Peter *Abrahams's novels of the 1940s and 1950s registered the plight of black city-dwellers, often deracinated, living in unfamiliar and squalid conditions in urban slums and brutally exploited by industry. His famous *Mine Boy* (1946) is the quintessential "Jim comes to Jo'burg" novel: the protagonist Xuma loses his bucolic innocence when he comes to the city and begins work as a mine laborer. He gains an understanding of the way he is exploited by virtue of his race and class position and comes at the end of the novel to assert his identity as a member of the black working class. The novel is informed by Abrahams's Marxist leanings, and this is one of the earliest manifestations of the increasing radicalization of South African (and mainly black) fiction in the postwar period. Alex *La Guma's novels also reflect this tendency. His first longer work of fiction, the novella *A Walk in the Night* (1962), is set in District Six and deals with the disenchantment of a young Coloured man who loses his job for talking back to a white foreman, and who then accidentally kills a man and joins a gang. His descent into a criminal way of life is clearly meant to be seen as a function of his degrading environment. A similar concern with the plight of the poor underclasses of Cape Town's slums is evident in his next work, *And a Threefold Cord* (1964). In his later novels *In the Fog of the Seasons' End* (1972) and *Time of the Butcherbird* (1979), La Guma shifts to more overtly political concerns and these works contain an implicit call to action on the part of the oppressed classes. *In the Fog of the Seasons' End* focuses on a general strike in Cape Town and sounds the call to armed revolt, while *Time of the Butcherbird* deals with black land dispossession in rural South Africa.

The Soweto disturbances of 1976 spawned a number of novels by black writers, including Miriam *Tlali's *Amandla* (1980), Mongane Wally *Serote's *To Every Birth Its Blood* (1981), Sipho *Sepamla's *A Ride on the Whirlwind* (1981), and Mbulelo *Mzamane's *The Children of Soweto* (1982). These novels further entrenched the tendency toward increased politicization and radicalization in the fiction of black South African writers.

Running in parallel with these developments are the novels of one of South Africa's foremost novelists, Nadine *Gordimer. Her early novels, including *The Lying Days* (1953), *A World of Strangers* (1958), and *Occasion for Loving* (1963), show the development of a writer concerned with portraying the minutiae of human relationships in a classic realist style. Her novels of the late 1970s and the 1980s—most notably *Burger's*

Daughter (1979) and *July's People* (1981)—reflect the hardening of South Africa's race relations and the deepening divisions in South African society. Gordimer's shift to a more radical political stance is expressed in the more "committed" nature of her fiction of this period, a tendency that continues until *My Son's Story* (1990). In a novelistic career spanning the period from 1950 to the present, Gordimer perhaps more than any other South African writer has charted the changing nature of twentieth-century South African society.

Other important novelists of the last quarter of the twentieth century are André *Brink and Christopher *Hope. Hope's satirical, deeply iconoclastic style—most in evidence in *Kruger's Alp* (1984) and *The Hottentot Room* (1986)—has long distinguished him as a unique voice in South African fiction. Like Gordimer, Brink's long career as a novelist in some ways mirrors developments in South African society. His novels of the 1970s—*An Instant in the Wind* (1976), *Rumours of Rain* (1978) and *A Dry White Season* (1979)—deal with human relationships in a racially divided society in a social-realist manner. His later work—*A Chain of Voices* (1982), *The Wall of the Plague* (1984), *The First Life of Adamastor* (1993), and particularly *Devil's Valley* (1998)—are concerned as much with the style in which they are written as with the content they convey.

This increasing tendency toward literary self-consciousness and metafictional sophistication is most marked, however, in the novels of J. M.* Coetzee. Indeed, with the appearance of his first novel *Dusklands* in 1974, Coetzee introduced a new dimension to fiction in South Africa. From an almost obsessive concern among South African writers with the details of South African society and politics, Coetzee turned attention to the aesthetic and philosophical underpinnings of fiction. His novels explore issues directly relevant to South African life (colonialism, greed, racism, and the ineradicable differences separating people), but in a manner that is self-conscious and philosophically sophisticated. His settings vary widely from the highly specific—a Karoo farm in *In the Heart of the Country* (1977), Cape Town in *Age of Iron* (1990) and *Disgrace* (1999)—to the indeterminate: an outpost of empire in *Waiting for the Barbarians* (1980), an unspecified island in *Foe* (1986). His concern throughout, however, is to probe at the nature of language and the writing of fiction, and to challenge more orthodox assumptions about the role of writing in a deeply politicized and divided society.

Coetzee's metafictional writing has opened up new vistas for South African fiction, and his Booker Award–winning *Disgrace* was a major event in South African literature. Novelists whose work may differ fairly substantially in style to his but who are in some way indebted to him include Mike *Nicol (*The Powers That Be*, 1989; *Horseman*, 1994; *The Ibis Tapestry*, 1998), Ivan *Vladislavić (*The Folly*, 1993), Elleke *Boehmer (*Screens Against the Sky*, 1990; *An Immaculate Figure*, 1993), and Damon *Galgut (*Small Circle of Beings*, 1988; *The Good Doctor*, 2003). Zakes *Mda's novels, such as *She Plays with the Darkness* (1995) and *Ways of Dying* (1995), also deploy features of metafiction and fantasy, suggesting that a decisive break with the predominantly social-realist, overtly political novels of the 1970s and 1980s has been made.

Nyatsumba, Kaizer (b. 1963) Short-story writer, poet, journalist. Born in White River in the Eastern Transvaal (now Mpumalanga), he is a graduate of the University of Zululand. He also studied in the United States at Georgetown University in Washington DC and the Newspaper Institute of America in New York. Returning to South Africa in 1985, he worked for the *Argus* newspaper group, later doing an advanced training course in news editing in Manchester, England. He is a founder member of the African Writers Association (AWA).

Nyatsumba has published two collections of short stories: *A Vision of Paradise* (1991) and *In Love with a Stranger and Other Stories* (1995). He has also published two volumes of poetry: *When Darkness Falls* (1990) and *Silhouettes* (1999). Nyatsumba endeavored, in his critical and creative writing, to formulate a mode of expression that goes beyond what he saw as the artistically stifling obsession with apartheid and the formulaic writing that has resulted from this obsession. He is also the author of *All Sides of the Story: A Grandstand View of South Africa's Political Transition* (1997).

FURTHER READING

Sikhumbuzo Mngadi, "Some Thoughts on Black Male Homosexualities in South African Writing: Zakes Mda's 'The Hill' and Kaizer Nyatsumba's 'In Happiness and in Sorrow,'" *English in Africa* 32, no. 2 (2005): 155–168.

O

Oliphant, Andries Walter (b. 1955) Poet, short-story writer, critic and editor. Born in Heidelberg, Oliphant was educated at the University of the Western Cape and the University of Oregon in the United States, where he was a Fulbright Scholar. He holds a master's degree in comparative literature. He has been involved in independent publishing in South Africa as an editor of Ravan Press and *Staffrider* magazine and later as general editor of the publishing house of the Congress of South African Writers. He played a leading role in the development of arts, culture, and media policies for a democratic South Africa in his capacities as chair of the National Arts Coalition and later as chair of the Arts and Culture Task Group appointed by the Minister of Arts, Culture, Science and Technology.

His poetry is collected in *At the End of the Day* (1988). He has edited numerous collections of South African fiction and criticism, including *Ten Years of Staffrider, 1978–1988* (1988; coedited with Ivan Vladislavić); *The Finishing Touch: Stories from the Nadine Gordimer Short Story Award* (1992); *Essential Things: An Anthology of New South African Poetry* (1992); *Culture and Empowerment: Writings, Art and Photography from the Zabalaza Festival* (1993); *The Change of Seasons and Other Stories* (1995); *A Writing Life: Celebrating Nadine Gordimer* (1998); and *At the Rendezvous of Victory and Other Stories* (1999). A leading voice in the debate on transforming the arts in the new South Africa, his essays and reviews on South African literature, art, and culture have appeared regularly in local and international newspapers and journals. He is also the author of a book on the artist Kagiso Pat Mautloa (2003) and collaborated with Peter Delius and Lalou Meltzer on *Democracy X: Marking the Present, Re-Presenting the Past* (2004).

He was awarded an Amstel Playwright of the Year Award for his play "The Bicycle" in 1979; the Hippogriff Award for Children's Poetry in 1988; the English Academy of Southern Africa's Thomas Pringle Award for Short Stories in 1992 and the International Literary Scholarship of the Foundation for the Creative Arts in 1994. In 1998 he received the National Book Journalist of the Year Award.

FURTHER READING

Colin Gardner, "Negotiating Poetry: A New Poetry for a New South Africa," *Theoria* 77 (1991): 1–14.

P

Packer, Joy (1905–1977) Novelist and autobiographer. Born in Cape Town and married to a high-ranking British naval officer, she lived in the Far East, Turkey, Greece, Yugoslavia, and London before retiring in the Cape.

Packer published six autobiographical works: *Pack and Follow: One Person's Adventures in Four Different Worlds* (1945), *Grey Mistress* (1949), *Apes and Ivory* (1953), *Home from the Sea* (1963), *The World Is a Proud Place* (1966), and *Deep as the Sea* (1977). She also published ten popular novels: *Valley of the Vines* (1955), *Nor the Moon by Night* (1957), *The High Roof* (1957), *The Glass Barrier* (1961), *The Man in the Mews* (1964), *The Blind Spot* (1967), *Leopard in the Fold* (1969), *Veronica* (1970), *Boomerang* (1972), and *The Dark Curtain* (1977).

FURTHER READING

John A. Stotesbury, *Apartheid, Liberalism and Romance: A Critical Investigation of the Writing of Joy Packer* (1996).

Padayachee, Deena (b. 1953) Short-story writer. Born in Durban and raised in Umhlali, north of Durban, Padayachee trained at the University of Natal as a medical doctor. His short stories, which have won him prizes from the Grahamstown Festival of the Arts and the South African Writers' Circle, are collected as *What's Love Got to Do With It?* (1992). He is recipient of the 1991 Nadine Gordimer Short Story Award for his story "The Finishing Touch," which concerns a conscience-stricken Indian businessman who adopts a European name after much tribulation. Another of his stories, "The Guests," touches deftly on the subject of forced removals by focusing on a personal friendship that develops between a teenage Indian girl and a young white boy whose family occupies her former home. Padayachee is also the author of the collection of poetry *A Voice from the Cauldron* (1986).

Patel, Essop (1943–2007) Poet and editor. Born in Germiston, he lived in Europe for several years before returning to South Africa to study law at the University of the Witwatersrand. He practiced as an advocate in Botswana and South Africa, concentrating on human rights and public interest matters.

Patel published three volumes of poetry: *They Came at Dawn* (1980), *Fragments in the Sun* (1985), and *The Bullet and the Bronze Lady* (1987). His poems also appeared in the anthology *Exiles Within: An Anthology of Poetry* (1986). They are largely poems of revolt in which aesthetic considerations are subordinated to political exigencies.

Patel edited *The World of Nat Nakasa* (1975) and *The World of Can Themba* (1985), and coedited *The Return of the Amasi Bird: Black South African Poetry 1891–1981* (1982) with Tim *Couzens. Patel was cited on the 1991 Kwanzaa Honors List.

FURTHER READING

Jane Wilkinson, ed., *Talking with African Writers: Interviews with African Poets, Playwrights and Novelists* (1992); Rajendra Chetty, *South African Indian Writings in English* (2002).

Pater, Elias (1916–1999) Poet. Pen name for Jacob Friedman. Born in Cape Town and trained as a doctor, he left South Africa to study for the priesthood in England.

From 1954 he served as a Carmelite monk at Stella Maris Monastery in Israel.

Pater published five volumes of poetry: *In Praise of Night* (1969), *Variations on Bialik Themes* (1970), *Jerusalem Sonnets: Collected Poems* (1983), *Mount Carmel: Poems from a Garden* (1988), and *Views from a Window: The Selected Poems of Elias Pater* (1992). Intensely spiritual, the poems deal with experiences of doubt and revelation. Pater received the 1971 Olive Schreiner Award for Literature.

Paton, Alan (Stewart) (1903–1988) Novelist, poet, short-story writer, biographer. Born in Pietermaritzburg, Paton began his working life as a teacher, first at Ixopo High and then at his old school, Maritzburg College. In 1935 he was appointed principal at Diepkloof Reformatory, near Johannesburg, for African juvenile offenders. He held this post for thirteen years, and it was during this period that he wrote his famous novel *Cry, the Beloved Country* (1948). In South Africa this novel has outsold all books with the exception of the Bible, and between sixteen million and seventeen million copies have been sold worldwide. It has been translated into seventeen languages and is never out of print.

Cry, the Beloved Country is the story of two families, the Kumalos and the Jarvises, whose lives are brought into violent intersection by the actions of their sons, Absalom and Arthur. Absalom has left Ndotsheni, near Ixopo in rural Natal, for Johannesburg, where he falls into bad company and a life of crime. He kills Arthur Jarvis (ironically, an outspoken proponent of liberal reform) in his Johannesburg home during a robbery and is convicted and hanged for the crime. The novel deals principally with the journey each father takes to Johannesburg to "find" his son (in both a literal and metaphorical sense). After this period of hardship and suffering, the two families return to rural Natal, where they have been neighbors (although scarcely aware of each other), to a new life of reconciliation and cooperation.

The novel's lament at the breakdown of traditional rural community life and the consequences of this for South Africa struck a prophetic note at the time of its publication: thereafter, the gathering pace of National Party–inspired racial legislation in the 1950s and 1960s brought about the irreversible degeneration of rural communities and the social fabric of South Africa. This process is adumbrated by the thematic patterning in *Cry, the Beloved Country*: rural innocence (Ndotsheni) becomes contrasted with urban degeneration (the slums of Johannesburg), where hope and pride are subverted by crime and degradation.

Paton's second novel, *Too Late the Phalarope* (1953), deals with the familiar South African theme of "miscegenation" by exploring the tragic consequences of a young Afrikaans man's illicit sexual liaison with a Coloured woman. Paton brings to this familiar theme a penetrating analysis of the psychosis of racial prejudice and poignantly evokes the plight of the young man caught between the repressive Calvinism of his family and community and his increasingly uncontrollable sexual desires. Critics have argued that it is formally a better work than its illustrious predecessor and deserves to be better known. His last novel, *Ah, But Your Land Is Beautiful* (1981), is set in the years 1952 to 1958 and deals with actual events and characters of the 1950s in a semifictionalized mode.

In 1953 Paton cofounded the South African Liberal Party, and, until its disbanding in 1968, was involved in its service: for three years as national chairman and then as national president for ten years. When the Liberal Party disbanded, largely due to the passing of the Political Interference Act (which prohibited multiracial party membership), he resigned from politics and devoted himself to writing.

His other works include two volumes of autobiography, *Towards the Mountain* (1980), which deals with his life up to 1948, and *Journey Continued* (1988), which begins in 1948, with the publication of *Cry, the Beloved Country* and the fateful National Party election victory, and ends in 1968 with the disbanding of the Liberal Party. His short stories are collected in *Debbie, Go Home* (1961) (published abroad as *Tales from a Troubled Land*) and *More Tales of South Africa* (1967). He also published two substantial biographies: *Hofmeyr* (1964) and *Apartheid and the Archbishop: The Life and Times of Geoffrey Clayton, Archbishop of Cape Town* (1973), and an autobiographical work, *Kontakion for You Departed* (1969), written in tribute to his first wife. Selections of his shorter writings appeared as *The Long View* (1968) and *Knocking on the Door* (1975), which includes some of his poems. A full selection of his poems appeared as *Songs of Africa: Collected Poems* (1995), and a hitherto unknown manuscript was edited for publication by Herman Wittenberg as *Lost City of the Kalahari* (2005).

FURTHER READING

Peter Alexander, *Alan Paton: A Biography* (1994); Edward Callan, *Alan Paton* (1968; rev. ed. 1982); Anne Paton, *Some Sort of Job: My Life with Alan Paton* (1992); Roy Sargeant, *The Principal: Alan Paton's Years at Diepkloof Reformatory* (1997); Richard Peck, *A Morbid Fascination: White Prose and Politics in Apartheid South Africa* (1997); Randolph Vigne, *Liberals Against Apartheid: A History of the Liberal Party in South Africa, 1953–1968* (1997); Jolyon Nuttall, *A Literary Friendship: Alan Paton and Neville Nuttall* (2001); Harold Bloom, ed., *Alan Paton's "Cry, the Beloved Country"* (2004).

Penny, Sarah (b. 1970) Novelist. Born in Cape Town and educated at the universities of Cape Town, Rhodes and St Andrews, Scotland, Penny currently lives in London and as a creative writing tutor at Brunel, as well as a freelancer for a number of publications in Britain and South Africa. She is the author of the memoir *The Witness of Bones* (1997) and the novel *The Beneficiaries* (2002). The latter explores the emergence into adulthood of Lally, whose withdrawal from South African society as she lives in self-imposed exile in London is challenged when she receives a letter from the Truth and Reconciliation Commission requesting her to participate in a hearing into the disappearance of a young black activist. This leads her to embark on a journey of renewal back into her own rural childhood in the Eastern Cape.

Plaatje, Sol T. *See* Writers Before 1945

Plomer, William (Charles Franklyn) (1903–1973) Novelist, short-story writer, poet. Born in Pietersburg to English parents, Plomer spent his early childhood years in the Northern Transvaal (now Limpopo) and was educated at St. John's College, Johannesburg, and Rugby, England. Plomer's father retired to the Natal north coast in 1922, where the family ran a trading station. This provided the setting for some of Plomer's most important fiction, including his controversial novel *Turbott Wolfe* (1926) and the stories "Ula Masondo" (1927) and "The Child of Queen Victoria" (1933).

Turbott Wolfe, which Plomer started when he was nineteen and completed when he was twenty-one, is a precociously intelligent work that stirred white society at the time. It was published by the Hogarth Press, run by Leonard and Virginia Woolf, and the modernist tendencies of the novel are conspicuous. It purports to be the narrative of one Turbott Wolfe, as told to "William Plomer," and concerns Wolfe's experiences in Africa, from whence he has come to England to die (although still a young man). Wolfe (often taken by critics as a representation of the author himself) is employed in a trading store in "Lembuland" (northern Natal) and encounters a range of people, including the missionary Rupert Friston, Caleb Msomi, and his cousin Zachery, who marries Mabel van der Horst and thus introduces the theme of "miscegenation." This group styles itself "Young Africa" and has lengthy discussions about how to shape Africa's future; Wolfe runs up against the police authorities, however, and returns to England. His attraction to a young African girl also broaches the topic of forbidden love across the color bar, but the relationship is never consummated. (This subject is handled more maturely in "The Child of Queen Victoria.") Episodic and fragmented, the novel is frequently criticized for being unsure of its own direction, for attempting too much and resolving too little. The central character himself is also insufficiently developed and motivated, and yet the book has a raw power and sense of urgency that has elicited much debate (much of it vituperative) and controversy.

While *Turbott Wolfe* was being prepared for the press, Plomer met Roy *Campbell and was invited to spend some time with the Campbells at their home on the Natal south coast. There he met Laurens *van der Post, and the three collaborated on producing the literary magazine *Voorslag* in 1926. In September of the same year, Plomer and Van der Post took a ship to Japan; at this time, Plomer's collection of stories *I Speak of Africa* and *Notes for Poems* (both 1927) appeared. Later volumes of short stories are *Paper Houses* (1929), a set of stories about Japan, and *The Child of Queen Victoria* (1933), set in South Africa, Greece, and France. Plomer subsequently made a selection of his stories entitled *Four Countries* (1949); and *Selected Stories* (1985), edited by Stephen *Gray, is a gathering of his African stories.

I Speak of Africa contains the well-known "Ula Masondo," a tale in the "Jim comes to Jo'burg" mold. Ula Masondo leaves his home village in Lembuland for the goldfields of Johannesburg symbolically wrapped in a traditional African blanket. He soon falls into bad company and a life of crime, abandoning his earlier ways; at the story's end, he returns to the village dressed in "European" clothes and with a changed attitude. The twist at the end is that it is he who rejects his family and former way of life (not the other way round) and becomes a pathetic, deracinated figure. The title story of *The Child of Queen Victoria* centers on the dilemma of a traditional Englishman whose attraction to a young African woman in rural Natal threatens to disrupt his conceptual and moral universe. Other memorable stories from this volume are "When the Sardines Came," a tale set on the Natal south coast about an unlikely affair that develops between a married woman and a young Russian man who injures himself while fishing, and "Down on the Farm," about the rivalry between two cousins who live and work on adjoining farms in the Stormberg area of the Eastern Cape.

In 1929, Plomer left Japan for England, where he was to live the rest of his life, working for the publishing house of Jonathan Cape. These years, in which he became a distinguished man of letters and knew many of the important literary figures of the day, are recounted in his two volumes of autobiography *Double Lives* (1943) and *At Home* (1958). These were later revised and combined into one volume entitled *The Autobiography of William Plomer* (1975), with the sections dealing with his life in South Africa appearing posthumously as *The South African Autobiography* (1984).

A prolific writer, Plomer's novels set in England include *Sado* (1931; published in the United States as *They Never Came Back*, 1932), *The Case Is Altered* (1932), *The Invaders* (1934), and *Museum Pieces* (1952). Further volumes of poetry include *The Family Tree* (1929), *The Fivefold Screen* (1932), *Visiting the Caves* (1936), *The Dorking Thigh and Other Satires* (1945), *A Shot in the Park* (1955), *Taste and Remember* (1966), and *Celebrations* (1972). Selections of his poems have appeared as *Selected Poems* (1940) and *Collected Poems* (1960; rev. ed. 1973), with a further *Selected Poems* (with a more South African focus) appearing in 1985. Memorable among these many poems are "A Transvaal Morning," "The Scorpion," "Conquistadors," and the harshly critical "The Boer War."

A miscellany of commentaries, stories and poems was published as *Electric Delights* (1978). He also published a biography, *Cecil Rhodes* (1933), wrote several libretti for operas by Benjamin Britten, and edited *Selections from the Diary of the Rev. Francis Kilvert (1870–1879)* in three volumes (1938–1940; republished in one volume, 1944).

FURTHER READING

John Robert Doyle, *William Plomer* (1969); Peter F. Alexander, *William Plomer: A Biography* (1989); David Ward, *Chronicles of Darkness* (1989); Michael Chapman et al., eds., *Perspectives on South African English Literature* (1992); Michael Wade, *White on Black in South Africa: A Study of English-Language Inscriptions of Skin Colour* (1993); Ann Blake et al., *England Through Colonial Eyes in Twentieth Century Fiction* (2001).

Poetry British settlement of the Cape in the early nineteenth century, together with the founding of an English-language press, created the conditions for the emergence of South African English poetry. In the course of the nineteenth century, Cape newspapers and periodicals published poetry written on a variety of colonial subjects. Ranging from the balladic and heroic to the picturesque and the sentimental, these contributions emulated, in form and style, nineteenth-century poetry published in British magazines of the time.

Michael Chapman has argued that this nineteenth-century Cape poetry reveals two tendencies, the "educated" and the "colloquial." The educated tendency speaks in measured tones and constitutes the mouthpiece of a liberal-humanist perspective. The colloquial tendency employs a racy idiom and popular rhythms and comments satirically on various colonial themes. The former tendency is traditionalist. It is associated with the interests of the intellectual class of administrators and missionaries, and it is characterized by a philanthropic sentiment toward the indigenous inhabitants and an inspired relationship with the natural environment. The latter tendency is populist. It is associated with the disruptive energy of frontier settlers and miners, and is characterized by a cynical view of official colonial policies and a sardonic attitude toward the rough-and-tumble of colonial life.

Poetry anthologies of the nineteenth and early twentieth centuries favor the traditionalist style. In anthologies such as *The Poetry of South Africa*, (1887), *Centenary Book of South African Verse* (1925), and *A Book of South African Poetry* (1959), a pedagogical poetry of sanitized sentiment is promoted at the expense of a poetry of the dissenting voice. Given the fact that readers of poetry are (in the Western tradition) the leisured and moneyed classes, it is not surprising that anthologies of South African poetry have represented middle-class needs and tastes. It was only in the 1970s and 1980s, under the twin influence of political struggle and a radicalized intellectual class, that alternative anthologies, such as *Black Voices Shout* (1974) and *Voices from Within* (1982), began to appear, featuring new or formerly marginalized voices, specifically those of black writers. Academic interest in such voices was subsequently extended to include writing by women, and resulted in anthologies such as *Breaking the Silence: A Century of South African Women's Poetry* (1990).

Thomas *Pringle inaugurated the traditionalist style of poetry. Reared in Scotland, Pringle practiced as an editor, journalist, and poet before emigrating to the Cape in 1820, bringing with him a tradition of neoclassical poetic diction, picturesque detail, and philanthropic sentiment. Demonstrating keen powers of observation, Pringle's *African Sketches* (1834) combines prose journal and poetic description in providing a vivid account of colonial life at the Cape between 1820 and 1826, when Pringle returned to England. After Pringle, there was a relative dearth of significant poetry in this educated, traditionalist style until William Charles *Scully's *The Wreck of the Grosvenor and Other South African Poems* (1886), a collection similarly characterized by a sensitive apprehension of the particularities of the South African landscape and people, but lacking the verbal felicity and visionary intensity of Pringle's poetry.

Andrew Geddes Bain, a contemporary of Pringle, inaugurated the populist style of poetry. Bain's poetry, while politically conservative insofar as it presents the perspective of the settlers rather than of the philanthropists, captures the inflections of the local Cape dialect of English and Dutch. A similarly populist style is evident in Albert Brodrick's *Fifty Fugitive Fancies in Verse* (1875), the first book of poetry to be published in the former Transvaal Republic. Rather than expressing idealistic sentiments, as the educated poetry tends to do, Brodrick's poetry, like the poetry of Bain, projects a realistic, unsentimental voice, employing the ballad and the public epic to comment wryly on politics and society.

It is often noted that between the poetry of Pringle in the 1820s and the poetry of the twentieth century, there is nothing of interest. This depends, of course, on what the reader is looking for. While the effusiveness of Victorian versifying is cloying to contemporary taste, there is much of historical interest in this nineteenth-century poetry, and some literary interest, particularly with regard to the poets mentioned before. Nevertheless, there is a sense in which South African poetry does indeed project a distinctive voice for the first time in the writings of Francis Carey *Slater and Roy *Campbell, who represent important tendencies in the poetry of the early twentieth century.

In his first volumes of poetry, Slater perpetuates the refined, mellifluent style characteristic of much nineteenth-century poetry. However, with the publication of *The Karroo and Other Poems* (1924), languid discursiveness gives way to a taut focus on concrete impressions in which the South African experience is rendered powerfully vivid. This style is carried over to the long poem *Drought: A South African Parable* (1929), an evocative and mesmeric description in which the parched landscape is employed as an analogue of spiritual aridity. Two further volumes are worth mentioning. *Dark Folk and Other Poems* (1935) is a sensitive account of African tribal life in an idiom derived from long familiarity with the Xhosa language and customs. *The Trek* (1938), written to commemorate the centenary of the historical event and intended as a gesture of reconciliation between Afrikaner and Briton, offers an epic account of the heroism as well as fractiousness of the Voortrekker leaders. Slater's *Collected Poems* appeared in 1957.

Innovative to a degree in terms of diction, rhythm, and voice, Slater remains committed to an aesthetics of verbal restraint and emotional equilibrium. The extent of this is evident when his poetry is set alongside Campbell's South African poetry, which, by contrast, exhibits a fierce energy that seeks to rattle the polite tones of middle-class expression. Campbell's long poem *The Flaming Terrapin* (1924), with its vivid imagery, vigorous rhythms and brash pronouncements, extols the qualities of heroic masculinity in the face of what is perceived as Europe's cultural enervation. *The Wayzgoose: A South African Satire* (1928) savages the mediocrity and pretentiousness of the colonial way of life. *Adamastor* (1930), containing those poems for which Campbell is best known in South Africa, touches many themes. Most notable are those poems that celebrate the wild splendor of nature and those that predict a popular insurrection in response to South African racial politics. Campbell's robust poetry makes an interesting contrast to the poetry of his contemporary, William *Plomer, whose ironic and detached comments on South African society reflect a refined and urbane response.

Like Pringle and Bain in respect of nineteenth-century poetry, Slater and Campbell may be seen as representing two tendencies in twentieth-century South African poetry. Slater's poetry extends the cultured style, employing a largely conventional poetic diction, natural imagery, and relying, if not always on fixed metrical schemes, then at least on regular rhythms. Campbell's poetry, on the other hand, is more experimental, and is characterized by unusual diction, a charged symbolic imagery, and flexible, individualized speech patterns.

Aside from the poetry of white South Africans, who, through paying attention to the African context, attempt to provide English-language poetry with a local habitation, the twentieth century also gives rise to black poets such as Herbert Isaac Ernest *Dhlomo. Dhlomo's long poem *Valley of a Thousand Hills* (1941) simultaneously employs a Romantic idiom derived from the British poetic tradition in celebrating the natural beauty of the KwaZulu-Natal landscape, and seeks to invoke an authentic African tribal past. In this regard, the poem prefigures the dilemma later black poets writing in English were to confront. Simply stated, the dilemma revolves around the question of how to reconcile the language of the colonizer with the requirements of a liberatory poetic discourse.

Writing after World War II, Guy *Butler is, in some respects, the last of the colonial poets, imposing closure on a poetic tradition running from Pringle through Scully to Slater. He differs from his predecessors in that he evinces a self-reflexivity absent from their work, confronting head-on the colonial context within which he writes. The title of Butler's first volume of poetry, *Stranger to Europe: Poems 1939–1949* (1952), alludes to the theme of identity that was to preoccupy him throughout his literary career, the parameters of which are established in terms of the relationship between Europe and Africa. What Butler characteristically seeks in his poetry is a synthesis between the two frames of reference, conceived as an integration of the principles of rationality and sensuality represented by Europe and Africa respectively. Subsequent volumes of poetry include *South of the Zambezi: Poems from South Africa* (1966), *Selected Poems* (1975), *Pilgrimage to Dias Cross: A Narrative Poem* (1987), and *Collected Poems* (1999).

At a time when Butler and other white South African poets such as R. N. *Currey and Roy *Macnab were endeavoring to locate themselves as Europeans in an African context, Arthur *Nortje was struggling with his identity as a Coloured of mixed racial origin. Exiled from his home country in the mid 1960s, he employs a confessional style that lyrically explores a cluster of themes converging on love and loss. His particular achievement lies in relating the political and the personal in such a way as to convey a sense of the divided nature of existence, one in which there is no sure ground upon which to establish a system of belief. Influenced by the English poets whom he had studied, and showing a remarkable felicity for image making and a sure ear for rhythm and sound, he nevertheless, like Dennis *Brutus, anticipates the poetry of resistance that was to emerge soon after his early death at twenty-eight years of age. A collection of Nortje's poems, *Anatomy of Dark* (2000), was published posthumously.

Similarly desolate in its evocation of psychic pain is the poetry of Ruth *Miller and Wopko *Jensma. Miller's work, in particular, has been acclaimed for its sensitive, and indeed surgical, anatomy of despair. Appearing in the 1960s, her work has been brought together posthumously in *Ruth Miller: Poems, Prose, Plays* (1991). The individualism of this introverted style of poetry, its formalism and self-involvement bordering, at times, on the incommunicable, becomes, in the poetry of Sydney *Clouts, a contemporary of Miller's, self-absorption in the act of creation itself.

Douglas *Livingstone published the bulk of his poetry at a time of political turmoil in South Africa, when cultural expression was increasingly mobilized as a weapon in the struggle against apartheid. Seemingly out of step with the tenor of his times, when revolutionary content took precedence over formal accomplishment, his poetry is now recognized as embodying individual vision and skilled craftsmanship. While it would be going too far to say that the poetry shares an affinity with the poetry of Campbell, the respective oeuvres are similarly vigorous in style, masculine in perspective, and concerned, at a thematic level, with the instinctual rather than the picturesque aspects of nature. Employing a mixture of the lyrical and the ironic in his examination of both the human condition and the conditions of nature, Livingstone's poems characteristically match the complexities of life with a complex verbal and musical structure. His first significant volume of poetry, *Sjambok and Other Poems from Africa* (1964), establishes the range of themes—nature, sexuality, colonialism, and religion—that typify the later volumes *Eyes Closed Against the Sun* (1970), *A Rosary of Bone* (1975), and *The Anvil's Undertone* (1978). His volume *A Littoral Zone* (1991), which alludes to the area where sea meets land, is particularly interesting in the way it incorporates his interests as marine biologist, resulting in a poetry that is at once focused on empirical particularities and suggestive of the mysteries of existence.

The 1970s were characterized by an efflorescence of poetry inspired by the Black Consciousness movement and its tenets of self-liberation. Poets such as Oswald *Mtshali, Sipho *Sepamla, and Mafika *Gwala rose to prominence in a context where those who had been marginalized by apartheid found an audience receptive to the incipient voices of resistance. The most significant black poet to emerge during this period was Mongane Wally *Serote. At once introspective and rhetorical, poignant and bitter, his poetry seeks to make readers aware of the human degradation and desolation of township life under apartheid rule. The title of his first volume of poetry, *Yakhal'inkomo* (1972), draws attention to the way in which the violence of apartheid is internalized and becomes a force of self-destruction in the victims. This concern with community is evident also in the second volume *Tsetlo* (1974). The most engaging expressions of his individuality are to be found in the subsequent volumes *No Baby Must Weep* (1975) and *Behold Mama, Flowers* (1978), where an increasing militancy against social repression is evident. Invoking personal and national history, these volumes, each constituting long poems employing a stream of consciousness technique, delve into the past in an attempt to project a viable future. The later volumes, *Third World Express* (1992), *Come Hope with Me* (1994), and *Freedom Lament Song* (1997), while still concerned with the past, are generally orientated toward the future, addressing themselves to issues of liberation and reconstruction.

Revealing a different affiliation from that of Serote, Mazisi *Kunene has sought, like Dhlomo before him, to reconstruct a tribal African past in a modern idiom. *Zulu Poems* (1970), *Emperor Shaka the Great* (1979), *Anthem of the Decades* (1981), and *The Ancestors and the Sacred Mountain* (1982) reveal a trajectory that moves from history to mysticism as Kunene endeavors increasingly to convey the spiritual essence of African culture rather than simply its external historical and cultural achievements.

The oral tradition of Africa has been incorporated into contemporary poetic forms in various ways, where it has tended to serve a sociopolitical rather than strictly aesthetic function. In the work of Mzwakhe *Mbuli, whose live performances roused audiences at political rallies during the 1980s, the oral tradition merges with dub and rap. Mbuli's albums *Change Is Pain* (1986), *Resistance and Defence* (1992), and *Africa* (1993) employ a discourse of liberation that is eclectic in its use of biblical allusion and the rhetoric of mass mobilization. In the performances of another oral poet, Alfred Qabula, the oral tradition is even more directly evident. Here the praise poem is adapted to the concerns of workers in strengthening union organization and lambasting the exploitative capitalist bosses.

While black poetry in the 1970s and 1980s tended toward political expression, white poetry, with some exceptions, continued to explore more private themes. In his eschewal of direct political statement in favor of a depiction of personal relationships and an invocation of natural and urban landscapes, Stephen Watson continues the preoccupations of poets such as Lionel Abrahams, Douglas Reid Skinner, Patrick Cullinan, and Don Maclennan. Introspective and reflective, Watson's poetry evinces a disenchanted romanticism in the volumes *In This City* (1986), *Cape Town Days* (1989) *Presence of the Earth* (1995), and *The Other City: Selected Poems* (2000), where absence seems to be the condition of possibility of human desire. *Return of the Moon* (1991) differs markedly from the other volumes in form and content. Drawing on transcriptions of Khoisan lore, it seeks to convey something of the worldview of this remarkable hunter-gatherer people, whose spirituality is brought vividly to life.

In some respects the division evident in nineteenth-century and early twentieth-century poetry, between the traditionalist and the popular, has continued to operate in South African poetry, and is evident most noticeably in the split between white poetry and black poetry. If white poetry has become increasingly individualistic and academic, black poetry has been characterized by a foregrounding of the communal rather than the individual, and by a directness of expression defying the poetics of restraint. Nevertheless, there have been white poets such as Peter *Horn, Jeremy *Cronin, and Kelwyn *Sole who have attempted, in their work, to bridge the divide between the personal and the political, the erudite and the everyday. Horn has consistently presented the struggle in South Africa as a class struggle rather than a racial or even a nationalist one, offering fresh possibilities of identification and opposition. *Civil War Cantos* (1987) employs colloquial speech patterns, a communal voice, and a political frame of reference in articulating popular resistance to capitalist oppression. "The Plumstead Elegies" (*Selected Poems*, 1991) makes use of psychoanalytic and materialist perspectives in giving expression to a vision of freedom at once psychical and political. Then there have also been black poets who, like Lesego *Rampolokeng, have eschewed the poetry of community to project a highly individualistic vision of contemporary social malaise.

Another kind of bridging of discursive boundaries is evident in the work of Tatamkulu *Afrika, who published his first volume of poetry, *Nine Lives* (1991), when he was already seventy years old. Afrika subsequently published *Dark Rider* (1992), *Maqabane* (1994), *Flesh and the Flame* (1995), *The Lemon Tree and Other Poems* (1995), and *The Angel and Other Poems* (2000). Passionate in his portrayal of all forms of social oppression, his poetry evinces his strong Islamic faith, which infuses his writing with a deep humanity and spirituality, establishing a link between political rhetoric and spiritual fervor. His focus is on common forms of suffering and loss, which he renders symbolically meaningful and lyrically intense.

Despite a small readership and a struggling publishing industry, South African poetry continues to show vigorous life. Journals such as *New Contrast*, *New Coin Poetry*, and *Upstream* have ensured that poetry continues to be published regularly. Publishers such as Carrefour Press, Snailpress, Carapace, and Gecko Poetry have, against the odds, brought out significant volumes of poetry. Through the encouragement of committed editors, many new poets have emerged in recent years, most notably Ken *Barris, Basil *Du Toit, Mzi *Mahola, Seitlhamo Motsapi, Mteto Mzongwana, Mxolisi Nyezwa, Ian Tromp, Dan *Wylie, and others. Anthologies such as *The Paperbook of South African English Poetry*, *The Heart in Exile*, and *The Lava of This Land* continue to make past and current South African poetry available to the general reader. Poetry events are also regularly held in the major cities. From being a colonial import, South African English poetry is now a thoroughly local pursuit.

Poland, Marguerite (b. 1950) Novelist and children's writer. Born and reared on a farm in the Eastern Cape, she attended the universities of Rhodes, Stellenbosch, and Natal, Durban.

Poland has published several novels, including *Train to Doringbult* (1987), *Shades* (1993), *Iron Love* (1999) and *Recessional for Grace* (2003). She has also published numerous children's books inspired by Khoisan and African folklore and mythology, including *The Mantis and the Moon: Stories for the Children of Africa* (1979), *The Fiery-Necked Nightjar* (1980), *Once at KwaFubesi* (1981), *The Bush-Shrike* (1982), *The Wood-Ash Stars* (1983), *The Small Clay Bull* (1986), *Shadow of the Wild Hare* (1986), and *When the Boerboon Flower Falls* (1989). Poland was awarded the 1979 Percy Fitzpatrick Award, the 1980 Katrine Harries Award, and the 1984 Sankei Award for Children's Books.

FURTHER READING

Denise A. Godwin, "Discovering the African Folk-Tale in Translation," *South African Journal of African Languages* 11, no. 4 (1991): 109–118; David Medalie, "'Such Wanton Innocence': Representing South African Boyhoods," *Current Writing* 12, no. 1 (2000): 41–61; Wendy Woodward, "Postcolonial Ecologies and the Gaze of Animals: Reading Some Contemporary Southern African Narratives," *Journal of Literary Studies* 19, nos. 3 & 4 (2003): 290–315.

Press, Karen (b. 1956) Poet. Born in Cape Town, Press was educated at the University of Cape Town. She has worked in alternative education projects, was cofounder of a publishing collective, and now works as a fiction editor. She is the author of several volumes of poetry. The first, *Bird Heart Stoning the Sea* (1990), has three sections carrying separate titles: *Bird Heart Stoning the Sea*, a series of personal lyrics; *Krotoa's Story*, a poetic interpretation of the life story of the Khoikhoi protégée of Jan van Riebeeck and his wife (published in a separate edition, *Krotoa*, 1990, illustrated by Jeff Rankin); and *Lines of Force*, a short story subtitled "A Small Mystery Murder." Written in the wake of the politically turbulent late 1980s, this debut collection reveals a poet poised between public political attestation and individualized poetic statement.

The promise of her first collection is more fully realized in the carefully crafted *The Coffee Shop Poems* (1993) and *Echo Location: A Guide to Sea Point for Residents and Visitors* (1998). These were followed by *Home* (2000) and *The Little Museum of Working Life* (2004). She is coeditor (with Ingrid *de Kok) of *Spring Is Rebellious: Arguments About Cultural Freedom* (1990), and coauthor (with Mike van Graan) of *Popular and Political Culture for South Africa: Towards a Revolutionary Artistic Practice in South Africa* (1990). She is also the author of a book of children's stories, *Children of Africa* (1987; also released in Xhosa and Afrikaans), and *Nongqawuse's Prophecy* (1990; illustrated by Jeff Rankin).

FURTHER READING

Pieter Conradie, "The Story of Eva (Krotoa): Translation Transgressed," *Journal of Literary Studies* 14, nos. 1–2 (1998): 55–66; Mary West, "The Co-Ordinates of (Post-)Colonial Whiteness: A Reading of Karen Press's *Echo Location: A Guide to Sea Point for Residents and Visitors*," *English in Africa* 33, no. 1 (2006): 93–111.

Pringle, Thomas *See* Writers Before 1945

Prison Literature Herman Charles *Bosman's semifictionalized prison memoir, *Cold Stone Jug* (1949), is often given as the foundational text for the shamefully large body of South African prison literature. This is so despite the text's uneasy relationship with the overtly political prison memoirs of the 1960s and later. For Bosman was a common criminal (he murdered his stepbrother) and never sought to deny this, while later practitioners of the genre were invariably incarcerated for political offenses. Bosman's chronicle describes the four years he spent in Pretoria Central Prison, initially in the shadow of the gallows, until his sentence was commuted to ten years of imprisonment with hard labor. Despite the fact that Bosman was not a political prisoner, many of the features of prison life that he records—the brutality, the boredom, the denial of individuality and full humanity to prisoners—are common to virtually all narratives about South African prisons. Indeed, in his commentary on the book, Jeremy *Cronin (a political prisoner who himself served seven years) asserts that Bosman achieves a continuity with other writers in this genre mainly because many of the details he supplies about prison life remain substantially unchanged up to the present day. One important difference, however, according to Cronin, is that whereas Bosman was able to write honestly about prison experience as though it were an unusual occurrence, the more contemporary writer would not be able to escape the moral consequences of writing about a system that made prison life an ordinary experience for a far wider spectrum of South African society.

The fact that such large numbers of South Africans have been jailed for political activities as well as for minor offenses (mainly for breaking the Pass Laws) has meant that many South African literary texts that are not prison memoirs per se deal in part with prison life. Athol *Fugard's *The Island* (1973) portrays political prisoners on Robben Island, while the author himself saw firsthand, as a clerk in a Native Commissioner's Court in Johannesburg in the 1950s, the devastating effects of the Pass Laws, which criminalized vast numbers of ordinary work-seekers in urban areas. The upshot of this experience was the play *Sizwe Bansi Is Dead* (1972). Other examples of fictional works that deal with prison life include Christopher *Hope's story "Learning to Fly" (1976); Bessie *Head's stories "The Prisoner Who Wore Glasses" (1973) and "The Collector of Treasures" (1977), in which the woman protagonist is sentenced to life imprisonment for killing her abusive husband in self-defense; the closing part of Nadine *Gordimer's *Burger's Daughter* (1979), in which Rosa Burger's imprisonment is described; Mtutuzeli *Matshoba's story about forced labor on farms, "A Glimpse of Slavery" (1979), as well as his "A Pilgrimage to the Isle of Makana" (1979), in which the protagonist journeys to Robben Island to see a relative imprisoned there. J. M. *Coetzee explores the psychology of detention and torture through the sinister Colonel Joll in *Waiting for the Barbarians* (1981), while Miriam *Tlali's "detour into detention" is described in her collection *Mihloti* (1984). These are merely a small sample of the vast body of works of fiction that deal with prison life in South Africa.

The first full-length political prison memoir was Ruth First's *117 Days: An Account of Confinement and Interrogation under the South African Ninety-Day Detention Law* (1965). First, the only woman associate of the Rivonia group, was detained in 1963 under the ninety-day detention without trial law. *117 Days* recounts not only her own experiences, but also those of other political prisoners of different race and class positions, and this gives a sense of the broad political resistance to the apartheid state. Although it at times appears detached and strives for the longer, historical view, rather than the immediate personal one, First does describe the gradual breakdown of her personality and her demoralization after being released, only to be detained again—a detail that finds its way into many prison memoirs.

In his *The Jail Diary of Albie Sachs* (1966), *Sachs, a young advocate at the time, describes his attempt to thwart his interrogators by maintaining a rule of silence. Sachs spent 168 days in detention without ever being brought to trial. Like First, he was arrested under the ninety-day provision, released, and then immediately rearrested. Sachs's account is a deeply personal one in which he reflects on the psychological effects of detention without trial in solitary confinement.

Dennis *Brutus's *Letters to Martha and Other Poems from a South African Prison* (1968) is necessarily different from the other works in the genre in that it takes the form of a series of poems actually written in jail. The poems were included in letters to his sister and decoded afterward. In these personal musings Brutus attempts to grasp and articulate the larger significance of imprisonment on the grounds of political belief, which involves a crushing not only of the individual spirit, but also of the lives of people on the outside.

D. M. Zwelonke's *Robben Island* (1973) is not notable for its literary artistry, but nonetheless makes a powerful impact on the reader. Cast in the form of fiction, the narrator Danny recounts his experience of eight years on the island. Fragmented and confusing in places, in its immediacy it is nonetheless compelling, especially in its detailed eyewitness accounts of the sufferings of fellow prisoners.

Hugh *Lewin, a journalist who was one of the leaders of the National Union of South African Students (NUSAS), was sentenced to seven years for his activities as a member of the African Resistance Movement, a sabotage organization. His chronicle of his years in prison appeared in 1974 as *Bandiet: Seven Years in a South African Prison. Bandiet* is Afrikaans for convict (although it carries the connotations of bandit or outlaw). Before being relocated to a prison built especially for political prisoners, Lewin spent some time among common criminals in Bosman's Pretoria Central, and his account includes insights into the minds and motives of ordinary criminals.

Breyten *Breytenbach's *The True Confessions of an Albino Terrorist* (1984) is notable for its self-reflexiveness. Breytenbach was arrested by the security police upon his secret return to South Africa and sentenced to seven years' imprisonment in Pretoria Maximum Security Prison. These details find their way into his text, but *True Confessions* is also a metafictional commentary on the process of writing about interrogation and confession. This aspect of the text is discussed in the concluding "Note About Torture in South African Cells and Interrogation Rooms": "The detainee and the interrogator both know that there is, obscurely, a measure of ritual involved in their relationship, a ritual as old as the history of human intercourse."

Jeremy *Cronin's *Inside* (1983) is a series of poignant and powerful poems about his period of imprisonment after he was charged in 1976 under the Terrorism Act and sentenced to seven years' imprisonment. During this period his wife died, and he was denied permission to attend her funeral. Like Bosman, Brutus, and Breytenbach, Cronin demonstrates considerable skill in turning the deadening experience of prison into subject matter for masterly artistic treatment.

Other accounts of prison experience which appeared in the 1980s include Indres Naidoo's *Island in Chains: Ten Years on Robben Island by Prisoner 885/63* (1982; as told to Albie Sachs); Molefe Pheto's *And Night Fell: Memoirs of a Political Prisoner in South Africa* (1985), described by the author as "the narrative of a nightmare that lasted for 281 days in South African prisons, 271 of them in solitary confinement"; Tshenuwani Simon Farisani's *Diary from a South African Prison* (1987); Michael Dingake's *My Fight*

Against Apartheid (1987); and Caesarina Kona Makhoere's *No Child's Play: In Prison Under Apartheid* (1988). Makhoere was incarcerated after the school and township disturbances of 1976 and testifies to the fact that, in the way the authorities treated political prisoners, imprisonment became a continuation of the kind of control exerted during the periods of slavery and indentured labor. Emma Mashinini's experience of detention and interrogation was so extreme that it took many years before she could write *Strikes Have Followed Me All My Life: A South African Autobiography* (1989). Indeed, her narrative was prompted by the therapy she received at the Danish Rehabilitation Centre for Torture Victims and became a way of exorcising the trauma she had experienced, a telling example of which was her inability to recall her youngest daughter's name.

Accounts of imprisonment for political activity find their way into the autobiographies of a number of prominent South Africans. These include Nelson Mandela's *No Easy Walk to Freedom* (1965) and his *Long Walk to Freedom* (1994); Winnie Mandela's *Part of My Soul* (1984); Frank Chikane's *No Life of My Own: An Autobiography* (1988); Govan Mbeki's *Learning from Robben Island: The Prison Writings of Govan Mbeki* (1991); and Mosiuoa Patrick Lekota's *Prison Letters to a Daughter* (1991).

Writings about detention and imprisonment have also appeared in anthologies containing autobiographical material. Diana Russell's *Lives of Courage: Women for a New South Africa* (1989) contains some such accounts, while Barbie Schreiner's *A Snake with Ice Water: Prison Writings by South African Women* (1992) is wholly devoted to the subject. The Detainees' Parents Support Committee published *Cries of Freedom: Women in Detention in South Africa* (1988), and Don Foster, Dennis Davis, and Diane Sandler jointly wrote *Detention and Torture in South Africa* (1987).

FURTHER READING

Paul Gready, "Autobiography and the 'Power of Writing': Political Prison Writing in the Apartheid Era," *Journal of Southern African Studies* 19, no. 3 (1993): 489–523; J. U. Jacobs, "Prison Literature: South Africa," *Encyclopaedia of Post-Colonial Literatures in English* (1994): 1312–1314; David Schalkwyk, "Confession and Solidarity in the Prison Writing of Breyten Breytenbach and Jeremy Cronin," *Research in African Literatures* 25, no. 1 (1994): 23–45; David Schalkwyk, "The Rules of Physiognomy: Reading the Convict in South African Prison Writing," *Pretexts* 7, no. 1 (1998): 81–96.

R

Rampolokeng, Lesego (b. 1965) Poet. Born and raised in Soweto, he studied law at the University of the North but failed to complete his degree. Widely appreciated as a performance poet, Rampolokeng has published several volumes of poetry, including *Horns for Hondo* (1990), *Talking Rain* (1993), *Blue V's: Rap-Poems* (1998), *The Bavino Sermons* (1999), and *The Second Chapter* (2003). Drawing on a wide range of influences, including traditional oral poetry, Black Consciousness poetry, and rap poetry, and employing a stream-of-consciousness technique in rapid rhyme, Rampolokeng's poems constitute a scornful denunciation of the violence, corruption, and hypocrisy that have characterized South African society, both during and after apartheid. His poetry is aimed, as he phrases it, at those who put "vanity before humanity."

Rampolokeng has also published two novels: *Blackheart: Epilogue to Insanity* (2004) and *Whiteheart: Prologue to*

Hysteria (2005). He was awarded the 1990 Sydney Clouts Memorial Prize and has appeared on the 1991 Kwanzaa Honors List.

FURTHER READING

Frank Schulze-Engler, "Literature and Civil Society in South Africa," *Ariel* 27, no. 1 (1996): 21–40; Flora Veit-Wild, "Carnival and Hybridity in Texts by Dambudzo Marechera and Lesego Rampolokeng," *Journal of Southern African Studies* 23, no. 4 (1997): 553–564; James Ogude, "Writing Resistance on the Margins of Power: Rampolokeng's Poetry and the Restoration of Community in South Africa," *Alternation* 5, no. 2 (1998): 251–262; Russell Kaschula, "Imbongi to Slam: The Emergence of a Technologised Auriture," *Southern African Journal for Folklore Studies* 14, no. 2 (2004): 46–58.

Reitz, Deneys *See* Writers Before 1945

Renault, Mary (Eileen Mary Challans) (1905–1983) Novelist. Born in London, and educated at St Hugh's College, Oxford, she trained as a nurse and served in that capacity until the end of World War II. This experience produced her "hospital" novels, published under her own name: *Purposes of Love* (1939), *Kind Are Her Answers* (1940), *The Friendly Young Ladies* (1944), and *Return to Night* (1947). She emigrated to South Africa in 1948 and began publishing historical novels about ancient Greece, starting with *The Last of the Wine* (1956), perhaps her best-known work. *The King Must Die* (1958) and *The Bull from the Sea* (1962) deal with the Theseus legend and are products of meticulous research, as is the trilogy on Alexander the Great, entitled *The Persian Boy* (1972). *The Lion in the Gateway* (1964) is a history of Greece for young readers based on Herodotus and Plutarch. She wrote no novels with a South African setting.

Rive, Richard Moore (1931–1989) Novelist, short-story writer, literary critic. Born in District Six, Rive was educated at the universities of Cape Town, Columbia, and Oxford, where he wrote his doctoral thesis on Olive Schreiner. He traveled and lectured widely as a recipient of several fellowships. His first collection of stories, banned in South Africa, appeared as *African Songs* (1963). He edited the anthology *Modern African Prose* (1963) and *Quartet: Four Voices from South Africa* (1964), which includes some of his stories alongside those of Alex *La Guma, James *Matthews, and Alf Wannenburgh. "Rain," one of his best-known stories, is among these. It is typical of Rive's style in its impressionistic evocation of the social milieu of District Six as Rive himself knew it. It is a tale about the woman Siena and her hopeless quest to find the lover who has deserted her. In this thumbnail sketch of District Six, Rive deftly manages to evoke the texture of life in the slum—its hardships and hopelessness, but also its compassion for the plight of those in distress.

Rive's first novel, *Emergency* (1964), focuses on events during the State of Emergency following Sharpeville and was banned in South Africa. *Selected Writings* (1977) contains stories, essays, and plays, including *Make Like Slaves*, which won the BBC African Theatre Competition in 1972. *Writing Black* (1981) is an autobiography that describes his childhood in District Six, his entry into academia, his association with numerous writers and critics, and his extensive travels in Africa, Europe, and America. The title, the author says in a preface, was "deliberately chosen in order to focus attention on my experiences as a South African who is still voteless because of the color of my skin. I look forward to the day when it will not be necessary for writing in my country to be tied to ethnic labels, when the only criteria will be writing well and writing South African."

Advance, Retreat: Selected Short Stories (1983), with woodcuts by Cecil Skotnes, contains a selection of his stories written between 1955 and 1982. Rive revised many of his earlier stories for this edition, the first collection to be published in South Africa. This was followed by his second novel, *'Buckingham Palace,' District Six* (1986), which focuses on the lives of the inhabitants of a dingy row of five cottages in the heart of the slum. The novel has three parts—"Morning 1955," "Afternoon 1960," and "Night 1970"—the last of which charts the beginning of the demise of District Six when the first houses are bulldozed. *Emergency Continued* (1990), as its title suggests, is a sequel to *Emergency*: it traces the lives of a group of political activists who experienced Sharpeville in 1960 and who now, decades later, are again caught up in the turbulence of protest and resistance to the regime. One of these is now a dedicated Coloured teacher who is reluctantly drawn into the maelstrom of violence in the mid-1980s. The novel was completed just two weeks before Rive was murdered at his home in Cape Town in 1989.

An acknowledged Schreiner scholar, Rive edited her *Diamond Fields: Only a Story of Course* for publication in *English in Africa* in 1974 (rev. ed. 1995). His *Olive Schreiner: Letters, 1871–99* appeared in 1987.

FURTHER READING

Dennis Duerden and Cosmo Pieterse, eds., *African Writers Talking: A Collection of Interviews* (1972); Dieter Welz, ed., *Writing against Apartheid: South African Writers Interviewed* (1987); Catherine Dubbeld, ed., *Richard Rive: A Select Bibliography* (1990); Stephen Gray, *Free-lancers and Literary Biography in South Africa* (1999); Grant Farred, *Midfielder's Moment: Coloured Literature and Culture in Contemporary South Africa* (2000).

Roberts, Sheila (1937–2009) Short-story writer, novelist, poet, critic. Born in Johannesburg, Roberts attended school in Potchefstroom and studied at the University of South Africa, where she gained an MA degree. Her doctorate, completed in 1977, was awarded by the University of Pretoria for a study of the novels of Patrick White. Having worked in a variety of occupations, she left South Africa in the late 1970s to settle in the United States, where she was a professor of English at the University of Wisconsin in Milwaukee.

Roberts contributed prolifically to South African literature in the 1970s and 1980s. Her first volume of stories *Outside Life's Feast* (1975) received the Olive Schreiner Prize; it is remarkable for its uncompromising insights into white working-class society in South Africa. A second collection of stories, *This Time of Year* (1983), again explores the frustrations and prejudices of her working-class white protagonists with an uncompromising commitment to detail, although these stories have a more subtle, arguably superior, quality. The title story centers on the character Hannah, who knows that her future hinges on the decision she will shortly have to make about remarrying her feckless former husband Sam. As the details of her former life with Sam unfold it becomes clear that she is in danger of following the same route to financial ruin and familial disintegration experienced by Mary Vosloo, the neighbor who has recently committed suicide. The sordid details about Sam and their former life together that filter into the narrative accumulate to provide a compelling portrait of suffering and deprivation. A further collection of stories appeared as *Coming In and Other Stories* (1993).

Roberts's first collection of poems, *Lou's Life and Other Poems* (1977), appeared in a volume jointly with three other South African poets. The same year also saw the appearance of her first novel *He's My*

Brother (published in America as *Johannesburg Requiem*), which was banned at the time for sexual explicitness. Her second novel, *The Weekenders*, appeared in 1981. Her critical study *Dan Jacobson* (1984) was followed by another collection of poems, *Dialogues and Divertimenti* (1985), and the novels *Jacks in Corners* (1987) and *Purple Yams* (2001).

Roberts is best known for her skillful short stories in which she portrays the tawdriness and vulgarity of the lives of the white underclass in South Africa with an unflinching honesty. Her familiarity with the milieu allows her an intimate insight into this society and at the same time frees her writings from the white middle-class guilt so pervasive in South African fiction. Sexuality, smells, colors, tactile sensations, and the telling minutiae of her characters' physiques are all very immediate to her, conveyed with a candor and precision frequently uncomfortable to readers familiar with her milieu. In her later stories she moves away from this realist mode and experiments with a more reflexive narrative style. This is most conspicuous in her humorous and playful "Carlotta's Vinyl Skin" (included in *Coming In and Other Stories*). Roberts was awarded the Thomas Pringle Prize by the English Academy of South Africa for stories published in the literary periodical *Contrast*.

FURTHER READING

Cherry Wilhelm, "Trends in Recent English Fiction and Criticism in South Africa," *English in Africa* 5, no. 2 (1978): 17–27; Craig MacKenzie and Cherry Clayton, eds., *Between the Lines: Interviews with Bessie Head, Sheila Roberts, Ellen Kuzwayo, Miriam Tlali* (1989); Margaret Lenta, "Two Women and Their Territories: Sheila Roberts and Miriam Tlali," *Tulsa Studies in Women's Literature* 11, no. 1 (1992): 103–111; M. J. Daymond, "Gender and 'History': 1980s South African Women's Stories in English," *Ariel* 27, no. 1 (1996): 191–213.

Rooke, Daphne (1914–2009) Novelist. Born in Boksburg, Transvaal (now Gauteng), she was educated at Durban Girls' High School and later emigrated to Australia.

Rooke published ten novels: *The Sea Hath Bounds* (1946, reissued as *A Grove of Fever Trees* in 1950), *Mittee* (1951, translated into fourteen languages and recently reissued as a Penguin Twentieth Century Classic), *Ratoons* (1953), *Wizard's Country* (1957), *Beti* (1959), *A Lover for Estelle* (1961), *The Greyling* (1962), *Diamond Jo* (1965), *Boy on a Mountain* (1969), and *Margaretha de la Porte* (1974). She also published three children's books: *The South African Twins* (1953), *The Australian Twins* (1954), and *The New Zealand Twins* (1957).

Merging romance and realism, the novels explore the South African past from different points of view, employing perspectives as diverse as a crazed white male narrator, a Coloured Afrikaans female narrator, an English settler girl, and a hunchbacked African tribesman to articulate, in a frequently controversial manner, what remains unspoken in the grand narratives of socially sanctioned history.

Once rated at least the equal of Nobel laureates Gordimer and Lessing (in the 1950s a reviewer for *The Guardian* paid tribute to young women writers from the region by saying: "Gordimer, Lessing, Rooke, and the greatest of these is Rooke"), Rooke has for decades suffered critical and popular neglect. The 2008 reissue of three of her novels by the Toby Press in the United Kingdom may help to revive her reputation.

FURTHER READING

Helen Camberg, *Daphne Rooke—Her Works and Selected Literary Criticism: A Bibliography*

(1969); Michael Cawood Green, *Novel Histories: Past, Present and Future in South African Fiction* (1997); J. M. Coetzee, *Stranger Shores: Essays, 1986–1999* (2001).

Rose-Innes, Henrietta (b. 1971) Novelist and short-story writer. Based in Cape Town, Rose-Innes teaches creative writing at the University of Cape Town and works as literary editor, scriptwriter, and script editor. She has been recipient of several prizes for her short stories, which have been anthologized in various publications, including *Dinaane: Short Stories by South African Women, South African Short Stories Since 1994, A City Imagined, 180 Degrees, Leaves to a Tree, Open: An Erotic Anthology by South African Women, New Writing from Southern Africa 2007*, and *Jambula Tree and Other Stories*. She is the author of two novels, *Shark's Egg* (2000) and *The Rock Alphabet* (2004). *Shark's Egg* chronicles the life of a young woman through high school and university in Cape Town of the 1980s and 1990s, charting, through friendship and love, a trajectory of loss and recovery. *The Rock Alphabet* weaves together the stories of Ivy, whose search for missing archeological material leads her to the mountains and their mysterious rock paintings, and Jean, who as a child had been found wandering in these mountains with his missing brother and continues to be haunted by the call of the wild.

S

Sachs, Albie (b. 1935) Autobiographer and cultural critic. Detained in solitary confinement during the 1960s, Sachs went into exile in Mozambique, where he was the victim of a letter bomb rigged by the South African security forces. A prominent figure in the African National Congress (ANC), he has practiced as a lawyer and has served as a justice of the Constitutional Court of South Africa.

Sachs has published four autobiographical works: *Jail Diary* (1969), *The Soft Vengeance of a Freedom Fighter* (1990), *Running to Maputo* (1990), and *The Free Diary of Albie Sachs* (2004). He is also coauthor of a collection of literary-critical essays, *Spring Is Rebellious: Arguments About Cultural Freedom* (1990), edited by Karen *Press and Ingrid *de Kok.

It is as a cultural critic that Sachs has had the greatest impact on the South African literary scene, arguing, controversially, that the clichés and limitations of resistance literature should be abandoned in favor of forms of expression that are better able to convey the subtleties of imaginative engagement with experience. Sachs received the 1991 *Sunday Times* Alan Paton Award.

FURTHER READING

Duncan Brown and Bruno van Dyk, eds., *Exchanges: South African Writing in Transition* (1991); Kevin Goddard and Andries Wessels, eds., *Out of Exile: South African Writers Speak: Interviews with Albie Sachs, Lewis Nkosi, Mbulelo Mzamane, Breyten Breytenbach, Dennis Brutus, Keorapetse Kgositsile* (1992); S. V. Menager-Everson, "The Albie Sachs Debate," *Research in African Literatures* 23, no. 4 (1992): 59–66; Paul Gready, "Autobiography and the 'Power of Writing': Political Prison Writing in the Apartheid Era," *Journal of Southern African Studies* 19, no. 3 (1993): 489–523; Immanual Suttner, ed., *Cutting Through the Mountain: Interviews with South African Jewish Activists* (1997); Paul Gready, *Writing as Resistance: Life Stories of Imprisonment, Exile, and Homecoming from Apartheid South Africa* (2003).

Sam, Agnes (b. 1942) Short-story writer. Born in Port Elizabeth to an Indian Catholic family, Sam was educated at a private school and later studied in Lesotho and Zimbabwe. She went into exile in England in the 1970s and returned to South Africa twenty years later. Her stories are collected in *Jesus Is Indian and Other Stories* (1989). Using a variety of narrative perspectives and locales, Sam's stories explore aspects of childhood, young adulthood, and community history. "The Story Teller," for instance, presents itself as an item of oral history and describes the way in which children were tricked into boarding a ship carrying indentured Indian laborers to South Africa. The last story, "And They Christened It Indenture," explores the gradual resistance to indentured labor among the South African Indian community and Christianity's complicity in the exploitation of people.

FURTHER READING

Miki Flockemann, "Asian Diasporas, Contending Identities and New Configurations: Stories by Agnes Sam and Olive Senior," *English in Africa* 25, no. 1 (1998): 71–86.

Schoeman, Karel (b. 1939) Novelist and historian. Born in the Orange Free State (now Free State), and having spent time abroad, Karel Schoeman worked as a librarian in Cape Town for many years before his retirement to Trompsberg, in the Free State.

He is the author of more than ten award-winning novels in Afrikaans, four of which have been translated into English: *Promised Land* (1979), winner of the CNA Literary Prize; *Another Country* (1991); *Take Leave and Go* (1993); and *This Life* (2005). Set in an imagined future after the collapse of white rule, *Promised Land* describes the return to South Africa of a young man who has inherited a farm from his mother, and who encounters a landscape that has changed utterly from the one imbedded in his childhood memory. *Another Country* tells the story of a wealthy and sophisticated Dutch bachelor who arrives in the nineteenth-century Free State capital of Bloemfontein, hoping to find a cure for the tuberculosis that is eating away at his life. Detailed evocation of domestic and social life together with subtle psychological analysis of character and close observation of manners are characteristic also of *This Life*, with its portrait of a woman lying on her deathbed recalling, in the space of a night, her life as spinster on the family farm.

Schoeman has published a number of historical works in English of literary-cultural importance, including *Olive Schreiner: A Woman in South Africa 1855–1881* (1989, 1991), *Only an Anguish to Live Here: Olive Schreiner and the Anglo-Boer War, 1899–1902* (1992), and *Irma Stern: The Early Years, 1894–1933* (1994), and he has also edited several works of historical interest.

FURTHER READING

Michael Green, *Novel Histories: Past, Present and Future in South African Fiction* (1997); Willie Burger, "Karel Schoeman's Voices from the Past: Narrating the Anglo-Boer War," *Current Writing* 12, no. 1 (2000): 1–16; Ralph Pordzik, "Nationalism, Cross-Culturalism, and Utopian Vision in South African Utopian and Dystopian Writing 1972–92," *Research in African Literatures* 32, no. 3 (2001): 177–197.

Scholefield, Alan (Tweedie) (b. 1931) Novelist. Born in Cape Town and educated at Queen's College, Queenstown, and the University of Cape Town, Scholefield worked for a short time on the *Cape Argus* and *Cape Times* newspapers before settling in England, where he has lived and worked as a journalist since 1953.

His first novel, *A View of Vultures*, appeared in 1966 and was followed by several other popular novels deploying a variety of historical settings. These include *Great Elephant* (1967), set in the time of Shaka;

The Eagles of Malice (1968), a story of the German-Herero war in German West Africa (now Namibia); *Point of Honour* (1979), set in wartime Dunkirk; *The Stone Flower* (1982), set in the early days of the Kimberley diamond fields; *King of the Golden Valley* (1985), about Trans-Asian car races; and *The Last Safari* (1987), set in Kenya and straddling the pre- and postindependence eras.

His *The Young Masters* (1971), a perceptive exploration of a white South African boyhood, is often considered his best South African work. With his wife, the journalist Anthea Goddard, he wrote the thriller *Cat's Eyes* (1981) under the pseudonym Lee Jordan.

Schreiner, Olive *See* Writers Before 1945

Scully, W. C. *See* Writers Before 1945

Sepamla, Sydney Sipho (1932–2007)
Poet and novelist. Born in Krugersdorp, Sepamla trained as a teacher and taught at secondary school level before working as a personnel officer. He was for many years director of the Federated Union of Black Artists (FUBA) in Johannesburg.

His collections of poetry are *Hurry Up To It!* (1975), *The Blues Is You in Me* (1976), *The Soweto I Love* (1977), *Children of the Earth* (1983), and *From Goré to Soweto* (1988); his *Selected Poems* appeared in 1984. His poems deploy blues rhythms, township argot, and a lively mixture of linguistic registers to probe at the ironies and injustices of racial discrimination. Along with poets such as Mbuyiseni Oswald *Mtshali, Mongane Wally *Serote, and Mafika Pascal *Gwala, he was at the forefront of the explosion of black poetry in the 1970s.

In "The Work Song" (from *The Blues Is You in Me*), the speaker celebrates the secret subversiveness of a work-gang chant and the strength and resilience the gang itself represents. "Da Same, Da Same" (from the same collection) is a witty appeal to the reader to recognize the human commonality binding together people of different races in South Africa, whether black, white, "India," or "clearlink." The title poem of the volume conveys a strident protest message typical of the era in sonorous, elegant phrasings infused with blues refrains: "I want to holler the how-long blues / because we are the blues people all / the whiteman bemoaning his burden / the blackman offloading the yoke."

He is also the author of several novels, including *The Root Is One* (1979); *A Ride on the Whirlwind* (1981), about the Soweto uprisings of 1976; *A Scattered Survival* (1989); and *Rainbow Journey* (1996). A former editor of the literary periodicals *S'ketsh* and *New Classic*, he wrote several short stories and was the joint recipient (with Lionel *Abrahams) of the 1976 Thomas Pringle Poetry Award.

FURTHER READING

Tony Emmett, "Oral Political and Communal Aspects of Township Poetry in the Mid-Seventies," *English in Africa* 6, no. 1 (1979): 72–81; Michael Chapman, ed., *Soweto Poetry* (1982); Jacques Alvarez-Pereyre, *The Poetry of Commitment in South Africa* (1984); John Haynes, *African Poetry and the English Language* (1987); Kelwyn Sole, "The Days of Power: Depictions of Politics and Community in Four Recent South African Novels," *Research in African Literatures* 19, no. 1 (1988): 65–88; Jane Watts, *Black Writers from South Africa: Towards a Discourse of Liberation* (1989); Raoul Granqvist and John A. Stotesbury, eds., *African Voices: Interviews with Thirteen African Writers* (1989); Johan Geertsema, "Fictionalization, Conscientization and the Trope of Exile in *Amandla* and *Third Generation*," *Literator* 14, no. 3 (1993): 109–128; Thengani H. Ngwenya, "Interview with Sipho Sepamla," *English Academy Review* 11 (1994): 73–82.

Serote, Mongane Wally (b. 1944)
Poet and novelist. Born in Sophiatown, Serote attended primary school in Alexandra Township outside Johannesburg and high school in Lesotho and Soweto. Detained under the Terrorism Act in 1969, he was released nine months later without being charged. He worked in advertising and studied fine art at Columbia University, graduating with an MFA in 1977. He moved to Botswana in 1979, where he cofounded the Medu Arts Ensemble, and to London in 1986, where he held a position on the ANC cultural desk. He returned to South Africa in the early 1990s and took up work in the Department of Arts and Culture.

His collections of poetry are *Yakhal'inkomo* (1972; winner of the 1973 Ingrid Jonker Prize), *Tsetlo* (1974), *No Baby Must Weep* (1975), *Behold Mama, Flowers* (1978), *The Night Keeps Winking* (1982), *A Tough Tale* (1987), *Third World Express* (1992), *Come and Hope with Me* (1994), and *Freedom Lament and Song* (1997). His *Selected Poems* appeared in 1982. The early poems introduced the militant voice of Black Consciousness to South African literature and, in their reliance on elements of African oral culture, challenged accepted poetic norms. His later poems are long, epic pieces.

His novel *To Every Birth Its Blood* (1981), like *Sepamla's *A Ride on the Whirlwind* and *Mzamane's *Children of Soweto*, deals with the 1976 Soweto uprising and its dramatic aftermath, and was met with critical acclaim. The novel embodies what one critic called "the irruption of history" into Serote's artistic project, shifting from an individualistic modernist aesthetic to a collective, populist one. Serote has also produced two collections of essays on South African culture and politics, *On the Horizon* (1990) and *Hyenas* (2000). His most recent works include the novels *Gods of Our Time* (1999) and *Scatter the Ashes and Go* (2002) and the long poem *History Is the Home Address* (2004). Also the author of several short stories, he received a Creative Writing Award from the English Academy of Southern Africa in 1983 for his significant contribution to South African literature in the 1970s.

FURTHER READING

Tony Emmett, "Oral Political and Communal Aspects of Township Poetry in the Mid-Seventies," *English in Africa* 6, no. 1 (1979): 72–81; Michael Chapman, ed., *Soweto Poetry* (1982); Jacques Alvarez-Pereyre, *The Poetry of Commitment in South Africa* (1984); Nick Visser, "Fictional Projects and the Irruptions of History: Mongane Serote's *To Every Birth Its Blood*," *English Academy Review* 4 (1987): 67–76; Anne McClintock, "'Azikwelwa': We Will Not Ride: Politics and Value in Black South African Poetry," *Critical Inquiry* 13, no. 3 (1987): 597–623; Kelwyn Sole, "The Days of Power: Depictions of Politics and Community in Four Recent South African Novels," *Research in African Literatures* 19, no. 1 (1988): 65–88; Jane Watts, *Black Writers from South Africa: Towards a Discourse of Liberation* (1989); Raoul Granqvist and John A. Stotesbury, eds., *African Voices: Interviews with Thirteen African Writers* (1989); Jane Wilkinson, *Orpheus in Africa: Fragmentation and Renewal in the Work of Four African Writers* (1990); Jane Wilkinson, ed., *Talking with African Writers: Interviews with African Poets, Playwrights and Novelists* (1992); Rolf Solberg and Malcolm Hacksley, eds., *Reflections: Perspectives on Writing in Postapartheid South Africa* (1996); Michael Green, *Novel Histories: Past, Present and Future in South African Fiction* (1997); Michael Titlestad, "Mongane Serote's *To Every Birth Its Blood*: History and the Limits of Improvisation," *Journal of Literary Studies* 19, no. 2 (2003): 108–124.

Sharpe, Tom (b. 1928) Novelist. Born in England, he came to South Africa in 1951 and worked in the Native Affairs Department in Pietermaritzburg and later as a teacher and photographer. He returned to England in 1961. He is the author of several satirical novels, two of which deal with South Africa: *Riotous Assembly* (1971) and *Indecent Exposure* (1973). Later works include *Porterhouse Blue* (1974), *Blott on the Landscape* (1975), *Wilt* (1976), *The Great Pursuit* (1977), *The Throwback* (1978), *Ancestral Vices* (1980), *Vintage Stuff* (1982), and *Wilt on High* (1985).

Short Story It is arguably in the genre of short fiction that South African literature has most consistently excelled: three of South Africa's most prominent writers in English (Pauline *Smith, H. C. *Bosman, and Nadine *Gordimer) have built their reputations substantially from writing short stories; and a host of others—including W. C. *Scully, William *Plomer, Jack *Cope, Doris *Lessing, Dan *Jacobson, Es'kia *Mphahlele, Bessie *Head, Sheila *Roberts, Ahmed *Essop, and Njabulo *Ndebele (to name just a few)—have used the short story form extensively.

The history of the South African short story goes back further than is generally assumed. Stories with recognizable South African settings, characters and preoccupations appeared in literary journals like *The Cape of Good Hope Literary Magazine* in the 1840s. Two of the earliest book collections of South African tales, however, are R. Hodges's *The Settler in South Africa and Other Tales* (1860) and A. W. *Drayson's *Tales at the Outspan, or Adventures in the Wild Regions of Southern Africa* (1862). Olive *Schreiner was the earliest female short-story writer of note with her *Dreams* (1891), although she was preceded by the lesser-known Marguerite de Fenton (Marguerite Mostyn Cleaver) with *Tales Written in Ladybrand* (1885) and Mary Anne Carey-Hobson with *South African Stories* (1886). Schreiner's "Eighteen-Ninety-Nine" (1923), about the devastating effects of the Second Boer War on the Boer women in particular, stands out as one of the most powerful and moving short stories of this early period.

The late nineteenth century saw a proliferation of short-story collections, many of them demonstrating in their titles their affinity with an oral milieu, which was a strong tendency in the early South African short story. Some examples are J. Forsyth *Ingram's *The Story of a Gold Concession and Other African Tales and Legends* (1893), W. C. *Scully's *Kafir Stories* (1895), and his *The White Hecatomb and Other Stories* (1897), Ernest *Glanville's *Tales from the Veld* (1897), H. A. *Bryden's *Tales of South Africa* (1896) and his *From Veldt Camp Fires: Stories of Southern Africa* (1900), and Percy *FitzPatrick's *The Outspan: Tales of South Africa* (1897).

Among this group of early writers, Scully and FitzPatrick are the only two whose short stories have been reissued. Selected stories by Scully have appeared in Jean Marquard's useful edition entitled *Transkei Stories* (1984), and several of these display Scully's abiding interest in oral history and folklore. Sir Percy FitzPatrick's *The Outspan* (rereleased in 1987) is an outstanding example of the kind of colonial fiction occasioned by the presence of the motley band of expatriate adventurers who flocked to the South African diamond and goldfields in the last two decades of the nineteenth century. The title story employs a fictional narrator and evokes the fireside ethos of the oral tale.

Perceval *Gibbon raised this "fireside tale" genre to new heights in his collection of stories *The Vrouw Grobelaar's Leading Cases* (1905). In comparison with Scully and FitzPatrick, Gibbon demonstrates greater skill with literary artifice and the art of storytelling, and this technical skill is accompanied by a more complex social vision. His use of a storyteller figure—the redoubtable Vrouw Grobelaar—is not sporadic or opportunistic as it is in the case of the other two writers. The result is a well-crafted collection of mutually compatible stories anticipating Pauline *Smith's *The Little Karoo* (1925) and *Bosman's *Mafeking Road* (1947).

Pauline Smith's *The Little Karoo* is probably South Africa's earliest collection of short stories to achieve lasting recognition. Each of the ten stories included in *The Little Karoo* (two were added to the original eight of the first edition) exemplifies Smith's remarkable ability to capture the stark, elemental quality of her rural Dutch characters and the ponderous biblical cadences of their speech, the harsh oppressiveness of a life spent wresting the barest of yields from the reluctant earth, the austerity of their Protestant faith, and the tragic dimension in their human fallibilities.

In the stories of R. R. R. *Dhlomo, whose work of the late 1920s and the 1930s can be taken to represent the emergence of black South African short fiction, there are traces of a residual orality, although these are masked by a heavy reliance on Western literary models. A pioneer of the black short story, Dhlomo's numerous stories and journalistic sketches of life on the mines appeared in the black newspapers of the time. A selection of his pieces, edited by Tim *Couzens, that appeared in *English in Africa* in 1975 has recently been reissued as *20 Short Stories* (1996).

William *Plomer's stories appeared in *I Speak of Africa* (1927) and *The Child of Queen Victoria and Other Stories* (1933). The title story of the second volume is one of his best known and, as its title suggests, concerns the dilemma of a traditional Englishman whose attraction to a young African woman in rural Natal threatens to disrupt his conceptual and moral universe. A selected edition of Plomer's stories appeared in 1984.

Herman Charles Bosman is probably South Africa's most popular short-story writer, and his stories have appeared in numerous collections over the years. Among these are *Unto Dust* (1963), which includes his artful "Old Transvaal Story," *Bosman at His Best* (1965), *A Bekkersdal Marathon* and *Jurie Steyn's Post Office* (both 1971), all edited by Bosman's pupil and literary executor Lionel *Abrahams. The appearance in 1981 of his *Collected Works* (also edited by Abrahams) confirmed Bosman's stature in the world of South African literature. The efforts of another notable Bosman scholar, Stephen *Gray, have resulted in *Selected Stories* (1980), *Bosman's Johannesburg* (1986), and *Makapan's Caves and Other Stories* (1987), which has the distinction of being one of Bosman's rare successes on the overseas market.

Mafeking Road (1947), however, is by far Bosman's best-known collection, and was the only one to appear in his own lifetime. Bosman's storyteller figure, the wily backveld raconteur Oom Schalk Lourens, features in all but one of the stories in *Mafeking Road*. Schalk Lourens was first introduced to the South African reading public in "Makapan's Caves" (first published in 1930), which memorably begins: "Kaffirs? (said Oom Schalk Lourens). Yes, I know them. And they're all the same. I fear the Almighty, and I respect His works, but I could never understand why He made the kaffir and the rinderpest." From the very outset, then, Bosman was to make use of his very distinctive brand of irony to undermine white assumptions of superiority, a technique that has not always been properly interpreted by all readers of the Schalk Lourens stories.

Between 1930 and 1951 dozens of stories appeared in this sequence, most of which have been taken up in posthumous collections of his work. The later "Voorkamer" stories, which feature a number of narrators in a "conversation-forum" format, also testify to Bosman's consummate skill as a storyteller.

The trajectory of the South African short story from the 1860s to the 1950s parallels the demographic shifts in South Africa from countryside to city that were occasioned by the mineral discoveries of the late nineteenth century and subsequent industrialization and urbanization. The effects of this demographic shift can be traced in the changing texture of the short story over this period. From stories which have a predominantly rural setting, and which bear a close relationship to oral lore, legend, and small-town gossip, the South African short story of the 1950s and after is city-based, increasingly fragmented, and predominantly social realist.

The best-known postwar short-story writers working in this mode are Alan *Paton and Nadine *Gordimer. Paton is renowned for what is possibly South Africa's single most famous novel, *Cry, the Beloved Country* (1948), but some of the biting social realism and pathos of his novel are contained in the short stories in *Debbie Go Home* (1961) (also published as *Tales from a Troubled Land*) and *More Tales of South Africa* (1967). All of these are gathered in *The Hero of Currie Road: Complete Short Pieces* (2008).

Nadine Gordimer is South Africa's most prolific and successful short-story writer. Some fifteen collections of her stories have appeared over the years, beginning with *Face to Face* in 1949. Among these are *The Soft Voice of the Serpent and Other Stories* (1952), *Six Feet of the Country* (1956), *Not for Publication and Other Stories* (1965), *Livingstone's Companions* (1971) and *Something Out There* (1984). Selections of her stories have appeared as *Selected Stories* (1975), *Crimes of Conscience* (1991), and *Why Haven't You Written? Selected Stories 1950–1972* (1992).

As is the case with her novels, Gordimer's stories trace, in penetrating and often painful detail, the effects of South African politics and society on the individual. A powerful example is "Six Feet of the Country," which explores the contradictory emotions of a white farming couple when a young man, an illegal immigrant from Rhodesia, dies of pneumonia on their farm. (See the commentary section for more discussion of this story.)

In "The Train from Rhodesia," another famous Gordimer story, a young white woman on a train which has pulled into a small country station haggles with an old black man who has a wooden carving of a lion the girl desires. The old man's price is too high, and the girl, while recognizing the artistic merits of the piece, turns him down. As the train pulls out of the station, the girl's husband triumphantly presents her with the carving, which he has acquired for less than half the price the old man asked. With the "heat of shame" rising through her body, the girl turns her back on her bewildered husband, utterly disgusted and wearied by his inability to understand her genuine appreciation for the work of art and her shame at having acquired it in such a degrading manner.

Another prolific story-writer is Dan *Jacobson, whose stories have appeared in several collections over the years, including *A Long Way from London* (1958), *Beggar My Neighbour* (1964), *Through the Wilderness and Other Stories* (1968), *A Way of Life and Other Stories* (1971), and *Inklings: Selected Stories* (1973). One of Jacobson's best-known stories, "Beggar My Neighbour," is the story of a young white boy who befriends two black children and later has to come to terms with the harsh implications of rigid racial segregation, which consigns the children to disparate futures largely determined by race.

Stuart *Cloete achieved brief popularity with his many collections, among them *The Soldier's Peaches* (1959), *The Silver Trumpet* (1961), *The Looking Glass* (1963) and *The Honey Bird* (1964), while Jack *Cope's reputation, also established in the 1960s—by his *The Tame Ox* (1960) and *The Man Who Doubted* (1967)—is more solid, largely as a consequence of his deeper engagement with the worsening social relations in the South Africa of the time. Doris *Lessing was another writer of this period, her African stories appearing in *This Was the Old Chief's Country* (1951), *The Habit of Loving* (1957) and *African Stories* (1964). These stories deal mostly with the lives of the white colonials of Rhodesia. Her well-known "Witchcraft for Sale" (from *This Was the Old Chief's Country*) demonstrates her acute awareness of the racial prejudices and insecurities of this society.

Among black writers, the pioneering work of R. R. R. Dhlomo was followed in 1946 by the publication of Es'kia *Mphahlele's first collection of stories *Man Must Live and Other Stories*. This heralded an era of unprecedented literary activity among black writers of the 1950s and 1960s, most of which centered on the magazine *Drum*. The short story (often taking the form of a magazine column or anecdote) was the dominant genre of the period, and *Drum* published the bulk of these stories, including stories by Nat *Nakasa, Can *Themba, and Casey *Motsisi. Posthumous collections of stories and sketches by these writers have appeared under the titles *The World of Nat Nakasa* (1975), *The Will to Die* (1972, 1982) and *The World of Can Themba* (1985), and *Casey and Co.: Selected Writings of Casey "Kid" Motsisi* (1983). *Drum* magazine itself is significant in that it ushered in a new era in black writing and black self-awareness, and its contributors laid an important foundation for later black writing in South Africa. Mphahlele was the most prolific writer of the era. His classic "Mrs Plum," which appeared in his *In Corner B* (1967), deftly explores the lives of black servants in relation to their privileged mistresses. His *The Unbroken Song: Selected Writings* appeared in 1981.

The magazine *Staffrider*, which first appeared in the late 1970s, was *Drum*'s more radical successor. Like *Drum*, it spawned a wealth of talented black writers, many of them writers of short stories. Mtutuzeli *Matshoba, Mbulelo *Mzamane, Mothobi *Mutloatse, and Njabulo *Ndebele are among the writers whose work first appeared in *Staffrider* and whose collections of stories were later put out by the publishers of the magazine, Ravan Press. Matshoba's *Call Me Not a Man* (1979), Mzamane's *Mzala* (1980), and Mutloatse's *Mama Ndiyalila* (1982) share a concern with presenting the life of black people in starkly realistic mode, and they often incorporate elements of African oral culture in an attempt to shrug off Western literary influence. Ndebele's *Fools and Other Stories* (1983) has enjoyed more sustained success than the collections of his *Staffrider* contemporaries. His stories are rich in detail and vividly evoke township life as seen mainly through the eyes of a young and sensitive protagonist.

Another highly accomplished short-story writer is Bessie *Head, whose *The Collector of Treasures* (1977) is set in a village in Botswana and successfully employs many techniques and devices germane to the oral milieu of the village. Head's stories engage effectively with the issues that emerge in Botswanan village life: tribal history, the arrival of the missionaries, religious conflict, witchcraft, rising illegitimacy, and, throughout, problems that the women in the society encounter.

Other accomplished short-story writers of the 1970s and 1980s include Christopher *Hope, Ahmed *Essop, Peter *Wilhelm, and Sheila *Roberts. Hope's witheringly satirical view of apartheid South Africa is well represented in his *Private Parts and Other Tales* (1981, 1982), which includes his "Learning to Fly," a mordant fable about the changing of the guard in the state security apparatus. Essop's *The Hajji and Other Stories* (1978), *Noorjehan and Other Stories* (1990), and *The King of Hearts and Other Stories* (1997) examine in fine detail and with gentle irony the life of the Asian community in and around Johannesburg. The issues that Essop explores are those that beset the day-to-day life of a community squeezed by the interests of the dominant racial groups in South Africa. Wilhelm's collections include *LM and Other Stories* (1975), *At the End of the War* (1981), and *Some Place in Africa* (1987). Roberts's *Outside Life's Feast* (1975) and *This Time of Year* (1983) explore the frustrations and prejudices of her working-class white protagonists with an uncompromising frankness and commitment to detail. Her *Coming in and Other Stories* appeared in 1993.

Cape Town's District Six, demolished in the 1960s, is the setting for a number of short stories, among them stories by Alex *La Guma, Achmat *Dangor, James *Matthews and Richard *Rive. Rive's well-crafted stories, collected in *Advance, Retreat: Selected Short Stories* (1983), mainly explore the effects of South Africa's racial laws on the individual. Dangor's writing centers on the iniquitous effects of racial segregation and forced removals, themes that are explored very powerfully in his award-winning prose collection *Waiting for Leila* (1981). The title story of *Waiting for Leila* is a novella that describes the demolition of District Six and features the drunken, degenerate Samad struggling to come to terms with the errors he has made in his life. Another story, "Jobman" (which became a short feature film), concerns a deaf farm worker who is brutally hunted down and killed on a Karoo farm after he comes back to reclaim his wife.

The contemporary South African short story manifests a fascinating diversity of techniques. The social realism so prominent in the 1970s and 80s has given way to metafictional experimentation in a variety of forms. Predictably, this development involves a further movement away from forms of story writing that draw on oral culture, the milieu in which the South African short story first emerged. The voices heard in Ivan *Vladislavić's *Missing Persons* (1989), for example, are those of alienated city-dwellers, cut off not only from forms of community embedded in the oral tale, but even from the communality of neighbors across the fence. Vladislavić's offbeat vision is consolidated very effectively in his *Propaganda by Monuments and Other Stories* (1996). Zoë *Wicomb's story-cycle, *You Can't Get Lost in Cape Town* (1987), explores a South African girl's childhood and the contradictory emotions experienced by her protagonist who ends up positioned uncomfortably between home and exile. The style of her stories is bold and experimental. Maureen *Isaacson's *Holding Back Midnight* (1992) is a similar display of imagination and linguistic skill. Her stories range widely in scope—from a depressingly believable projection of South Africa on the cusp of the millennium, to a portrait of regulation-bound life in ice-bound Sweden, to descriptions of growing up as a young Jo'burger in the freewheeling 1970s.

The astonishing diversity in style one encounters in the recent South African short story makes for rewarding reading. One encounters the tale sprung from oral origins, with distinct folkloristic undertones; the story written in the tradition of realism, with a heavy dose of social realism; the narrative fragment rendered in the spirit of journalistic reportage; the fantasy tale which reaches back into the past of myth and legend and that which looks forward to the kind of fictive experimentation loosely termed "magical realism." The genre of the South African short story has undergone a renaissance in recent years and the signs are that the form is destined to play a major role in bodying forth South Africa's future in imaginative terms.

Shukri, Ishtiyaq (b. 1968) Novelist. Born in Johannesburg, Ishtiyaq Shukri studied at the universities of the Western Cape and Witwatersrand before leaving South Africa to study South Asian literature in London.

He has published one novel, *The Silent Minaret* (2005), which was winner of the EU Literary Award for Best First Novel. Set in the Western Cape in the period before the democratic elections of 1994, and in post–September 11 London, *The Silent Minaret* explores the circumstances around the disappearance of Issa, a South African student living abroad, wrestling with questions of migrancy and struggling to reconcile the personal and the political in the context of global events.

Simon, Barney (1933–1995) Playwright, short-story writer, theater director. He was cofounder, with Mannie Manim, of the Market Theatre in Johannesburg, and he has had an enormous influence on the development of South African theater.

Simon published several plays, including *Cold Stone Jug: The Play* (1982), *Woza Albert!* (with Percy Mtwa and Mbongeni Ngema, 1983), *Cincinnati* (in *South African Theatre*, 1984), *Hey, Listen* (in *Market Plays*, 1986), and *Born in the RSA: Four Workshopped Plays* (1997), which includes *Born in the RSA*, *Outers*, *Black Dog Inj'emnhama*, and *Score Me the Ages*. He has also written and produced numerous unpublished plays: "Phiri," "Miss South Africa," "Joburg," "Sis!", "Storytime," "Call Me Woman," "So What's New," "The Lion and the Lamb: The Life of Christ," "People and Other Monologues," "Show Me Yours," "The Suit," "The Fourth Day of Christmas," "The Dybbuk," and "Starbrites." In addition, he wrote several screenplays: *Silent Movie*, *Rosa and the Eagle*, *Senhor Ventura*, *Martha Quest*, *Enemies: A Love Story*, *The Late Bourgeois World* (an adaptation of a novel by Nadine *Gordimer), *City Lovers*, *Six Feet of the Country*, and *Good Climate, Friendly Inhabitants* (the last three based on short stories by Gordimer). He contributed to a collection of short stories, *Twenty Stories* (1953), and published one collection of his own stories, *Joburg, Sis!* (1974). He also edited *Familiarity Is the Kingdom of the Lost* by Dugmore *Boetie (1984). Simon's approach of workshopping plays around a storytelling technique resulted in productions that were acclaimed for their energy and authenticity. Several times over he received the Breytenbach Epathlon for best director. He was also awarded a 1984 OBIE Award, a 1994 DALRO Award, and a 1995 FNB Vita National Theatre Award.

FURTHER READING

Anne Fuchs, *Playing the Market: The Market Theatre, Johannesburg, 1976–1986* (1990); Immanual Suttner, ed., *Cutting Through the*

Mountain: Interviews with South African Jewish Activists (1997); Mary Benson, *Athol Fugard and Barney Simon: Bare Stage, a Few Props, Great Theatre* (1997); Irene Stephanou et al. (2005), *The World in an Orange: Creating Theatre with Barney Simon* (2005).

Sitas, Ari (b. 1952) Poet and playwright. He studied at the University of the Witwatersrand. As founding member of the Junction Avenue Theatre Company, he was involved in its many productions, including the well-known *Fantastical Journey of a Useless Man* (1978). In 1983 he moved to Durban, where he was instrumental in the formation of the Durban Workers' Cultural Union and the Culture and Working Life Project. He was also involved in the formation of the Congress of South African Writers (COSAW) in 1987. One of his plays, *William Zungu: A Xmas Story*, was published in 1991.

Sitas has published three volumes of poetry, *Tropical Scars* (1989), *Songs, Shoeshine and Piano* (1992), and *Slave Trades and an Artist's Notebook* (2000). *Tropical Scars* is a long epic poem that is syntactically pared down to represent, grammatically, the wounds inflicted by apartheid. *Slave Trades* is similarly epic in scope, recreating, from archival sources and personal travel in Ethiopia, the experience of Arthur Rimbaud in late-nineteenth-century Africa. It employs the voice not only of Rimbaud himself but also of such figures as the Emperors Makkonen and Menelek and the poet Constantine Cavafy. Set in a period of high imperialism, and located at a geographical juncture of cultures and beliefs, the poem represents, as stated in the preface, "a song of loss and yearning," creating an emotional space for the past to speak to the present.

Sithebe, Angelina (b. 1962) Novelist. Born and raised in Soweto, Sithebe matriculated from Inanda Seminary School in Durban and trained as a geologist at Brooklyn College in New York. She has worked as a public relations officer for Codesa and in scholarship administration, communications, human resources, geotechnical engineering, and mining. She has published two novels. *Three Letters Three Words* (2006) is about a professional woman whose married, middle-class life is disrupted by her past. *Holy Hill* (2007) tells the story of Nana, who emerges from a Roman Catholic convent school in Zululand as a troubled young woman haunted by spirits, and whose encounter with Claude, former child soldier and drug addict turned born-again Christian, leads her back to the school after an absence of sixteen years.

Skinner, Douglas Reid (b. 1949) Poet, editor, publisher. Born in Upington, Northern Cape, he is a graduate of Rhodes University. Between 1974 and 1984 he lived in England and the United States, working in computer information systems. On his return to South Africa, he worked as freelance writer and publisher. He has since moved permanently to London.

Skinner has published five volumes of poetry: *Dreams from a World Place* (1979), *Reassembling World* (1981), *The House in Pella District* (1985), *The Unspoken* (1988), and *The Middle Years* (1993).

Avoiding contemporary political themes that characterized much South African literature of the time, the poems seek to discover histories beyond what the moment has to offer, providing links with the natural and the ancient worlds. In these poems, understanding is secondary to experiencing and "now" is always more immediate than "then," though what is apprehended in the present is mediated through images and language that serve both to distance the experience and to give it resonance. This resonance is precisely what the poems aspire to achieve.

Skinner is also the editor of *Soundings: An Anthology of Poems* (1989) and *Signs: Three Collections of Poetry* (1992), and, with Israel Aharon Ben Yosef, of *Approximations: Translations from Modern Hebrew Poetry* (1989). He was editor and publisher of *Upstream* magazine and founder of Carrefour Press.

Slabolepszy, Paul (b. 1948) Playwright. Born in England, he immigrated to South Africa as a child. He is a graduate of the University of Cape Town and makes his living acting in plays that he has written himself.

Slabolepszy has published two works, *Saturday Night at the Palace* (1985) and the collection of plays *Mooi Street and Other Moves* (1994), which includes *Mooi Street Moves, Boo to the Moon, Over the Hill, The Return of Elvis du Pisanie, Smallholding,* and *Under the Oaks*. He has also written several unpublished plays: "Renovations" (1979), "Defloration of Miles Koekemoer" (1980), "Karoo Grand" (1983), "Pale Natives" (1993/4), "Victoria Almost Falls" (1994), "Tickle to Fine Leg" (1995), "Heel Against the Head" (1995), "Fordsburg's Finest," and "Packing for Perth." He is the author of two teleplays, "Highrise Cowboy" and "Hands of Stone."

Topical and satirical, and making effective use of the rhythms, accents, and idiom of South African English, the plays use conventional characters and situations in sending up the preoccupations of a society obsessed with racial politics, sport, and parochial pursuits.

Slabolepszy has received numerous awards for drama, including the 1981 Amstel Award, a 1987 Sicilian Festival Annual Award, a 1988 AA Life Vita Award, the 1992 Amstel Pick of the Fringe Award, a 1993 DALRO Award, a 1993 Fleur Du Cap Theatre Award, a 1993 IGI Life Vita National Theatre Award, the 1994 Paper Boat Award (Mayfets—Scotland), and a 1995 FNB Vita National Theatre Award.

FURTHER READING

Geoffrey V. Davis, "Theatre for a Postapartheid Society," *Journal of Commonwealth Literature* 30, no. 1 (1995): 5–21; André Brink, "Challenge and Response: The Changing Face of Theater in South Africa," *Twentieth Century Literature* 43, no. 2 (1997): 162–176; Marietjie van Deventer, "Paul Slabolepszy's Angst-Ridden Elvis," *Literator* 21, no. 1 (2000): 121–137; Loren Kruger, "Theatre, Crime, and the Edgy City in Postapartheid Johannesburg," *Theatre Journal* 53, no. 2 (2001): 223–252; M. A. van Deventer, "Communicating Social Inclusiveness: Paul Slabolepszy's 'Fordsburg's Finest' (1997)," *Literator* 25, no. 2 (2004): 79–96.

Slater, Francis Carey *See* Writers Before 1945

Sleigh, Dan (b. 1938) Historian and novelist. A graduate of Stellenbosch University, a conservationist, and a former editor in the transcription department of the Cape Archives, Sleigh specializes in the Dutch Seaborne Empire (1602–1795). He has published widely in Afrikaans and rose to prominence with the translation into English of his novel *Islands* (2004), which has been awarded the M-Net prize, the Sanlam/Insig Prize, the WA Hofmeyr Award, and the Helgard Steyn Prize 2004. The novel tells the story of Krotoa-Eva and her daughter Pieternella. Krotoa-Eva was a Khoikhoi woman employed in the household of Jan van Riebeeck, head of the Dutch East India Company at the Cape, who subsequently married the Danish surgeon Peter Havgard. *Islands* re-creates the early encounter between the Dutch and the Khoi population.

Slovo, Gillian (b. 1952) Novelist and autobiographer. Daughter of the political activist Joe Slovo and Ruth *First, who was assassinated in Maputo in 1982 by agents of the apartheid regime, she has spent her life in exile in London since 1964. Slovo has published numerous works of fiction. Five of these are the Kate Baeier detective novels: *Morbid Symptoms* (1984), *Death by Analysis* (1986), *Death Comes Staccato* (1987), *Catnap* (1994), and *Close Call* (1995). Slovo has said that she writes detective fiction in response to a childhood characterized by clandestine political activity. The other fictional works are political novels dealing directly with South Africa: *Ties of Blood* (1989), *The Betrayal* (1991), *Façade* (1993), and *Red Dust* (2000). The last is about a South African woman living and working as a lawyer in New York who is drawn back to South Africa and into the tangled workings of the Truth and Reconciliation Commission in a rural town. It has been made into a film of the same name. All of these works, detective fiction and political fiction, address, in some way, the issues of history and memory, with main characters modeled on actual persons. The fiction has been described as an attempt to engage with a reality of dislocation and loss. Slovo has also published an autobiography, *Every Secret Thing: My Family, My Country* (1997), which similarly attempts to come to terms with and understand the past, with events revealing both more and less than the author had anticipated.

FURTHER READING

Claudia Braude, "The Archbishop, the Private Detective and the Angel of History: The Production of South African Public Memory and the Truth and Reconciliation Commission," *Current Writing* 8, no. 2 (1996): 39–65; Sarah Nuttall, "Popular Stories of Apartheid: Gillian Slovo's South African Novels," *Journal of Commonwealth Literature* 32, no. 1 (1997): 79–92; Marian Mesrobian MacCurdy, "Truth, Trauma, and Justice in Gillian Slovo's *Every Secret Thing*," *Literature & Medicine* 19, no. 1 (2000): 115–132; Sue Kossew, *Writing Woman, Writing Place: Contemporary Australian and South African Fiction* (2004); Georgina Horrell, "A Whiter Shade of Pale: White Femininity as Guilty Masquerade in 'New' (White) South African Women's Writing," *Journal of Southern African Studies* 30, no. 4 (2004): 765–776; Judith Lütge Coullie et al., eds., *Selves in Question: Interviews on Southern African Auto/biography* (2006).

Small, Adam (b. 1936) Poet and playwright. Born in Wellington, he studied at the universities of Cape Town, London, and Oxford and lectured at the universities of Fort Hare and the Western Cape. He is founder of the Cape Flats Players and is credited with providing the philosophical basis for Black Consciousness in the 1970s. A prominent writer in Afrikaans, his most famous Afrikaans play has been translated as *Kanna, He Is Coming Home* (1990). He has also written in English, most notably the quatrains *Black, Bronze, Beautiful* (1975) and the memoir *Elections and Erections* (2003). He is the author of *District Six* (1986). Modeled on the biblical Song of Solomon, and drawing on the poetics of blackness characteristic of the negritude movement, *Black, Bronze, Beautiful* celebrates sensory pleasure as life-affirming value.

Smith, Pauline *See* Writers Before 1945

Smith, Wilbur (Addison) (b. 1933) Novelist. Born in Northern Rhodesia (now Zambia), he was educated at Michaelhouse, in Natal, and Rhodes University, where he gained a degree in commerce. He now lives in Cape Town. One of South Africa's most commercially successful popular novelists, he made his name with his debut work, *When the Lion Feeds* (1964), which was banned for a time for its racy content. All of his twenty-odd novels have African settings and an adventure-thriller basis. They include *The Dark of the Sun* (1965), set in the Congo; *The Sound of Thunder* (1966), set at the time of the Boer War; *The Sunbird* (1972), which draws on the work of H. Rider *Haggard; *Eagle in the Sky* (1974), which sets up parallels between the South African and Israeli situations; and *A Time to Die* (1989), which deals with the Mozambican conflict. The Ballantyne family saga, which covers Rhodesian colonial history, is pursued in a series of novels: *A Falcon Flies* (1980), *Men of Men* (1981), *The Angels Weep* (1982), and *The Leopard Hunts in Darkness* (1984). Other novels include *The Burning Shore* (1985), *Power of the Sword* (1986), *Rage* (1987), and *Golden Fox* (1990), all of which feature the exploits of the Courtney family against the backdrop of South African history. His more recent work includes several more Courtney novels—*Birds of Prey* (1997), *Monsoon* (1999), *Blue Horizon* (2003), *The Triumph of the Sun* (2005), and *Assegai* (2009)—and a number set in ancient Egypt, *River God* (1993), *The Seventh Scroll* (1995), *Warlock* (2001), and *The Quest* (2007).

FURTHER READING

Martin Trump, ed., *Rendering Things Visible: Essays on South African Literary Culture* (1990); John A. Stotesbury, "The Function of Borders in the Popular Novel on South Africa," *English in Africa* 17, no. 2 (1990): 71–89; Richard Peck, *A Morbid Fascination: White Prose and Politics in Apartheid South Africa* (1997); Lindy Stiebel, *Imagining Africa: Landscape in H. Rider Haggard's African Romances* (2001).

Sole, Kelwyn (b. 1951) Poet and critic. Born in Johannesburg and educated at the universities of the Witwatersrand and London, he has worked in Botswana and Namibia and is now a professor of English at the University of Cape Town.

Sole has published several volumes of poetry, including *The Blood of Our Silence* (1987), *Projections in the Past Tense* (1992), *Love That Is Night* (1998), *Mirror and Water Gazing* (2001), and *Land Dreaming: Prose Poems* (2006).

The early volumes are distinguished by their depiction of how all aspects of experience, even the most intimate, are invaded by the political struggle waged in South Africa in the 1980s. This is referred to by one poem as the merging of the self with history: the stones that clatter against armored cars in the townships rattle, also, the dreams of lovers seeking a meager comfort in each other's arms. Written from a position of what Sole calls "personal fracture," the poems eschew fixed and stereotypical attitudes in favor of a life lived dangerously, in which the individual is constantly at risk. The more recent volumes extend the concerns of the earlier volumes, attacking the restrictive ethos of a soul-numbing, bureaucratized commodity existence and affirming the power of an imaginative and erotic mode of existence, a transgressive "love that is night." Sole was awarded the 1989 Olive Schreiner Award for Literature and the 1989 Thomas Pringle Award. He was also awarded second place in the 1993 and first place in the 1994 Sydney Clouts Memorial Prize.

In his criticism, he has for many years brought a sophisticated Marxist perspective to bear on South African culture and society.

FURTHER READING

David Attwell, "Resisting Power: A Reply to Kelwyn Sole and Isabel Hofmeyr," *Pretexts* 3, nos. 1 & 2 (1991): 130–134; Peter Horn, "A Radical Rethinking of the Art of Poetry in an Apartheid Society," *Journal of Commonwealth Literature* 28, no. 1 (1993): 97–113; Kelwyn Sole, "Democratising Culture and Literature in a 'New South Africa': Organisation and

Theory," *Current Writing* 6, no. 2 (1994): 1–37; Lewis Nkosi, "Sole and the Symptoms of Nervous Breakdown," *Current Writing* 6, no. 2 (1994): 55–59; Gareth Cornwell, "Mapmaking in the Missionary Position: A Response to Kelwyn Sole," *Current Writing* 6, no. 2 (1994): 53–54; Isabel Hofmeyr, "Kelwyn Sole, Postcolonialism, and the Challenge of the Local," *Current Writing* 6, no. 2 (1994): 49–52; Guy Willoughby, "Meeting of Soles: Overhearing Democratizing Culture and Literature," *Current Writing* 6, no. 2 (1994): 38–48; John Higgins, "The Sole Measure of Poetic Value: A Response to Kelwyn Sole," *Pretexts* 12, no. 1 (2003): 97–102.

Stander, Siegfried (1935–1988) Novelist. A journalist by profession, Stander wrote a number of novels in Afrikaans but is best known for two CNA Award–winning novels: *This Desert Place* (1961), about cattle ranching in the Bechuanaland Protectorate (now Botswana), and *The Horse* (1968). His other novels include *The Emptiness of the Plains* (1963), *The Fortress* (1972), *Leopard in the Sun* (1973), and *Flight from the Hunter* (1977). His novel *Into the Winter* (1983) deals with race relations in the changing South Africa of the 1980s. He also wrote a children's story, *The Journeys of Josephine* (1968), coauthored three novels with the famous heart surgeon Chris Barnard—*The Unwanted* (1974), *In the Night Season* (1977), and *The Faith* (1984)—and wrote *Like the Wind: The Story of the South African Army* (1985).

Steinberg, Jonny (b. 1970) Journalist and freelance writer. Born in South Africa, Jonny Steinberg holds a doctoral degree in political science from Oxford University. Although he is not a literary figure as such, the three books cited here employ a biographical method and a personal style in exploring the condition of contemporary South African society.

Midlands (2002) investigates the issue of farm murders in the postapartheid countryside of KwaZulu-Natal, bringing to light the racial tensions that remain unresolved in these communities. *The Number* (2004) provides insight into the "number gangs" in the prison system, through the biography of an individual member who attempts to free himself from the gangster ethos in the wake of what he regards as its compromises in contemporary times. Both books have received the *Sunday Times* Alan Paton Award for nonfiction. *Midlands* also received the National Booksellers' Choice award in 2003. *Three-Letter Plague* (2008) chronicles the resistance of a shopkeeper to the introduction of antiretroviral drugs in his Eastern Cape village.

Strauss, Peter (b. 1941) Poet, critic, editor. Born in Pietermaritzburg, he is a graduate of the universities of Natal and Cambridge. He lectured for many years at the University of Natal, Durban, before his retirement.

Strauss has published several volumes of poetry, including *Poems* (1973; jointly published alongside poems by Christopher *Hope, Ruth Keech, and Douglas *Livingstone), *Photographs of Bushmen* (1974), *Bishop Bernward's Door and Other Poems* (1983), and *The Owl and the Moon* (1999), as well as a study of poetry, *Talking Poetry: A Guide for Students, Teachers and Poets* (1993). He has also collaborated on a children's book, *Noah's Ark* (1994). Seeking to discover the mythical and the symbolic in the mundane and the everyday, the poems are delivered in a deceptively simple conversational style. Strauss is past editor of the literary magazine *Donga*. He was awarded the 1971, 1973, and 1981 Thomas Pringle Award, and is cited in the 1996 Children's Book Forum Honours List.

Swart, Vincent (1911–1962) Poet and editor. Born in Heilbron in the Free State, Swart studied and lectured at the University of the Witwatersrand, during which time he wrote poems for periodicals in South Africa and abroad. He was awarded a scholarship to Cambridge but was forced to return to South Africa in 1940 with the outbreak of World War II. He was editor of the left-wing periodical *Contemporary Issues* and became increasingly involved in politics in the postwar years. He was briefly jailed in 1960 for his political activities and banned thereafter. His poems appeared in *Contrast* and various anthologies and were edited by Marcia Leveson as *Collected Poems* (1981).

Swift, Mark (b. 1946) Poet. Born in Queenstown, Eastern Province, and educated in Cathcart, Cape Town, and East London, he studied toward an arts degree and subsequently became a journalist. He has worked for the *Cape Times* and *The Argus*, and has served on the editorial staff of the literary magazine *Contrast*. He emigrated to England, where he is currently employed by the *Cambridge Evening News*. Swift has published four volumes of poetry: *Treading Water* (1974), *Gentlewoman* (1978), *Seconds Out* (1983), and *Testing the Edge* (1996). The condition of exile explored in *Testing the Edge* is a pervasive experience of strangeness and displacement, conveyed in a voice that is not nostalgic so much as doggedly enduring, one that has become toughened against despair despite what one poem calls the "ambush of history." The images have a nuggetlike permanence retrieved from the instabilities of change. Swift was awarded the 1975 Ingrid Jonker Prize and the 1987 Thomas Pringle Award. His poems have been broadcast by the BBC, the SABC, and Canadian radio.

T

Themba, Daniel Canadoise D'Orsay (Can) (1924–1968) Short-story writer. Born in Marabastad, outside Pretoria, Themba was educated at the University of Fort Hare. He qualified as a teacher and taught for several years in Western Native Township on the outskirts of Johannesburg. After winning a *Drum* short-story competition in 1953 with his "Mob Passion," he was taken on as a staff writer by the magazine, to which he contributed five of his stories and a stream of journalistic pieces. He later worked on *Drum*'s sister publication *Golden City Post*, and his writing also appeared in *The Classic* and *Africa South*. In 1963 he went into voluntary exile in Swaziland and taught there until his alcohol-related death five years later. In 1966 he was declared a "statutory communist" under South Africa's 1965 Suppression of Communism Amendment Act, and his writing was banned in South Africa.

His work has been made available in three posthumous collections: *The Will to Die* (1972), edited by Donald Stuart and Roy Holland; *The World of Can Themba* (1985), edited by Essop *Patel; and *Requiem for Sophiatown* (2006), edited by Stephen *Gray. His work straddles the genres of fiction, autobiographical reminiscence, and journalistic reportage, and it frequently recounts, with humor and imagination, his exploits in the shebeens of Sophiatown. "Requiem for Sophiatown" and "The Bottom of the Bottle" are two well-known examples of this. His best-known story, however, is the much-anthologized "The Suit." Set in Sophiatown in the 1950s, it explores the idyllic relationship between a husband and wife, which takes a dramatic turn for the worse when the wife's infidelity is discovered. The story thus deals with the age-old theme of personal betrayal and its tragic consequences. Intertwined with this main concern are the subsidiary themes of the harshness of township life (but also its resilience and cheerfulness), racial segregation, and the lot of black people in general. Of particular interest is the story's style, which is effusive, even perhaps melodramatic. Themba also evinces a love of intricate phrases and unusual combinations of words, in this way demonstrating his (declared) affinity with stylists like Oscar Wilde.

FURTHER READING

Bob Gosani and Jürgen Schadeberg, *The Fifties People of South Africa* (1987); Paul Gready, "The Sophiatown Writers of the Fifties: The Unreal Reality of Their World," *Journal of Southern African Studies* 16, no. 1 (1990): 139–164; Mike Nicol, *A Good-looking Corpse* (1991); Anthony Sampson, *Drum: The Making of a Magazine* (2005).

Thomas, Gladys (b. 1935) Short-story writer, playwright, poet, children's writer. Born in Salt River, Cape Town, of a mixed-race family, she left school at fifteen to work in a clothing factory. She attended the International Writing Program at the University of Iowa in 1983. Strongly critical of apartheid, her work was banned under the apartheid regime and resulted in her being detained.

Thomas has published a collection of short stories, *Children of Crossroads* (1986), a play, *Avalon Court: Vignettes of Life of the 'Coloured' People on the Cape Flats of Cape Town* (1992), and a biographical study, *The Wynberg Seven* (1987). She has also been published in various anthologies of poetry, including *Cry Rage!* (1972) and *Exiles Within* (1986). She is the author of a collection of children's stories, *Spotty Dog and Other Stories* (1987). Her work documents the victims of apartheid's social policies. *Children of Crossroads* recounts the stories of children dispossessed by the forced removals of the Crossroads community. *The Wynberg Seven* deals with circumstances and parental perceptions of the youngsters on trial for politically motivated actions against the state. Thomas appeared on the 1980 Kwanzaa Honors List and received the 1990 Bertrams VO Award for African Literature.

Tlali, Miriam (b. 1933) Novelist and short-story writer. Tlali was the first black woman writer to publish a novel in English in South Africa. Born in Doornfontein, she grew up in Sophiatown and presently lives in Soweto. She studied at the universities of the Witwatersrand and Lesotho but was forced to abandon her studies after experiencing financial difficulties. She is the author of two novels. The first of these is *Muriel at Metropolitan* (1975), a largely autobiographical work about her experiences as a bookkeeper at a Johannesburg furniture store. The novel was banned for a long time in South Africa. Her second novel, *Amandla* (1981), concerns the Soweto disturbances and their aftermath. It sold well before being banned and achieved considerable popularity. Her stories have been collected in two volumes: *Mihloti* (1984) and *Footprints in the Quag: Stories and Dialogues from Soweto* (1989; published internationally as *Soweto Stories*). A consistent strain in her work is her concern with women's issues and the struggle of women to take control of their own lives in a patriarchal society.

FURTHER READING

Craig MacKenzie and Cherry Clayton, eds., *Between the Lines: Interviews with Bessie Head, Sheila Roberts, Ellen Kuzwayo, Miriam Tlali* (1989); Raoul Granqvist and John A. Stotesbury, eds., *African Voices: Interviews with Thirteen African Writers* (1989); Rolf Solberg and Malcolm Hacksley, eds., *Reflections: Perspectives on Writing in Postapartheid*

South Africa (1996); Paul Gready, *Writing as Resistance: Life Stories of Imprisonment, Exile, and Homecoming from Apartheid South Africa* (2003); Christina Cullhed, *Grappling with Patriarchies: Narrative Strategies of Resistance in Miriam Tlali's Writings* (2006).

Travel Literature The oral traditions of Africa probably contain the earliest accounts of travel in the southern African subcontinent, but these are lost to modernity as a consequence of the fugitive nature of all oral culture. Vestiges of such accounts survive in adulterated form in African literature: Bessie Head's story "The Deep River: A Story of Ancient Tribal Migration" (from her *The Collector of Treasures*, 1977) is one fairly recent example of this. But it is to written (invariably European) accounts that one has inevitably to turn in order to trace the literature of travel in Africa.

South African travel literature in its early manifestations is inextricably tied to the phenomena of exploration, missionary activity, and colonial conquest. The ancient Greeks, and most notably Ptolemy, had some vague knowledge of Africa, for Greek and Arab traders had ventured south down the east coast of Africa as far as Zanzibar. But it was the Portuguese explorers of Renaissance times, and Bartolomeu Dias and Vasco da Gama in particular, who were the most significant early explorers of the subcontinent. Their voyages of discovery stimulated later writings about the region such as Joao de Barros's *Decades of Asia* (1552–1615), an ambitious history of Portugal's overseas conquests that includes a reliable account of Dias at the Cape of Good Hope, and Bernardo Gomes de Brito's *Historia Tragica-Maritima* (1735–6).

Portuguese maritime power declined after the country's loss of independence to Spain at the end of the sixteenth century. At this time the Dutch became increasingly interested in gaining a foothold at the Cape, a process that culminated in Jan van Riebeeck's arrival there in 1652. This period saw a proliferation of texts about the Cape and other parts of the coast of South Africa. Anecdotal accounts of voyages and shipwrecks began to give way to more specific accounts of the geography and human habitation of the Cape and its immediate hinterland. These texts, however, were mostly formulaic and derivative and consisted of recycled stock notions about the Khoi ("Hottentot")—their strange implosive language, dietary practices, sexual anatomy and propensity to "idleness." One of the most substantial texts of this period is Willem ten Rhyne's *Schediasma de Promonotorio Bonae Spei* (1686), in which a Khoi informant is used to provide information on aspects of native life.

Perhaps the most important example of travel writing in the early eighteenth century is Peter Kolb(en)'s *The Present State of the Cape of Good Hope* (1719). It is an extended description that takes the form of a survey and thus anticipates the more systematic and scientific texts of the post-Enlightenment period of the late eighteenth and early nineteenth centuries. Kolb's initial purpose was to make astronomical observations, but his work came to incorporate accounts of Khoi culture and the effects of European settlement. The last decades of the eighteenth century saw the appearance of works by two Swedish botanists, Anders Sparrman (*A Voyage to the Cape of Good Hope*, 1783) and Carl Peter Thunberg (*Travels in Europe, Africa and Asia*, 1794–95), whose purpose was to carry out scientific research in the classificatory spirit of their teacher, Carolus Linnaeus. The French naturalist François le Vaillant, inspired by the romanticism of Jean-Jacques Rousseau, explored parts of South Africa and collected specimens. His record of this expedition is his sometimes-flamboyant *Travels Into the Interior Parts of Africa* (1790) and *Second Voyage . . .* (1794–95). He developed a close relationship with two of his Khoi helpers, observing with approval their preference for the simplicity of their lives.

The first period of British rule at the Cape (1795–1803) produced John Barrow's *An Account of Travels into the Interior of Southern Africa in the Years 1797 and 1798* (1801). Barrow was secretary to the British governor, and his role as a diplomat may have influenced his writing style, for his account is remarkably detached and impersonal. This also reflected the new spirit of scientific objectivity with which travel writers now sought to imbue their texts. However, Robert Semple's *Walks and Sketches at the Cape of Good Hope* (1803), another work of this period, is more in the vein of fictionalized travel writing, and deploys an imaginary traveling companion and interlocutor in discussion with whom the writer-protagonist expounds his views. The brief return to Dutch rule at the Cape (1803–1806) is reflected in the German Martin Hinrich Carl Lichtenstein's *Travels in Southern Africa in the Years 1803–1806* (1811).

Perhaps the most influential work in this genre in the first half of the nineteenth century, following Britain's resumption of rule at the Cape after 1806, is William Burchell's *Travels in the Interior of Southern Africa*, published in two volumes in 1822 and 1824. Burchell's work, the product of extensive travels in South Africa between 1811 and 1815, is a remarkable blend of systematic scientific observation and an inclusive romantic vision. His sympathy with the non-European inhabitants at the Cape recalls Le Vaillant. For Burchell, the Khoi were an admirable race with good military and herding skills, and he urged a humane and rational approach to these people on the part of the colonial authorities. His work also set a new standard of scientific rigor in the field of natural history in South Africa.

The steadily growing missionary activity in the interior of South Africa spawned works such as John Campbell's *Travels in South Africa* (1815), Allen Gardiner's *Narrative of a Journey to the Zoolu Country in South Africa* (1836), Robert Moffat's *Missionary Labours and Scenes in Southern Africa* (1842), and David Livingstone's *Missionary Travels and Researches in Southern Africa* (1857). The nineteenth century was also the era of the hunter-explorer. Sir William Cornwallis Harris was an early exponent of the big-game hunting narrative with his *The Wild Sports of Southern Africa* (1839). Harris was both hunter and naturalist, and he frequently made drawings of the animals he hunted. Others who worked in this genre are R. Gordon Cumming (*Five Years of a Hunter's Life in the Far Interior of South Africa*, 1850) and Frederick Courtney Selous, whose accounts of explorations in present-day Zimbabwe and beyond the Zambezi appeared as *A Hunter's Wanderings in Africa* (1891) and *Travel and Adventure in South-East Africa* (1893). H. A. Bryden produced several travel books, including *Kloof and Karroo: Sport, Legend, and Natural History in the Cape Colony* (1889), *Gun and Camera in Southern Africa* (1893), and *Travel and Big Game* (1887; cowritten with P. Selous). The exploration activity that preceded and accompanied the colonial expansion northward, notably under Cecil Rhodes's aggressive expansionist policies, is reflected in several works of the late nineteenth and early twentieth century, including Baden-Powell's *The Matabele Campaign* (1897) and *Sketches in Mafeking and East Africa* (1907), and Percy FitzPatrick's well-known *Through Mashonaland with Pick and Pen* (1892).

The relentless process of exploration and colonial conquest by European powers from the Renaissance period to the early twentieth century (the Anglo-Boer War was perhaps the last major event in this process in South Africa) effectively gave rise to the travel literature of South Africa. The more settled conditions of the twentieth century—at least as far as boundaries and territorial rights are concerned—has meant that the literature of travel and exploration has given way to the literature of protest and contestation regarding the rights to tracts of land within the boundaries of South Africa. Sol Plaatje's *Native Life in South Africa* (1916) is the classic example of literature in this vein.

Troost, Heinrich (b. 1961) Novelist. Having qualified at Stellenbosch University and worked for a while as legal consultant and manager at an insurance company, Troost currently practices as an attorney in the Western Cape. His novel *Plot Loss* (2007) tells the story of newly qualified Harry van As, who returns to Pretoria from the Cape to take up a job and encounters a city much changed, in his perspective, in the postapartheid years, where he is increasingly compelled to confront the meaning of his life.

U

Uys, Pieter-Dirk (b. 1945) Playwright, actor, cartoonist. Born in Cape Town, he has lived in Johannesburg, where he was director of P. D. Uys Productions, and now lives in Darling, on the Cape West Coast. He writes and performs in his own plays.

Uys has published numerous plays, including *Paradise Is Closing Down* (in *Theatre One: New South African Drama*, 1978); *God's Forgotten* (in *Theatre Two: New South African Drama*, 1981); *Karnaval* (1982); *Selle Ou Storie* (1983), *Farce About Uys: A Legal Assembly in Two Riotous Acts* (1983); *Appassionata* (in *Market Plays*, 1986); *Paradise Is Closing Down and Other Plays* (1989), which includes *God's Forgotten*, *Panorama*, and *Paradise Is Closing Down*; *Just Like Home* (in *South Africa Plays*, 1993); *No Space on Long Street; Marshrose: Two Plays* (2000); and *Foreign Aids* (2002). He has also published a film script, *Skating on Thin Uys*. Several unpublished plays, revues and cabarets have been written, including "Snow White and the Special Branch," "Black Beauty and BOSS," "Adapt or Dye," "Total Onslaught" (1984), "Rearranging the Deckchairs on the S.A. Bothatanic," "An Audience with Evita Bezuidenhout," "One Man One Volt" (1994), "God's Forgotten" (1995), "Bambi Sings the FAK Songs" (1995), and "You ANC Nothing Yet" (1995). He is also author of a number of prose works: *No One's Died Laughing* (1986), *P. W. Botha in His Own Words* (1987), *A Part Hate A Part Love: The Biography of Evita Bezuidenhout* (1990, rev. ed. 1994), *Funigalore: Evita's Real-Life Adventures in Wonderland* (1995), *The Essential Evita Bezuidenhout* (1997), and the novel *Trekking to Teema* (2001). Books in an autobiographical vein include *Elections & Erections: A Memoir of Fear and Fun* (2002) and *Between the Devil and the Deep: A Memoir of Acting and Reacting* (2005).

The primary target of Uys's satirical plays is racial policies and politicians. In the figure of Evita Bezuidenhout, who is Uys dressed up in drag, he has created an endearing persona who acts as mouthpiece for his barbed comments on topical political issues.

Uys's numerous awards include the 1989 and the 1993 Fleur Du Cap Theatre Awards, the 1990 South African Playwright of the Year Award, and a 1997 FNB Vita National Theatre Award.

FURTHER READING

Stephen Gray, "Die Van Aardes: Pieter-Dirk Uys's Popular Nuclear Detergent," *English in Africa* 6, no. 2 (1979): 78–84; Anne Fuchs, *Playing the Market: The Market Theatre, Johannesburg, 1976–1986* (1990); Mervyn McMurtry, "'The Rise of the First Ambassador Bezuidenhout': Pieter-Dirk Uys's Creation of Evita Bezuidenhout, Her Fictional Actuality and His Approach to Female Impersonation," *South African Theatre Journal* 8, no. 2 (1994): 79–107; Daniel Lieberfeld, "Pieter-Dirk Uys: Crossing Apartheid Lines," *The Drama Review: A Journal of Performance Studies* 41, no. 1 (1997): 61–71.

V

Van Der Merwe, Carel (b. 1964) Novelist. Born in Johannesburg, van der Merwe now lives in Stellenbosch, where he practices as a chartered accountant. His novel *No-Man's Land* (2007) was short-listed for the Commonwealth Writers' Prize Best First Book, Africa 2008. Set in postapartheid South Africa, it tells the story of Paul du Toit, a former Special Forces operative, who is called to appear before the Truth and Reconciliation Commission on account of an operation during which two civilians were killed. Shamed and disenchanted, and in search of the wife who left him after the revelations of the commission hearings, Paul finds himself in exile from his home country, adrift in the South African expatriate community in London.

Van Der Post, Laurens (1906–1996) Novelist and travel writer. Born into a rural Afrikaner family near Philippolis in the Orange Free State (now Free State), van der Post served the allies in World War II in Africa, Indonesia, and Burma, gathering experience that finds its way into several of his works. Between 1945 and 1947 he assisted in quelling the nationalist insurrections in Java and Sumatra.

His first novel, *In a Province* (1934), traces the short and eventful life of Johan van Bredepoel, an orphaned boy who is brought up by his well-to-do aunt and uncle, and who later comes to reject his heritage and begin an association with left-wing political activists in Port Benjamin (fictionalized Cape Town). He strikes up a friendship with Kenon Badiakgotla, a young man who has come to Port Benjamin from his rural home and who soon falls into bad company. The two meet "in a province" some years later and fall victim in different ways to reactionary white commandos bent on preventing the extension of political and social liberties to the black population. A raw and in some ways poorly resolved work, *In a Province* nonetheless acutely registers the injustice of the policies inflicted upon black people at the time and explores the white mindset that sustains such policies. Later novels include *The Face Beside the Fire* (1953), *Flamingo Feather* (1955), *The Hunter and the Whale* (1967), *A Story Like the Wind* (1972), and its sequel *A Far-off Place* (1974), about two teenagers who come of age and fall in love while being guided by a Bushman through a guerilla war.

Van der Post's wartime experiences are captured in *The Seed and the Sower* (1963), three connected stories relating to Japanese prisoner-of-war camps (made into a film entitled *Merry Christmas, Mr Lawrence* in 1983), and the memoir *The Night of the New Moon* (1970). His nonfictional works on the African hinterland include *Venture to the Interior* (1952), an account of his expedition into the British Protectorate of Nyasaland (now Malawi) to gather information for the British government on this region, *The Lost World of the Kalahari* (1958), his exploration of the San culture, and its sequel, *The Heart of the Hunter* (1961). *A Mantis Carol* (1975) and *Testament to the Bushmen* (1984; with Jane Taylor) are later works in this vein, while *First Catch Your Eland* (1977) is a cultural guide to Africa. Other works of nonfiction include a collection of penetrating essays on Africa's travails, *The Dark Eye in Africa* (1955), *Journey into Russia* (1964; published as *A View of All the Russias* in the United States), *A Portrait of Japan* (1968), and *Jung and the Story of Our Time* (1976), inspired by his friendship with the Swiss psychologist Carl Jung. Works in an autobiographical vein include *Yet Being Someone Other* (1982), a collection of seven narratives about South Africa and Japan, *A Walk with a White Bushman: Laurens van der Post in Conversation with Jean-Marc Pottiez* (1986), and *The Admiral's Baby* (1996), a return to his years spent fighting rebels in Indonesia.

FURTHER READING

Frederic A. Carpenter, *Laurens van der Post* (1969); Neil McEwan, *Africa and the Novel* (1983); David Ward, *Chronicles of Darkness* (1989); Richard Peck, *A Morbid Fascination: White Prose and Politics in Apartheid South Africa* (1997); J. D. F. Jones, *Storyteller: The Many Lives of Laurens van der Post* (2002).

Van der Vyver, Marita (b. 1958) Novelist. Born in Cape Town, van der Vyver holds a master's degree in journalism from the University of Stellenbosch. She is a prolific writer of Afrikaans fiction and several of her books have been translated into English, including *Entertaining Angels* (1994), *Childish Things* (1996), *Breathing Space* (2000), *Travelling Light* (2005), *Short Circuits* (2005), *Time Out* (2006), *Where the Heart Is* (2006), and *There Is a Season* (2007).

Entertaining Angels tells the story of Griet, who, having been dumped by her husband and lost her baby, draws comfort from the folktales imparted by her grandmother and meets an angel in the guise of a surfer. *Travelling Light* deals with an older Griet whose affair with an Italian puppeteer provokes a host of dilemmas concerning her past, her family and her country. In *Childish Things*, the protagonist Mart, who has emigrated to London, recollects her seventeenth year as teenager in a 1970s South Africa heading for revolution. *Breathing Space* describes the interweaving of personal and political conflict in the lives of ten friends during the period 1985 to 1995. The autobiographical work *Where the Heart Is* describes the writer's life in a village in Provence.

Van Heerden, Etienne (b. 1954) Novelist and short-story writer. Born in Johannesburg, van Heerden taught in the Afrikaans and Nederlands Department at Rhodes University before moving to the University of Cape Town.

He writes in Afrikaans but several of his novels have been translated into English, including *Ancestral Voices* (1989), winner of the CNA Literary Award and the Hertzog prize for Prose, *Casspirs and Camparis* (1993), *Leap Year* (1997), *Kikuyu* (1998), and *The Long Silence of Mario Salviati* (2002). He has also published a collection of short stories in English, *Mad Dog and Other Stories* (1992).

Evoking the rhythms and the textures of rural life, *Ancestral Voices* infuses realism with the qualities of myth and magic to offer a rewriting of the traditional *plaasroman* (farm novel) of Afrikaans literature. It describes a magistrate's attempts at discovering the circumstances surrounding the death of an otherworldly young boy. He finds that his investigations threaten to expose the secrets of a family torn between a legitimate line and an illegitimate line, where cousins live on opposite sides of the racial divide in this conservative Afrikaner community, and where past and present, truth and fantasy, threaten to blur. Like the earlier novel, *Leap Year* concerns itself with communities that have been socially and politically segregated, but which inhabit a shared historical and geographical world. Set in a coastal community in the Eastern Cape in the period immediately after the 1994 election, it describes how events conspire to draw together a family of white farmers and a family of township inhabitants. *Kikuyu* invokes the events that occurred one summer when the protagonist was a child on his parents' Karoo holiday farm. The events are seen partly through the eyes of the child and partly through the eyes of the adult who recalls this experience. *The Long Silence of Mario Salviati* represents, in a sense, a culmination of the motifs and techniques that characterize the early works, portraying families fractured by the politics of race, invoking the ghosts of history that haunt the present, providing shifting perspectives and fantastical occurrences. It tells the story of an art collector who travels to a small town to persuade a local sculptor to part with a famous piece. She finds herself accosted by the spirits of the dead and drawn into the mystery of the imagination.

FURTHER READING

Louise Viljoen, "Re-presenting History: Reflections on Two Recent Afrikaans Novels," *Current Writing* 5, no. 1 (1993): 1–24; Michiel Heyns, "Overtaken by History: Obsolescence-Anxiety in André Brink's *An Act of Terror* and Etienne van Heerden's *Casspirs and Campar-is*," *English Academy Review* 11 (1994): 62–72; Zoë Wicomb, "Five Afrikaner Texts and the Rehabilitation of Whiteness," *Social Identities* 4, no. 3 (1998): 363–383; Hein Viljoen and Chris N. van der Merwe, *Storyscapes: South African Perspectives on Literature, Space & Identity* (2004).

Van Niekerk, Marlene (b. 1954) Novelist, short-story writer, and poet. Born and raised in the Caledon district of the Western Cape, van Niekerk studied at the universities of Stellenbosch, Amsterdam, and the Witwatersrand. She is currently professor in the Department of Afrikaans and Dutch at Stellenbosch University. Writing in Afrikaans, she is the author of two collections of poetry, a collection of short stories, and two novels, among other publications. The novels have been translated into English. *Triomf* (2002) won the M-Net prize, the CNA Literary Award and the Noma Award for African Literature. *Agaat* (2006) was short-listed for the South African Booksellers' Choice Award 2005, won the *Sunday Times* Fiction Prize 2007, and was also short-listed for the *Independent* Foreign Fiction Prize 2008.

Set in the suburb of Triomf, a lower-class white neighborhood built on the ruins of the predominantly black Sophiatown, which had been razed by the apartheid government, the novel *Triomf* explores the lives of the inhabitants of a house in Martha Street. The microscopic lens employed in *Triomf* is used again in *Agaat* to examine the intertwined lives of two women, the white farmer Milla and her Coloured maidservant Agaat, whose relationship follows the twists in the country's political history from the 1950s through to the postapartheid period. The novels provide detailed evocations of the circumstances of individual lives, weaving together the political and the personal, and exposing the psychological compromises that result from a politically corrupt public sphere.

FURTHER READING

Jack Shear, "Haunted House, Haunted Nation: *Triomf* and the South African Postcolonial Gothic," *Journal of Literary Studies* 22, nos. 1–2 (2006): 70–95; Matthew Brophy, "Shadowing Afrikaner Nationalism: Jungian Archetypes, Incest, and the Uncanny in Marlene van Niekerk's *Triomf*," *Journal of Literary Studies* 22, nos. 1–2 (2006): 96–112; Nicole Devarenne, "'In Hell You Hear Only Your Mother Tongue': Afrikaner Nationalist Ideology, Linguistic Subversion, and Cultural Renewal in Marlene van Niekerk's *Triomf*," *Research in African Literatures* 37, no. 4 (2006): 105–120.

Van Wyk, Christopher (b. 1957) Poet, novelist, autobiographer. Born in Newclare, Johannesburg, van Wyk graduated from Riverlea High School and has worked as a clerk, as editor of *Staffrider* magazine, and as an educational writer for the South African Council for Higher Education (SACHED). He is cofounder, with Fhazel Johennesse, of the literary magazine *Wietie*.

Van Wyk has published a volume of poetry, *It is Time to Go Home* (1979), a novel, *The Year of the Tapeworm* (1996), and the autobiography *Shirley, Goodness & Mercy: A Childhood Memoir* (2004). He has collaborated on a number of historical books on major South Africa figures, including *Sol Plaatje* (1992), *Z. K. Matthews* (1992), *Yusuf Dadoo* (1993), *Oliver Tambo* (1994), *Mohandas Gandhi: The South Africa Years* (1994), *Chris Hani* (1994), and *They Fought for Freedom* (1996), and has edited several collections of short stories, including *Voices from Young Africa: The Best Writing from Upbeat Readers* (with Lizeka Mda, 1991), *Well Known Stories* (with Njabulo *Ndebele and Lois Head, 1992), *On the Banks of the Zambezi* (with Sousa Jamba and Carol Howes, 1993), *Fires and Shadows: Stories from Southern Africa* (with Karen *Press, 1995), and *New Stories* (with Carol Howes and Vusi Malindi, 1995). He is also the author of numerous children's books and books for newly literate adults. He was awarded the 1980 Olive Schreiner Prize, the 1982 Maskew Miller Prize for the Junior Adventure Novel in English, and the 1996 Sanlam Literary Award.

It is perhaps in his poetry that Van Wyk has established himself most clearly as a literary presence in South Africa. *It Is Time to Go Home* employs a colloquial voice that seems to speak from within the troubled townships of the 1970s, articulating the fears, dreams, and outrage that fueled the liberation struggle at the height of its assertion. The poetry is closely associated with the Black Consciousness philosophy of the time, espousing its values of self-pride and self-reliance.

FURTHER READING

Mbulelo V. Mzamane, "New Poets of the Soweto Era: Van Wyk, Johennesse, and Madingoane," *Research in African Literatures* 19, no. 1 (1988): 3–11; Sten Moslund, "Chris van Wyk's *The Year of the Tapeworm*: Beyond the Realism of Struggle in South Africa," *Journal of Cultural Studies* 3, no. 2 (2001): 412–431.

Van Wyk Louw, N. P. (1906–1970) Poet and playwright. Born in Sutherland in the Cape Province (now Northern Cape), van Wyk Louw studied at the University of Cape Town and taught at the Universities of Amsterdam and the Witwatersrand. He published widely in Afrikaans, and individual poems as well as the verse play *Raka* (1983) have been translated into English. First published in Afrikaans in 1941, *Raka* dramatizes the conflict between Koki, political leader and embodiment of culture and spirituality, and Raka, rebel usurper of power and embodiment of sensuality and appetite. The play touches on many issues that resonate with colonial and postcolonial literary themes.

Venter, Eben (b. 1954) Novelist. Born and raised in South Africa, and having worked as a chef in Melbourne, Venter currently divides his time between Australia and South Africa. Of his numerous novels written in Afrikaans, two have been translated into English, *My Beautiful Death* (2006) and *Trencherman* (2008).

While *My Beautiful Death* describes the difficult adjustments the emigrant who has left South Africa has to face in making a new start abroad, *Trencherman* describes a return trip to South Africa imagined as a journey to the heart of darkness. Using Conrad's novel as structural principle, *Trencherman* invokes a postapocalyptic landscape where central government has ceased to function, services and infrastructure have collapsed, the countryside is ravaged, and food has become scarce. It is into this nightmare world that Marlouw returns from Australia to locate his nephew Koert, who has created for himself an empire of meat on Ouplaas, the former family farm.

Vladislavić, Ivan (b. 1957) Short-story writer and novelist. Born in Pretoria and educated at the University of the Witwatersrand, Vladislavić lives and works in Johannesburg as a writer and freelance editor. He has developed a reputation as an iconoclast with an innovative and humorous style.

His first collection of stories, *Missing Persons* (1989; winner of the 1991 Olive Schreiner Prize), mixes black humor and sharp satire in a style that is linguistically inventive and witty. In "Journal of a Wall," the narrator incongruously devotes an inordinate amount of attention to the trivial event of a neighbor building a garden wall. The diligence with which he records the event verges on the pathological, and yet the humor of the story is located partly in the reader's shock of recognition. Contemporary South African city-dwellers, we realize, are perhaps only a few stages away from the pathology displayed by Vladislavić's narrator. As the story progresses the narrator's intense isolation becomes more and more apparent, and when his emotional investment in the event of the wall building is not rewarded by closer contact with his neighbors, he becomes violently angry and retreats still deeper into himself. It becomes clear, then, that Vladislavić's satire is directed chiefly at the walls that divide us in modern urban society. At the edges of the stories in *Missing Persons* the daily horrors of life in South Africa during the 1980s obtrude, and this gives them their satirical depth.

A novel, *The Folly* (1993; winner of the CNA Literary Award), followed this successful debut. Similar in style to the stories, it concerns the quirky relationship that develops between Mr. and Mrs. Malgas and the appropriately named Nieuwenhuizen when the latter occupies a plot of land next to them and begins to hatch his grand plan of building a house. Mr. Malgas becomes more and more absorbed in his eccentric neighbor's fantastic schemes, while Mrs. Malgas retreats in disgust behind her net curtain to watch the dismemberment of South Africa on television. In this novel, Vladislavić manages to merge the extraordinary and the mundane in a compelling display of linguistic virtuosity.

Vladislavić's second collection of stories is *Propaganda by Monuments and Other Stories* (1996). Like the earlier works it evokes a suburban South African world at once bizarre and instantly recognizable. In "The Tuba," a game of darts on the verandah of a white home is interrupted by the arrival of a black Salvation Army band playing Christmas carols. One of the darts players, Sergeant Dundas, plays the tuba in the Correctional Services orchestra, and, after initially expressing his resentment at the intrusion of the Salvation Army band and passing racial slurs, ends up joining the band and marching off with them into the distance. The title story is a surreally comic tale about the importation of a discarded Soviet monument by a black South African who plans to open a tavern bearing the name of V. I. Lenin. In "Autopsy," Elvis Presley is spotted in Hillbrow, while "The Omniscope (Pat. Pending)" describes the invention of a machine for seeing everything.

Vladislavić's recent creative work includes the novel *The Restless Supermarket* (2001; winner of the *Sunday Times* Literary Award) in which he continues his quirky and distinctive satirical treatment of South African society, *The Exploded View* (2004), a collection of four long stories, and *Portrait with Keys: Joburg and What-What* (2006). In *The Restless Supermarket*, Aubrey Tearle, the first-person narrator, is a proofreader who is dedicated "to matter in its proper order," and whose principal aim in life is "to determine *species* of error, and to assist in eliminating them." He sees the changes in contemporary South African society as a lowering of standards and attempts to "correct" them, much as a proofreader corrects textual grammatical errors. *Portrait with Keys* (winner of the 2007 Alan Paton Award and the 2007 University of Johannesburg Literary Prize) is a collection of musings, commentaries, and reminiscences on Johannesburg (past and present), and the author's sense of place in the shifting Jo'burg cityscape. It has cemented the author's place as one of South Africa's major contemporary writers.

Vladislavić has contributed substantially to commentary on contemporary South African art and architecture. His work in this arena includes *Blank __: Architecture, Apartheid and After* (1998; with Hilton Judin), *T'kama-Adamastor: Inventions of Africa in a South African Painting* (2000), *The Model Men* (2004), and *Willem Boshoff* (2005), the last being an appraisal of the work of one of South Africa's most important artists of recent times.

FURTHER READING

Sue Marais, "Ivan Vladislavić's Re-Vision of the South African Story Cycle," *Current Writing* 4, no. 1 (1992): 41–56; Sue Marais, "Getting Lost in Cape Town: Spatial and Temporal Dislocation in the South African Short Fiction Cycle," *English in Africa* 22, no. 2 (1995): 29–43; Elaine Young, "Or Is It Just the Angle? Rivalling Realist Representation in Ivan Vladislavić's *Propaganda by Monuments and Other Stories*," *English Academy Review* 18 (2001): 38–45; Felicity Wood, "Taking Fun Seriously: The Potency of Play in Ivan Vladislavić's Short Stories," *English Academy Review* 18 (2001): 21–37; Mike Marais and Carita Backström, "An Interview with Ivan Vladislavić," *English in Africa* 29, no. 2 (2002): 119–128; Mike Marais, "Visions of Excess: Closure, Irony and the Thought of Community in Ivan Vladislavić's *The Restless Supermarket*," *English in Africa* 29, no. 2 (2002): 101–117; Mike Marais, "Reading Against Race: J. M. Coetzee's *Disgrace*, Justin Cartwright's *White Lightning* and Ivan Vladislavić's *The Restless Supermarket*," *Journal of Literary Studies* 19, nos. 3–4 (2003): 271–289; Stefan Helgesson, "'Minor Disorders': Ivan Vladislavić and the Devolution of South African English," *Journal of Southern African Studies* 30, no. 4 (2004): 777–787; Gerald Gaylard, "Postcolonial Satire: Ivan Vladislavić," *Current Writing* 17, no. 1 (2005): 129–148; Susan van Zyl, "A Homo Calculator at Large: Reading the Late Work of Foucault in the Light of Ivan Vladislavić's 'Villa Toscana,'" *Journal of Literary Studies* 22, nos. 3–4 (2006): 257–275; Marita Wenzel, "Liminal Spaces and Imaginary Places in *The Bone People* by Keri Hulme and *The Folly* by Ivan Vladislavić," *Literator* 27, no. 1 (2006): 79–96.

Voysey-Braig, Megan (b. 1976) Novelist. Voysey-Braig's debut novel *Till We Can Keep an Animal* (2008) is narrated by a fifty-five-year-old woman who, in the course of an armed robbery, has been raped and murdered. Kept alive through the narrative intervention of the author, she uses this violent event as an opportunity to reflect on the violence that has characterized South African society over the course of its four-hundred-year history.

W

Ward, Harriet *See* Writers Before 1945

Watson, Mary (b. 1975) Short-story writer. Born and raised in Cape Town, Watson completed a master's degree in creative writing at the University of Cape Town and studied film and TV production at Bristol University. She lectures in film studies at the University of Cape Town. *Moss* (2004) comprises a collection of interrelated stories in which characters and motifs recur to create a dense pattern of reference and meaning that explores the relationship between good and evil, spirit and flesh, purity and contamination. The story "Jungfrau," which won the Caine Prize for African writing, focuses on a child's perception of family tensions and social relationships in postapartheid South Africa.

Watson, Stephen (b. 1954) Poet and critic. Born in Cape Town, he lectures at the University of Cape Town. Watson has published several volumes of poetry, including *Poems 1977–1982* (1982), *In This City* (1986), *Cape Town Days* (private edition, 1989), *Return of the Moon: Versions from the /Xam* (with woodcuts by Cecil Skotnes, 1991), *Selected Poems 1961–1994* (with illustrations by Judith Mason, 1994), *Presence of the Earth* (1995), *The Other City: Selected Poems 1977–1999* (2000), and *The Light Echo and Other Poems* (2007). The poems characteristically use Cape Town and its inhabitants as a primary source of inspiration, exploring the moods of a city cudgeled by autumn winds and cowled in winter rain. With a keen eye for details of landscape and weather, and a melancholic sense of absence and loss, particularly in respect of love, the poems are at once visionary and disenchanted, lyrical and embittered. Aside from poems set in Cape Town, several sequences of poems invoke the Cederberg as a place of spiritual connection. Some poems meditate on the nature of poetry.

Watson has also published a collection of literary-critical essays, *Selected Essays 1980–1990* (1990), and a study of the creative process, *A Writer's Diary* (1997). His prose writings reveal a passionate defense of the poetic imagination and a broad interest in contemporary poetry. He has edited *Patrick Cullinan: Selected Poems 1961–1991* (1992), *Guy Butler: Essays and Lectures 1949–1991* (1994), coedited *Critical Perspectives on J. M. Coetzee* (1996), coedited (with Patrick *Cullinan) *Dante in Africa: A Collection of Essays, Poems and Artwork* (2005), and edited *A City Imagined* (2006).

He was awarded the 1820 Settler's Foundation Festival Poetry Prize of 1985, the 1989 Maja Kriel Essay Prize, the 1992 Sydney Clouts Memorial Prize, and the 1993 UCT Book Award.

FURTHER READING

Andrew Foley, "A Sense of Place in Contemporary White South African Poetry," *English in Africa* 19, no. 2 (1992): 35–53; Dirk Klopper, "Native from the Start," *Current Writing* 7, no. 1 (1995): 125–138; Elsie Cloete, "Writing Around the Bushmen: The !Kung, Anthropology and Feminism," *Alternation* 4, no. 1 (1997): 45–59; Henriette Roos, "Moon, Man, Women, Bushmen: Reconciling the Irreconcilable?" *Alternation* 4, no. 2 (1997): 26–35; Dirk Klopper, "On the Edge of Darkness: Stephen Watson and the Return of the Romantic Imagination," *English in Africa* 25, no. 1 (1998): 87–98; Annie Gagiano, "'By What

Authority?': Presentations of the Khoisan in South African English Poetry," *Alternation* 6, no. 1 (1999): 155–173.

Wicomb, Zoë (b. 1948) Short-story writer and novelist. Born near Vanrhynsdorp in Namaqualand, Wicomb was educated at the universities of the Western Cape and Reading, England. She lived in Britain from 1970 until 1991, when she returned to South Africa to teach at the University of the Western Cape. She has since returned to Britain to resume her academic career at Strathclyde University in Glasgow. She is the author of two collections of stories and two novels, and has published a number of critical articles on South African literature and feminism.

You Can't Get Lost in Cape Town (1987) is a collection of connected short stories that all concern the character Frieda Shenton. The sequence has some of the qualities of the *bildungsroman*, as we see the protagonist coming to terms with her childhood and early experiences as a Coloured woman growing up in racist South Africa. It also has innovative metafictional qualities that are particularly apparent in its bold mixing of autobiography with reflexive narrative strategies that undercut a straightforward reading of the text as autobiography. "A Trip to the Gifberge," the last story in the sequence, deals with the return home of the protagonist after many years in Britain. It probes at the issues of exile and homecoming, of living a life outside the constraints of parental control and coming home to confront them again. In its switching between past and present, the story provides insight into the interior world of a young woman struggling to break free from a background that threatens to engulf her again. Another collection of short stories has subsequently appeared under the title *The One That Got Away* (2008), spanning Scotland and South Africa and evoking a complex world of intercontinental connections and disjunctions.

The novel *David's Story* is set in the period immediately before the election of 1994, when the armed wing of the ANC was in the process of disbanding. Focusing on the protagonist David, the novel weaves together the historical narrative of the Griqua people under the leadership of Andre le Fleur and the contemporary narrative of a cadre whose commitment to the armed struggle is challenged by events around a female activist who is subjected to disturbing forms of violation. David's growing consciousness of his ethnic affiliations is conveyed through a complex postmodernist narrative structure that fractures the very notions of a knowable subject and a determinate identity. *Playing in the Light* deals with a woman who, having lived her whole life as a white, discovers that she is of mixed-race descent. The seemingly straightforward realism is undercut through an unexpected switch of narrative authority that forces a reconsideration of the question of perspective.

FURTHER READING

Eva Hunter and Craig MacKenzie, eds., *Between the Lines II: Interviews with Nadine Gordimer, Menán du Plessis, Zoë Wicomb, Lauretta Ngcobo* (1993); Mary K. Deshazer, *A Poetics of Resistance: Women Writing in El Salvador, South Africa and the United States* (1994); Sarah Nuttall, "Reading in the Lives and Writing of Black South African Women," *Journal of Southern African Studies* 20, no. 1 (1994): 85–98; Sue Marais, "Getting Lost in Cape Town: Spatial and Temporal Dislocation in the South African Short Fiction Cycle," *English in Africa* 22, no. 2 (1995): 29–43; Rob Gaylard, "Exile and Homecoming: Identity in Zoë Wicomb's *You Can't Get Lost in Cape Town*," *Ariel* 27, no. 1 (1996): 177–189; M. J. Daymond, "Gender and 'History': 1980s South African Women's Stories in English,"

Ariel 27, no. 1 (1996): 191–213; Miki Flockemann, "Fictions of Home and (Un)Belonging: Diasporan Frameworks in Michelle Cliff's 'Abeng' and Zoë Wicomb's 'Journey to the Gifberge,'" *Alternation* 8, no. 1 (2001): 116–133; Stephan Meyer and Thomas Olver, "Zoë Wicomb Interviewed on 'Writing' and 'Nation,'" *Journal of Literary Studies* 18, nos. 1–2 (2002): 182–198; Hein Willemse, "Zoë Wicomb in Conversation with Hein Willemse," *Research in African Literatures* 33, no. 1 (2002): 144–152; Thomas Olver and Stephan Meyer, "Zoë Wicomb on *David's Story*," *Current Writing* 16, no. 2 (2004): 131–142; Annie Gagiano, "Adapting the National Imaginary: Shifting Identities in Three Post-1994 South African Novels," *Journal of Southern African Studies* 30, no. 4 (2004): 811–824; Mike Marais, "Bastards and Bodies in Zoë Wicomb's *David's Story*," *Journal of Commonwealth Literature* 40, no. 3 (2005): 21–36; Constance C. Richards, "Nationalism and the Development of Identity in Postcolonial Fiction: Zoë Wicomb and Michelle Cliff," *Research in African Literatures* 36, no. 1 (2005): 20–33.

Wilhelm, Peter (b. 1943) Poet, novelist, short-story writer, journalist. Born in Cape Town, he qualified as a teacher before pursuing a career as journalist. He has worked at the *Financial Mail* and has edited *Leadership* magazine.

Wilhelm has published two volumes of poetry, *White Flowers* (1977) and *Falling Into the Sun* (1993). He has also produced three novels, *The Dark Wood* (1977), *The Healing Process* (1988), and *The Mask of Freedom* (1994). In addition, he has published three collections of short stories: *L. M. and Other Stories* (1975), *At the End of a War* (1981), and *Some Place in Africa* (1987). He is the author of a children's book, *Summer's End* (1984).

Dealing with the violence and social degradation of colonial and postcolonial Africa, Wilhelm's fiction offers a bleak perspective on the continent's past and its future. Similarly, the poetry, terse and somber, portrays a world that, in the words of one poem, is a "stone" on which we are "beaten." Paradoxically, however, the very harshness of the world, its dumb material intractability, makes spiritual redemption in the form of love a human imperative.

Wilhelm is coeditor of *Poetry South Africa: Selected Papers from Poetry '74* (1976). His most recent work includes a selection of his columns, *The State We're In* (1999) and *The Bayonet Field: Selected Stories* (2000). He was awarded the 1976 Mofolo-Plomer Prize for Literature, the 1982 Thomas Pringle Award, and the 1995 Sanlam Literary Award.

FURTHER READING

Cherry Wilhelm, "Trends in Recent English Fiction and Criticism in South Africa," *English in Africa* 5, no. 2 (1978): 17–27; Sheila Roberts, "Character and Meaning in Four Contemporary South African Novels," *World Literature Written in English* 19, no. 1 (1980): 19–36.

Winterbach, Ingrid (b. 1948) Artist and novelist. Winterbach lives in Durban and has published eight novels in Afrikaans, three of which have been translated into English, *The Elusive Moth* (2005), *To Hell with Cronje* (2007), and *The Book of Happenstance* (2008).

Set at the end of the apartheid era, *The Elusive Moth* tells the story of Karolina, an entomologist, who travels to a small town in the Free State to research a rare moth species, where she is drawn into the political and personal intrigues of the town. The Afrikaans version of the novel was awarded the M-Net Book Prize in 1994 and the Old Mutual Literary Prize in 1997. *To Hell with Cronje* returns to an earlier period of South African history. Set in February 1902, three months before the end of the Anglo-Boer War, the novel describes the events that befall a party of Boer soldiers who are taking a traumatized youth from deep in the Cape Colony to his home in the Free State. The protagonists Reitz, a geologist, and Ben, a natural historian, each keep a journal in which they record the natural phenomena they have encountered during their various campaigns across the country, and spend their nights listening to war stories recounted with varying degrees of disillusion by fellow burghers. The Afrikaans version of the novel was awarded the Hertzog Prize for prose in 2002.

Wright, David (1920–1994) Poet and editor. Born in Johannesburg, and deaf from childhood, he left South Africa for England in 1934, when he was fourteen years old, to attend the Northampton School for the Deaf. A graduate of Oriel College, Oxford, he was coeditor of *Magazine X*.

Wright published eleven volumes of poetry: *Poems* (1947), *Moral Stories* (1954), *Monologue of a Deaf Man* (1958), *A South African Album* (1976), *To the Gods the Shades: New and Collected Poems* (1976), *A View of the North: Poems* (1976), *Selected Poems* (1980, reissued 1988), *Metrical Observations* (1980), *Four Voices: Poetry from Zimbabwe* (with Rowland Molony, John Eppel, and Noel Brettell, 1982), *Elegies* (1990), and *Poems and Versions* (1992). He also published a literary study, *Roy Campbell* (1961), and a prose work, *Deafness: A Personal Account* (1969).

Employing a leisurely, discursive style, densely worded but lucid, the poems are accounts of travel, records of journeys undertaken, pictures of places seen and people met. The calm, reflective surface of the poems belies a restless, migratory energy that invigorates their emotional depths and perturbs their pensive certainties.

Wright is coeditor, with John Heath-Stubbs, of the *Faber Book of Twentieth Century Verse* (1955; rev. ed. 1975), and editor of *South African Stories* (1960). He was awarded the 1950 Atlantic Award, the 1958 and 1960 Guinness Poetry Prize, the Gregory Fellowship in Poetry at Leeds University 1963–1967, and the 1988 Eleanor Anderson Award.

FURTHER READING

Guy Butler, "David Wright at Sixty," *English in Africa* 7, no. 1 (1980): 91–96.

Wylie, Dan (b. 1959) Poet and critic. Raised in Rhodesia (now Zimbabwe) and educated at Rhodes University, he has worked as writer and teacher, and currently lectures at Rhodes University. Wylie has published four volumes of poetry: *Migrant: Poems* (1994); *The Road Out* (1996), winner of the Ingrid Jonker Prize and Olive Schreiner Prize; *Original Forest* (2001); and *Road Work* (2007). *The Road Out* comprises poems of existential exploration that seek out significance not in an intellectual realm of ideas but in the here and now of phenomenal existence, in the blood-pulse of life, which begins to beat when, as one poem has it, intellectuality temporarily goes on vacation. *Road Work* presents the observations of a traveler in locations as diverse as the Patagonian glaciers, the Australian desert, and European pastoral retreats.

Wylie is also the author of two historical studies on Shaka: *Savage Delight: White Myths of Shaka* (2001) and *Myth of Iron: Shaka in History* (2006), and has written a memoir, *Dead Leaves: Two Years in the Rhodesian War* (2002).

Z

Zadok, Rachel (b. 1972) Novelist. Born in South Africa, Zadok studied fine art and worked as a freelance graphic designer before moving to London, where she wrote *Gem Squash Tokoloshe* (2005). Set in the Northern Transvaal (now Limpopo Province), the novel describes the return of Faith to the family farm, where she and her mother had been abandoned years before by her father, and which, along with buried memories of childhood, is bequeathed to her at the death of her mother in Sterkfontein mental asylum many years later.

Zwi, Rose (b. 1928) Novelist and short-story writer. Born in Mexico to Jewish refugees from Lithuania, Zwi moved to South Africa as a young girl and completed her studies at the University of the Witwatersrand, moved briefly to Israel, returned to South Africa, and then, in 1988, relocated to Sydney, Australia, where she currently lives. She is the author of the novels *Another Year in Africa* (1980), *The Inverted Pyramid* (1981), *Exiles* (1984), *The Umbrella Tree* (1990), and *Safe Houses* (1993); a family history, *Last Walk in Naryshkin Park* (1997); and a collection of short stories, *Speak the Truth, Laughing* (2002). Much of Zwi's writing draws on her own family history in exploring the experience of immigration. This is evident as much in *Safe Houses*, which deals with families of different backgrounds during the antiapartheid struggle, as it is in *Another Year in Africa*, which presents the efforts of immigrant Jews to make a home for themselves in South Africa of the 1920s, and *Last Walk in Naryshkin Park*, which reconstructs the massacre of Jews in Lithuania in 1941. *Speak the Truth, Laughing* deals with immigrant experience in Africa and Australia, focusing, like the earlier work, on issues of identity and belonging, displacement and community.

PART TWO

Writers Before 1945

B

Bancroft, Francis (Frances Slater) (1862–1947) Novelist. An aunt of the prolific poet Francis Carey *Slater, Frances Slater was born on the family farm, Carnavon Dale, near Grahamstown, and worked as a teacher for some years before training as a nursing sister. Under the pen name Francis Bancroft, she published fifteen novels and a volume of short stories between 1903 and 1933. Her work is a mixture of romantic potboilers and treatments of more serious subjects, such as women's suffrage, pacifism, the temperance cause, and Afrikaner-English relations. Her most celebrated novel is *Of Like Passions* (1907), a lurid but ideologically conflicted saga of the tragic consequences of interracial sexual dalliance.

FURTHER READING

Gareth Cornwell, "Francis Bancroft's *Of Like Passions* and the Politics of Sex in Early Twentieth-Century South Africa," *English in Africa* 25, no. 2 (1998): 1–35.

Black, Stephen (1880–1931) Journalist, playwright, novelist, short-story writer. Born in Cape Town and educated at Saint Saviour's Upper Boys' High School and Diocesan College, he worked as a sports and crime reporter on the *Cape Argus* from 1906. In 1910 he formed his own theatre company and toured South Africa and Rhodesia (now Zimbabwe). He lived in England from 1913 to 1915, where he wrote articles for London's *Daily Mail*, and in France from 1918 to 1927. He again toured Rhodesia with a theater company in 1928. A selection of his journalistic writings was published in *English in Africa* (September 1981).

A number of Black's plays have been published. *Three Plays* (1984; edited by Stephen *Gray) contains *Love and the Hyphen* (1908, revised 1928–29), *Helena's Hope, Ltd.* (1910) and *Van Kalabas Does His Bit* (1916). *The Peacemaker* (date unknown) has been published in *Modern Stage Directions: A Collection of Short Dramatic Scripts* (1984). His unpublished plays include "The Flapper" (1911), "The

Uitlanders" (1911), "I.D.B." (1912), and "A Boer's Honour" (1912), subsequently revised as "A Backveld Boer" (1928). He is the author of two novels, *The Dorp* (1920) and *The Golden Calf: A Story of the Diamond Fields* (1925), as well as of two collections of short stories, *Cloud Child: Selected Stories 1908–1920* (date unknown) and the unpublished "The Adventures of Oom Kalabas." He also wrote the film script *The Life of Rhodes*.

Sometimes referred to as the founder of South African theater, Black offered a caustic satirical portrait of early twentieth-century South African society. Dramatizing topical issues, his plays portray stereotypical South African characters using a language that is recognizably local. The plays are credited for their comic timing and keen ear for dialogue.

Black was founder of the literary magazine *The Sjambok* (1929–1931). He received the 1904 Rhodes Prize for Literature.

FURTHER READING

Stephen Gray, "Stephen Black: South African dramatist, novelist," *Encyclopaedia of Post-Colonial Literatures in English* (1994).

Blackburn, Douglas (1857–1929) London-born Douglas Blackburn came to South Africa in the early 1890s and returned to England only in 1908, thus spending nearly two decades in the country. First and foremost a pressman, Blackburn was the precocious young editor of *The Brightonian* before its bankruptcy in 1884, worked in Fleet Street as a drama reviewer for nearly a decade, and then came out to South Africa in the 1890s to work on *The Star*. At the time of the Jameson Raid he became the proprietor-editor of the weekly newspaper *The Sentinel*, and during the Boer War years he worked on both sides of the front as a correspondent.

As an editor and journalist, Blackburn was staunchly anti-imperialistic and pro-republican, and it is these sentiments that also infuse his novels, the most important of which are *Prinsloo of Prinsloosdorp: A Tale of Transvaal Officialdom* (1899; reissued in 1978 and 1989), *A Burger Quixote* (1903; reissued in 1984) and *Leaven: A Black and White story* (1908; reissued in 1991). The last of these is an early example of the "Jim comes to Jo'burg" genre. The first two are important precursors in style and theme to the work of Pauline *Smith and, in particular, Herman Charles *Bosman. They both use a larger-than-life narrator who relates his various picaresque adventures in a tongue-in-cheek manner.

Blackburn's other novels are *Kruger's Secret Service, by One Who Was In It* (1900), *Richard Hartley, Prospector* (1905), *I Came and Saw* (1908), and *Love Muti* (1915). He is also author of the autobiography *Secret Service in South Africa* (1911). A selection of his journalism was published in *English in Africa* (March 1978).

In his extensive journalistic and creative output Blackburn was to prove himself a shrewd and incisive interpreter of South African society in the turbulent years spanning the Jameson Raid (1895) and Union (1910). In many ways a pioneer of the satirical turn in South African literature, particularly in his treatment of the Afrikaner as subject, Blackburn enjoyed a brief vogue in the first two decades of the twentieth century, but is now almost completely forgotten.

FURTHER READING

Stephen Gray, *Douglas Blackburn* (1984).

Brownlee, Frank (1875–1952) Novelist and short-story writer. Son of Charles Brownlee, secretary for native affairs in the Cape, he was born in Claremont, Western Cape, and educated at Dale College and the Lovedale

Institute. He worked in the Department of Justice and the Native Affairs Department before taking up various posts as native commissioner in the Transkei. An ethnologist at heart, he was an authority on Bantu law and customs and on San culture and folklore.

Brownlee published two novels, *Ntsukumbini: Cattle Thief* (1929), reissued as *Cattle Thief: The Story of Ntsukumbini* in 1932 and republished as *Cattle Thief* in 2007, and *Corporal Wanzi* (1937). He also published a collection of Khoikhoi folklore, *Lion and Jackal* (1938), and wrote an unpublished collection of sketches, "Chats with Christina." He is in addition the author of the historiographical study *Historical Records of the Transkeian Native Territories* (1923). His work reveals both his sensitivity toward and his knowledge and understanding of indigenous African customs and beliefs.

Bryden, H. A. (Henry Anderson) (1854–1937) Novelist, travel writer, and short-story writer. Born in Surbiton, England, Bryden came to South Africa in 1876. He traveled extensively in southern Africa and wrote many works about the region. These include *Kloof and Karroo: Sport, Legend, and Natural History in the Cape Colony* (1889), *Gun and Camera in Southern Africa* (1893), *Travel and Big Game* (1897; with P. Selous), and *Enchantments of the Veld* (1930). His novels and short stories with a South African setting include *Tales of South Africa* (1896), *From Veldt Camp Fires: Stories of Southern Africa* (1900), and *The Gold Kloof* (1907). His historical works include *The Victorian Era in South Africa* (1899) and *A History of South Africa: From the First Settlement of the Dutch, 1652, to the Year 1903* (1904).

Buchan, John (1875–1940) Novelist, biographer, and essayist. Born in Perth, Scotland, and educated at Glasgow University and Oxford, Buchan was private secretary to the high commissioner in South Africa, Lord Milner, from 1901 to 1903. He wrote many adventure stories, including *The Watcher by the Threshold* (1902) and the famous *The Thirty-Nine Steps* (1915), but it is for his story set in South Africa, *Prester John* (1910), that he is best remembered in the country. The novel tells the story of David Crawfurd and his dealings with a black minister, Rev. John Laputa, who instigates an abortive rebellion against white colonial authority. Buchan's one hundred works include biographies of major historical figures and writers and various collections of essays, including *The African Colony: Studies in the Reconstruction* (1903).

C

Camoëns, Luis de (1524?–1580) Portuguese Renaissance poet. Camoëns wrote the epic poem *The Lusiads*, which describes Vasco da Gama's journey around the Cape. The poem has inspired many literary and literary-critical responses, particularly as regards its projection of the spirit of the Cape of Storms in the mythical figure of Adamastor, a slain Titan. In subsequent rewritings, Adamastor is portrayed as the primal African who threatens to awake from his sleep of enslavement and oppression and to expel, with violence, the invading colonizers.

FURTHER READING

Malvern van Wyk Smith, ed., *Shades of Adamastor: Africa and the Portuguese Connection—An Anthology of Poetry* (1988).

Colenso, Frances Ellen (1849–1887) Novelist and historian. Born in Norfolk, she came out to South Africa with her family in 1853 upon her father's appointment as Anglican bishop of Natal. The family settled at Bishopstowe outside Pietermaritzburg and, apart from a short spell (1862–1865) at school in England, Frances was educated at home. She never married, and worked as a teacher while pursuing her own intellectual interests. Like her father, she often took an independent line on colonial affairs. In her best-known work, *My Chief and I, or Six Months in Natal after the Langalibalele Outbreak* (1880), she sympathetically retells the story of Lieutenant Colonel Anthony Durnford, who was given the task of sealing off the passes between Natal and Basotholand in order to prevent the escape of the Hlubi chief, Langalibalele, after his rebellion against the colonial authorities. The sequel to this narrative, *Five Years Later*, remained unpublished until the appearance of Margaret Daymond's edition in 1994, which gathered the two narratives into a single volume. Colenso is also the author of two two-volume studies: *History of the Zulu War and Its Origins* (1880), and *The Ruin of Zululand: An Account of British Doings in Zululand Since the Invasion of 1879* (1884, 1885).

Cornell, Fred (Frederick Carruthers) (1867–1921) Short-story writer and poet. Born in England and educated at Bedford Grammar School, Cornell came to South Africa in 1902. His interest in Namaqualand and South-West Africa (Namibia) is reflected in his memoir *The Glamour of Prospecting* (1920) and the better-known *A Rip van Winkle of the Kalahari and Other Tales of South-West Africa* (1914). The latter evokes the life of the prospector in the African hinterland. In several of the tales a narrator, simply called "Jason," tells his companions tales about the Kalahari and German South-West Africa. "The Follower" is a ghost story, while "The Proof" deals with the old myth about a human being brought up by baboons. In "The Drink of the Dead," Jason again features, although this time as a character, the narrator of the embedded ghost tale being, appropriately enough, the ghost of a Portuguese adventurer who had perished in an ill-fated treasure-seeking expedition. Cornell's use of the frame narrative places him in a tradition of this kind of storytelling that includes writers such as A. W. *Drayson, William Charles *Scully, James *FitzPatrick, Ernest *Glanville, and F. C. *Slater. Cornell is also the author of *East and West; or, War Songs and Verses for South African Soldiers* (1916).

D

Dhlomo, H. I. E. (Herbert Isaac Ernest) (1903–1956) Playwright, poet, short-story writer, critic, journalist. Born in Siyamu, Natal (now KwaZulu-Natal) and educated at the missionary school of Adams College, where he graduated as teacher, Dhlomo taught in Johannesburg before pursuing a career as journalist, first as reporter on the *Bantu World* and later as assistant editor of *Ilanga laseNatal.* He served as library organizer of the Transvaal Committee of the Carnegie Library Service, played an active role in the Bantu Dramatic Society at the Bantu Men's Social Centre, and was one of the founders of the Youth League of the ANC in 1946.

Dhlomo published two plays: "The Girl Who Killed to Save: Nongquase the Liberator" (1935) and "Dingana" (1954). He also wrote and produced many unpublished plays, including "Cetshwayo, Chaka: A Tragedy," and "Moshoeshoe" (known collectively as "The Black Bulls"), "Malaria," "Men and Women," "Ntsikana," "Ruby,"

"The Bazaar," "The Expert," "The Pass," "The Workers," "The Living Dead," and "Umhlola Wasensimini." In addition, he published the epic poem *Valley of a Thousand Hills* (1941) as well as the prose work *Zulu Life and Thought* (1945). His essays on literary theory and criticism have been collected in *English in Africa* (September 1977). His *Collected Works* was published in 1985.

Although Dhlomo's plays are generally seen to be derivative and stilted, his long poem *Valley of a Thousand Hills* has enduring value. Contrasting the disharmony of human society with the harmony of nature, the poem is an interesting example of the application of a romantic sensibility to the African context. Dhlomo's literary critical writings are regarded, moreover, as making an important intervention in the articulation of a South African aesthetic. Broadly, they espouse the view that Western literary tradition should be employed in such a way as to enhance rather than suppress African tradition.

FURTHER READING

Tim Couzens, *The New African: A Study of the Life and Works of H. I. E. Dhlomo* (1985).

Dhlomo, R. R. R. (Rolfes Reginald Raymond) (1906–1971) Short-story writer and novelist. The younger brother of H. I. E. Dhlomo, he was born near Pietermaritzburg and educated as a teacher at John Dube's Ohlange Institute (Inanda, Natal) and at Adams College (Amanzimtoti). When the family moved to Johannesburg, Dhlomo found work as a mine clerk, an experience that finds its way into many of his stories and sketches. In the 1920s he became a freelance writer for the Zulu daily *Ilanga lase Natal* and contributed a stream of articles about life on the reef under a variety of pseudonyms. His novella about life in the black urban slums, *An African Tragedy* (1928), was the first extended piece of prose fiction in English published by a black South African and brought him the attention of the Johannesburg literary world. He began to contribute pieces to Stephen *Black's satirical magazine *Sjambok* (1929–1931). In 1932 he became sub-editor on *Ilanga lase Natal* and in the same year was appointed assistant editor of the recently launched *Bantu World*. In 1943 he returned to Durban as editor of *Ilanga lase Natal*, a position he held until retirement.

Most of his work is in Zulu and takes the form of historical novels: *uDingane* (1936), *uShaka* (1937), *uMpande* (1938), *uCetshwayo* (1952), and *uDinizulu* (1968). His stories in English, first collected by Tim *Couzens and published in *English in Africa* (March 1975; republished as *20 Short Stories*, 1996), can be taken to represent the emergence of the black South African short story in English. Notable among these are "Murder on the Mine Dumps" (1930), which explores the conflict that develops between miners when they fall under the influence of their malevolent ringleader, "The Dog Killers" (1930), about the brutal killing of dogs in a mine compound, and "Magic in a Zulu Name" (1933), in which a father calls a witchdoctor to treat his son who is lying trembling in a corner of the hut after a fierce thunderstorm; the witchdoctor reveals that the boy's ailment is caused by a curse put on his mother by a spurned lover.

While they often lack the technical accomplishment usually associated with the modern short story, Dhlomo's stories are of considerable literary and sociological importance. In them can be seen many of the elements that came to characterize the themes of later black South African writing: the drift to the cities, the breakdown of traditional life, and the often tragic consequences of old customs encountering new and unaccommodating social circumstances.

Drayson, A. W. (Alfred Wilks) (1827–1901) Travel writer and short-story writer. Captain Alfred Wilks Drayson was an English sojourner in South Africa and the author of several travelogues about the region. His works include *Sporting Scenes Amongst the Kaffirs of South Africa* (1858), *Among the Zulus: The Adventures of Hans Sterk, South African Hunter and Pioneer* (1879), and *The Diamond Hunters of South Africa* (1889). Perhaps the most interesting of his works is *Tales at the Outspan, or Adventures in the Wild Regions of Southern Africa* (1862)—probably South Africa's first collection of fireside tales. In its use of a frame narrator and a set of internal narrators who tell the stories, it anticipates a tradition in the South African short story that includes writers such as William Charles *Scully, Percy *FitzPatrick, Ernest *Glanville, Perceval *Gibbon, Pauline *Smith, and Herman Charles *Bosman.

F

Fairbridge, Dorothea Ann (1862–1931) Novelist and historian. Cousin to Kingsley Fairbridge, she was born in Cape Town and educated in England. Her lifelong interest in South African history is reflected in both her fiction and historical works. She wrote a novel based on the life of Willem Adriaan van der Stel, *That Which Hath Been* (1910). Her second novel, *Piet of Italy* (1913), deals with the Cape Coloured and Malay communities. Her other novels are *The Torch Bearer* (1915), *Skiddle* (1925) and *The Uninvited* (1926). Her nonfiction works include *A History of South Africa* (1918), *The Historic Houses of South Africa* (1922), *A Pilgrim's Way in South Africa* (1928), *Along Cape Roads* (1928), and *The Historic Farms of South Africa* (1931). She also edited the letters of Lady Anne Barnard (*Lady Anne Barnard at the Cape of Good Hope*, 1924) and Lady Duff Gordon (*Letters from the Cape by Lady Duff Gordon*, 1927).

FURTHER READING

Peter Merrington, "Pageantry and Primitivism: and the 'Aesthetics of Union,'" *Journal of Southern African Studies* 21, no. 4 (1995): 643–656.

Fairbridge, Kingsley (1885–1924) Poet. Born in Grahamstown, he grew up in Rhodesia and studied in England as the first Rhodes Scholar at Oxford. Founder of the Child Emigration Society and the Fairbridge Farm Schools, a scheme whereby the slum children of overcrowded England were established as farmers in the relatively sparsely populated lands of the British Empire, he emigrated to Australia, where he established a school near Pinjarra, described by his wife Ruby Whitmore in *Pinjarra, the Building of a Farm School* (1937). The school became the model of similar schools opened subsequently.

Fairbridge published one volume of poetry, *Veld Verse* (1909), as well as his *Autobiography* (1927). He is also author of *Juvenile Emigration and the Farm School System*.

Praised for their pursuit of a valid South African mythology with which to embody a sensitive response to the indigenous landscape and its people, the poems are said to demarcate a kind of temporal boundary between an Africa of the past and a modern Africa.

FitzPatrick, Sir James Percy (1862–1931) Novelist, short-story writer, political polemicist. Born in King William's Town, where his father was a judge in what was then British Kaffraria, the FitzPatrick family moved to Cape Town, where Percy went to school. His father's death forced

Percy to leave school and begin work to help support the family. He worked rather unhappily as a bank clerk in Cape Town for a few years; upon turning twenty-one, he left for the Eastern Transvaal goldfields, where he became a transport rider based at Barberton. With the decline of these fields he moved on to the Witwatersrand.

The world of gold diggers, prospectors, and transport riders is vividly evoked in FitzPatrick's first published work, *The Outspan: Tales of South Africa* (1897). The long, rambling title story of the collection employs a fictional narrator and evokes the fireside ethos of the oral tale. The story draws on the familiar theme of "miscegenation": it concerns an unusual Englishman who takes two Swazi wives and adopts an African lifestyle but eventually fetches up among the prospectors in Barberton and dies a sudden death from fever. "Induna Nairn" has a similar peripatetic quality to "The Outspan": it is a lengthy, somewhat fragmented narrative steeped in a chauvinistic Victorian morality. Another story, "The Pool," mixes the racism of colonial ideology with the melodrama favored by the age.

This world is also evoked in FitzPatrick's best-known work, *Jock of the Bushveld* (1907). Intended as a story for children, the novel recounts the growth to maturity of a young boy and his bull terrier pup. They share the excitement of camp life among the gold diggers and wildlife adventure in the African veld (when Jock is lost and has to learn to survive on his own). The story is told in an unsentimental fashion and is redolent of the smells and sounds of the campfire and the wide-open African veld. Lavishly illustrated by E. Caldwell, *Jock* has gone into numerous impressions and editions since it was first published and has established itself as a classic adventure story, enjoyed by children and adults alike.

FitzPatrick later worked for Alfred Beit and became a partner in a mining house. His account of his travels north appeared as *Through Mashonaland with Pick and Pen* (1892). His association with Cecil Rhodes and Dr Jameson led to a brief spell of imprisonment after the Jameson Raid. In *The Transvaal from Within* (1899) he made a case for the Transvaal Republic "Uitlanders" shortly before the outbreak of the Second Boer War. Knighted in 1902, he played a leading role as a "unionist" in 1910 and spent his last years on his citrus farm in the Uitenhage area. His reminiscences appeared posthumously as *South African Memories* (1932; rev. ed. 1979).

FURTHER READING

J. P. R. Wallace, *Fitz: The Story of Sir Percy FitzPatrick* (1955); A. P. Cartwright, *The First South African: The Life and Times of Sir Percy FitzPatrick* (1971); Andrew Duminy and Bill Guest, *Interfering in Politics: A Biography of Sir Percy FitzPatrick* (1987); Gareth Cornwell, "FitzPatrick's 'The Outspan': Deconstructing the Fiction of Race," *English in Africa* 10, no. 1 (1983): 15–28.

G

Gibbon, Perceval (Reginald Percival) (1878–1926) Novelist, short-story writer, poet. Born in Trelach, Wales, Gibbon died in Guernsey, Channel Islands. He spent the years 1898–1903 in South Africa, where he worked as a journalist on *The Natal Witness*, *The Rand Daily Mail*, and *The Rhodesian Times*. He published short stories alongside his journalism of the time, and some of these stories reappeared in subsequent collections.

Gibbon produced five works that employ African settings: a volume of poems, *African Items* (1903); three novels, *Souls in*

Bondage (1903), *Salvatore* (1908) (set in the territory then known as Portuguese East Africa), and *Margaret Harding* (1911); and a collection of stories, *The Vrouw Grobelaar's Leading Cases* (1905). A gradual development from the racism typical of the age to a more enlightened view is discernible in his work.

Souls in Bondage, which explores the theme of racial mingling, is a sensationalistic potboiler and very uneven in quality. *The Vrouw Grobelaar's Leading Cases* employs the storyteller of the collection's title to narrate stories about the rural Afrikaans community of Dorpfontein, and Gibbon creates a cognitive and ideological distance between himself and this figure. With her raconteur's gift for deploying powerful storylines and concealed endings, Gibbon's storyteller is a forerunner of *Bosman's Oom Schalk Lourens figure. *Margaret Harding* is even more critical of blind racial prejudice and explores the effects of a transgression of racial boundaries in early twentieth-century rural South Africa. The protagonist of the novel's title is newly arrived in the Karoo and encounters an unusual black man who is a descendant of a local chief but has been brought up in England and trained as a doctor. The relationship that develops disrupts the time-honored social codes of the small community, and it allows Gibbon to reflect critically on the irrational race prejudices of the time.

Later works by Gibbon that do not employ African settings include *The Adventures of Miss Gregory* (1912), *The Second-Class Passenger* (1913), *Those Who Smiled* (1920), and *Dark Places* (1926).

Glanville, Ernest (1856–1925) Novelist and short-story writer. Born in Wynberg in the Cape, the son of T. Burt Glanville, once a member of the Cape Parliament, Glanville attended St. Andrews College in Grahamstown. His education was interrupted when he accompanied his father to the diamond fields at Kimberley in 1870. The two transported a printing press through the Karoo to the fields, where they set up the mining camp's first newspaper. This launched Glanville's long career in journalism.

Returning to Grahamstown, he joined *The Grahamstown Journal* as subeditor, and thereafter he went to London, where he and his brother edited a weekly, the *South African Empire*. When the Zulu War broke out in 1879 he returned to South Africa as war correspondent for the London *Daily Chronicle*. Later he became assistant editor on the *Daily Telegraph* and began a career as a prolific writer of books on South Africa. He returned to South Africa in 1903 to join the *Cape Argus* and thereafter worked on the Bulawayo *Chronicle* and the Johannesburg *Star*. A newspaperman to the end, he was contributing articles to the *Weekend Argus* at the time of his sudden death in Rondebosch.

Glanville is remembered today as the author of several Eastern Cape frontier romances and animal tales. Early novels include *The Lost Heiress: A Tale of Love, Battle and Adventure* (1891), set against the background of the Anglo-Zulu War, *A Fair Colonist* (1894), and *The Kloof Bride; or, the Lover's Quest* (1898), which deals with an African rebellion against colonial rule. The South African War formed the backdrop to *The Despatch Rider* (1900), *Max Thornton* (1901), and *A Beautiful Rebel* (1902). Later animal adventure stories include *Tyopa: A Bush Romance* (1920), *Claw and Fang* (1923), and *The Hunter: A Story of Bushman Life* (1927). With the exception of a few short stories, Glanville's works (some twenty in all) have been out of print for many years.

His most memorable fictional creation is the character "Uncle Abe Pike"—a frontiersman with a gift for telling tall tales. These tales, set on the Eastern Cape frontier in the last part of the nineteenth century, are collected in *Kloof Yarns* (1896) and in expanded form in *Tales from the Veld* (1897). Whereas earlier practitioners of this kind of tale such as A. W. *Drayson, Joseph *Ingram and William Charles *Scully tended not to subvert and render ironic the tales told by their narrators, Abe Pike's tales are indisputably "tall tales," told chiefly to amuse and divert rather than to instruct and enlighten. In this, Glanville anticipates later writers working in this mode such as Perceval *Gibbon and Herman Charles *Bosman.

Goudvis, Bertha (1876–1966) Dramatist, novelist, short-story writer. Born in Cumbria, England, Goudvis came out to South Africa in 1881 as part of the early wave of Jewish migration to the country. She worked as a hotelier and journalist in South Africa, Rhodesia, and Mozambique. She contributed a weekly column to the *Natal Mercury* in Durban and later worked on the *Evening Standard*, the *Star*, and the *Rand Daily Mail* in Johannesburg. Her early works were plays: *A Husband for Rachel* (1924) is about a young Jewish woman who wishes to escape an arranged marriage but, ironically, falls in love with the man with whom her marriage has been arranged; *The Way the Money Goes*, set in contemporary Johannesburg, *Patriots*, set during the Boer War, and *The Sergeant-in-Charge*, set in rural South Africa, were all performed in 1925 and published together with *A Husband for Rachel* as *The Way the Money Goes and Other Plays* (1925). Her other plays are *Wedding Prelude* (first performed in 1931) and *The Aliens* (1936). Her only novel, *Little Eden* (1949), is set in Zululand and traces the fortunes of a shrewd female hotelier who has to deal with a Rand magnate who comes to the area to inspect minerals on a nearby farm. Goudvis is best known, however, for *The Mistress of Mooiplaas and Other Stories* (1956), a collection of tales set in various parts of rural South Africa and dealing astutely with human relationships, mainly from a woman's point of view.

H

Haggard, Sir Henry Rider (1856–1925) Novelist. Born in London, the eighth of the ten children of a Norfolk squire, Haggard was educated at a London day school and at Ipswich Grammar School. He joined the Colonial Service as a personal aide to Sir Henry Bulwer and spent two terms in South Africa: 1875–79 and 1880–81. He took part in Sir Theophilus Shepstone's annexation of the Transvaal in 1877 and remained loyal to the British colonial effort for the remainder of his life. He studied law and was called to the bar in 1885, but the successes of his early novels meant that he was able to pursue the life of a writer instead.

His early works include *Cetewayo and His White Neighbours* (1882), *Dawn* (1884), *The Witch's Hand* (1884), and the hugely popular *King Solomon's Mines* (1885). This romantic tale of an expedition to the African interior was followed by other popular novels employing an African setting: *Allan Quatermain* (1887), *Jess* (1887), *She* (1887), and *Nada the Lily* (1892). His "Zulu trilogy" consists of *Marie* (1912), *Child of Storm* (1913), and *Finished* (1917), while *Allan's Wife and Other Tales* (1890) contains several stories with a southern African setting.

FURTHER READING

Lilias Rider Haggard, *The Cloak That I Left: A Biography of the Author Henry Rider Haggard*

K. B. E. (1951); Morton Cohen, *Rider Haggard: His Life and Work* (1960).

Howarth, Anna (1854–1943) Novelist. Born in London, she came out to South Africa in 1894 and worked as a nurse's aide in Grahamstown. Her association with Eastern Cape families provided her with material about frontier life, the focus of her first and best-known novel, *Jan: An Afrikander* (1897). Notable for its honesty and judicious use of factual detail, the novel deals with the social consequences of miscegenation and is a very early example of this preoccupation in colonial South African writing. Her later novels are *Katrina: A Tale of the Karoo* (1898), *Sword and Assegai* (1899), and *Nora Lester* (1902).

I

Ingram, Joseph Forsyth (1858–1923) Travel writer and poet. Born in Belfast, he grew up in Scotland until his family was forced by financial circumstances to emigrate to South Africa in the 1860s. The family settled on a farm in Natal, and Ingram made trading trips into Zululand and elsewhere in South Africa. He served in the Zulu and Boer wars in the 1880s and contributed articles to the *Natal Mercury* and newspapers abroad. A fellow of the Royal Geographical Society, he wrote a handbook on South Africa, *The Land of Gold, Diamonds, and Ivory*, and published a volume of verse entitled *Poems of a Pioneer* (1893). His *The Story of a Gold Concession and Other African Tales and Legends* (1893) is a collection of narratives gleaned from his encounters with the tribespeople of southeastern Africa.

L

Leipoldt, C. Louis (Christiaan Frederick Louis) (1880–1947) Novelist, poet, playwright, autobiographer. Born in Worcester, the son of a Rhenish missionary, he is regarded as one of the pioneering figures in Afrikaans literature, although much of his nonfiction writing was in English. While still at school, Leipoldt contributed articles to local newspapers, and during the Boer War he was a correspondent for local and foreign newspapers. After the war he studied medicine at Guy's Hospital in London. Returning to South Africa in 1914, he became a medical inspector of schools, an experience recounted in his autobiography *Bushveld Doctor* (1937). Other works in English in this period include *Medicine and Faith* (1935) and *Jan van Riebeeck: A Biographical Study* (1936). His poetry on the Second World War and other topics was collected as *The Ballad of Dick King and Other Poems* (1949), while his *300 Years of Cape Wine* (1952) was published posthumously. Stephen *Gray has edited and had published the typescript of three novels, *Chameleon on the Gallows*, *Stormwrack*, and *The Mask*, subsequently republished as *The Valley Trilogy* (2002). Set in a semirural Cape community, the novels cover a historical period from the Great Trek to the 1940s.

Lewis, Ethelreda (1875–1946) Novelist. Born in Derbyshire, England, she came to South Africa in 1904. She wrote poems and stories for local newspapers and magazines but made her name as a novelist. Her novels include *The Harp* (1924), *The Flying Emerald* (1925), and *Mantis* (1926), which are all set in South Africa. Under the pseudonym R. Hernekin Baptist, she published *Four Handsome Negresses* (1931), about the harrowing experiences of four

African women captured from the coast of Guinea; *Wild Deer* (1933; republished in 1984 under her own name); *Love at the Mission* (1938); and *A Cargo of Parrots* (1938). She is best known, however, as the editor of the multivolume *The Life and Times of Trader Horn—The Ivory Coast in the Earlies* (1927), *Harold the Webbed* (1928), and *The Waters of Africa* (1929)—a prose chronicle that records the life of the adventurer Alfred Aloysius Horn (A. A. Smith, 1851–1931).

M

Marais, Eugene (1871–1936) Short-story writer, poet, essayist. Born near Pretoria, he worked as newspaper editor in the Transvaal Republic before studying medicine and law in London. He fought in the Boer War on the side of the Boers and thereafter practiced as country doctor and lawyer. As is evident in his books on nature, he brought a philosophical and poetic eye to the study of the natural sciences. Some of his Afrikaans writings have been translated into English.

Marais published one volume of poems in Afrikaans, which was also translated into English, *Poems* (1956). A collection of essays translated into English appeared under the title *The Road to Waterberg* (1972). He is also author of two animal studies, *The Soul of the White Ant* (1937) and *My Friends the Baboons* (1939, reissued as *The Soul of the Ape* in 1969).

Millin, Sarah Gertrude (1889–1968) Novelist, short-story writer, biographer, autobiographer. Born in Lithuania to a Russian Jewish family, Millin came to South Africa as a young child, grew up in the Transvaal and was educated in Kimberley. She married Philip Millin, who later became a supreme court judge, and established an influential group of friends (which included Jan Smuts and Jan Hofmeyr), and maintained contact with writers like Pauline Smith.

A prolific writer and an influential literary figure in the period between the two world wars, her fourth novel, *God's Step-Children* (1924), established her reputation and is still the work for which she is best known. It deals with the theme of miscegenation and became controversial for its implicit racism. The story takes the form of a generational saga beginning with the Rev. Andrew Flood, an English missionary, who marries a "Hottentot" woman. His line of descendents finally issues in the "white" Barry Lindsell, who graduates from Oxford and brings home an English bride. When his jealous half-sister betrays him by revealing the secret of his Coloured ancestry, his wife leaves him and he eventually returns to the "brown people" in the community at Griqualand West, thus resolving this "tragedy of blood," as the author calls it. The novel has been pilloried for its racism, especially once the racial policies in South Africa began to have an impact on the society in general, but it remains a powerful exploration of a dominant thematic trope in South African literature and reflects the scientific thought concerning evolution and biological racial determinism current at the time.

Millin's seventeen novels include the "River" trilogy—*The Dark River* (1919), in which her obsession with racial mingling first found expression, *Adam's Rest* (1922), and *The Sons of Mrs Aab* (1931)—and the trilogy dealing with the "Coloured race": *God's Step-Children*, *King of the Bastards* (1949), and *The Burning Man* (1952). She was alarmed at the Nazi appropriation of *God's Step-Children* in the 1930s and wrote

The Herr Witchdoctor (1941), which warned against the rise of Nazi ideas in South Africa at the time. Later novels include *The Wizard Bird* (1962) and *Goodbye, Dear England* (1965).

Her two collections of short stories are *Men on a Voyage* (1930) and *Two Bucks Without Hair* (1957), which includes the Alita stories, about a Sotho maid and her relationship with her white "madam." Her impressionistic account of South African history and society, *The South Africans* (1926; revised in 1951 as *The People of South Africa*), was intended as an explanation of South Africa to a metropolitan audience; it brought her considerable acclaim in South Africa, however. She is also the author of two biographies on political figures whom she admired—*Rhodes* (1933) and *General Smuts* (1936; in two volumes)—and wrote two autobiographies: *The Night Is Long* (1941) and *The Measure of My Days* (1955). Her detailed account of World War II appeared in five volumes as *War Diaries 1944–1948*.

FURTHER READING

J. P. L. Snyman, *The Works of Sarah Gertrude Millin* (1955); Martin Rubin, *Sarah Gertrude Millin: A South African Life* (1977); J. M. Coetzee, *White Writing: On the Culture of Letters in South Africa* (1988); Michael Chapman, Colin Gardner, and Es'kia Mphahlele, eds., *Perspectives on South African English Literature* (1992).

P

Plaatje, Sol T. (Solomon Tshekisho) (1876–1932) Novelist, nonfiction writer, linguist, translator. Sol T. Plaatje is remembered today as the pre-eminent writer, newspaper editor and linguist of his time and, most particularly, as a political spokesman for the African National Congress from its inception in 1912. He was born on the farm Doornfontein, an outstation some fifty miles southwest of the Berlin Mission Society's main mission at Pniel in the Orange Free State. His early education was received at the Pniel Mission school, where he passed Standard III, the highest level of education offered by the school.

In 1894 he became a messenger for the Kimberley Post Office. He married in 1898 and in the same year was appointed as an interpreter at the magistrate's court in Mafeking, a post in which he distinguished himself. Over these years he taught himself languages, and became fluent in English, Dutch, Sotho, Tswana, Xhosa, and German. During the famous siege of Mafeking he kept a diary that was eventually published in 1973 as *The Boer War Diary of Sol T. Plaatje*.

The diary was never intended for publication, and its style is often telegraphic and elliptical. It begins three weeks into the siege (which lasted from October 11, 1899, to May 17, 1900) and ends several weeks before its lifting. An intensely personal and emotional work, it records the daily events Plaatje experienced and also contains some revealing details gleaned from his work as official Court Interpreter. Its enduring value lies in the fact that it is an inside view of a conflict by a black man caught between the contending forces.

In 1902, after eight years in the Cape Civil Service, he resigned to become editor of the newly established *Koranta ea Becoana*, which began as a Setswana-language supplement to the *Mafeking Mail*. With the eventual collapse of the newspaper in 1909, Plaatje began work as a labor recruiter for various mining companies. The South African Native Convention was formed in March 1909 in response to the color-bar clauses in the draft South Africa

Act. Plaatje became an office-bearer at the second annual meeting of the convention in Bloemfontein in March 1910. In the same year Plaatje moved back to Kimberley and became editor of the new newspaper *Tsala ea Becoana*, which first appeared in June 1910.

The South African Native National Congress, in which Plaatje was a key figure from the start, was formed in January 1912. Plaatje was elected general secretary of the Congress. The next year saw the introduction of the Natives' Land Act. This was to prove one of the most important pieces of legislation in South African history and one of the central events in Plaatje's life. The act introduced into the legislation of the Union the principle of territorial segregation. In the years to follow Plaatje was in the forefront of organizing African opposition to the act. Five delegates, including Plaatje, were elected from the Congress to act as a deputation to the British government. From 1914 to 1917, after the failure of this deputation to extract concessions from the government, Plaatje stayed in England, where, after a series of setbacks, he managed in 1916 to publish his examination of the effects of the Land Act, *Native Life in South Africa*.

Native Life was intended as a direct appeal to the British government to intervene in South Africa, particularly in respect of the recent Land Act, which allocated just seven percent of the South Africa's total area to the country's five million Africans. An underlying theme in the book (and, indeed, in all of Plaatje's work) is the common humanity of all of South Africa's people. Written in order to solicit favorable British public opinion, Plaatje was careful to apply British analogies for every important instance of social injustice he cited in relation to South Africa. He also cannily linked the hardships that were currently being endured in wartime Britain with the hardships suffered by black South Africans. Using his journalist's skill at giving a human dimension to the general misery occasioned by the Land Act, he cited examples of evictions he himself witnessed. The result is a moving and compelling protest against the most devastating of all apartheid laws.

The last part of his life he devoted increasingly to literature and in 1930, after ten years of difficulties with publishers, he saw his novel *Mhudi: An Epic of South African Native Life a Hundred Years Ago* appear under the Lovedale Press imprint. This was one of the earliest novels by a black man to appear in South Africa. Set in the 1830s, a time of unparalleled social upheaval caused by the *mfecane*, the dispersion of the tribes following the wars that erupted between the Zulus and other tribes in Natal, and the Great Trek, it tells the story of Mhudi and Ra-Thaga and their struggle to secure land and a means of existence in this turbulent time. At the beginning of the novel, the Barolong capital, Kunana, is destroyed after the Barolong kill Mzilikazi's tax collectors. This triggers a diaspora of the tribe, and Ra-Thaga and Mhudi, the young Barolong hero and heroine, meet in the wilderness. They make their way to Thaba Nchu, where members of their tribe and of other tribes displaced by the wars have sought refuge under the protection of the Basuto king Moshoeshoe. At this point the Boers are making their way up from the Cape into the hinterland, and the Barolong ally themselves with the Boers in their common struggle against the marauding Matabele under Mzilikazi. In the ensuing battle the Matabele are defeated, and Mhudi and Ra-Thaga are reunited and depart at the end for Thaba Nchu in a wagon given them by their Boer friends.

Mhudi had a mixed reception upon its publication, something that has persisted until today. Its detractors pointed to its curiously hybrid form—part history, part romance, part allegory—its incongruously outdated language and its stilted dialogue. Its champions, while conceding its unevenness, have identified its rootedness in oral African forms and its important role as a pathbreaker for subsequent black South African fiction.

Plaatje is also remembered as one of the earliest translators of Shakespeare into an African language (he translated *The Comedy of Errors* and *Julius Caesar* into Tswana). He also compiled a book of Tswana proverbs (*Sechuana Proverbs with Literal Translations and Their European Equivalents*, 1916), and wrote political pamphlets, including *The Mote and the Beam: An Epic on Sex-Relationships 'Twixt White and Black in British South Africa* (1921). Brian Willan's *Sol Plaatje: Selected Writings* appeared in 1996.

FURTHER READING

Brian Willan, *Sol Plaatje: A Biography* (1984); Peter Midgley, *Sol Plaatje: An Introduction* (1996).

Pringle, Thomas (1789–1834) Poet and journalist. Born in the year of the French Revolution, at Kelso, Scotland, Pringle was educated at Edinburgh University, where he developed a keen interest in the poetry of Burns and other Scottish poets. Leaving university without taking a degree, he worked for some years as a clerk and used his spare time to write poetry, essays, and journalism. In 1816 his verse epistle "The Autumnal Excursion" appeared and attracted the attention of Sir Walter Scott. A year later he was appointed coeditor of the newly founded *Edinburgh Monthly Magazine* (later *Blackwood's*). He did not prove successful as an editor of this and the other Scottish journals to which he turned, however, and in 1819 he joined a government-sponsored emigration scheme to the Eastern Cape. Before he left Scotland, however, he had the satisfaction of seeing *The Autumnal Excursion, or, Sketches in Teviotdale; with Other Poems* (1819) published.

Pringle's party arrived at the Cape in April 1820 and then moved on to Algoa Bay, in which district his family had been allotted a settlement. He very soon encountered the harsh laws governing the lives of people of color and became an opponent of this sort of injustice from the start. Nonetheless, as a settler and colonist he found himself in the dilemma of decrying a system in which he was himself complicit. In 1822, leaving the family farmstead Glen-Lynden in the hands of his brother, Pringle set out for Cape Town, where he took up a post at the new Government Library (later the South African Library). It was at this point that he initiated the idea of starting a journal and petitioned the conservative Governor, Lord Charles Somerset, to this end. Somerset reluctantly gave permission on the proviso that the journal would not be detrimental to the safety of the Colony, and Pringle was joined by John Fairbairn, a friend from his student days, to launch the proposed *South African Journal*. In 1824, however, the London printer Robert Greig launched *The South African Commercial Advertiser* and invited Pringle and Fairbairn to become coeditors. The latter publication soon ran afoul of Somerset, who summarily suspended it when it reported a case of legal action against him. Soon after this the second issue of Pringle's *South African Journal* appeared, which criticized Somerset's handling of the Albany settlers. Somerset responded by summoning Pringle to appear before him and answer a charge of flouting his authority. Pringle resigned his position and went back to Glen-Lynden, where he sold his remaining possessions and returned to England in 1826.

Although Pringle's brief sojourn in South Africa seemed a failure, it did provide him with a wealth of experience that he could later work into his poetry. His journalistic writing on slavery at the Cape led to his being appointed secretary to the Anti-Slavery Society in 1827. In the same year he edited George Thompson's *Travels and Adventures in Southern Africa*, to which he added poems and sketches of his own. One of these, "Afar in the Desert," attracted the attention of Samuel Taylor Coleridge, and the two became acquaintances. In 1828 his *Ephemerides, or Occasional Poems, written in Scotland and South Africa* appeared and this further enhanced his literary reputation. His major prose work *Narrative of a Residence in South Africa* appeared in 1834 alongside his *Poems Illustrative of South Africa* in a volume entitled *African Sketches*. Later in that year it was discovered that he was suffering from advanced tuberculosis, and he died before the year was out.

Pringle is best remembered for a number of poems dealing with his years as a settler in South Africa, which are among the earliest attempts to adapt European language and sentiments to an alien African landscape. "The Bechuana Boy" is remarkable for its sympathy with its forlorn subject, an African boy who tells his tale of bereavement at the hands of bandits: "I am in the world alone!" "Afar in the Desert" recounts the speaker's sense of wonder and awe at traversing a vast empty landscape with only a "silent Bush-boy" at his side. The poem has considerable power and technical skill, and its evangelical fervor is evident in its concluding affirmation: "Man is distant, but God is near!" Pringle's criticism of colonial society is particularly conspicuous in "The Forester of the Neutral Ground," which deals with what would become a dominant theme in South African literature: a marriage across the color bar and the banishment of the offending parties. "Makanna's Gathering" has been considered South Africa's first "protest poem," dealing as it does with a call to arms by the "Amakosa" to drive the white men into the sea. Although the linguistic register used in his poems appears quaint to the modern reader, Pringle's achievement was to open up possibilities for future attempts by South African poets to find the means to give expression to the African landscape.

FURTHER READING

Jane Meiring, *Thomas Pringle: His Life and Times* (1968); John Robert Doyle, *Thomas Pringle* (1972); Ernest Pereira and Michael Chapman, eds., *African Poems of Thomas Pringle* (1989); Damian Shaw, "Thomas Pringle's 'Bushmen': Images in Flesh and Blood," *English in Africa* 25, no. 2 (1998): 36–61; Matthew Shum, "Thomas Pringle and the 'Xhosa,'" *English in Africa* 27, no. 2 (2000): 1–28; Michael Chapman, ed., *Postcolonialism: South/African Perspectives* (2008).

R

Reitz, Deneys (1882–1944) Autobiographer. Born and educated in Bloemfontein, at age seventeen he joined the Boer forces when the Boer War broke out in 1899. He fought in many of the major engagements of the war, and he was with Jan Smuts when the latter invaded the Cape Colony toward the end of the war. He chose to go into exile rather than take the oath of allegiance, and spent three years in exile in Madagascar. He served with distinction in the First World War and later became High Commissioner for South Africa in London. His memoir of his experience in the Boer War, *Commando: A Boer Journal of the Boer War* (1929), is one of the most vivid and readable accounts of the war. He tells his story in an understated yet engaging manner, always downplaying his remarkable feats. *Trekking On* (1933) and *No Outspan* (1943) are accounts of his later experiences as a diplomat and statesman. These three works were reissued in one volume as *The Trilogy of Deneys Reitz* (1994) and later as *Adrift on the Open Veld: The Boer War and Its Aftermath* (1999).

S

Schreiner, Olive Emilie Albertina (1855–1920) Novelist, short-story writer, political essayist. Born at Wittebergen Mission Station in the northeastern Cape (near Lesotho), Schreiner was ninth of the twelve children of Rebecca and Gottlob Schreiner, a Wesleyan missionary. Her childhood, the first six years of which were spent at Wittebergen, was a difficult one. Rebecca, remembered by the children as cold and distant, adhered to strict Christian standards and her children's upbringing was puritanical and restrictive. Her father was warmer by nature but less of a powerful presence in the home. He, too, was devoutly Christian and pursued his missionary vocation with zeal. He proved incompetent, however, and in 1865 was forced to leave the ministry. He also failed as a trader and was declared bankrupt; this led to the breakup of the family home.

Olive lived a peripatetic and for the most part unhappy life in Cradock, at the Kimberley diamond diggings, and as a governess mainly on isolated Karoo farms. She began writing during this time, and her first novel, *Undine* (published posthumously in 1928, but written between 1875 and 1877), is a semiautobiographical account of a young woman's life as a governess and her desire to free herself from the physical and intellectual constraints of the day. Schreiner's desire for intellectual freedom was spurred at this time by her encounter with Herbert Spencer's *First Principles* (1862), one of the many contemporary books on the emerging conflict between conventional religion and scientific rationalism. The ideal of "free thinking" that Spencer espoused was crucial to Schreiner's own development as a thinker: it provided her with an intellectual basis for her religious doubts and enabled her to break the shackles of her dogmatic religious upbringing. Readings of the works of Darwin and John Stuart Mill would follow, and these reinforced her increasingly skeptical, nonconformist attitudes.

Her life as a governess was hard and unrewarding, but she poured her remaining energies into writing. While working for the Fouchés at their farm, Klein Gannahoek, near Cradock, she worked on *The Story of an African Farm* (1883). The stark isolation of the landscape around her she registered as an artistic challenge to be overcome. In a passage from the famous preface to the novel, she notes that the artist must "sadly squeeze the colour from his brush, and dip it into the grey pigments around him." In her steady, although somewhat forlorn, focus on what lay before her, she broke the mould of much colonial fiction of the time, which saw the barren, alien landscapes of the colonies as unsustaining of novelistic endeavor.

In 1881, aged twenty-six, she left South Africa for England to seek a publisher for *The Story of an African Farm* and to explore the possibility of a medical education. The latter came to nothing when she was forced to withdraw from training at the Royal Infirmary in Edinburgh, but the novel did find a publisher. After doing the rounds of several publishing firms, the book was finally accepted by Chapman and Hall and appeared early in 1883 under the pseudonym of Ralph Iron. The book was an instant success and a decisive turning point in her life.

The novel traces the lives of the three main characters, Lyndall, Waldo, and Em from childhood to young adulthood. The children live on a Karoo farm headed by Em's stepmother, Tant Sannie, a crude Afrikaner woman with a venal and selfish streak. Em is a plain, compassionate, practical girl who will eventually inherit the farm. Her cousin Lyndall is a free spirit, strong-minded and rebellious, and destined for an unhappy end. Waldo, the German farm manager Otto's son, is a boy who thinks deeply about ultimate questions like life and death, God and the meaning of the universe, and the place of human beings in it. When Tant Sannie takes in an itinerant charlatan, Bonaparte Blenkins, the household becomes a tyranny. Old Otto is summarily dismissed and dies shortly afterwards; Waldo feels compelled to disavow any belief in God; and the two girls turn inward upon their own resources. In due course Blenkins is revealed for the rogue he is and is forced to leave. Lyndall leaves the farm with a lover in search of a more fulfilling life; she gives birth to a baby, who dies shortly afterward; turns down her lover's proposal of marriage; and dies tended by Gregory Rose, a man she had earlier rejected. When Waldo returns to the farm after working in various small towns in menial positions and receiving mostly abuse and derision, he discovers that Lyndall has died and he too some days later walks out into the sun and succumbs.

The novel has been criticized for being uneven and marred by lengthy philosophical passages that disrupt the narrative flow, but its strengths are its powerful evocation of setting, and its strong portrayals of character—especially that of Waldo. In its progressive views on feminism and marriage it also broke new ground, and its pervasive sense of a baneful fate that presides over the affairs of the characters in this harsh setting is keenly realized and moving.

While in London Schreiner made the acquaintance of young intellectuals such as Havelock Ellis, Edward Carpenter, Eleanor Marx, and Karl Pearson, all of whom were critical of prevailing social and political norms and influenced her own thought. She traveled around Europe from 1886 to 1888, returning to England briefly and then back to South Africa. Although her reputation as a writer was firmly established, she herself was haunted by a sense of personal failure and incompleteness. She went back to England the following year to meet old friends and revise *From Man to Man* (1926), the novel she had been working on for years but which was destined to remain unfinished.

Like *African Farm*, *From Man to Man* examines the lives of two women: Rebekah, a woman who makes a conventional marriage and whose life appears set for fulfillment and happiness; and her younger sister, Bertie, who is seduced at a young age by her tutor and is later jilted by her fiancé when she confesses this to him. Rebekah, intelligent and articulate, is patronized by her conventional husband. She also has to endure his unfaithfulness as he begins to have a series of sexual liaisons. He refuses her a divorce, and she is forced to forgo the opportunity of a more fulfilling relationship with another man and turn her energies toward her children. A loving and able mother, Rebekah also has a rich interior life and, like Lyndall from *African Farm*, a capacity for abstract philosophical thought. Her pursuit of truth, whatever the personal cost, also strongly recalls Lyndall's quest. Another central theme is relations between the sexes, where the ideal of relationships founded on love and justice is articulated. Bertie is condemned to a downward course in life, and at the end of the novel Rebekah finds her dying in a brothel. Schreiner's portrayal of Bertie is a powerful critique of a society that would condemn a woman for an indiscretion while hypocritically turning a blind eye to the same behavior in men.

Two other important works of this period are *Dreams* (1890) and *Dream Life and Real Life* (1893). As their titles suggest, dreams, fantasies and allegories play a significant role in these collections. In "Three Dreams in a Desert," for example, the narrator falls asleep under a mimosa tree and has three allegorical dreams about the subjugation of women and the path they must tread in order to achieve liberation from male domination. The "real world" of the Karoo—the African plain, the hot sun, and the parched bushes briefly alluded to in the opening lines—is abandoned for the world of fantasy, where ideas triumph over the quotidian materiality of everyday life, a life the more attractive aspects of which would in any event be denied a woman growing up in a late-nineteenth-century colony.

Schreiner returned to South Africa at the end of 1893 and in 1894, at the age of thirty-eight, married Samuel Cron Cronwright, a Cradock farmer several years her junior. (Cronwright changed his name to Cronwright-Schreiner, an indication of Schreiner's commitment to her feminist principles.) Her steadily deteriorating asthmatic condition soon made it necessary for them to seek a more congenial climate. They moved to Kimberley, where Olive fell pregnant and gave birth, in 1895, to a daughter, who died the following day. This event had a profound effect on Schreiner: she lay for hours with the dead body in her arms before she allowed it to be placed in a lead coffin. The coffin was moved from Kimberley to Hanover, and then to De Aar, where it was placed in a brick-lined grave.

Olive now became increasingly involved in the political life of South Africa, which at that time was dominated by Cecil John Rhodes. Initially an admirer of Rhodes, she after a time became disillusioned with him and what he represented. Her allegorical novel *Trooper Peter Halket of Mashonaland* (1897) is a thinly veiled attack on Rhodes and his Chartered Company. During the Boer War the Schreiners espoused the Boer cause and were active in lobbying anti-imperialistic support in both South Africa and Britain. Their jointly written political tract *The Political Situation* (1896) appeared at this time and was followed by Schreiner's *An English South African's View of the Situation* (1899), a plea for the prevention of war. Another significant work set in this period is her long story "Eighteen-ninety-nine," about the devastation wrought during the Second Boer War.

As the contours of postwar South African society began to emerge, however, Olive grew less supportive of the Boer cause, and turned her attention increasingly to the conflict between capital and labor and, in particular, the struggle of women for enfranchisement and liberation. Her *Woman and Labour* (1911) argues that without access to remunerative work, women will be forced into a worthless parasitical role in society. In 1914 Olive left for Europe once more. She spent most of the First World War in Britain, where she supported the cause of the pacifists and conscientious objectors. Her health failing, she left for South Africa in August 1920, only to die in Cape Town before the year was out.

Her other works are *Closer Union* (1909), *Thoughts on South Africa* (1923), and *Stories, Dreams and Allegories* (1923). Recent collections of her work include *The Women's Rose: Stories and Allegories* (1986), *An Olive Schreiner Reader: Writings and Women in South Africa* (1987), and *Words in Season* (2005).

FURTHER READING

S. C. Cronwright-Schreiner, *The Life of Olive Schreiner* (1924); S. C. Cronwright-Schreiner, *The Letters of Olive Schreiner* (1924); Ridley Beeton, *Olive Schreiner: A Short Guide to her Writings* (1974); Ruth First and Anne Scott, *Olive Schreiner: A Biography* (1980); Cherry Clayton, ed., *Olive Schreiner* (1983); Malvern van Wyk Smith and Don Maclennan, eds., *Olive Schreiner and After* (1983); Joyce Avrech Berkman, *The Healing Imagination of Olive Schreiner* (1989); Karel Schoeman, *Olive Schreiner: A Woman in South Africa* (1991); Karel Schoeman, *Only an Anguish to Live Here: Olive Schreiner and the Anglo-Boer War, 1899–1902* (1992); Tina Barsby, *Olive Schreiner: An Introduction* (1995).

Scully, W. C. (William Charles) (1855–1943) Novelist, short-story writer, poet, autobiographer, historiographer. Born in Dublin, Ireland, he and his family emigrated to South Africa in 1867. He was a diamond prospector in Kimberley and a gold prospector in Lydenburg and Pilgrim's Rest before joining the Cape Civil Service in 1876, where he served later as magistrate and civil commissioner in the Transkei, Namaqualand, and the Transvaal.

Scully published two volumes of poetry, *The Wreck of the Grosvenor and Other South African Poems* (1886) and *Poems* (1892). He published four novels: *A Vendetta of the Desert* (1898), *Between Sun and Sand* (1898), *The Harrow* (written in 1904 and published in 1921), and *Daniel Vananda: The Life Story of a Human Being* (1923). He also published four collections of short stories: *Kafir Stories* (1895), *The White Hecatomb and Other Stories* (1897), *By Veldt and Kopje* (1907), and *Lodges in the Wilderness* (1915), as well as a miscellany of sketches, poems and stories, *Voices of Africa* (1943). A selection of his stories appeared posthumously as *Transkei Stories* (1984). In addition, he published three autobiographical works: *The Ridge of the White Waters ("Witwatersrand"), or, Impressions of a Visit to Johannesburg* (1912), *Reminiscences of a South African Pioneer* (1913), and *Further Reminiscences of a South African Pioneer* (1913). He is also author of the biography, *Sir J H Meiring Beck: A Memoir* (1921), and the historical work, *A History of South Africa from the Earliest Days to Union* (1922).

Although as an employee in the colonial civil service he supported imperialism and adhered, in some respects, to European perceptions of Africans as simple and primitive, his writings evince a sympathetic response to landscape and to the indigenous people whom he came to know. Employing an ethnological eye for the details of customs and beliefs, his novels and short stories portray a way of life characterized by physical hardship and spirituality, the integrity of which was increasingly threatened by imperial incursion.

FURTHER READING

John Robert Doyle, *William Charles Scully* (1978).

Slater, Francis Carey (1876–1958) Poet, short-story writer, novelist, editor. Born in Alice, Eastern Cape, and reared on a farm where he learned to speak fluent Xhosa, he was educated at Lovedale. He worked for the Standard Bank and took early retirement to devote himself to literature.

Slater published ten volumes of poetry: *Footpaths Thro' the Veld* (1905), *From*

Mimosa Land (1910), *Calls Across the Sea* (1917), *Settlers and Sunbirds* (1919), *The Karroo and Other Poems* (1924), *Drought: A South African Parable* (1929), *Dark Folk and Other Poems* (1935), *The Trek* (1938), *The Distraught Airman and Other Wartime Verses* (1940), and *Veld Patriarch and Other Poems* (1949). His *Collected Poems* was published in 1957. He also published two collections of short stories, *The Sunburnt South* (1908) and *The Secret Veld* (1931), as well as one novel, *The Shining River* (1925), and an autobiography, *Settler's Heritage* (1954).

With the publication of *The Karroo and Other Poems,* Slater revealed a distinctive voice capable of articulating the particularities of the local context. This voice grew in assurance and poetic strength with the publication of his subsequent volumes of poetry, three of which stand out. *Drought* conveys with mesmeric force the impact of drought on the landscape and people, and uses this physical phenomenon as a metaphor for racial hatred to suggest barrenness of spirit. *Dark Folk* comprises lyrical but also realistic evocations of African life. *The Trek* was published to coincide with the centenary of the Great Trek and celebrates the pioneering spirit of the Voortrekkers.

Slater is editor of *The Centenary Book of South African Verse* (1925) and *New Centenary Book of South African Verse* (1945).

FURTHER READING

John Robert Doyle, *Francis Carey Slater* (1971).

Smith, Pauline (Janet) (1882–1959) Short-story writer and novelist. Born in Oudtshoorn to British parents; Smith's father was a medical doctor who came out to South Africa and established a practice in the town. Smith attended schools in South Africa and Britain, but her education was interrupted by ill health (from which she suffered intermittently her whole life), and she never completed her schooling. The death in 1898 of her father, to whom she was very attached, meant that she never returned to the Colony permanently, and lived for most of her life in Dorset, making several return trips to South Africa when health and finances allowed.

In 1902 her first story, "A Tenantry Dinner," appeared in the Aberdeen *Evening Gazette* under the pseudonym Janet Tamson. Other stories and poems followed. In 1904 she returned to South Africa, where she started a diary in which she recorded observations about South African society and landscape. In 1908, on a visit to Switzerland, she met the writer Arnold Bennett, who was henceforth to encourage her in her writing. Her next trip to South Africa in 1913 was nearly a year in duration, much of which she spent in the Little Karoo area, again recording incidents and observations about people she met.

She spent the First World War years in England, where she published the first of her *Little Karoo* stories, "The Sisters," in 1915. In the early 1920s other stories appeared, including "The Pain" and "The Schoolmaster," and in 1925 *The Little Karoo* was published (with an introduction by Arnold Bennett). At this stage it was a collection of eight stories; the revised 1930 edition would add two more. Less than a year later her novel, *The Beadle* (1926), was published. This was to be her last major work, although several other works appeared, both in her lifetime and posthumously.

In 1929 the BBC broadcast her play *The Last Voyage*, as well as readings of several of the stories from *The Little Karoo* and extracts from *The Beadle* in the late 1940s. In 1933, *A. B.*, her memoir of Arnold Bennett (who had died two years earlier), appeared. Toward the end of this year she made another trip to South Africa, this time staying for over two years. Her collection of children's stories, *Platkops Children* (1935), appeared at this time. Her 1937–38 trip to South Africa was to be her last. The Second World War intervened, and Smith spent these years in England, depressed and in increasingly poor health. She struggled from 1949 onward to complete her second novel, *Winter Sacrament*, but, dogged by ill health (neuralgia and chronic heart problems) she was forced eventually to abandon it.

In 1993 a collection of her miscellaneous works appeared under the title *The Unknown Pauline Smith*. This includes the *Winter Sacrament* fragment, extracts from her diaries and several out-of-print stories. Among the last are her "Koenraad tales," which employ a narrator ("Koenraad") and deal with the pranks of farmers in the Little Karoo district in a manner that anticipates Bosman's "Oom Schalk Lourens" stories. Another recent publication is *Secret Fire: The 1913–1914 South African Journal of Pauline Smith* (1997), edited by Harold Scheub.

Each of the ten stories in *The Little Karoo* exemplifies Smith's remarkable ability to capture the stark, elemental quality of her rural Dutch characters and the ponderous biblical cadences of their speech, the harsh oppressiveness of a life spent wresting the barest of yields from the reluctant earth, the austerity of their Protestant faith, and the tragic dimension in their human fallibilities. So compatible are the stories in terms of theme and setting that they have been profitably read as a "cycle."

In "The Pain" (often considered Smith's best story), Juriaan van Royen undertakes a journey to Platkops Dorp to seek help for his terminally ill wife at the newly established hospital there. The humble, rustic lifestyle of the simple peasant couple—a life closely tied to the soil and the elements, and presided over by a benign but frugal God—comes up against a newer world of modern medicine and impersonal efficiency, a world with new rhythms and rationales. In this bewilderingly new setting, Juriaan's God deserts him and the central irony of the story unfolds: Deltje's physical pain, which persuaded them to undertake the journey, is not cured in hospital but merely eclipsed by the greater pain of spiritual suffering. The couple secretly resolve to leave the hospital, and the closing passage sees them on their way back to their isolated homestead, where Deltje will await a lingering but certain death and, with her passing—the reader is left to presume—will come the inescapable fact of Juriaan's own demise.

"The Schoolmaster" concerns the youthful, selfless love Engela feels for Jan Boetje, a man on the run from his own past. Jan Boetje becomes the teacher to the young children on Engela's grandparents' farm. He tells the children and Engela about the far-off wonders of Europe, while Engela instructs him in local veld lore. One day, in a fit of rage (which signifies something about his troubled past), Jan Boetje blinds a pair of mules when they refuse to cross a stream and subsequently banishes himself to a life of drawing a handcart across the veld, buying and selling goods to eke out an existence. In the depths of her anguish upon his departure, Engela draws comfort from the thought that what she taught him about the veld would help him in the physical and spiritual wilderness that he has damned himself to inhabit for life. In a tragically ironic final twist, the family discovers that Jan Boetje has drowned in a flood at the drift near the farm.

The story illustrates Smith's immense power as a writer in the tragic mode, and marks her position in this tradition in South African literature. "The Miller" is another example of this tendency in Smith's work. Andries Lombard, the miller, is described as "a stupid kindly man whom illness had turned into a morose and bitter one." His illness causes him to become estranged from his wife and children and this culminates in his refusal to attend the annual Thanksgiving ceremony at the local church. At the last moment, when the service is already fully underway, he suddenly desires to be reunited with his wife. He makes his way down to the Thanksgiving but collapses outside the church, coughing up blood and, slipping from her arms, dies without achieving full reconciliation. (Significantly, the person who helps him when he collapses is Esther Sokolowsky—the "Jew-woman"—a refugee persecuted in Russia and now condemned to be an outsider in this rigidly Calvinistic community. This detail, like the minute description of the way the church congregation is segregated by gender and race, testifies to Smith's acute perceptiveness regarding matters of oppression.)

Smith's skill as a writer manifests itself chiefly in the austere economy of her stories—a quality perfectly commensurate with the frugal, self-denying lifestyles of the people of the Little Karoo. This gives the stories an archetypal, timeless quality: the ageless themes of thwarted love, familial conflict and betrayal, and the depredations of a baneful fate all surface again in these stories and are stripped of ornamentation and reduced to their bare, elemental features.

The Beadle shares the stories' setting and thematic concerns. Andrina, the central character, is a warm and innocent young girl who works for the Van der Merwe family on their farm, Harmonie, in the Aangenaam valley area of the Little Karoo. In much the same pattern as "The Schoolmaster," a stranger comes into this caring, God-fearing household: he is the self-centered and feckless Englishman Henry Nind, who seduces Andrina before leaving the district. Finding herself pregnant, Andrina leaves Harmonie in search of Nind, who is believed to be in the north of the country.

The story of the beadle, a morose and embittered man, shadows Andrina's story: it emerges that he is Andrina's secret father, having forced himself on Andrina's mother, who died in childbirth. He has for years been watching his daughter growing up and now nurses an intense hatred of the young Englishman, whom he sees as a version of himself, committing the same errors and ruining a young girl's life. (There is also a distinct suggestion of racial enmity mixed in with personal grievance.) Andrina's plight precipitates the beadle's confession of guilt to the community, the Englishman goes back to England, and the end of the novel sees father and daughter reconciled, with Andrina quite unashamed of giving birth to a child under these circumstances. Smith thus offers a highly sympathetic rendering of the "fallen woman" theme and presents at the novel's conclusion a sense of hope and regeneration largely absent in her unrelievedly tragic short stories.

FURTHER READING

Geoffrey Haresnape, *Pauline Smith* (1969); Dorothy Driver, ed., *Pauline Smith* (1983).

W

Ward, Harriet (1808–1873) Novelist. Born in Norfolk, England, Ward came out to the Eastern Cape Frontier with her soldier husband, Captain John Ward, in 1842. The couple spent the next five years in the colony and returned to Britain in 1848. This experience produced *Five Years in Kaffirland; with Sketches of the Late War in that Country, to* *the Conclusion of Peace* (1848). This work was reissued in 1851 with a new title: *The Cape and the Kaffirs: A Diary of Five Years' Residence in Kaffirland, with a chapter of advice to emigrants based on the latest official returns and the most recent information regarding the colony.* Some of this material found its way into the novel *Jasper Lyle: A Tale of Kaffirland* (1851). Her later novels include *Lizzy Dorian: The Soldier's Wife* (1854) and *Hardy and Hunter: A Boy's Own Story* (1858). Ward also wrote *Recollections of an Old Soldier: A Biographical Sketch of the Late Colonel Tidy* (1849) and edited Edward Napier's memoir *Past and Future Emigration, or, The Book of the Cape* (1849).

Bibliography

PRIMARY TEXTS

Abrahams, Lionel. *The Celibacy of Felix Greenspan: A Novel in Eighteen Stories.* Johannesburg: Bateleur, 1977.
——. *Lionel Abrahams: A Reader.* Ed. Patrick Cullinan. Johannesburg: Ad Donker, 1988.
——. *A Dead Tree Full of Live Birds.* Cape Town: Snailpress; Johannesburg: Hippogriff Press, 1995.
——. *The White Life of Felix Greenspan.* Johannesburg: M&G Books, 2002.
——. *Chaos Theory of the Heart and Other Poems.* Johannesburg: Jacana, 2005.
Abrahams, Peter. *Mine Boy.* London: Dorothy Crisp, 1946.
——. *Wild Conquest.* London: Faber, 1951.
——. *The Path of Thunder.* London: Faber, 1952.
——. *Return to Goli.* London: Faber, 1953.
——. *Tell Freedom.* London: Faber, 1954.
——. *A Wreath for Udomo.* London: Faber, 1956.
——. *A Night of Their Own.* London: Faber, 1965.
——. *The Coyaba Chronicles: Reflections on the Black Experience in the Twentieth Century.* Kingston: Ian Randle; Cape Town: David Philip, 2000.
Afrika, Tatamkhulu. *Nine Lives.* Cape Town: Carrefour/Hippogriff, 1991.
——. *Dark Rider.* Ed. Robert Berold. Cape Town: Snailpress/Mayibuye Books, 1992.
——. *The Innocents.* Cape Town: David Philip, 1994.
——. *The Flesh and the Flame.* Cape Town: Silk Road International, 1995.
——. *Mad Old Man Under the Morning Star: The Poet at Eighty.* Cape Town: Snailpress, 2001.
——. *Bitter Eden.* London: Arcadia, 2002.
——. *Nightrider: Selected Poems.* Ed. Shabbir Banoobhai et al. Cape Town: Kwela/Snailpress, 2003.
——. *Mr Chameleon: An Autobiography.* Johannesburg: Jacana, 2005.
Altman, Phyllis. *The Law of the Vultures.* London: Cape, 1952.
Baderoon, Gabeba. *The Dream in the Next Body.* Cape Town: Kwela/Snailpress, 2005.
——. *A Hundred Silences.* Cape Town: Kwela/Snailpress, 2006.
Bailey, Brett. *The Plays of Miracle & Wonder: Bewitching Visions and Primal High-Jinx from the South African Stage.* Cape Town: Double Storey, 2003.
Barris, Ken. *The Jailer's Book.* Cape Town: Kagiso, 1996.

——. *Evolution*. Halfway House: Zebra Press, 1998.
——. *Summer Grammar*. Howick: Brevitas, 2004.
Becker, Jillian. *The Keep*. London: Chatto & Windus, 1967.
——. *The Virgins: A Novel*. London: Gollancz, 1976.
Behr, Mark. *The Smell of Apples*. Cape Town: Queillerie, 1993.
Benson, Mary. *At the Still Point*. London: Chatto & Windus, 1971.
Berold, Robert. *The Door to the River*. Johannesburg: Bateleur Press, 1984.
——. *The Fires of the Dead: Poems*. Cape Town: Carrefour Press, 1989.
——. *Rain Across a Paper Field*. Pietermaritzburg: Gecko Poetry, 1999.
——, ed. *It All Begins: Poems from Postliberation South Africa*. Pietermaritzburg: Gecko Poetry, 2002.
Blacklaws, Troy. *Karoo Boy*. Cape Town: Double Storey, 2004.
——. *Blood Orange*. Cape Town: Double Storey, 2005.
Blignaut, Aegidius Jean. *Dead End Road*. Johannesburg: Ad Donker, 1980.
Bloom, Harry. *Episode*. London: Collins, 1956.
Bloom, Harry, and Pat Williams. *King Kong: An African Jazz Opera*. London: Collins, 1961.
Boetie, Dugmore. *Familiarity Is the Kingdom of the Lost*. Ed. Barney Simon. London: Barrie and Rockliff, 1969.
Bosman, Herman Charles. *Jacaranda in the Night*. Johannesburg: A P B Bookstore, 1947.
——. *Mafeking Road*. Johannesburg: Central News Agency, 1947.
——. *Cold Stone Jug*. Johannesburg: A.P.B. Bookstore, 1949.
——. *Willemsdorp*. Cape Town: Human & Rousseau, 1977.
——. *Idle Talk: Voorkamer Stories I*. Ed. Craig MacKenzie. Cape Town: Human & Rousseau, 1999.
——. *Old Transvaal Stories*. Ed. Craig MacKenzie. Cape Town: Human & Rousseau, 2000.
——. *Seed-Time and Harvest and Other Stories*. Ed. Craig MacKenzie. Cape Town: Human & Rousseau, 2001.
——. *Verborge Skatte*. Ed. Leon de Kock. Cape Town: Human & Rousseau, 2001.
——. *A Cask of Jerepigo*. Ed. Stephen Gray. Cape Town: Human & Rousseau, 2002.
——. *Unto Dust and Other Stories*. Ed. Craig MacKenzie. Cape Town: Human & Rousseau, 2002.
——. *My Life and Opinions*. Ed. Stephen Gray. Cape Town: Human & Rousseau, 2003.
——. *Young Bosman*. Ed. Craig MacKenzie. Cape Town: Human & Rousseau, 2003.
——. *Wild Seed*. Ed. Stephen Gray. Cape Town: Human & Rousseau, 2004.
——. *Homecoming: Voorkamer Stories II*. Ed. Craig MacKenzie. Cape Town: Human & Rousseau, 2005.
Breytenbach, Breyten. *Mouroir: Mirrornotes of a Novel*. London: Faber, 1984.
——. *The True Confessions of an Albino Terrorist*. Johannesburg: Taurus, 1984.
——. *Memory of Snow and Dust*. London: Faber, 1989.
——. *Dog Heart: A Travel Memoir*. Cape Town: Human & Rousseau, 1998.
Brink, André. *The Ambassador*. Johannesburg: Central News Agency, 1964.
——. *Looking on Darkness*. New York: Morrow, 1975.
——. *An Instant in the Wind*. New York: Morrow, 1977.
——. *A Dry White Season*. London: Allen, 1979.
——. *A Chain of Voices*. London: Faber, 1982.
——. *The Wall of the Plague: A Novel*. New York: Summit Books, 1984.
——. *An Act of Terror: A Novel*. London: Secker & Warburg, 1991.
——. *The First Life of Adamastor*. London: Secker & Warburg, 1993.
——. *On the Contrary: Being the Life of a Famous Rebel, Soldier, Traveller, Explorer, Reader, Builder, Scribe, Latinist, Lover and Liar*. London: Secker & Warburg, 1993.
——. *Imaginings of Sand*. London: Secker & Warburg, 1996.
——. *Devil's Valley: A Novel*. London: Secker & Warburg, 1998.

——. *The Rights of Desire: A Novel.* London: Secker & Warburg, 2000.
——. *The Other Side of Silence.* London: Secker & Warburg, 2002.
——. *Before I Forget.* London: Secker & Warburg, 2004.
——. *Praying Mantis.* London: Secker & Warburg, 2005.
Brink, André, and J. M. Coetzee, eds. *A Land Apart: A South African Reader.* London: Faber, 1986.
Brown, Andrew. *Coldsleep Lullaby.* Ed. Martha Evans. Cape Town: Zebra, 2005.
Brownlee, Russel. *Garden of the Plagues.* Cape Town: Human & Rousseau, 2005.
Brutus, Dennis. *Sirens, Knuckles, Boots: Poems.* Ibadan: Mbari, 1963.
——. *Letters to Martha and Other Poems from a South African Prison.* London: Heinemann, 1968.
——. *A Simple Lust: Selected Poems.* London: Heinemann, 1973.
——. *Leafdrift.* Ed. Lamont B. Steptoe. Camden, N.J.: Whirlwind Press, 2005.
——. *Poetry & Protest: A Dennis Brutus Reader.* Ed. Lee Sustar and Aisha Karim. Chicago: Haymarket Books, 2006.
Burgess, Yvonne. *A Life to Live.* Johannesburg: Ad Donker, 1973.
——. *The Strike: A Novel.* Johannesburg: Ad Donker, 1975.
——. *Say a Little Mantra for Me.* Johannesburg: Ravan, 1979.
——. *Measure of the Night Wind.* Johannesburg: Penguin, 2002.
Butler, Guy, ed. *A Book of South African Verse.* London: Oxford University Press, 1959.
——. *Karoo Morning: An Autobiography (1918–35).* Cape Town: David Philip, 1977.
——. *Essays and Lectures, 1949–1991.* Ed. Stephen Watson. Cape Town: David Philip, 1994.
——. *Collected Poems.* Ed. Laurence Wright. Cape Town: David Philip, 1999.
Butler, Guy, and Chris Mann, eds. *A New Book of South African Verse in English.* Cape Town: Oxford University Press, 1979.
Campbell, Roy. *Light on a Dark Horse: An Autobiography 1901–1935.* London: Hollis and Carter, 1951.
——. *Collected Works.* Johannesburg: Ad Donker, 1985.
Cartwright, Justin. *Freedom for the Wolves.* London: Hamish Hamilton, 1983.
——. *Interior.* London: Hamish Hamilton, 1988.
——. *Look at It This Way.* London: Macmillan, 1990.
——. *Masai Dreaming.* London: Macmillan, 1994.
——. *Not Yet Home: A South African Journey.* London: Fourth Estate, 1996.
——. *Half in Love.* London: Hodder & Stoughton, 2001.
——. *White Lightning.* London: Hodder & Stoughton, 2002.
——. *The Promise of Happiness.* London: Bloomsbury, 2004.
Case, Maxine. *All We Have Left Unsaid.* Cape Town: Kwela, 2006.
Chapman, Michael, ed. *A Century of South African Poetry.* Johannesburg: Ad Donker, 1981.
——. *The Paperbook of South African English Poetry.* Johannesburg: Ad Donker, 1986.
——. *The "Drum" Decade: Stories from the 1950s.* Pietermaritzburg: University of Natal Press, 1989.
——. *The New Century of South African Poetry.* Johannesburg: Ad Donker, 2002.
——. *The New Century of South African Short Stories.* Johannesburg: Ad Donker, 2004.
Chapman, Michael, and Achmat Dangor, eds. *Voices from Within: Black Poetry from Southern Africa.* Johannesburg: Ad Donker, 1982.
Cloete, Stuart. *Rags of Glory.* London: Collins, 1963.
Clouts, Sydney. *Sydney Clouts: Collected Poems.* Cape Town: David Philip, 1984.
Coetzee, J. M. *Dusklands.* Johannesburg: Ravan, 1974.
——. *In the Heart of the Country: A Novel.* Johannesburg: Ravan, 1978.
——. *Waiting for the Barbarians.* Johannesburg: Ravan, 1981.
——. *Life & Times of Michael K.* Johannesburg: Ravan, 1983.
——. *Foe.* Johannesburg: Ravan, 1986.

——. *Age of Iron*. London: Secker & Warburg, 1990.
——. *Doubling the Point: Essays and Interviews*. Ed. David Attwell. Cape Town: David Philip, 1992.
——. *The Master of Petersburg*. London: Secker & Warburg, 1994.
——. *Boyhood: Scenes from Provincial Life*. London: Secker & Warburg, 1997.
——. *Disgrace*. London: Secker & Warburg, 1999.
——. *The Lives of Animals*. Ed. Amy Gutmann. Princeton: Princeton University Press, 1999.
——. *Stranger Shores: Essays 1986–1989*. London: Secker & Warburg, 2001.
——. *Youth*. London: Secker & Warburg, 2002.
——. *Elizabeth Costello: Eight Lessons*. London: Secker & Warburg, 2003.
——. *Slow Man*. London: Secker & Warburg, 2005.
——. *Inner Workings: Literary Essays 2000–2005*. London: Harvill Secker, 2007.
——. *Diary of a Bad Year*. London: Harvill Secker, 2007.
Cope, Jack. *The Fair House*. London: Macgibbon & Kee, 1955.
——. *The Golden Oriole*. London: Heinemann, 1958.
——. *Albino*. London: Heinemann, 1964.
——. *The Dawn Comes Twice*. London: Heinemann, 1969.
——. *Selected Stories*. Cape Town: David Philip, 1986.
Cope, Jack, and Uys Krige, eds. *The Penguin Book of South African Verse*. Harmondsworth: Penguin, 1968.
Cope, Michael. *Spiral of Fire*. Cape Town: David Philip, 1987.
——. *Intricacy: A Meditation on Memory*. Cape Town: Double Storey, 2005.
Coullie, Judith Lütge, ed. *The Closest of Strangers: South African Women's Life Writing*. Johannesburg: Wits University Press, 2004.
Couzens, Tim, and Essop Patel, eds. *The Return of the Amasi Bird: Black South African Poetry, 1891–1981*. Johannesburg: Ravan, 1982.
Cronin, Jeremy. *Inside*. Johannesburg: Ravan, 1983.
——. *Even the Dead: Poems, Parables and a Jeremiad*. Cape Town: Mayibuye/David Philip, 1997.
——. *Inside & Out: Poems from Inside and Even the Dead*. Cape Town: David Philip, 1999.
Cullinan, Patrick. *Selected Poems, 1961–1994*. Ed. Stephen Watson. Cape Town: Snailpress, 1994.
——. *Matrix*. Plumstead: Snailpress, 2002.
——. *Escarpments: Poems 1973–2007*. Cape Town: Umuzi, 2008.
Currey, Ralph Nixon. *Collected Poems*. Oxford: James Currey; Cape Town: David Philip, 2001.
Dangor, Achmat. *Waiting for Leila*. Johannesburg: Ravan, 1981.
——. *Kafka's Curse: A Novella & Three Other Stories*. Cape Town: Kwela, 1997.
——. *Bitter Fruit*. Cape Town: Kwela, 2001.
Daymond, Margaret, and Florence Howe, eds. *Women Writing Africa: The Southern Region*. New York: Feminist Press at the City University of New York, 2003.
De Kok, Ingrid. *Familiar Ground: Poems*. Johannesburg: Ravan, 1988.
——. *Seasonal Fires: New and Selected Poems*. Cape Town: Umuzi, 2006.
Dhlomo, H. I. E. *Collected Works*. Ed. Nick Visser and Tim Couzens. Johannesburg: Ravan, 1985.
Dike, Fatima. *The First South African: A Play*. Johannesburg: Ravan, 1979.
Dikeni, Sandile. *Guava Juice*. Cape Town: Mayibuye, 1992.
——. *Telegraph to the Sky*. Pietermaritzburg: University of Natal Press, 2000.
Dikobe, Modikwe. *The Marabi Dance*. London: Heinemann, 1973.
Dowling, Finuala. *What Poets Need*. Johannesburg: Penguin, 2005.
Driver, C. J. *Elegy for a Revolutionary*. London: Faber, 1969.
——. *Send War in Our Time, O Lord*. London: Faber, 1970.
——. *Shades of Darkness: A Novel*. Johannesburg: Jonathan Ball, 2004.
Duiker, K Sello. *Thirteen Cents*. Cape Town: Ink, 2000.

——. *The Quiet Violence of Dreams*. Cape Town: Kwela, 2001.
Du Plessis, Menán. *A State of Fear*. Cape Town: David Philip, 1983.
——. *Longlive!* Cape Town: David Philip, 1989.
Ebersohn, Wessel. *A Lonely Place to Die: A Novel*. London: Gollancz, 1979.
——. *Store up the Anger: A Novel*. Johannesburg: Ravan, 1980.
Eglington, Charles. *Under the Horizon: Collected Poems of Charles Eglington*. Ed. Jack Cope. Cape Town: Purnell, 1977.
Eprile, Tony. *The Persistence of Memory*. Cape Town: Double Storey, 2005.
Essop, Ahmed. *The Hajji and Other Stories*. Johannesburg: Ravan, 1978.
——. *The Visitation*. Johannesburg: Ravan, 1980.
——. *The Emperor: A Novel*. Johannesburg: Ravan, 1984.
——. *Noorjehan and Other Stories*. Johannesburg: Ravan, 1990.
——. *The Third Prophecy*. Johannesburg: Picador Africa, 2004.
Feinberg, Barry, ed. *Poets to the People: South African Freedom Poems*. London: Allen & Unwin, 1974.
First, Ruth. *117 Days*. Harmondsworth: Penguin, 1965.
Freed, Lynn. *Home Ground*. London: Heinemann, 1986.
Fugard, Athol. *The Blood Knot: A Play in Seven Scenes*. Johannesburg: Simondium, 1963.
——. *Hello and Goodbye: A Play in Two Acts*. Cape Town: Balkema, 1966.
——. *Boesman and Lena: A Play in Two Acts*. Cape Town: Buren, 1969.
——. *People Are Living There: A Play in Two Acts*. Cape Town: Buren, 1969.
——. *Sizwe Bansi Is Dead*. London: Hansom Books, 1973.
——. *Three Port Elizabeth Plays: The Blood Knot, Hello and Goodbye, Boesman and Lena*. London: Oxford University Press, 1974.
——. *Sizwe Bansi Is Dead and The Island*. New York: Viking, 1976.
——. *Dimetos and Two Early Plays*. Oxford: Oxford University Press, 1977.
——. *Tsotsi: A Novel*. New York: Random House, 1979.
——. *A Lesson from Aloes: A Play*. New York: Random House, 1981.
——. *'Master Harold' . . . and the Boys*. Oxford: Oxford University Press, 1983.
——. *Notebooks, 1960–1977*. Johannesburg: Ad Donker, 1983.
——. *The Road to Mecca: A Play in Two Acts Suggested by the Life of Helen Martins of New Bethesda*. London: Faber, 1985.
——. *A Place with the Pigs: A Personal Parable*. London: Faber, 1988.
——. *My Children! My Africa! and Selected Shorter Plays*. Ed. Stephen Gray. Johannesburg: Witwatersrand University Press, 1990.
——. *Playland*. London: Faber, 1993.
——. *The Township Plays: No-Good Friday, Nongogo, The Coat, Sizwe Bansi Is Dead, The Island*. Ed. Dennis Walder. Cape Town: Oxford University Press, 1993.
——. *My Life and Valley Song*. Johannesburg: Hodder & Stoughton/Witwatersrand University Press, 1996.
——. *The Captain's Tiger*. Johannesburg: Witwatersrand University Press, 1997.
——. *Interior Plays*. Ed. Dennis Walder. Oxford: Oxford University Press, 2000.
——. *Port Elizabeth Plays*. Ed. Dennis Walder. Oxford: Oxford University Press, 2000.
——. *Sorrows and Rejoicings*. New York: Theatre Communications Group, 2002.
——. *Exits and Entrances*. Cape Town: David Philip, 2005.
——. *Karoo and Other Stories*. Cape Town: David Philip, 2005.
Fugard, Athol, and Ross Devenish. *The Guest: An Episode in the Life of Eugène Marais*. Johannesburg: Ad Donker, 1977.
——. *Marigolds in August: A Screenplay*. Johannesburg: Ad Donker, 1982.
Fugard, Athol, John Kani, and Winston Ntshona. *Statements: Two Workshop Productions*. Oxford: Oxford University Press, 1974.
——. *Statements, Sizwe Bansi Is Dead, The Island*. New York: Theatre Communications Group, 1986.

Fugard, Athol, and Don Maclennan. *The Coat and The Third Degree: Two Experiments in Play-Making*. Cape Town: Balkema, 1971.
Galgut, Damon. *Small Circle of Beings*. Johannesburg: Lowry, 1988.
——. *The Beautiful Screaming of Pigs*. London: Scribner, 1991.
——. *The Quarry*. Johannesburg: Viking, 1995.
——. *The Good Doctor*. New York: Grove Press, 2003.
——. *The Imposter*. Johannesburg: Penguin, 2008.
Gordimer, Nadine. *Face to Face: Short Stories*. Johannesburg: Silver Leaf, 1949.
——. *The Soft Voice of the Serpent and Other Stories*. New York: Simon & Schuster, 1952.
——. *The Lying Days: A Novel*. London: Gollancz, 1953.
——. *Six Feet of the Country: Short Stories*. London: Gollancz, 1956.
——. *A World of Strangers*. London: Gollancz, 1958.
——. *Friday's Footprint*. London: Gollancz, 1960.
——. *Occasion for Loving*. London: Gollancz, 1963.
——. *Not for Publication*. London: Gollancz, 1965.
——. *The Late Bourgeois World*. London: Cape, 1966.
——. *A Guest of Honour*. New York: Viking, 1970.
——. *Livingstone's Companions: Stories*. London: Cape, 1972.
——. *The Conservationist*. London: Cape, 1974.
——. *Burger's Daughter*. London: Cape, 1979.
——. *A Soldier's Embrace: Stories*. London: Cape, 1980.
——. *July's People*. Johannesburg: Ravan, 1981.
——. *Something Out There*. Johannesburg: Ravan, 1984.
——. *A Sport of Nature*. Cape Town: David Philip, 1987.
——. *The Essential Gesture: Writing, Politics, Places*. Johannesburg: Taurus, 1988.
——. *My Son's Story*. Cape Town: David Philip, 1990.
——. *Jump and Other Stories*. Cape Town: David Philip, 1991.
——. *None to Accompany Me*. Cape Town: David Philip, 1994.
——. *Writing and Being*. Cambridge, Mass.: Harvard University Press, 1995.
——. *The House Gun*. Cape Town: David Philip, 1998.
——. *Selected Stories*. London: Bloomsbury, 2000.
——. *The Pickup*. Cape Town: David Philip, 2001.
——. *Loot and Other Stories*. Cape Town: David Philip, 2003.
——. *Get a Life*. Cape Town: David Philip, 2005.
——. *Beethoven Was One-Sixteenth Black and Other Stories*. London: Bloomsbury, 2007.
Gordon, Gerald. *Four People: A Novel of South Africa*. Cape Town: Purnell, 1964.
Goudvis, Bertha. *Little Eden*. Johannesburg: Central News Agency, 1949.
——. *The Mistress of Mooiplaas and Other Stories*. Johannesburg: Central News Agency, 1956.
Govender, Ronnie. *At the Edge and Other Cato Manor Stories*. Pretoria: Manx, 1996.
Gray, Stephen. *Selected Poems 1960–1992*. Cape Town: David Philip, 1992.
——, ed. *Modern South African Stories*. Cape Town: Ad Donker, 1980.
——, ed. *Modern South African Poetry*. Johannesburg: Ad Donker, 1984.
——, ed. *The Penguin Book of Southern African Stories*. Harmondsworth: Penguin, 1985.
——, ed. *The Penguin Book of Southern African Verse*. London: Penguin, 1989.
——, ed. *The Penguin Book of Contemporary South African Short Stories*. Johannesburg: Penguin, 1993.
——, ed. *South African Plays*. Johannesburg: Heinemann-Centaur, 1993.
Gwala, Mafika Pascal. *Joli'inkomo*. Johannesburg: Ad Donker, 1977.
Head, Bessie. *When Rain Clouds Gather*. London: Heinemann, 1968.
——. *Maru*. London: Heinemann, 1971.
——. *A Question of Power: A Novel*. New York: Pantheon, 1973.

——. *The Collector of Treasures and Other Botswana Village Tales*. Cape Town: David Philip, 1977.
——. *A Bewitched Crossroad: An African Saga*. Johannesburg: Ad Donker, 1984.
——. *A Woman Alone: Autobiographical Writings*. Ed. Craig MacKenzie. London: Heinemann, 1990.
——. *The Cardinals: With Meditations and Stories*. Cape Town: David Philip, 1993.
Hendricks, Katie. *The Bend in the Road*. Cape Town: Timmins, 1953.
Heyns, Michiel. *The Children's Day*. Johannesburg: Jonathan Ball, 2002.
——. *The Reluctant Passenger: A Novel*. Johannesburg: Jonathan Ball, 2003.
——. *The Typewriter's Tale*. Johannesburg: Jonathan Ball, 2005.
Hirson, Denis. *The House Next Door to Africa*. Cape Town: David Philip, 1986.
——. *We Walk Straight So You Better Get out the Way*. Johannesburg: Jacana, 2005.
Hope, Christopher. *A Separate Development*. Johannesburg: Ravan, 1980.
——. *Private Parts and Other Tales*. Johannesburg: Bateleur, 1981.
——. *White Boy Running*. London: Secker & Warburg, 1988.
Horn, Peter. *Poems, 1964–1989*. Johannesburg: Ravan, 1991.
——. *My Voice Is Under Control Now and Other Stories*. Cape Town: Kwela, 1999.
Hutchinson, Alfred. *Road to Ghana*. London: Gollancz, 1960.
Isaacson, Maureen. *Holding Back Midnight and Other Stories*. Johannesburg: COSAW, 1992.
Jabavu, Noni. *Drawn in Colour: African Contrasts*. London: John Murray, 1960.
——. *The Ochre People: Scenes from a South African Life*. London: John Murray, 1963.
Jacobs, Rayda. *The Slave Book*. Cape Town: Kwela, 1998.
Jacobson, Dan. *The Zulu and the Zeide: Short Stories*. Boston: Little, Brown, 1953.
——. *A Long Way from London*. London: Weidenfeld and Nicolson, 1953.
——. *The Trap: A Novel*. London: Weidenfeld and Nicolson, 1955.
——. *A Dance in the Sun: A Novel*. London: Weidenfeld and Nicolson, 1956.
——. *Time of Arrival and Other Essays*. New York: Macmillan, 1958.
——. *The Evidence of Love: A Novel*. London: Weidenfeld and Nicolson, 1959.
——. *The Beginners: A Novel*. London: Weidenfeld and Nicolson, 1962.
——. *A Way of Life and Other Stories*. London: Longman, 1971.
Jamal, Ashraf. *Love Themes for the Wilderness*. Cape Town: Kwela and Random House, 1996.
——. *The Shades*. Howick: Brevitas, 2002.
Jensma, Wopko. *Sing for Our Execution*. Pretoria: Ophir, 1971.
——. *Sing for Our Execution: Poems and Woodcuts*. Johannesburg: Ophir and Ravan, 1973.
——. *Where White Is the Colour, Where Black Is the Number*. Johannesburg: Ravan, 1974.
——. *I Must Show You My Clippings*. Johannesburg: Ravan, 1977.
Johnson, Shaun. *The Native Commissioner: A Novel*. Johannesburg: Penguin, 2006.
Junction Avenue Theatre Company. *At the Junction: Four Plays*. Ed. Martin Orkin. Johannesburg: Witwatersrand University Press, 1995.
Kani, John. *Nothing but the Truth*. Johannesburg: Witwatersrand University Press, 2002.
Karodia, Farida. *Daughters of the Twilight*. London: The Women's Press, 1986.
——. *Coming Home and Other Stories*. London: Heinemann, 1988.
——. *Against an African Sky and Other Stories*. Cape Town: David Philip, 1995.
——. *Boundaries*. Johannesburg: Penguin, 2003.
Kgositsile, Keorapetse. *My Name Is Afrika*. New York: Doubleday, 1971.
——. *This Way I Salute You: Selected Poems*. Cape Town: Kwela/Snailpress, 2004.
Khumalo, Fred. *Bitches' Brew*. Johannesburg: Jacana, 2006.
——. *Touch My Blood: The Early Years*. Cape Town: Umuzi, 2006.
Kozain, Rustum. *This Carting Life: Poems*. Cape Town: Kwela/Snailpress, 2005.
Kraak, Gerald. *Ice in the Lungs*. Johannesburg: Jacana Media, 2006.

Krog, Antjie. *Country of My Skull*. Johannesburg: Random House, 1998.

——. *A Change of Tongue*. Johannesburg: Random House, 2003.

Kunene, Mazisi. *Emperor Shaka the Great: A Zulu Epic*. London: Heinemann, 1979.

Kuzwayo, Ellen. *Call Me Woman*. Johannesburg: Ravan, 1986.

La Guma, Alex. *A Walk in the Night*. Ibadan: Mbari, 1962.

——. *And a Threefold Cord*. Berlin: Seven Seas, 1964.

——. *The Stone Country*. Berlin: Seven Seas, 1967.

——. *A Walk in the Night and Other Stories*. London: Heinemann, 1968.

——. *In the Fog of the Seasons' End*. London: Heinemann, 1972.

——. *Time of the Butcherbird*. London: Heinemann, 1979.

Landsman, Anne. *The Devil's Chimney*. London: Granta, 1998.

Langa, Mandla. *Tenderness of Blood*. Harare: Zimbabwe Publishing House, 1987.

——. *A Rainbow on the Paper Sky*. London: Kliptown Books, 1989.

——. *The Naked Song and Other Stories*. Cape Town: David Philip, 1996.

——. *The Memory of Stones*. Cape Town: David Philip, 2000.

Lanham, Peter, and A. S. Mopeli-Paulus. *Blanket Boy's Moon*. London: Collins, 1953.

——. *The Road Awaits*. London: Collins, 1955.

Leipoldt, C. Louis. *Stormwrack*. Ed. Stephen Gray. Cape Town: David Philip, 1980.

Lewin, Hugh. *Bandiet: Seven Years in a South African Prison*. London: Heinemann, 1974.

Livingstone, Douglas. *A Ruthless Fidelity: Collected Poems of Douglas Livingstone*. Ed. Malcolm Hacksley and Don Maclennan. Johannesburg: Ad Donker, 2004.

Luthuli, Albert. *Let My People Go: An Autobiography*. Johannesburg: Collins, 1962.

Lytton, David. *The Goddam White Man*. London: Macgibbon & Kee, 1960.

——. *A Place Apart*. London: Macgibbon & Kee, 1961.

——. *The Paradise People*. London: Macgibbon & Kee, 1962.

Maclennan, Don. *Reckonings*. Cape Town: David Philip, 1983.

——. *Collecting Darkness*. Johannesburg: Justified Press, 1988.

——. *Letters: New Poems*. Cape Town: Carrefour, 1992.

——. *The Poetry Lesson: New Poems*. Cape Town: Snailpress, 1995.

——. *Solstice: Poems*. Cape Town: Snailpress/Scottish Cultural Press, 1997.

——. *Notes from a Rhenish Mission*. Cape Town: Carapace Poets, 2001.

——. *The Road to Kromdraai*. Cape Town: Snailpress, 2002.

——. *Under Compassberg*. Grahamstown: Privately published, 2003.

——. *Reading the Signs*. Cape Town: Carapace, 2005.

——. *The Necessary Salt*. Grahamstown: Privately published, 2006.

——. *Selected Poems*. Johannesburg: Quartz Press; Cape Town: Snailpress, 2006.

——. *The Owl of Minerva*. Grahamstown: Privately published, 2007.

——. *Through a Glass Darkly*. Grahamstown: Privately published, 2008.

Macnab, Roy. *Testament of a South African*. London: Fortune, 1947.

Macnab, Roy, and Charles Gulston, eds. *South African Poetry: A New Anthology*. London: C. A. Roy for Collins, 1948.

Madingoane, Ingoapele. *Africa My Beginning*. Johannesburg: Ravan, 1979.

Magona, Sindiwe. *To My Children's Children*. Cape Town: David Philip, 1990.

——. *Living, Loving, and Lying Awake at Night*. Cape Town: David Philip, 1991.

——. *Forced to Grow*. Cape Town: David Philip, 1992.

——. *Mother to Mother*. Cape Town: David Philip, 1998.

Mahola, Mzi. *Strange Things*. Cape Town: Snailpress, 1994.

——. *When Rains Come*. Cape Town: Carapace Poets, 2000.

——. *Dancing in the Rain: A Voice in My Father's House*. Somerset West: Samizdat/Snailpress, 2004.

Maimane, Arthur. *Victims: A Novel*. London: Allison & Busby, 1976.
Malan, Rian. *My Traitor's Heart*. London: The Bodley Head, 1990.
Manaka, Matsemela. *Beyond the Echoes of Soweto: Five Plays*. Ed. Geoffrey V. Davis. Amsterdam: Harwood Academic, 1997.
Mandela, Nelson Rolihlahla. *Long Walk to Freedom: The Autobiography of Nelson Mandela*. Randburg: Macdonald Purnell, 1994.
Maponya, Maishe. *Doing Plays for a Change: Five Works*. Johannesburg: Witwatersrand University Press, 1995.
Marquard, Jean, ed. *A Century of South African Short Stories*. Johannesburg: Ad Donker, 1978.
Matlou, Joël. *Life at Home and Other Stories*. Johannesburg: COSAW, 1991.
Matlwa, Kopano. *Coconut*. Johannesburg: Jacana, 2007.
Matshoba, Mtutuzeli. *Call Me Not a Man*. Johannesburg: Ravan, 1979.
——. *Seeds of War*. Johannesburg: Ravan, 1981.
Matthee, Dalene. *Circles in a Forest*. London: Viking, 1984.
——. *Fiela's Child*. London: Viking, 1986.
——. *The Mulberry Forest*. London: Michael Joseph, 1989.
——. *The Day the Swallows Spoke*. London: Michael Joseph, 1993.
——. *Dreamforest*. Johannesburg: Penguin, 2004.
——. *Driftwood*. Johannesburg: Penguin, 2005.
Matthews, James. *The Park and Other Stories*. Athlone: BLAC, 1974.
——. *Cry Rage: Odyssey of a Dissident Poet*. Athlone: Realities, 2006.
Matthews, James, and Gladys Thomas. *Cry Rage!* Johannesburg: Spro-Cas, 1972.
Matthews, James, ed. *Black Voices Shout! An Anthology of Poetry*. Athlone: BLAC, 1974.
Matthews, Z. K. *Freedom for My People: The Autobiography of Z. K. Matthews: Southern Africa 1901 to 1968*. Cape Town: David Philip, 1981.
Mbuli, Mzwakhe. *Before Dawn*. Johannesburg: COSAW, 1989.
Mda, Zakes. *We Shall Sing for the Fatherland and Other Plays*. Johannesburg: Ravan, 1980.
——. *The Plays of Zakes Mda*. Johannesburg: Ravan, 1990.
——. *And the Girls in Their Sunday Dresses: Four Works*. Johannesburg: Witwatersrand University Press, 1993.
——. *She Plays with the Darkness: A Novel*. Johannesburg: Vivlia, 1995.
——. *Ways of Dying*. Cape Town: Oxford University Press, 1995.
——. *The Heart of Redness*. Cape Town: Oxford University Press, 2000.
——. *Fools, Bells, and the Habit of Eating: Three Satires*. Johannesburg: Witwatersrand University Press, 2002.
——. *The Madonna of Excelsior*. Cape Town: Oxford University Press, 2002.
——. *The Whale Caller*. Johannesburg: Penguin, 2005.
——. *Cion: A Novel*. New York: Picador, 2007.
Medalie, David. *The Shadow Follows*. Johannesburg: Picador Africa, 2006.
Melamu, Moteane John. *Children of the Twilight*. Johannesburg: Vivlia, 1996.
Mhlongo, Nicholas. *Dog Eat Dog*. Cape Town: Kwela, 2004.
——. *After Tears*. Cape Town: Kwela, 2007.
Mhlophe, Gcina. *Love Child*. Pietermaritzburg: University of Natal Press, 2002.
Miller, Ruth. *Poems, Prose, Plays*. Ed. Lionel Abrahams. Cape Town: Carrefour, 1990.
Millin, Sarah Gertrude. *King of the Bastards*. London: Heinemann, 1950.
——. *The Burning Man: A Novel*. London: Heinemann, 1952.
——. *The Measure of My Days*. London: Faber and Faber, 1955.
Modisane, Bloke. *Blame Me on History*. New York: Dutton, 1963.
Mokgatle, Naboth. *The Autobiography of an Unknown South Africa*. Berkeley: University of California Press, 1975.
Mopeli-Paulus, A. S. *Turn to the Dark*. London: Cape, 1956.
Motsisi, Casey. *Casey & Co.: Selected Writings*. Ed. Mothobi Mutloatse. Johannesburg: Ravan, 1978.

Mpe, Phaswane. *Welcome to Our Hillbrow*. Pietermaritzburg: University of Natal Press, 2001.
Mphahlele, Es'kia (Ezekiel). *Man Must Live and Other Stories*. Cape Town: African Bookman, 1946.
——. *Down Second Avenue*. London: Faber and Faber, 1959.
——. *The Living and Dead and Other Stories*. Ibadan: Ministry of Education, 1960.
——. *The African Image*. London: Faber, 1962.
——. *In Corner B*. Nairobi: East African Publishing House, 1967.
——. *The Wanderers: A Novel*. New York: Macmillan, 1971.
——. *Voices in the Whirlwind and Other Essays*. New York: Hill & Wang, 1972.
——. *Chirundu*. Johannesburg: Ravan, 1979.
——. *The Unbroken Song: Selected Writings*. Johannesburg: Ravan, 1981.
Mtshali, Mbuyiseni Oswald. *Sounds of a Cowhide Drum: Poems*. Johannesburg: Renoster, 1971.
——. *Fireflames*. Pietermaritzburg: Shuter & Shooter, 1980.
Mtwa, Percy, Mbongeni Ngema and Barney Simon. *Woza Albert!* London: Methuen, 1983.
Muller, David. *Whitey: A Novel*. Johannesburg: Ravan, 1977.
Mutloatse, Mothobi. *Mama Ndiyalila: Stories*. Johannesburg: Ravan, 1982.
Mutloatse, Mothobi, ed. *Forced Landing: Africa South Contemporary Writings*. Johannesburg: Ravan, 1980.
——. *Reconstruction: 90 Years of Black Historical Literature*. Johannesburg: Ravan, 1981.
Mzamane, Mbulelo Vizikhungo. *Mzala: The Stories of Mbulelo Mzamane*. Johannesburg: Ravan, 1980.
——. *The Children of Soweto: A Trilogy*. Johannesburg: Ravan, 1982.
——. *The Children of the Diaspora and Other Stories of Exile*. Johannesburg: Vivlia, 1996.
Nakasa, Nat. *The World of Nat Nakasa: Selected Writings of the Late Nat Nakasa*. Ed. Essop Patel. Johannesburg: Ravan/Bataleur, 1975.
Ndebele, Njabulo S. *Fools and Other Stories*. Johannesburg: Ravan, 1983.
——. *The Cry of Winnie Mandela: A Novel*. Cape Town: David Philip, 2003.
Ngcobo, Lauretta. *Cross of Gold: A Novel*. London: Longman, 1981.
——. *And They Didn't Die*. Johannesburg: Skotaville; London: Virago, 1990.
Ngema, Mbongeni. *The Best of Mbongeni Ngema: An Anthology*. Johannesburg: Skotaville/Via Afrika, 1995.
——. *Mbongeni Ngema's "Sarafina!" The Times, the Play, the Man*. Cape Town: Nasou Via Afrika, 2006.
Nicol, Mike. *Among the Souvenirs*. Johannesburg: Ravan, 1978.
——. *The Powers That Be*. London: Bloomsbury, 1989.
——. *This Sad Place: Poems*. Plumstead: Snailpress, 1993.
——. *The Waiting Country: A South African Witness*. London: Gollancz, 1995.
Nkosi, Lewis. *The Rhythm of Violence*. London: Oxford University Press, 1964.
——. *Mating Birds*. New York: St. Martin's, 1986.
——. *Underground People*. Cape Town: Kwela, 2002.
——. *Mandela's Ego*. Cape Town: Umuzi, 2006.
Nortje, Arthur. *Anatomy of Dark: Collected Poems of Arthur Nortje*. Ed. Dirk Klopper. Pretoria: UNISA Press, 2000.
Paton, Alan. *Cry, the Beloved Country: A Story of Comfort in Desolation*. New York: Scribner, 1948.
——. *Too Late the Phalarope*. New York: Scribner, 1953.
——. *Debbie Go Home: Stories*. London: Cape, 1961.
——. *The Hero of Currie Road*. Cape Town: Umuzi, 2008.
Peteni, Randall Langa. *Hill of Fools: A Novel of the Ciskei*. Cape Town: David Philip, 1976.
Pheto, Molefe. *And Night Fell: Memoirs of a Political Prisoner in South Africa*. London: Heinemann, 1985.
Plomer, William. *Double Lives: An Autobiography*. New York: Noonday Press, 1945.
——. *Collected Poems*. London: Cape, 1973.
——. *The Autobiography of William Plomer*. London: Cape, 1975.

Prince, Frank Templeton. *Collected Poems.* London: Anvil Press Poetry/Menard Press, 1979.

Qangule, Z. S. *The Making of a Servant and Other Poems.* Trans. Robert Kavanagh. Pretoria: Ophir, 1971.

Ramgobin, Mewa. *Waiting to Live: A Novel.* Cape Town: David Philip, 1986.

Rampolokeng, Lesego. *Horns for Hondo.* Johannesburg: COSAW, 1990.

——. *Talking Rain.* Johannesburg: COSAW, 1993.

——. *The Bavino Sermons by Lesego Rampolokeng.* Durban: Gecko Poetry, 1999.

——. *The Second Chapter.* Berlin: Pantolea, 2003.

——. *Blackheart: Epilogue to Insanity.* Johannesburg: Pine Slopes, 2004.

——. *Whiteheart: Prologue to Hysteria.* Grahamstown: Deep South, 2005.

Rive, Richard. *African Songs.* Berlin: Seven Seas, 1963.

——, ed. *Quartet: New Voices from South Africa.* New York: Crown, 1963.

——. *Emergency: A Novel.* London: Collier-Macmillan, 1970.

——. *Selected Writings: Stories, Essays, Plays.* Johannesburg: Ad Donker, 1977.

——. *Writing Black.* Cape Town: David Philip, 1981.

——. *Advance, Retreat: Selected Short Stories.* Cape Town: David Philip, 1983.

——. *Buckingham Palace, District Six.* Cape Town: David Philip, 1986.

Roberts, Sheila. *Outside Life's Feast: Short Stories.* Johannesburg: Ad Donker, 1975.

——. *He's My Brother: A Novel.* Johannesburg: Ad Donker, 1977.

——. *This Time of Year and Other Stories.* Johannesburg: Ad Donker, 1983.

——. *Coming In and Other Stories by Sheila Roberts.* Johannesburg: Justified Press, 1993.

——. *Purple Yams.* Johannesburg: Penguin, 2001.

Rooke, Daphne. *The Sea Hath Bounds.* Johannesburg: A P B Bookstore, 1946.

——. *A Grove of Fever Trees.* London: Cape, 1951.

——. *Mittee.* London: Gollancz, 1951.

——. *Ratoons.* London: Gollancz, 1953.

——. *Wizard's Country.* London: Gollancz, 1957.

——. *A Lover for Estelle.* London: Gollancz, 1961.

——. *The Greyling.* London: Gollancz, 1962.

——. *Diamond Jo: A Novel.* London: Gollancz, 1965.

Rose-Innes, Henrietta. *The Shark's Egg.* Cape Town: Kwela, 2000.

——. *The Rock Alphabet.* Cape Town: Kwela, 2004.

Royston, Robert, ed. *To Whom It May Concern: An Anthology of Black South African Poetry.* Johannesburg: Ad Donker, 1973.

Sachs, Albie. *Jail Diary.* London: Sphere, 1969.

——. *The Soft Vengeance of a Freedom Fighter.* Cape Town: David Philip, 1990.

Sachs, Wulf. *Black Hamlet.* Boston: Little, Brown, 1947.

Segal, Ronald. *Into Exile.* New York: McGraw Hill, 1963.

Sepamla, Sipho. *Hurry up to It!* Johannesburg: Ad Donker, 1975.

——. *The Blues Is You in Me.* Johannesburg: Ad Donker, 1976.

——. *The Soweto I Love.* Cape Town: David Philip, 1977.

——. *The Root Is One.* Cape Town: David Philip, 1979.

——. *A Ride on the Whirlwind: A Novel.* Johannesburg: Ad Donker, 1981.

——. *Children of the Earth.* Johannesburg: Ad Donker, 1983.

——. *Selected Poems.* Ed. Mbulelo Vizikhungo Mzamane. Johannesburg: Ad Donker, 1984.

——. *Third Generation.* Johannesburg: Skotaville, 1986.

——. *A Scattered Survival.* Johannesburg: Skotaville, 1989.

——. *Rainbow Journey.* Johannesburg: Vivlia, 1996.

Serote, Mongane. *Yakhal'inkomo: Poems.* Johannesburg: Renoster and Bateleur, 1972.

——. *Tsetlo.* Johannesburg: Ad Donker, 1974.

——. *No Baby Must Weep.* Johannesburg: Ad Donker, 1975.

——. *Behold Mama, Flowers.* Johannesburg: Ad Donker, 1978.

——. *To Every Birth Its Blood.* Johannesburg: Ravan, 1981.

——. *Selected Poems*. Ed. Mbulelo Vizikhungo Mzamane. Johannesburg: Ad Donker, 1982.

——. *On the Horizon*. Foreword Raymond Suttner. Johannesburg: COSAW, 1990.

——. *Third World Express*. Cape Town: David Philip, 1992.

——. *Come and Hope with Me*. Cape Town: David Philip, 1994.

——. *Freedom Lament and Song*. Cape Town: Mayibuye/David Philip, 1997.

——. *Gods of Our Time*. Johannesburg: Ravan, 1999.

——. *Scatter the Ashes and Go*. Johannesburg: Ravan, 2002.

——. *History Is the Home Address*. Cape Town: Kwela/Snailpress, 2004.

Shore, Herbert L., and Megchelina Shore-Bos, eds. *Come Back, Africa*. New York: International Publishers, 1968.

Shukri, Ishtiyaq. *The Silent Minaret*. Johannesburg: Jacana, 2005.

Simon, Barney. *Joburg, Sis!* Johannesburg: Bateleur, 1974.

——. *Born in the RSA: Four Workshopped Plays*. Johannesburg: Witwatersrand University Press, 1997.

Skinner, Douglas Reid. *The House in Pella District*. Cape Town: David Philip, 1985.

——. *The Unspoken: Poems by Douglas Reid Skinner*. Cape Town: Carrefour, 1988.

——. *The Middle Years: Poems*. Cape Town: Carrefour, 1993.

Slabolepszy, Paul. *Saturday Night at the Palace: A Play in One Act by Paul Slabolepszy*. Johannesburg: Ad Donker, 1985.

——. *Mooi Street and Other Moves*. Johannesburg: Witwatersrand University Press, 1994.

Slovo, Gillian. *Ties of Blood*. London: Michael Joseph, 1989.

——. *Every Secret Thing: My Family, My Country*. London: Little, Brown, 1997.

——. *Red Dust*. London: Virago, 2000.

Small, Adam. *Black, Bronze, Beautiful: Quatrains*. Johannesburg: Ad Donker, 1975.

Smith, Wilbur. *When the Lion Feeds*. London: Heinemann, 1966.

Sowden, Lewis. *The Crooked Bluegum*. London: The Bodley Head, 1955.

Stein, Sylvester. *Second-Class Taxi*. London: Faber and Faber, 1958.

Steinberg, Jonny. *Midlands*. Johannesburg: Jonathan Ball, 2002.

Taylor, Jane. *Ubu and the Truth Commission*. Cape Town: University of Cape Town Press, 1998.

——. *Of Wild Dogs*. Cape Town: Double Storey, 2005.

Themba, Can. *The Will to Die*. London: Heinemann, 1972.

——. *Requiem for Sophiatown*. Johannesburg: Penguin, 2006.

Tlali, Miriam. *Muriel at Metropolitan*. Johannesburg: Ravan, 1975.

——. *Amandla!* Johannesburg: Ravan, 1981.

Troye, Des. *An Act of Immorality*. Johannesburg: Transworld, 1963.

Trump, Martin, ed. *A Century of South African Short Stories*. Johannesburg: Ad Donker, 1993.

Uys, Pieter-Dirk. *Karnaval: A Play by Pieter-Dirk Uys*. Johannesburg: Ad Donker, 1982.

——. *Selle Ou Storie: A Play by Pieter-Dirk Uys*. Johannesburg: Ad Donker, 1983.

——. *Paradise Is Closing Down & Other Plays*. London: Penguin, 1989.

Van der Post, Laurens. *Venture to the Interior*. London: Hogarth Press, 1952.

——. *Flamingo Feather: A Story of Africa*. London: Hogarth Press, 1955.

——. *The Lost World of the Kalahari*. London: Hogarth Press, 1958.

——. *The Heart of the Hunter*. London: Hogarth Press, 1961.

——. *A Story Like the Wind*. London: Hogarth Press, 1972.

——. *A Far-Off Place*. London: Hogarth Press, 1974.

Van de Ruit, John. *Spud*. Johannesburg: Penguin, 2005.

Van Wyk, Chris. *It Is Time to Go Home*. Johannesburg: Ad Donker, 1980.

——. *The Year of the Tapeworm*. Johannesburg: Ravan, 1996.

——. *Shirley, Goodness & Mercy: A Childhood Memoir*. Johannesburg: Picador Africa, 2004.

Vladislavić, Ivan. *Missing Persons: Stories by Ivan Vladislavić;*. Cape Town: David Philip, 1989.

——. *The Folly*. Cape Town: David Philip, 1993.
——. *Propaganda by Monuments and Other Stories*. Cape Town: David Philip, 1996.
——. *The Restless Supermarket*. Cape Town: David Philip, 2001.
——. *The Exploded View*. Johannesburg: Random House, 2004.
——. *Portrait with Keys: Joburg & What-What*. Cape Town: Umuzi, 2006.
Walker, Oliver. *Wanton City: An Escapade*. London: Werner Laurie, 1949.
——. *Shapeless Flame*. London: Werner Laurie, 1951.
Watson, Stephen. *In This City: Poems by Stephen Watson*. Cape Town: David Philip, 1986.
——. *Selected Essays 1980–1990*. Cape Town: Carrefour, 1990.
——. *Return of the Moon: Versions from the /Xam*. Cape Town: Carrefour, 1991.
——. *Presence of the Earth: New Poems*. Cape Town: David Philip, 1995.
——. *A Writer's Diary*. Cape Town: Queillerie, 1997.
——. *The Other City: Selected Poems 1977–1999*. Cape Town: David Philip, 2000.
——, ed. *A City Imagined*. Johannesburg: Penguin, 2006.
——. *The Light Echo and Other Poems*. Johannesburg: Penguin, 2007.
Webster, Elizabeth Charlotte. *Expiring Frog*. Johannesburg: Pers-Boekhandel, 1946.
Webster, Mary Morison. *A Village Scandal*. Johannesburg: A P B Bookstore, 1965.
Wicomb, Zoë. *You Can't Get Lost in Cape Town*. London: Virago Press, 1987.
——. *David's Story*. Cape Town: Kwela, 2000.
——. *Playing in the Light*. Cape Town: Umuzi, 2006.
Wilhelm, Peter. *LM and Other Stories*. Johannesburg: Ravan, 1975.
——. *The Dark Wood: A Novel*. Johannesburg: Ravan, 1977.
——. *At the End of a War*. Johannesburg: Ravan, 1981.
——. *Some Place in Africa*. Johannesburg: Ad Donker, 1987.
——. *The Healing Process: A Novel*. Johannesburg: Ad Donker, 1988.
——. *The Mask of Freedom*. Johannesburg: Ad Donker, 1994.
——. *The Bayonet Field: Selected Stories*. Johannesburg: Ad Donker, 2000.
Williams, John Grenfell. *I Am Black: The Story of Shabala*. Cape Town: Juta, 1949.
Woods, Donald. *Asking for Trouble: Autobiography of a Banned Journalist*. London: Gollancz, 1980.
Wright, David. *Selected Poems*. Johannesburg: Ad Donker, 1980.
Zwelonke, D. M. *Robben Island*. London: Heinemann, 1978.
Zwi, Rose. *Another Year in Africa*. Johannesburg: Bateleur, 1980.

SECONDARY TEXTS

Alexander, Peter F. *Alan Paton: A Biography*. Oxford: Oxford University Press, 1994.
Alvarez-Pereyre, Jacques. *The Poetry of Commitment in South Africa*. Trans. Clive Wake. London: Heinemann, 1984.
Attridge, Derek. *J. M. Coetzee & the Ethics of Reading: Literature in the Event*. Pietermaritzburg: University of KwaZulu-Natal Press, 2005.
Attridge, Derek, and Rosemary Jolly, eds. *Writing South Africa: Literature, Apartheid and Democracy, 1970–1995*. Cambridge: Cambridge University Press, 1998.
Attwell, David. *J. M. Coetzee: South Africa and the Politics of Writing*. Cape Town: David Philip, 1993.
——. *Rewriting Modernity: Studies in Black South African Literary History*. Pietermaritzburg: University of KwaZulu-Natal Press, 2005.
Barnard, Rita. *Apartheid and Beyond: South African Writers and the Politics of Place*. New York: Oxford University Press, 2007.
Barnett, Ursula A. *Ezekiel Mphahlele*. Boston: Twayne, 1976.
Benson, Mary. *Athol Fugard and Barney Simon: Bare Stage, A Few Props, Great Theatre*. Johannesburg: Ravan, 1997.
Boehmer, Elleke, Laura Chrisman, and Kenneth Parker, eds. *Altered State? Writing and South Africa*. Sydney: Dangaroo, 1993.
Brown, Duncan. *Voicing the Text: South African Oral Poetry and Performance*. Cape Town: Oxford University Press, 1998.

Callan, Edward. *Alan Paton*. New York: Twayne, 1968.

Chapman, Michael. *Southern African Literatures*. London: Longman, 1996.

Chapman, Michael, ed. *Soweto Poetry*. Johannesburg: McGraw-Hill, 1982.

Chapman, Michael, Colin Gardner, and Es'kia Mphahlele, eds. *Perspectives on South African English Literature*. Cape Town: Ad Donker, 1992.

Christie, Sarah, et al. *Perspectives on South African Fiction*. Johannesburg: Ad Donker, 1980.

Clingman, Stephen. *The Novels of Nadine Gordimer: History from the Inside*. Johannesburg: Ravan, 1986.

Coetzee, J. M. *White Writing: On the Culture of Letters in South Africa*. New Haven: Yale University Press, 1988.

——. *Giving Offense: Essays on Censorship*. Chicago: University of Chicago Press, 1996.

Conference of Writers, Publishers, Editors and University Teachers of English. *Proceedings of a Conference of Writers, Publishers, Editors and University Teachers of English Held at the University of the Witwatersrand, Johannesburg, 10–12 July 1956*. Johannesburg: Witwatersrand University Press, 1957.

Coullie, Judith, and J. U. Jacobs, eds. *A.K.A. Breyten Breytenbach: Critical Approaches to His Writings and Paintings*. New York: Rodopi, 2004.

Couzens, Tim. *The New African: A Study of the Life and Work of H. I. E. Dhlomo*. Johannesburg: Ravan, 1985.

Daymond, M. J., J. U. Jacobs, and Margaret Lenta, eds. *Momentum: On Recent South African Writing*. Pietermaritzburg: University of Natal Press, 1984.

De Kock, Leon, Louise Bethlehem, and Sonja Laden, eds. *South Africa in the Global Imaginary*. Pretoria: UNISA Press, 2004.

Dovey, Teresa. *The Novels of J. M. Coetzee: Lacanian Allegories*. Johannesburg: Ad Donker, 1988.

Eilersen, Gillian Stead. *Bessie Head: Thunder Behind Her Ears: Her Life and Writing*. Cape Town: David Philip, 1995.

Eve, Jeanette. *A Literary Guide to the Eastern Cape: Places and the Voices of Writers*. Cape Town: Double Storey, 2003.

Farred, Grant. *Midfielder's Moment: Coloured Literature and Culture in Contemporary South Africa*. Boulder, Colo.: Westview Press, 2000.

February, Vernon A. *Mind Your Colour: The 'Coloured' Stereotype in South African Literature*. London: Kegan Paul, 1981.

Friedman, Graeme, and Roy Blumenthal, eds. *A Writer in Stone: South African Writers Celebrate the 70th Birthday of Lionel Abrahams*. Cape Town: David Philip, 1998.

Gallagher, Susan VanZanten. *A Story of South Africa: J. M. Coetzee's Fiction in Context*. Cambridge, Mass.: Harvard University Press, 1991.

——. *Truth and Reconciliation: The Confessional Mode in South African Literature*. Portsmouth, N.H.: Heinemann, 2002.

Gordimer, Nadine. *The Black Interpreters: Notes on African Writing*. Johannesburg: Spro-Cas/Ravan, 1973.

Gray, Stephen. *Southern African Literature: An Introduction*. Cape Town: David Philip, 1977.

——. *Life Sentence: A Biography of Herman Charles Bosman*. Cape Town: Human & Rousseau, 2005.

Gray, Stephen, ed. *Athol Fugard*. Johannesburg: McGraw-Hill, 1982.

——. *Herman Charles Bosman*. Johannesburg: McGraw-Hill, 1986.

Gready, Paul. *Writing as Resistance: Life Stories of Imprisonment, Exile, and Homecoming from Apartheid South Africa*. Lanham, Md.: Lexington Books, 2003.

Green, Michael Cawood. *Novel Histories: Past, Present and Future in South African Fiction*. Johannesburg: Witwatersrand University Press, 1997.

Head, Dominic. *Nadine Gordimer*. Cambridge: Cambridge University Press, 1994.

——. *J. M. Coetzee*. Cambridge: Cambridge University Press, 1997.

Helgesson, Stefan. *Writing in Crisis: Ethics and History in Gordimer, Ndebele and Coetzee*. Pietermaritzburg: University of KwaZulu-Natal Press, 2004.

Heywood, Christopher. *Nadine Gordimer*. Windsor: Profile Books, 1983.

———. *A History of South African Literature*. Cambridge: Cambridge University Press, 2004.

Heywood, Christopher, ed. *Aspects of South African Literature*. London: Heinemann, 1976.

Huggan, Graham, and Stephen Watson, eds. *Critical Perspectives on J. M. Coetzee*. London: Macmillan, 1996.

Jolly, Rosemary Jane. *Colonization, Violence, and Narration in White South African Writing: André Brink, Breyten Breytenbach, and J. M. Coetzee*. Johannesburg: Witwatersrand University Press, 1996.

Jones, J. D. F. *Storyteller: The Many Lives of Laurens van der Post*. London: John Murray, 2001.

King, Bruce, ed. *The Later Fiction of Nadine Gordimer*. New York: St. Martin's, 1993.

Klima, Vladimir. *South African Prose Writing in English*. Prague: Oriental Institute, 1971.

Kossew, Sue. *Pen and Power: A Post-Colonial Reading of J. M. Coetzee and André Brink*. Amsterdam: Rodopi, 1996.

———, ed. *Critical Essays on J. M. Coetzee*. New York: G. K. Hall, 1998.

Koyana, Siphokazi Z., ed. *Sindiwe Magona: The First Decade*. Pietermaritzburg: University of KwaZulu-Natal Press, 2004.

MacKenzie, Craig. *Bessie Head*. New York: Twayne, 1999.

———. *The Oral-Style Short Story in English: A. W. Drayson to H. C. Bosman*. Atlanta: Rodopi, 1999.

Malan, Charles, ed. *Race and Literature/Ras en Literatuur*. Pinetown: Owen Burgess, 1987.

Manganyi, Noel Chabani. *Exiles and Homecomings: A Biography of Es'kia Mphahlele*. Johannesburg: Ravan, 1983.

Masilela, Ntongela. *The Cultural Modernity of H. I. E. Dhlomo*. Trenton, N.J.: Africa World Press, 2007.

Ndebele, Njabulo S. *Rediscovery of the Ordinary: Essays on South African Literature and Culture*. Johannesburg: COSAW, 1991.

———. *Fine Lines from the Box: Further Thoughts on Our Country*. Cape Town: Umuzi, 2007.

Newman, Judie. *Nadine Gordimer*. London: Routledge, 1988.

———, ed. *Nadine Gordimer's "Burger's Daughter": A Casebook*. Oxford: Oxford University Press, 2003.

Nkosi, Lewis. *Home and Exile and Other Selections*. London: Longman, 1983.

O'Brien, Anthony. *Against Normalization: Writing Radical Democracy in South Africa*. Durham, N.C.: Duke University Press, 2001.

Ogungbesan, Kolawole. *The Writing of Peter Abrahams*. London: Hodder & Stoughton, 1979.

Parker, Kenneth, ed. *The South African Novel in English: Essays in Criticism and Society*. London: Macmillan, 1978.

Penner, Dick. *Countries of the Mind: The Fiction of J. M. Coetzee*. New York: Greenwood Press, 1989.

Poyner, Jane, ed. *J. M. Coetzee and the Idea of the Public Intellectual*. Athens: Ohio University Press, 2006.

Raditlhalo, Sam, and Taban Lo Liyong, eds. *Es'kia: May You Grow as Big as an Elephant and Dwarf the Rhinoceros*. Johannesburg: Stainbank & Associates, 2006.

Roberts, Sheila. *Dan Jacobson*. Boston: Twayne, 1984.

Rosenberg, Valerie. *Sunflower to the Sun: The Life of Herman Charles Bosman*. Cape Town: Human & Rousseau, 1976.

Sanders, Mark. *Complicities: The Intellectual and Apartheid*. Durham, N.C.: Duke University Press, 2002.

Smit, Johannes A., Johan van Wyk, and Jean-Philippe Wade, eds. *Rethinking South African Literary History*. Durban: Y Press, 1996.

Smith, Malvern van Wyk. *Grounds of Contest: A Survey of South African English Literature*. Cape Town: Jutalit, 1990.

Smith, Malvern van Wyk, ed. *Shades of Adamastor: Africa and the Portuguese Connection: An Anthology of Poetry*. Grahamstown: Institute for the Study of English in Africa, Rhodes University, & NELM, 1988.

Smith, Rowland, ed. *Critical Essays on Nadine Gordimer*. Boston: G. K. Hall, 1990.

Stiebel, Lindy, and Liz Gunner, eds. *Still Beating the Drum: Critical Perspectives on Lewis Nkosi*. New York: Rodopi, 2005.

Titlestad, Michael. *Making the Changes: Jazz in South African Literature and Reportage.* Pretoria: University of South Africa Press, 2004.

Trump, Martin, ed. *Rendering Things Visible: Essays on South African Literary Culture.* Johannesburg: Ravan, 1990.

Vandenbroucke, Russell. *Truths the Hand Can Touch: The Theatre of Athol Fugard.* New York: Theatre Communications Group, 1985.

Wade, Michael. *Peter Abrahams.* Ed. Gerald Moore. London: Evans, 1972.

——. *Nadine Gordimer.* London: Evans, 1978.

Wagner, Kathrin. *Rereading Nadine Gordimer: Text and Subtext in the Novels.* Johannesburg: Witwatersrand University Press, 1994.

Walder, Dennis. *Athol Fugard.* London: Macmillan, 1984.

——. *Athol Fugard.* Tavistock: Northcote House and the British Council, 2003.

White, Landeg, and Tim Couzens, eds. *Literature and Society in South Africa.* Cape Town: Maskew Miller Longman, 1984.

Wilhelm, Peter, and James A. Polley, eds. *Poetry South Africa: Selected Papers from Poetry '74.* Johannesburg: Ad Donker, 1976.

Wright, Laura. *Writing "Out of All the Camps": J. M. Coetzee's Narratives of Displacement.* New York: Routledge, 2006.

Yousaf, Nahem. *Alex La Guma: Politics and Resistance.* Portsmouth, N.H.: Heinemann, 2001.

Index

JENNINGS LIBRARY
CALDWELL COLLEGE